AN INTRODUCTION

PENOLOGY

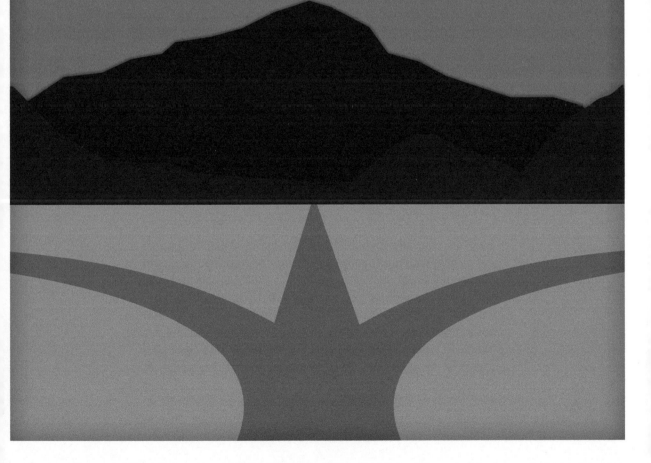

Sara Miller McCune founded SAGE Publishing in 1965 to support the dissemination of usable knowledge and educate a global community. SAGE publishes more than 1000 journals and over 800 new books each year, spanning a wide range of subject areas. Our growing selection of library products includes archives, data, case studies and video. SAGE remains majority owned by our founder and after her lifetime will become owned by a charitable trust that secures the company's continued independence.

Los Angeles | London | New Delhi | Singapore | Washington DC | Melbourne

Lol Burke & Helena Gosling

AN INTRODUCTION TO
PENOLOGY
PUNISHMENT, PRISONS & PROBATION

Los Angeles | London | New Delhi
Singapore | Washington DC | Melbourne

Los Angeles | London | New Delhi
Singapore | Washington DC | Melbourne

SAGE Publications Ltd
1 Oliver's Yard
55 City Road
London EC1Y 1SP

SAGE Publications Inc.
2455 Teller Road
Thousand Oaks, California 91320

SAGE Publications India Pvt Ltd
B 1/I 1 Mohan Cooperative Industrial Area
Mathura Road
New Delhi 110 044

SAGE Publications Asia-Pacific Pte Ltd
3 Church Street
#10-04 Samsung Hub
Singapore 049483

Editor: Natalie Aguilera
Editorial assistant: Rhoda Ola-Said
Production editor: Sarah Cooke
Marketing manager: Ruslana Khatagova
Cover design: Francis Kenney
Typeset by: C&M Digitals (P) Ltd, Chennai, India
Printed in the UK

Library of Congress Control Number: 2022938229

British Library Cataloguing in Publication data

A catalogue record for this book is available from
the British Library

ISBN 978-1-5264-9284-5
ISBN 978-1-5264-9283-8 (pbk)

At SAGE we take sustainability seriously. Most of our products are printed in the UK using responsibly sourced
papers and boards. When we print overseas we ensure sustainable papers are used as measured by the PREPS
grading system. We undertake an annual audit to monitor our sustainability.

Table of contents

Detailed table of contents

About the Authors

Lol Burke is Professor in Criminal Justice at Liverpool John Moores University and specialises in the areas of probation research, policy and practice. He has a particular interest in the impact of marketisation upon service delivery and way that occupational culture acts out in probation settings as well resettlement provision for people released from prison. As a former probation practitioner, he has experience working in both community and custodial settings. He has published extensively on probation-related issues and rehabilitation in general and is co-author of *Redemption, Rehabilitation and Risk Management* (Routledge 2012), *Delivering Rehabilitation: The Politics, Governance and Control of Probation* (Routledge 2015), *Reimagining Rehabilitation: Beyond the Individual* (Routledge 2019) and *Reimagining Probation Practice: Re-forming Rehabilitation in an Age of Penal Excess* (Routledge 2022).

Helena Gosling is a Senior Lecturer in Criminal Justice at Liverpool John Moores University. Prior to becoming an academic, she worked in the drug rehabilitation sector across community, residential and custodial settings. Her main research interests are situated in the design, delivery and commissioning of innovation and alternative practice within and beyond the criminal justice system. More recently, Helena has developed and extended her research interests to focus on ways in which higher education can work alongside current and potential students with experience of the criminal justice system in a more meaningful way.

Acknowledgements

This book is dedicated to all those who have experienced the sharp end of punishment directly or indirectly and those working towards a more just society. Lol would like to thank his family, Sandra, Megan and Daniel for all their support during the writing of this book. Helena would like to acknowledge Craig, James and Daniel for their love and laughter and especially Bernie and John for their unwavering commitment to grandparenting duties. Helena would also like to extend her thanks to Gareth Edwards and Jane Higham for their friendship, expertise and wisdom. In particular, Helena would like to acknowledge Cat Jones whose insight and generosity went some way to help shape the construction of Chapter 9. Your passion and drive to support change is contagious! Lol and Helena would also like to thank Natalie and the team at Sage for not only giving us the opportunity to write this book but also for the on going support and guidance provided throughout the production process.

INTRODUCTION

WHY PUNISHMENT, PRISONS AND PROBATION?

In a valedictory article marking her retirement as chief executive of the Howard League for Penal Reform, a position she held for 35 years, Frances Crook wrote that:

> **If a time traveller from 100 years ago walked into a prison today – whether one of the inner-city Victorian prisons or the new-builds where the majority of men are held – the similarities would trump the differences. They would recognise the smells and the sounds, the lack of activity and probably some of the staff. It is not only the buildings that have stayed the same – it is the whole ethos of the institution. (Crook, 2021)**

Crook's words capture the inertia inherent in our prison system as it lumbers from crisis to crisis. At present there are more than 80,000 people in the prison system in England and Wales (double what there was some 50 years ago) despite promises of reform and the development of so-called *alternatives to custody*. Decades of failed social policies mean that most of those who end up in prisons will have experienced a lifetime of family breakdown, poverty, addiction and long-standing health problems. A disproportionate number will die whilst in prison or under supervision by probation. Many will be homeless and unemployed on their release. It is perhaps unsurprising then that at the core of this book is the need for a radical rethinking of the way in which state punishment is conceptualised and administered in contemporary society. As such, the book is designed to provide a concise, informative, scholarly text that will speak to a variety of audiences interested in how the notion of punishment plays out in community and custodial settings with people who have broken the law.

WHY PUNISHMENT?

By focusing on attempts to justify *why* we punish people who break the law, rather than endeavours to understand *who* we punish, we can distance ourselves from the systemic problems which surround the design and delivery of criminal justice on a global scale. The long-standing, almost taken for granted, inclusion of harm as a hallmark of punishment further compounds this sense of distance, desensitising the gravity and extent of common penal practices whilst simultaneously limiting our ability to treat people who end up in the criminal justice system as equals (Coverdale, 2013). In this respect we would concur with Rob Canton that punishment should always respect the principle that the individual who commits a crime remains 'one of us, not an "other" and always take account of her interests and well-being, even when acting against her wishes' (2017: 213). By integrating questions about who we punish into the epicentre of ongoing penological debates, we become more able to critically engage with the idea of punishment and question whether, and on what grounds, we can rationalise the use of punitive measures and sanctions amongst those who have broken the law and more importantly been caught and convicted for their actions.

When we consider who we punish, we are more able to think pragmatically about ongoing penal practice as well as long-standing justifications of such endeavours. For instance, there is a commonly held belief that lawbreakers are sent to prison to protect the public. Yet official statistics document how 67 per cent of people serving a custodial sentence are convicted of a non-violent offence (Prison Reform Trust, 2019). If most people who are sent to prison pose little to no threat to the public, how can we continue to justify imprisonment based on such principles? This is just one of many examples that raise questions about the role of punishment as well as long-standing attempts to justify penal practices. Although laws and legislation provide sufficient guidance for the infliction of punishment, there remains a need to justify how and why we respond to lawbreaking in this fashion, given that, by definition, punishment involves an intentional imposition of suffering and harm that, in most cases, leaves a legacy on the person subject to such actions.

The inability to reach a consensus about punishment (as a concept and practice) draws attention to the role and functions of our penal institutions. This raises tough questions about how to respond to lawbreaking and, more importantly, whether punishment is justifiable. Hudson (1996) advocates a restriction and reduction in the use of punishment, suggesting that we should be profoundly uneasy about state-administered punishment in general, and therefore should approach it with caution and restraint. Rather than reinventing the wheel, Locke (1963) suggests that we should move beyond discussions about why we punish, towards a discussion of what the purpose of punishment should be. In doing so, we are better placed to engage with questions such as: is punishment the right response to lawbreaking? And does punishment achieve justice? What are the psychological, social, political, cultural and economic factors that either support or hinder the changes we are intending to seek by punishing individuals?

Though punishment is a central element of the criminal justice system, it is yet to be explicitly defined and universally understood. This raises a series of theoretical and practical problems, as it is difficult, if not impossible, to determine how to punish those who have broken the law if society is unable to define the notion of punishment and indeed, what it represents (van Ginneken and Hayes, 2017). Taking into consideration its varying forms, definitions and characteristics, Callender (2020) suggests that punishment should provide an ordered expression of the desire for justice, with a fundamental aim to prevent suffering. Though thought provoking, such sentiments do little to advance our ability to better understand what the term punishment means or how justice can be achieved through the application of punitive measures.

Establishing a universal definition of punishment has been described as unachievable given that it can be defined and understood in multiple ways, is value-laden and able to influence our learning about right and wrong. Nevertheless, attempts have been made to communicate what punishment entails. Generally speaking, such endeavours pivot around expressions of resentment and disapproval as well as pursuits to inflict pain and suffering on those who are deemed to have done wrong in some way. With this in mind, punishment can be described as a communicative act which informs people that they have done wrong (Duff, 1998). In sum, punishment is a term that can be used to refer to any way of responding to wrongdoing and lawbreaking to demonstrate disapproval or blame. While attempts to define punishment vary in content and clarity, the idea that punishment must be considered unpleasant for the wrongdoer is a consistent feature of most definitions, with the term punishment typically used to describe anything society deems painful, harmful or unpleasant to the recipient.

When grappling with the complexities that surround attempts to define punishment, we must recognise that the idea of punishment, in both theory and practice, is an evolutionary rather than static concept that varies over time, place and space to reflect differing interests, values and goals. This is particularly apparent in respect of the two penal organisations which are the main focus of this book – prisons and probation. For example, The Probation of Offenders Act 1907 provided the statutory foundation of the Probation Service and made it possible for Magistrates' Courts to appoint probation officers who were required to *advise, assist and befriend* people subject to supervision. Since the introduction of the Probation of Offenders Act 1907, the role of the probation officer has extended to include through-care (in prison support) and after-care (post-release supervision) and transformed, with probation officers now expected to *confront, control and monitor* individuals under their supervision (see Chapter 6 for a further discussion).

If you look at the guiding principles for prison and probation services in Denmark, alongside England and Wales, you will observe how punishment can vary across place and space. For example, in Denmark, the primary task of the prison and probation service is to implement sanctions imposed by the courts through control, security, support and motivation (Danish Prison and Probation Service, 2012). When compared to the stated ambitions of Her Majesty's Prison and Probation Service to 'deliver the government's vision and investment to make prisons places of safety and reform, and to continue to transform our work in the community' (HM Prison and Probation Service, 2022) it is possible to identify varying aims and ambitions between countries. That said, what is consistent across time, place and space is an inherent lack of clarity when it comes to attempts to define the aims and ambitions of penal practices across both community and custodial settings.

Alongside this, it is important to recognise that whether a person is punished (or not as the case may be) is not only a consequence of the act itself. Rather, in reality, whether someone is punished is dependent on several factors such as whether their behaviour is defined as a crime or not; whether their actions are visible to agents of criminal justice; whether they are believed to be guilty in the first instance; or whether they have the socio-economic resources to shield against inequality, disadvantage and deprivation. This is an important consideration for anyone interested in penology as research from around the world consistently illustrates how people involved in the criminal justice system disproportionately come from deprived communities, with most lawbreaking linked to petty and persistent crime. Taking this into consideration, the authors suggest that parallels can be drawn between pursuits to define punishment and justice given that there is no single way to define these terms. What is considered just (and indeed unjust) cannot be captured by one single perspective. Despite this, attempts have been made to differentiate between types of justice, including but not limited to:

Corrective justice (or retributive justice) has historical roots appearing in early accounts of law, theology and philosophy. It is a perspective that reflects a fundamental need for fairness, through the punishment of lawbreakers who must pay for what they have done and get their *just deserts*. Punishment from a corrective justice perspective must deter lawbreaking and be the most efficient means of doing so. Punishment must not harm the lawbreaker more than is required to repair the harms caused by their actions or harm a person to a degree that is entirely out of proportion to the harm caused and/or prevented.

Distributive justice, in its broadest sense, is about the socially just allocation of resources with a particular focus on how benefits and burdens are distributed amongst individuals as a matter of rights and entitlement. It is concerned with giving all members of society a fair share of benefits and resources available based upon principles of equity (one's rewards should be equal to one's contributions), equality (everyone gets the same amount regardless of their input) and need. Distributive justice is ultimately about fairness, from the perceived fairness of outcomes to resource allocation.

Natural justice has its origins in the concept *Jus Natural* which means a law of nature. Although quite a general idea, natural justice implies a general duty to act fairly and impartially. The right to a fair hearing is an example of natural justice as it requires that a person should receive fair and unbiased treatment before a decision is made that will negatively affect them. In doing so, the concept upholds principles of both procedural and administrative fairness.

Restorative justice can be difficult to define as it encompasses a wide variety of practices that can take place at varying points in the criminal justice process. That said, the Restorative

Justice Council (2016: para 1) offers a useful definition, noting how restorative justice 'brings together those harmed by crime or conflict and those responsible for the harm into communication, enabling everyone affected by a particular incident to play a part in repairing the harm and finding a positive way forward.'

Social justice is a political and philosophical concept which asserts that there are dimensions to the idea of justice that go beyond those embodied in principles of law, economics or traditional moral frameworks. Turnbull (2020: para 3) notes how 'social justice is all about working towards a more equal society' within which each individual matters, their rights are protected, and decisions are made in ways that are fair and honest.

Definitions of the term justice, summarised above, are not intended to be extensive nor exhaustive. Rather, they are designed to highlight how the idea of justice can be conceptualised in various ways through the application of philosophical, moral, social, legal, environmental and penological lenses, each of which expresses principles of justice in its own way, having different but equally important implications for penal institutions. In their broadest sense, theories of justice are attempts to understand society. In doing so, they offer a series of interpretations based on shared values, attitudes and beliefs with regard to lawbreaking and what is required to achieve justice for those who have been wronged.

Lucas (1972) suggests that the idea of justice has largely been replaced with that of legality, which restricts the range of factors that may be taken into consideration when working alongside people who have broken the law. This has not only restricted our vision of justice and what justice could embody in contemporary society but reinforced efforts to justify punitive measures rather than seek alternative ways to work alongside people who not only break the law but are subject to criminal proceedings. This hinders our ability to address the root causes of lawbreaking as well as pursuits to create a more equal, fair and just society. For this reason, we conclude this book by examining some alternative approaches that are based on the belief 'that those who have committed crimes should be restored to membership of a shared moral community' (Canton, 2017: 213).

WHY PRISONS AND PROBATION?

Modern societies deploy a wide range of sanctions in response to crimes (many of which are discussed in this book) that require moral justification. Penology is therefore often conceptualised as the study of punishment in prisons and in the community. Prisons and probation occupy a central position in the criminal justice system of all developed nations. Much is known about these services, their administration, their actual and/or perceived effectiveness and their subsequent limitations. However, the day-to-day administration, design and delivery has remained the subject of intense debate and controversy throughout their history. With a clear focus on theory, policy and practice readers will be encouraged to critically engage with long-standing penological debates that take into consideration long-standing justifications, aims and ambitions of punishment within and across community and custodial settings that are required to work alongside people who have broken the law and found themselves engulfed by the criminal justice system. Critically engaging with the design and delivery of contemporary sites and mechanisms of punishment is an important endeavour for any citizen – after all, such practices are executed in our name.

CONTENT OF THE BOOK

This book is divided into three separate but interconnected sections (*foundations, design and delivery*, and *implementation and impact*) to help you think practically and cohesively about the material that is presented to you in this text. In doing so, each section consists of a collection of four chapters that speak to the aims and ambitions of the section, whilst simultaneously providing you with the theoretical, practical and political insight required to critically engage with the notion of punishment within and across community and custodial environments. Chapters 1 to 4 come together to create the *foundations* section. This may be considered an introductory component of the book as its offerings explore some of the ideas, approaches and models that underpin contemporary penological thought. In doing so, the chapters in this section provide an important foundation for anyone interested in penology as they offer an opportunity for you to build your criminological insight which will subsequently prepare you for the discussions that evolve as the textbook unfolds.

Chapter 1 begins our journey into penological thought through an exploration of how systems of control, discipline and governance – which developed alongside the birth of the modern prison – have spread into the wider community. Drawing on a range of theorists such as Michel Foucault, Stan Cohen, David Garland and Fergus McNeill, we explore a range of perspectives that attempt to explain state punishment as well as the response of state penal institutions to the insecurities inherent in post-modern societies. In Chapter 2, we explore the development and application of prevalent models such as the Risk-Needs-Responsivity (RNR) model, desistance and Good Lives Model (GLM) to understand how and in what ways people involved in prison and probation services are supported to change their ways. To conclude this section, Chapters 3 and 4 explore the theories of prisons and probation, their role in the infliction of state punishment, the evidence-base for their efficacy, and some of the contemporary challenges which face the delivery of punishment in community and custodial settings.

Chapters 5 to 8 specifically focus on the *design and delivery* of prison and probation services in England and Wales. As you will see, these chapters mirror each other in considering a range of contemporary issues as they relate to each of the respective organisations. In Chapters 5 and 6, we consider the purposes of both prisons and probation and their respective roles within the sentencing framework, their organisational structures and mechanisms to ensure their governance and accountability. Both prisons and probation have separate occupational cultures that have developed over a long period. It is our contention that recent attempts to incorporate them into a single structure to achieve a *seamless sentence* have not paid sufficient heed to this. In Chapters 7 and 8 we therefore look at the work of both institutions from the perspective of occupational culture, how this is experienced by those in custodial and community settings, the formal and informal social structures that influence the day-to-day operation of both institutions, and skills involved in both prison and probation work.

Chapters 9 to 12 come together to form the *implementation and impact* section of the book. Through a particular focus on the concept of vulnerability, this section provides a series of carefully crafted discussions that support the reader to critically explore taken for granted ideas about the design and delivery of punishment at the coal face of service delivery. Through the lens of *what works* Chapters 9 and 10 explore the implementation and impact of interventions delivered across prison and probation services. Building on this, in Chapters 11 and 12, we explore how penal institutions respond to the needs of individuals with whom they work. As we have noted, people who find themselves in prison or on probation have often faced discrimination and deprivation and they sometimes present a range of behaviours that are considered *challenging* and *problematic*. In these chapters we explore the term vulnerability, consider the range of needs this encompasses and how they are experienced disproportionately by those in prison and on probation in comparison to the general population.

As we discussed at the start of this chapter, there is no doubt that notions of punishment are contested. Likewise, prisons are controversial institutions that are subject to intense debate and critique. Alongside this, there has been no shortage in the rethinking of probation, which has faced a succession of organisational changes driven by a perceived need to increase confidence amongst sentencers and the general public. As such we believe that it is important to end the book with an opportunity for you to consider what a penology of the future could look like given that what we do in our penal systems also shines a light on wider society given its ability to 'reflect society back to itself: they embody the ways we have failed, the people we have failed, and the policies that have failed, all at immense human – and economic – cost' (Crook, 2021). In the concluding chapter we therefore consider the potential of peacemaking criminology and restorative processes as an alternative paradigm for conflict resolution.

Throughout this textbook we have refrained where possible from using dehumanising labels such as 'prisoners' and '(ex)offenders' when referring to people who are or have been involved with criminal justice services. This is because taken for granted penological terminology can marginalise, stereotype and other people who are involved (or have previously been involved) with prison and/or probation services, as well as normalise the use of (largely unjustified) punishment in contemporary society and desensitise the collateral consequences of both community and custodial sentences. Rather, you will note that we have made a commitment to use respectful and person-centred language when referring to people who are in prison and/or on probation, their characteristics and experiences. The term 'offender' or 'prisoner' is however still used in the textbook when we have referred to government strategies (e.g. Female Offender Strategy) or drawn on direct quotes or ministerial rhetoric so as to be true to the original citation. Appropriate use of inclusive language in relation to race, sexuality and disability can be complex. For example, in our discussions around racial discrimination we use the term BAME as an abbreviation for individuals of Black, Asian and Minority Ethnic heritage. Whilst we acknowledge that this is a contested term, our intention is 'to be as inclusive as possible, and to reflect the ever-changing experience and identities of Asian and African/Caribbean peoples' (Wainwright, 2009: 511). Alongside this, we have made a conscious decision to confront long-standing penological issues that call into question the aims, ambitions and justifications of penal practices in both prison and probation services through a humanitarian lens, prioritising conversations about who is affected by contemporary penal policy and practice. In doing so, we encourage you to move beyond questions such as does prison work? and are community sentences effective? towards more meaningful questions, such as:

- For whom do prisons and probation work?
- In what ways do prison and probation work?
- How can we, as a society, create responses to lawbreaking and troublesome behaviour that are rooted in principles of social justice?

references

Callender, J. (2020) Justice, reciprocity and the internalisation of punishment in victims of crime. *Neuroethics*. 13, 43–54.

Canton R. (2017) *Why Punish? An Introduction to the Philosophy of Punishment*. London: Palgrave: Macmillan.

Coverdale, H. (2013) Punishing with care: treating offenders as equal persons in criminal punishment. PhD thesis. Available at: http://etheses.lse.ac.uk/1080 (last accessed 29 June 2022).

Crook, F. (2021) The reform of prisons has been my life's work, but they are still utterly broken. *The Guardian*. Available at: www.theguardian.com/commentisfree/2021/aug/10/reform-prisons-utterly-broken (last accessed 29 June 2022).

Danish Prison and Probation Service (2012) *The Danish Prison and Probation Service – in Brief*. Available at: www.prisonstudies.org/sites/default/files/resources/downloads/inbrief_updateddec.2012.pdf (last accessed 29 June 2022).

Duff, A. (1998) Desert and penance, in A. von Hirsch and A. Ashworth (eds) *Principled Sentencing. Readings on Theory and Policy*. Oxford: Oxford University Press, pp. 161–7.

HM Prison and Probation Service (2020) About us. Available at: www.gov.uk/government/organisations/her-majestys-prison-and-probation-service/about#priorities (last accessed 29 June 2022).

Hudson, B. (1996) *Understanding Justice*. Buckingham: Open University Press.

Locke, D. (1963) The many faces of punishment. *Mind*, 72(288), 568–72.

Lucas, J. (1972) Justice. *Philosophy*, 47(18), 229–48.

Prison Reform Trust (2019) *Bromley Briefings Prison Factfile*. Available at: https://prisonreformtrust.org.uk/wp-content/uploads/2020/01/Bromley-Briefings-Prison-Factfile-Winter-2019.pdf (last accessed 29 June 2022).

Restorative Justice Council (2016) *What is Restorative Justice?* Available at: https://restorativejustice.org.uk/what-restorative-justice (last accessed 25 June 2022).

Turnbull, E. (2020) *Social Justice and Human Rights*. The British Institute of Human Rights. Available at: www.bihr.org.uk/blog/social-justice-and-human-rights (last accessed 25 June 2022).

Van Ginneken, E. and Hayes, D. (2017) 'Just' punishment? Offenders' views on the meaning and severity of punishment. *Criminology and Criminal Justice*, 17(1), 62–78.

Wainwright, J. (2009) Racism, anti-racist practice and social work: Articulating the teach and learning experiences of Black social workers. *Race Ethnicity and Education*, 12(4), 495–516.

1

UNDERSTANDING CONTEMPORARY PENOLOGY

PERSPECTIVES

IN THIS CHAPTER, YOU WILL EXPLORE

1. The development of social control and surveillance against the background of the changing nature of supervision which is often characterised as a move from soft to hard control

2. The expansion of social control in contemporary society drawing on the classic work of Stan Cohen which first drew our attention see some of the more negative aspects of these developments

3. The notion of mass supervision using electronic monitoring as a case study par excellence of the nature of contemporary social control

---

INTRODUCTION

In the Introduction to this book, we discussed the contested nature of penology and the implications this has for how society responds to those who commit crimes. We argued that that these ideas can change over time and place and so in the next two chapters we consider a range of insights and approaches that have, and continue to, influence not only our contemporary understanding but also the work of penal agents in custodial and community settings. In this respect these chapters provide a foundation for the rest of the book and allow you to consider the broader context in which modern prison and probation work is undertaken. We do not claim that these developments provide a complete analysis of contemporary penology and in this respect we accept that our analysis is incomplete, but it is our contention that each significantly influences our contemporary understanding of the penal practices that we explore throughout this book. We start by examining the expansion of surveillance and social control in modern society and explore how this has been aided by the advancement of new technologies. We then go on to discuss the predominance of risk and public protection in contemporary penal policies and practice, which we would argue represents another, and closely linked, aspect of the sovereign state's desperate need to seek solutions to concerns about funding, prison conditions, high reoffending rates and the need to counter the increasing insecurity of its citizens.

David Garland (2001) argues that during the last quarter of the 20th century a new *collective experience* of crime and insecurity combined with a new range of technical possibilities and policy initiatives to produce a set of adaptations. The old form of the penal-welfare state (Garland, 1985), and the project of diagnosing, treating and rehabilitating individuals, which became known as the *rehabilitative ideal*, gave way to one in which responsibilities for control are simultaneously more dispersed and politicised. This move from modernity to post-modernity in crime control involved a combination of increased punitiveness accompanied by rising levels of punishment and technocratic managerialism involving the management and control of aggregate categories of deviants. According to Waquant (2009) the concentration of these new forms of control/ containment have been primarily aimed at the poor and have a racialised dimension. Conversely, the deviant behaviours of the rich and powerful have been ignored or subject to less scrutiny. Finally, we consider the role of privatisation and the outsourcing of penal justice. We explore both the efficacy and morality of what has increasingly become a key feature of contemporary crime policies against a backdrop of neo-liberal politics that promotes deregulation, lower taxation and reductions in state spending.

KEY QUESTIONS TO CONSIDER WHEN READING THIS CHAPTER

1. Should we be concerned about the expansion of social control within society?

2. Do we live in a risk society?

3. Should privatisation be a feature of criminal justice? Is your view shaped by practical or ethical concerns?

SURVEILLANCE, SOCIAL CONTROL AND NEW TECHNOLOGY

In broad terms social control refers to the control of a person or a group by wider society to enforce social norms, through socialisation, policing, laws or similar measures. There are two elements of social control that are relevant to the delivery of punishment within the penal system. The first of these is *supervision*, which is a holistic and supposedly humanistic concept. It implies the existence of a personal relationship based on periodic contact between supervisor and supervisee and entails a degree of watchfulness combined with the possibility guidance on the part of the supervisor but ultimately depends on the person under supervision acting in a trustworthy manner (Raynor and Robinson, 2009). The second concept is that of *surveillance*, which involves the continuous observation of a place, person, group or ongoing activity to gather information. Surveillance implies the existence of a form of impersonal technology – this offers the prospect (although not always the reality) of monitoring a person's whereabouts and movements. It gives the appearance of being backed by a more intensive and ostensibly more reliable enforcement regime that is less dependent on the trustworthiness of the individual. Both prison and probation work involve both surveillance and supervision. Both operate as mechanisms for ensuring the control of individuals and changing behaviours deemed illegal by wider society.

Since the advent of the modern prison, surveillance has always played a critical part. In British prison reformer Jeremy Bentham's famous late 18th century vision of the panopticon, people in prison would experience a feeling of being seen at all times, even if the guards were not always watching them. The architecture of the institution made it possible for them to view each person in prison at any moment while remaining unseen themselves. In most places, Bentham's literal vision of the panopticon never came to pass, but with today's electronic monitoring and curfews, we can feel its legacy in the creation of an environment where surveillance is constant, and intrusion is an ever-present possibility. Michel Foucault's analysis of the birth of the modern prison ponders on the fact that we have only been using imprisonment as a sentence since the turn of the 18th century (see Chapter 4). This leads him to examine the conditions which led to the establishment of the prison and its relationship to contemporary strategies of power. According to Foucault, within a disciplinary framework, institutions seek to normalise individuals through spatial–temporal techniques such as routines and solitary confinement. The main goal of these modern disciplinary systems is not revenge (as in the case of torture in pre-modern punishment) but to correct deviant behaviour and reform in the sense of living by society's standards or norms. In Foucault's view, new disciplinary sciences (such as criminology, psychiatry and psychology) made *deviance* visible and therefore correctable in ways that was impossible in the previous social order.

The Foucauldian concept of *governmentality* has also informed the work of those who maintain that risk focused penal regulation has become a mechanism for *governing through crime* (Simon, 2007). This primarily involves the application of risk-based technologies that enable governments to steer citizens to conformity without exerting visible force (Rose and Miller, 1992). In *Discipline and Punish*, Foucault (1977) discussed the carceral network as a system of confinement, punishment and discipline that begins within and extends beyond the prison. The logics and practices that regulate social life inside prisons have subsequently made their way into most other social institutions. The reform of people in prisons, the instruction of school children, the confinement of people with poor mental health, and the supervision of workers are all products of the new political and economic order under capitalism. The carceral imagination has therefore become deeply embedded within the structures of the social world.

The development of social control and its attendant surveillant technologies has tended to be presented as a progressive development and an inevitable component of contemporary society. In simple terms, when applied to criminal justice institutions the argument put forward is that firstly prison is a more humane sanction than capital punishment and secondly that probation is more humane than prison. Before prisons gained popularity, capital punishments and bodily harm were the preferred mode of state-inflicted punishment. The death penalty was routinely imposed for the most minor of offences. In the 18th and early 19th centuries, prison reformers in the United States and Europe promoted prison as a more humane alternative and a kind of substitute for the whip, the stocks and the branding iron. These early reformers were often from devoutly Christian backgrounds and many envisaged prisons as sites of redemption. They saw the penitentiary – a term that comes from the word penitent – as a place where people might, in isolation come to realise the nature of their sins and emerge remorseful, obedient and rehabilitated. The experience was not supposed to be pleasant and could include near constant solitary confinement or silence, and sometimes ruthless forced labour. The concept of discipline was also developed by Michel Foucault to characterise the attempt to transform the soul of the person who has offended and make them compliant to the rules of society.

Probation was traditionally seen as a progressive and more humanitarian response that developed at the beginning of the 20th century as a response to the overuse of imprisonment, particularly for those who committed first and minor offences. However, as Maurice Vanstone (2004) has pointed out, there is a dark side to probation development. Although many of the early pioneers of probation in England and Wales were motivated by their religion and humanitarian concerns, the rapid growth of early probation also corresponded with widespread concerns regarding the behaviour of the so-called *dangerous classes* of working-class itinerants who drank too much and committed petty crimes to finance their lifestyles. Offers of help were limited to those deemed deserving and were conditional in the sense that the individual had to take a pledge to give up drink before being placed on probation (McWilliams, 1983). And, of course, the offer of help was accompanied by the threat of being sent to prison if the person did not comply with the requirements of the sanction.

Stan Cohen viewed the whole of the community corrections movement as merely an extension of the overall pattern established in the 19th century whereby the mode of control founded on discipline was based on institutions such as the prison and the asylum. In a series of works that culminated in his 1985 book *Visions of Social Control*, Cohen painted the nightmarish vision of the city of the future as being increasingly subjected to a sophisticated social control network. Cohen argued that whereas the first transformation of the criminal justice system in the 18th and 19th centuries had the effect of concentrating the social control energies of the state on highly selected populations of deviants inside specially designed institutions like the prison and the asylum, this was no longer the case. Instead, he argued that penal developments associated with community corrections movements demonstrated how the state was now spreading its tentacles of control ever more deeply into the fabric of society by significantly widening the reach and scope of its social control apparatus. In this respect, Cohen merely considered these trends to be a continuation of the same disciplinary project of the state, albeit on a much more ambitious scale. Cohen described the key features of what he called a second transformation in criminal justice in several memorable metaphors of fishing nets.

Cohen describes *widening the net* as the process whereby community programmes can capture many people who would not normally formally have been subjected to the attentions of the criminal justice system. One example is when police caution is used not only as an alternative to prosecution but also for those who would otherwise have been informally dealt with. The end result is to increase rather than decrease the total number that gets into the system in the first place. By *thinning the mesh*, he is referring to the fact that not only are more people brought into the system, those who are dealt with by means of new and more intensive community orders also experience a greater degree of intervention than would have been the case if a more traditional alternative to custody such as fines, the traditional probation order or conditional discharge, had been used. As a result of these and other developments such as home curfews and electronic monitoring there is a *blurring* of the distinction between institutional and non-institutional forms of control – or even between what is or is not regarded as punishment. In this respect, Cohen argued that it is difficult to see at times where the prison stops and the community starts. This is particularly true of more intrusive forms of community sentences that place restrictions on the individual and deprive them of their liberty much as in the same way as the prison. The combined effect of these developments is that the system of social control is now extended more and more deeply into the informal networks of society. This is what Cohen termed *penetration*. Even more important, though, is the fact that these measures strengthen the existing prison system. They do not replace it, but on the contrary, they enable the prison to reach out into the community. This, he argues, will lead to the use of different nets with new agencies supplementing rather than replacing the original organisations of control in the criminal justice system.

Cohen's work is important on several levels. Firstly, it challenges the notion that the growth of forms of social control like probation were inherently a positive and progressive humanitarian development as opposed to imprisonment. He argues that more and different community-based sanctions do not necessarily mean less or less intensive forms of control. This points us to the unintended consequences of increased social control. A contemporary example is the introduction of the sentence of imprisonment for public protection within the English and Welsh criminal justice system which has left many individuals marooned unjustifiably within the prison system long after the requirements of formal justice have been met (see Chapter 4 for a further discussion). Additionally, on a more general level, the link between violation of community-based supervision and post-release imprisonment has become more problematic with recent changes in legislation affecting the supervision of all those sentenced to under 12 months terms of imprisonment. Dressed up as support – but without the practical and human resources to make it meaningful – and enforced through further periods of imprisonment, this appears also to be a newly designed but classic case of net widening. Secondly, Cohen's work alerts us to the fact that so-called alternatives to custody, particularly if they are not successful in diverting individuals from imprisonment, make control and surveillance more widespread. This is certainly true in England and Wales, as it is in most countries (Aebi et al., 2015). Recent years have seen community sentences grow alongside – rather than replacing – imprisonment, leading to a bloated criminal justice system.

Much of Cohen's vision has been vindicated to date. So far, the development of punishments in the community has done nothing to solve the penal crisis, and in some respects can be said to have made it worse. Community punishments were, as we have seen, developed and promoted as alternatives to custody in the hope that they would alleviate the crisis of prison resources. However, the strategy of toughening up community sentences to build public confidence has merely led to a general ratcheting up of penalties. Prison numbers have also increased, matched by a crisis of resources, morale and legitimacy within the Probation Service.

Cohen was of course writing before the advent of technological advances that have shaped contemporary crime control in ways that would have been on unimaginable in Cohen's time. Increasingly, technological advances such as CCTV and electronic monitoring are impacting on the way in which surveillance and supervision are enacted in contemporary society and it is perhaps all too easy to be seduced by the promise of technology to provide a technical fix to the deep moral and structural changes we face. Concerns about the intrusiveness of these measures and their potential to infringe the rights of the individual are often countered by utilitarian arguments (see Chapter 5 for a further discussion) that such developments are *for the greater good* and that there is nothing to fear if you have not done anything wrong. Maybe, we wonder, if we have CCTV cameras watching our every movement might help. Maybe we could use electronic monitoring to release people early from prison and so alleviate pressure on the system. After all, is it not better to be in your own home than in a prison cell? Isn't it better to have the support of a probation officer on your release from prison than being left to your own devices?

The ever-increasing enthusiasm by governments for new surveillance technologies seems destined to blur the boundaries between prison and the community further. As Thomas Mathiesen (1983: 139) observes:

> **TV cameras on subway stations and in supermarkets, the development of advanced computer techniques in intelligence and surveillance, a general strengthening of the police, a general strengthening of the large privately run security companies, as well as a whole**

range of other types of surveillance of whole categories of people – all of this is something we have begun to get and have begun to get used to.

When most people discuss the need to end the damaging impact of mass imprisonment, they typically define the problem of mass incarceration in the narrowest possible terms, focusing only on reducing the number of people who are currently behind bars. This is understandable perhaps given the over-use of imprisonment and the resultant problems this brings. However, as Schenwar and Law (2020: xi) point out:

> **if we limit our field of vision in this way – measuring progress solely by the number of people who are no longer locked up in prisons – we inevitably fail to take into account the millions of people who can be found in immigration detention centres or mental health facilities, as well as tens of millions of people on probation or parole worldwide.**

The term *mass imprisonment* makes it easy to forget that most people under some form of carceral control are not even in prison. More than three times as many people are currently on probation or parole as are held in prison. In England and Wales this is approximately 250,000 individuals in relation to a prison population of around 83,000.

So even if we significantly reduced the number of people imprisoned, we would still have large groups of people under surveillance in the form of probation, parole or electronic monitoring and therefore constantly under the gaze and control of the state. They may be free in the sense that they are no longer being held behind prison doors but instead maybe sentenced to their homes, placed under curfew or confined within their neighbourhoods through electronic monitoring devices that monitor their every movement. Such individuals may not be imprisoned but they would still be labelled criminals and subject to legal discrimination and often denied employment, housing and access to basic public goods. Again, this raises several fundamental questions that we would ask you to consider as you work through this book. Even if you are not monitored by a tracking device, what does it mean to have to report in with a probation officer before every life decision? To be bound by stringent curfew restrictions on Internet use, and constraints on whom you spend your time with? To be tested for drugs or alcohol under the threat of a return to prison?

Academic commentators such as Nils Christie (2015) have argued that a *prison industrial complex* has developed in modern society. The term prison industrial complex is used to describe the relationship between public and private interests that employ prisons, policing, probation, the courts and other criminal justice apparatus as a means of maintaining social, economic and political inequalities. The prison industrial complex brings together a web of punitive systems that mainly target people who are marginalised by virtue of their race, class, gender or who are simply considered surplus to society. It has been argued that we are now witnessing the growth of a *treatments industrial complex* (Schenwar and Law, 2020) with the expansion of the incarceration industry into some areas that traditionally were focused on treatment and care of individuals involved in the criminal justice system. This treatment industrial complex involves secure hospitals, treatment programmes and approved premises, and several private companies that have benefied from prisons and immigration detention centres have now entered the treatment business – and as with all businesses their bottom line depends on expansion. According to Miller (2014: 329) as these forms of 'carceral devolution' developed in the 20th and early 21st centuries, new and additional formal and informal mechanisms were added including:

- the activation of third parties to reward and punish former prisoners through employment, housing, and social service policy

- the expansion of community corrections, neighbourhood watches and gated communities to protect and contain social actors within designated geographic spaces

- the therapeutic logics that have come to animate emerging criminal justice initiatives

- and the targeting of marginalised and dishonoured groups for criminal justice and social welfare intervention.

From this perspective, this new rehabilitation paradigm is not just a matter of social control:

> **but of a recasting of the role, force, and consequence of the state. It has produced novel ways of being in the social world, contributing to how the former prisoner, as a criminalized, racialized, and otherwise dishonoured cultural category is understood by researchers, the public, and policy makers, while also contributing to how former prisoners understand themselves. (Miller, 2014: 329)**

It is important to stress that the need to reduce the prison population is important given not only the harm it can do to individuals but also its failure to bring about positive change. But when we say that we need more alternatives to prison it could be argued that it is a false and dangerous alternative if those institutions that are intended to replace the use of imprisonment merely function like prison, primarily concerned with control rather than healing the damaging effects of crime on communities or restoring the individual to the status of citizen. Moreover, our experience tells us that so-called alternatives to prison tend to act as alternatives to each other. Ultimately, the question is where will this all end?

In Fergus McNeill's (2019) recent work, *Pervasive Punishment: Making Sense of Mass Supervision*, which we will explore further in Chapter 3, he offers an analysis of contemporary penal supervision in the community both in Scotland and in England and Wales with reference to the North American and European contexts. Following in the tradition of Foucault and Cohen, McNeill challenges the commonplace liberal view that community sanctions and measures are relatively and sometimes substantially benign in comparison to imprisonment. McNeil argues that the scale and reach of community supervision and the intensity of the oversight and grip imposed on supervised individuals in late modernity is much more painful to undergo than scholars and practitioners have often realised.

RISK AND PUBLIC PROTECTION

Preoccupation with how we manage *risky* individuals has become perhaps one of the defining characteristics of contemporary criminal justice. On the one hand, we as citizens and consumers are increasingly rendered responsible for our own safety; on the other hand there are increasing calls for punishment for those who offend. The enhanced awareness of risk situates the pursuit of safety as 'normal, pragmatic and everyday' (Sparks 2010: 294). The concept of risk is both complex and contested and can mean many things to different people. It can refer to both the probability of an adverse event – such as a risk of reoffending – or to the severity of the consequences of an event – such as the risk of harm. It can also refer to different subjects or targets of risk, the risk of self-harm or the risks posed to specific individuals in a particular relationship with the person deemed a risk – such as children and/or significant others – or it can be a risk to the general public. Discussions of risk used to be concerned mainly with the identification of a small number of *dangerous offenders*, but risk has now become central to all aspects of probation work. The risks posed by all people on probation are now routinely assessed, and the outcome of that assessment determines the type and intensity of intervention that will follow. Indeed, as we will discuss later, the idea that people can be categorised on the basis of assessed risk was the basis of splitting probation into the National Probation Service (responsible for managing and supervising high-risk individuals) and the community rehabilitation companies (CRCs) (responsible for managing and supervising medium- and low-risk individuals). The dominance of risk and public protection has unsurprisingly impacted on the work of criminal justice staff in both custodial and community settings. It has led to:

- The extended use of custody for dangerous individuals and the use of preventative sentencing on the grounds of risk. Prison staff therefore have to manage high-risk populations safely, reduce violence to prisoners and staff and manage prisoner contacts with past and potential victims. They do this by addressing risky behaviours through sentence planning and intervention programmes. They also assess risk prior to release and consider appropriate licence conditions.

- Extended monitoring and surveillance of those who present a high risk of harm in the community and upon release from prison. This includes the use of registers, *tracking* systems and targeting high-risk individuals for more intensive interventions, restrictive conditions and control measures. Probation staff have to assess risk in all cases and advisee sentencers on the levels of risk in pre-sentence reports (see Chapter 10). They must ensure that individuals are safely managed in the community and enforce restrictive conditions when necessary to limit opportunities for further offending in order to protect both victims and the public.

Harrison (2011) notes that the construction of dangerousness moved from those individuals committing habitual property offences to those committing acts of violence and particularly those involving sexual violence. Whilst it is difficult to accurately pinpoint the timing of this transition (Kemshall, 2020) it was certainly given impetus by the risk-focused sentencing of the Criminal Justice Act 1991, which saw the lengths of custodial sentences increasing and the introduction of preventive sentencing for those deemed to pose a serious risk of harm. There are many complex and interrelated reasons for this *renaissance of dangerousness* that have been put forward. Firstly, there is the belief that we are currently living in a *risk society* – a term coined by Ulrich Beck (1992). Beck argued that modern society is highly *risk-aware*, anxious about the many hazards of 'modernisation' – such as the unforeseen impact of technological advances and innovations (for example, pollution, human activity on climate, nuclear waste, the proliferation of weapons of mass destruction). We therefore need to attempt to understand and control these uncertain threats, which increase our sense of vulnerability and risk awareness. This includes heightened sensitivity to the risks posed by some individuals because as Canton (2017: 127) notes, those who commit crimes 'are in principle more identifiable and controllable than most of the shapeless and unattributable threats generated by modern technologies, while retributive emotions countenance strong reactions to criminals'. Ward and Maruna (2007: 81) contend that risk-averse societies effectively quarantine people and this leads to (a) exaggerated public fears and anxiety about personal safety, (b) social exclusion of individuals with criminal records, and (c) increased risk because of offenders' lack of opportunities to pursue rewarding, pro-social lifestyles.

Secondly, *the politics of criminal justice* have meant that political parties in many countries have promised to make the public safer, partly through the identification and management of dangerous individuals. It has been argued that this has led to a change in penological focus that involves the identification and management of high-risk categories and sub-populations, which are sorted according to their levels of dangerousness. Such strategies and techniques have been in existence since the early 1990s. This was termed a *new penology* by Feeley and Simon (1992). Instead of focusing on the individual and trying to rehabilitate them, the new penology is focused on notions of risk and how groups of individuals can be managed according to these risk classifications. In particular, it seeks to regulate levels of deviance, rather than intervening or responding to individual deviants or social malformations. Under this model, risk management is much more important than rehabilitation, with a focus placed on surveillance, confinement and control.

In addition to the new penology, dangerousness legislation has also been influenced by what Anthony Bottoms (1995) describes as *populist punitiveness*. This has partly been in response to high-profile cases surrounding early release decisions, and when shortcomings in community supervision which were believed to have led to serious further offences. This has become embroiled in the politics of law and order. Bottoms argues that current law and order responses have been largely based on the belief that the public are in favour of harsh punishments, especially in relation to dangerous people. Thinking that this is true, and that the introduction of punitive penalties will garner public support, policy makers have increasingly introduced more severe measures for those classified as high-risk. As a result, by the early 2000s both prisons and probation had begun to be enmeshed in wider debates around crime control and in particular around high-risk individuals epitomised by the notorious cases of Sydney Cooke and Robert Oliver who were members of a paedophile ring. Plans for their release were leaked to the press and as a result, both were housed for a considerable time in a police station on their release – for their own safety. The vigilante action on the Paulsgrove Estate in 2000 against known and suspected paedophiles reflected not only a heightened level of public anxiety but also a distrust of the authorities to manage such risks accordingly. According to Kewley and Brereton (2022) the impact of dangerousness narrative has had a palpable impact on frontline workers with a blame culture infiltrating recent probation practice.

The management of people who commit sexually motivated offences, and in particular the management of those convicted of sexual offences in the community, subsequently dominated the policy agenda with a campaign for Sarah's Law – named after Sarah Payne (a nine-year-old girl who was abducted and murdered by a known individual with previous convictions for sexually motivated offences who was under supervision in the community at the time). Sarah's Law enabled members of the public to ask the police if an individual had previous convictions for sexual offending against a child. In practice, the scheme was quite limited as an enquiry must be made via the police, about a named person, the person must be in contact with or have access to a child or children, and the person making the enquiry will only be told something if the subject of the enquiry meets certain criteria of risk and has previous convictions for sexual offences against children. Crucially, a disclosure will only be made to the person who is in the best position to protect the child.

A parallel development was the introduction of the sex offenders register. People are placed on the register at the same time as they receive their sentence for a sexual offence. This requires them to notify the police every time their circumstances change. The severity of the sentence dictates how long a person has to stay on the register and this can be anything from two years to the rest of their lives. Regular risk assessments are undertaken but these are mainly used for increasing or decreasing the intensity of the intervention. As Thomas (2009: 257) observes, registration 'is a form of public protection and not part of the punishment'.

A summary of research on the impact of registration on sexual recidivism suggests that there has been no significant impact on outcomes (Prescott and Rockoff, 2011); furthermore, failure to register also does not appear to be associated with any significant increase in sexual recidivism. Surveys of public attitudes to notification tend to report positive responses and individuals on the register, when surveyed, often felt notification was a deterrent to recidivism. However, a large number of studies highlighted the negative impact of notification requirements on individuals convicted of sexual offences in terms of work, housing, harassment and disadvantage (Lobanov-Rostovsky, 2015). Conversely, as we mentioned earlier, the preoccupation with public protection and risk management has corresponded with *the rise of alternatives*. By this we mean the attempt to limit the size of the prison population through the provision of *alternatives to custody* and systems of early release. The starting point here is that prison should be reserved for people who engage in persistent and serious criminality. If resources are limited, it makes sense to concentrate them on people who are most likely to reoffend most seriously. This has led to a system of bifurcation aimed at reducing levels of punishment for those who commit less serious offences, whilst at the same time increasing them for those who commit more serious and dangerous acts. The thought that dangerous people are in prison brings a sense of reassurance, even if this feeling is often misleading and confuses prevention with mere postponement.

An enhanced focus on risk and public protection has led to an increasing emphasis on partnership and inter-agency work. Multi-Agency Public Protection Arrangements (MAPPA) involve the identification and management of high-risk categories and sub-populations, which are sorted according to their levels of dangerousness. Such strategies and techniques have been in existence since the early 1990s and, although such work is now accepted to be an essential function of the work of probation, it is not without controversy. As Robinson and McNeill (2010) note, in times of insecurity and pressure on scare resources, talking up probation's credentials to manage and reduce risks may seem sensible. However, as McNeill and Weaver point out, not all risks are predictable or harms preventable and in committing itself to assessing and managing risk, probation 'exposes itself not to the likelihood of failure, but to its inevitability' (2010: 14). Cases of serious further offending such as that of Joseph McCann can severely undermine public perceptions of probation's ability to deliver public protection. McCann committed a series of indiscriminate sexual assault and rape offences that ranged from an 11-year old boy to a 71-year-old woman, whilst under the supervision of the National Probation Service. Following his re-arrest McCann was sentenced to 33 life sentences of imprisonment.

MAPPA is a set of statutory arrangements established in the 2003 Criminal Justice Act to assess and manage risks posed by certain people who commit violent or sexual offences. A person is assessed under the Offender Assessment System (OASys) in England and Wales as being a high or very high risk of causing serious harm *and* presenting risks that can only be managed by a plan that requires close cooperation at a senior level due to the complexity of the case and/or because of the unusual resource commitments it requires. Or, although an individual is not assessed as a high or very high risk, the case is exceptional because the likelihood of media scrutiny and/or public interest in the management of the case is very high. The purpose of MAPPA is to help reduce the reoffending behaviour of sexual and violent individuals to protect the public, including previous victims, from serious harm. These purposes are achieved by ensuring that all the relevant authorities work effectively together so that relevant individuals are identified, appropriate risk assessments are completed and, leading on from this, suitable risk management plans are formulated. The key to this is the sharing of information between MAPPA agencies.

Both the prison and probation services are *responsible authorities* within the MAPPA arrangements, alongside the Police. The responsible authorities are also under a duty to decide whether they should disclose information regarding the previous convictions of those whom they supervise irrespective of whether information is requested. There is also a duty on what are known as *duty to co-operate agencies*, which includes housing, Children's Social Care and Adult Social Care, health and education, to co-operate with the responsible authorities. Panels are therefore often made up of police, probation, social services, health and housing. It is also good practice to involve, when appropriate, the expertise of forensic psychiatrists and psychologists. To qualify for MAPPA, a person must fall into one of three categories:

Category 1 Registered sex offenders: these will be managed by the police and, if under a court order or on licence from prison, by the Probation Service (PS) as well.

Category 2 Violent offenders, registered terrorist offenders and other sex offenders: includes people who have been sentenced to 12 months or more in custody or to detention in hospital with restrictions, now living in the community and subject to The Probation Service supervision and management.

Category 3 Other dangerous offenders: includes people who have committed an offence in the past, indicating a capacity to cause a serious risk of harm to the public and who because of their assessed risk it is thought need multi-agency management.

Once it has been identified that an individual is MAPPA eligible it will then be decided at what level that individual needs monitoring. There are three levels of MAPPA supervision as shown below:

Level 1: used in cases where the risk posed by the individual can be managed by one agency without actively or significantly involving other agencies.

Level 2: used where the active involvement of more than one agency is required but where either the level of risk or complexity of managing the risk is not so great as to require referral to level 3.

Level 3: used for the management of the 'critical few'.

Between 2017 and 2018, 587 level 2 and 3 MAPPA cases were returned to custody for breaching their licence conditions. This was a reduction of 16 per cent from the previous year and continues a steady decrease in recalls since 2006. During the same time period, however, 242 MAPPA cases were charged with a serious further offence (SFO), which was a 12 per cent increase from the previous year and the highest number for ten years. While 242 may sound high when put into the context of the total number of MAPPA eligible individuals this only represents 0.3 per cent of all cases (Bryant et al., 2015).

When a serious offence is committed by a person under supervision, an SFO review is undertaken to ascertain the circumstances which led to the commission of the offence and whether there are any lessons which need to be learnt. This will normally be delegated to HM Inspectorate of Probation. Since 2016 the rate of SFO notifications and resultant reviews has decreased by 27 per cent, including a reduction in the number related to rape and sexual offences (see Figure 1.1).

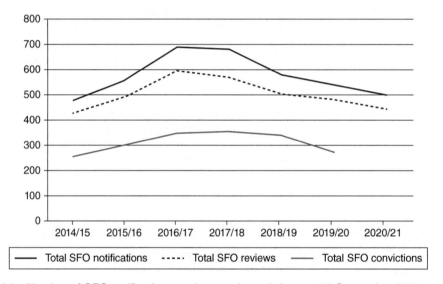

Figure 1.1   Number of SFO notifications, reviews and convictions at 30 September 2021

(*Source*: Ministry of Justice (2021) Serious Further Offences 2021 Bulletin, https://assets.publishing.service. gov.uk/government/uploads/system/uploads/attachment_data/file/1028666/Serious_Further_Offences_bulletin_ 2021_Final.pdf)

Enquiries sometimes discover that procedures were not followed and may attribute this to staff inexperience, high workloads, shortcomings in training, or perhaps to weaknesses in implementation or under-resourcing. However, as Canton and Dominey (2018: 161) note, 'few if any inquiries have taken the further step of claiming that had the procedures been appropriately followed, the serious offence would not have taken place'. Concerns have been raised that probation's ability to deliver effective public protection has been undermined by a succession of organisational changes that culminated in Transforming Rehabilitation (TR) reforms. HM Inspectorate of Probation (2018) found that the decline in the quality of public protection work was most marked among the CRCs, with many serious further offences committed by those who are judged to present a low or medium risk of serious harm. However, perhaps the biggest threat to the effectiveness of MAPPA is often not the individual themselves but the impossible expectations placed on it by politicians, the public and the lack of adequate resources to facilitate it. High-quality public protection work can reduce but cannot eliminate the potential for risk of harm to society.

There are a number of components to risk management work that include (but are not limited to) the following:

- *Intervention programmes* are defined as programmes designed to help individuals to change their criminal behaviour through control or management of thinking patterns, feelings, drives and attitudes. Intervention programmes may use a range of methods, but in practice have been based on intensive cognitive-behavioural methods delivered both in custody and in the community. These programmes are not the only types of interventions to reduce risk. Others include rehabilitative interventions (e.g., stable accommodation) and protective interventions (e.g., being part of a pro-social network).

- *Restrictive conditions* are those conditions that restrict where an offender can go, or live, what he or she can do, and whom he or she can contact. Offenders may have a condition to reside in a certain place (such as a hostel or approved premises) or not to enter a particular area. They can also be self-imposed (such as an offender committing to attend AA meetings). Restrictive conditions are specific to individual offenders. It is important that they match the assessed risk factors, and are proportionate, justified and workable in practice. It is also important that they are monitored and enforced if breached.

- *Monitoring, surveillance and control procedures* are those that provide a watching eye over the offender. They are usually used to monitor compliance with restrictive conditions, to monitor grooming activities and to gain further information on networks and criminal activities. These procedures can include electronic tagging, the use of CCTV, and police observation. In prison they can include monitoring mail and phone calls, and visitor and offender contact. (National Offender Management Service, 2016: 5)

Two key measures, Circles of Support and Accountability (COSA) and polygraph testing illustrate the different approaches to managing risky individuals in the community, especially those convicted of sexual offences. COSA were first developed in Canada in the mid-1990s based on the principles of restorative justice (Bates et al., 2011). In Canada, Circles can operate at three different points in the criminal justice process: as an alternative to custody or as well as custody; on release from prison as a means of supporting parole supervision; and at the end of a custodial sentence in the absence of statutory supervision (McCarten and Kemshall, 2020). Hanvey (2011) points out that the Circles approach is also closely associated with the strengths-based Good Lives Model (that we discuss in the next chapter) as it focuses on enhancing the person's capabilities to attain goals, or primary human goods, through socially acceptable means.

As we discuss in Chapter 13, isolation and loneliness can be potential risk factors in sexual offending (Edwards and Hensley, 2001; Marshall, 2010). As Clarke et al. (2017: 446) note, this means that 'communities that fail to reintegrate offenders may counter intuitively, also fail to quell important risk factors' in the type of offence. COSA is potentially a means of addressing this dilemma. Circles began as an informal community response to fears evoked by the release of high-risk people who had committed offences against children into the community, where individuals, mainly from the Mennonite Church, formed small groups or circles around the released person. The person (or core member as they are known) is given support by a group of four to six volunteers who are in turn supported by a Circle coordinator. Volunteers are from within the community, with a range of ages and backgrounds, and meet with the core member on a weekly and sometimes daily basis. COSA aims to promote community integration of people who have committed a criminal offence by helping them develop and maintain engagement in positive activities and supportive relationships within the community. Through COSA the individual is held to account and is subject to a degree of social control but is also able to access support. They typically involve a partnership between professionals and volunteers. In Canada, Circles are a community-driven and professionally supported model whereas in the British context they are professionally driven, community-supported projects (Wilson et al., 2007). Although COSA has restricted its remit to those who have committed sexual offences against children, some community projects for high-risk personality disordered offenders have been heavily influenced by the model and have adapted it to work with those with adult victims and histories of physical violence. In a series of studies based in Canada, it was found that involvement in a Circle suggested a reduction in general reconviction rates among those assessed as most likely to reoffend sexually (Clarke et al., 2017). However, studies have been hampered by low base rates for sexual recidivism, small sample sizes, and short follow-up periods. Moreover, the goals of COSA are broader than just reducing reoffending. They aim to achieve greater social cohesion and community engagement.

The introduction of polygraph testing (or lie detector as it is sometimes referred to) in relation to the post-sentence management of those convicted of sexual offences has been highly contested. The basis of the polygraph examination involves individuals being asked a series of questions while linked up to sensors measuring blood pressure, breathing and perspiration based on the notion that lying induces a *stress response* in the autonomic nervous system (Marshall and Thomas, 2015). The Offender Management

Act 2007 sets out the statutory position regarding the mandatory testing of those convicted of sexual offences on parole – those over 18 years who have served at least one year in prison and are deemed to pose a high risk of recidivism are subject to six-monthly testing on release. Post-custodial polygraph testing was piloted between 2009 and 2011 and rolled out across England and Wales in 2013. In England and Wales, the polygraph tests have focused primarily on compliance with the terms and conditions of probation or parole, although tests may take place when there is a concern that an individual may have breached a licence condition or reoffended. In probation trials, over 90 per cent of offender managers rated polygraphy as being helpful, and none considered it to have a negative impact. However, this is different from concluding that polygraphy results have improved treatment outcomes or genuinely reduced sexual recidivism. There have been two United Kingdom studies that have examined the efficacy of polygraphy in facilitating relevant disclosures in comparison with a group of individuals with whom polygraphy was not used. The first trial was voluntary and the second mandatory, and both confirmed that the use of polygraphy was associated with greatly increased odds of making relevant disclosures (Marshall and Thomas, 2015). Interestingly, whilst 73 per cent of interviewed probation officers believed the people they supervised were open with them, this was the case for only 25 per cent of those who supervised polygraphed individuals.

There is an error rate with polygraphy of around 10 to 20 per cent (Craissati 2019: 147). In the United Kingdom, a released person cannot be recalled to prison on the basis of a *failed* polygraphy test, although it is of course the case that if disclosures reveal significant breaches of release conditions, then an offender will be recalled on that basis. The error rate is one of the main criticisms of polygraphy and is certainly a concern among those people with personality disorders, some of whom may be particularly prone to making false confessions. There is also a prevailing myth that the polygraph is a *lie detector* test, and it may therefore be the case that they make disclosures, expecting to be *found out*. Rigorous training and supervision of polygraph assessors is therefore vital to counter the very real risk otherwise of a drift towards unethical practice. The use of polygraph testing brings into sharp focus a range of ethical and professional issues, and as Marshall and Thomas (2015: 137) note, 'might be just the start of a slippery slope that will lead to a more widespread use once the polygraph has been embedded in the public's consciousness'.

PRIVATISATION, OUTSOURCING AND COMPETITION

The third development, which we would contend has had a significant impact on shaping contemporary penology, has been that of privatisation, outsourcing and competition.

According to Bell (2011), this has signalled a transformation in the role of the state from a provider of public services to that of a facilitator of market solutions. Those who promote and support privatisation usually contend that it does not matter who delivers the service as long as it is delivered to those who need it in a timely manner, efficiently and at a lower cost to the public purse – in other words, it delivers value for money. Muir (2012), however, has argued that there are services which are generally unsuitable for private sector delivery because there are:

- Services where the outcomes wanted by or required for the consumer are far too complex to be to be easily contracted for

- Relational services which engage the public very intensively and where the introduction of the profit motive may undermine the trust upon which good quality relationships depend

- Services which are there to uphold the law, such as the police and the judiciary, where it is particularly important that private interests are excluded and that there is direct public accountability

- Services that are particularly important for the inculcation of values.

The fundamental difference between public and state provision is in its type of ownership. In the public sector the service is owned and managed by the government whereas in the private sector it is owned by shareholders who invest in the company in return for a dividend on its profits. When thinking about this issue it is important to look at the terms that are used to underpin it and that are used in debates interchangeably although in reality they have different meanings. *Privatisation* in its purest form refers to the transfer of ownership, property or business from the government to the private sector. The government therefore ceases to be the owner of the entity or business. So, for example, a private prison will be built, owned and managed by a private corporation under contract to the government. *Outsourcing*, on the other hand, involves the practice of hiring a provider to deliver services that traditionally were performed in-house by the company's own employees and staff. *Competition* involves trying to produce a better service or goods than your competitors. This can be achieved through being more efficient or being able to produce the good or service at a lower cost. Competition depends on the existence of a market because if you do not have anyone to compete with or anyone that is challenging you then you have a monopoly on the goods or services and so in theory there is no incentive to produce them more efficiently or at a lower cost because people and organisations will have to purchase your goods simply because there is no alternative. This is known as marketisation. Often privatisation of state-owned monopolies occurs alongside deregulation – that is, the introduction of policies to allow more firms to enter the industry and increase the competitiveness of the market. *Contestability* is a term which is closely allied to marketisation. Traditionally, marketisation has been used as a mechanism to introduce private sector provision and to break down state monopolies and replace goods and services that were formally delivered by the public sector. Contestability, on the other hand, is less ideologically driven in the sense that whilst it also attempts to create a market based on competition, it argues that contracts should be awarded to whoever can provide the best service at the cheapest cost irrespective of whether they are from the public, private or voluntary sectors. Finally, *commodification* is the act of turning something into an item that can be bought and sold.

It is important to note that privatisation is a long-standing feature of criminal justice. In 15th-century England, for example, basements of ale houses were used as jails to hold people awaiting trial and the inn keepers were compensated by a combination of fees paid to the county and payments made to families of the accused. When there was a death penalty in England and Wales, hangmen were contracted to the state and paid on a *per-neck* basis (that is, for every person they hanged). The first modern form of mass punishment (transportation) was driven not by the state but by private contractors who saw a means of making profit from law-and-order concerns in England and labour shortages in the New World. However, towards the end of the first half of the 20th century the belief that some things were too important to be left in private hands – and so could only be guaranteed to be delivered in everyone's interest – formed the basis for *nationalisation* of public services in England and Wales. So, for example, gas, electricity, water, transport, etc. were all brought under public control because we all need them and so people should not be able to exploit them for commercial gain. The arguments for bringing prisons and probation under public control in the 18th and 19th centuries was based on the belief that state punishment and protecting the public were too important to be left to private and voluntary provision and required state intervention to ensure that they were delivered appropriately and consistently. However, this all started to change in the 1980s. In the next section, we will look at the reasons behind this major reversal in government policy.

One of the main arguments for privatisation is that the state cannot, and indeed should not, deliver everything. As mentioned earlier, private companies have always had a role to play in providing specialist services to the public sector although in recent years this has changed and their role has been to provide services that would formerly have been provided by the public sector. Even those who oppose the privatisation of public goods would perhaps concede that private sector specialisms and expertise are still needed in a complex contemporary society. The introduction of private investment can be *a useful means of dealing with pressures within the system* – for example, prison overcrowding – and relieves pressure on the police. Many public sector prisons date back to Victorian times and so are now not fit for purpose. It is probably true that private prisons tend to be newer, cleaner and provide a much better environment.

Secondly, it is claimed that private companies are more efficient and thereby deliver better value for money and more choice. One of the main arguments for privatisation is that private companies have a profit incentive to cut costs and be more efficient. If you work for a government-run industry, managers do not usually share in any profits. However, a private firm is interested in making a profit, and so it is more likely to cut costs and be efficient. Since privatisation, companies such as British Telcom and British Airways have shown degrees of improved efficiency and higher profitability. It is argued that public sector organisations are less efficient than their private sector counterparts because they are not subject to competition in the same way that the private sector is and that they continue to receive money from the government purse even if they fail to deliver services as expected. Public sector organisations find it hard sometimes to sack surplus workers because the cost of unemployment will still be borne by the state. The private sector, on the other hand, because they have to make a profit to stay in business, are incentivised to be more efficient and achieve cost reductions – and thereby more profit – by introducing new technology and increasing the productivity of its labour force (or sacking them!). Moreover, a government may think only in terms of the next election. Therefore, they may be unwilling to invest in infrastructure improvements which will bring benefits in the long term because they are more concerned about projects that give a benefit before the election.

It is also argued that private sector companies are *more accountable*. This is because they deliver services under contract to the state, and in theory if the state is unhappy with what they are providing then the state can end the contract or look for another provider. Each private prison, for example, has a controller responsible for ensuring its compliance with the law. Contracts have therefore been used to enforce minimum standards within private prisons and there is some evidence that private prisons provide a better range of services, programmes and out-of-cell activities for those in their care. An example is the decency agenda, which was first introduced in the private sector and then rolled out across the prison estate. It is unlikely that this would have happened as quickly had it been left solely to the public sector. The introduction of the private sector can lead to *sharing of good practice between sectors*. Public prisons have been around for over a century in their contemporary form and of course, as with any organisation, they have developed baggage over time. Traditionally, prisons have been dominated by a white male macho culture and have recruited significantly from ex-armed- forces personnel. Private prisons have led the way in the recruitment of more women and people from BAME groups. Having considered the arguments for privatisation, we now consider the case against it.

Firstly, it is argued that some goods and services are by their nature a *natural monopoly*. A natural monopoly occurs when the most efficient number of firms in an industry is one. For example, tap water has very significant fixed costs. Therefore, there is little or no scope for having competition amongst several firms. Therefore, in this case, privatisation would just create a private monopoly which might seek to set higher prices which exploit consumers. Secondly, there are many industries which perform an important public service, such as healthcare, education and public transport. In these industries, the profit motive should not be the primary objective of firms and the industry. For example, in the case of healthcare, it is feared that privatisation would mean greater priority being given to profit than to patient care. Also, in an industry like healthcare, arguably we do not need a profit motive to improve standards. When doctors treat patients, they are unlikely to try harder if they get a bonus. Thirdly, there is the argument that the *government loses out on potential dividends*. Many of the privatised companies in the United Kingdom are quite profitable. This means the government does not benefit from their dividends, which instead go to wealthy shareholders. Selling state-owned assets to the private sector was seen as politically attractive because it raised significant sums for the United Kingdom government. However, the counterargument to this is that this is a one-off benefit. It also means we lose out on future dividends from the profits of public companies as these are paid out to shareholders instead. Fourthly, because of the high capital costs involved, privatisation creates private monopolies, such as the water companies and rail companies. This needs regulating to prevent abuse of monopoly power. Therefore, there is still a need for government regulation, as there is under state ownership.

Government may be motivated by short-term pressures, but so might private firms. To please shareholders, they may seek to increase short-term profits and avoid investing in long- term projects. Privatisation can therefore encourage *cost cutting to maximise profit*. This is because in practice their motives are very different. Governments can put social benefits above profit motive whereas private firms may ignore *external costs*, such as pollution and other environmental harm. This is because ultimately governments are answerable to the general public whereas private companies are primarily answerable to their shareholders.

Government spends approximately £292 billion (more than a third of all public spending) on procuring goods, works and services from external suppliers. Most of this spending is with private companies (with around 4 per cent accounted for by voluntary organisations). Private companies operate prisons, assess benefit claimants, provide employment training, offer routine National Health Service (NHS) operations and deliver social care. They provide immigration enforcement and accommodate asylum seekers. They provide catering in schools and collect waste for more than half of Britain's local authorities. They run the IT systems that government relies on to collect taxes, pay pensions, look after savings and manage medical and criminal records. They are responsible for Britain's largest infrastructure projects, building hospitals, schools and roads. This has led to concerns that they are too big to fail. This has become extremely important considering a series of high-profile contract failures. One of the most high-profile cases was that involving electronic monitoring (Dearden, 2019). The companies were investigated by the Serious Fraud Squad on the grounds that they were defrauding the Government by claiming that they were providing tagging services to people who were either in prison or in some cases had died.

As we mentioned earlier, the appeal of privatisation is to break the monopoly of the state. However, as we have also seen, there is a danger that these public monopolies merely become replaced with private monopolies. This is because building a prison or running an electronic monitoring system, for example, are extremely costly and require substantial investment of the kind that only multinational corporations can provide. This has certainly been the case in England and Wales where we have seen a small number of companies control the market for both prison and probation services. For example, Serco and G4S received over two-thirds of government contracts for contracted-out prisons, detention centres and electronic monitoring. Twenty of the 21 CRCs which were formed as part of the probation reform we will discuss in Chapters 4 and 6 were owned by private sector organisations. More than half of the CRCs were owned by just two companies, Interserve and Sodexo. Neither of these companies had an established record of delivering rehabilitative services and their expertise lay in the provision of a range of other services that have been outsourced through recent government contracting out activity. The scale and nature of outsourcing in England and Wales means that the market for delivering public services is inevitably dominated by giant conglomerates with similar business models that are heavily dependent on securing public contract revenues. They rely on winning new contracts by undercutting their competitors and an unrelenting growth strategy accelerated through acquisition. This creates a complex web of corporate governance that lacks transparency and undermines accountability.

Private companies can walk away from contracts if for whatever reason they are unable to deliver or they feel that they are not delivering a big enough return on their investments. This raises the fundamental question, in whose interest do they operate? If a private company walks away from delivering a prison or probation service, then the government has to step in because it has a moral duty, and indeed a legal duty, to protect its citizens. In this respect, although the attractiveness of privatisation is that it is claimed that it transfers risks away from the public sector to the private, in reality it is much more complex. It also brings into question the belief that private sector organisations are by definition always more efficient than their public counterparts.

How then do we evaluate the benefits of privatisation based on all experiences over the past 50 years in England and Wales? Whether privatised provision brings benefits to the public seems to depend on three key factors. Firstly, it depends on the type of *industry in question*. An industry like telecoms is a industry where the incentive of profit can help increase efficiency. However, as we have noted, if you apply it to industries like healthcare and criminal justice then the profit motive is less important. Secondly, it depends on *the quality of regulation*. Do the regulators ensure that the privatised firm meets certain standards of service and keeps prices low? It could be argued that in the case of some former public provision like electricity and gas that competition has actually increased the price to the consumer. Thirdly, it depends on *whether the market is contestable and competitive*. Creating a private monopoly, as we have seen in the case of electronic monitoring, may actually lead to higher costs. But if, on the other hand, the market is highly competitive then there is certainly greater scope for efficiency savings. Outsourcing seems to work best in sectors that are relatively simple to contract for and deliver. When these services were first outsourced in the 1980s and 1990s, they brought about large savings – sometimes around 20 per cent of overall operating costs. However, over time the public sector has also become more efficient in these areas, meaning that the comparative advantage of the private sector has become smaller or disappeared. For frontline services – such as prisons – the picture is much more mixed but there is one sector, probation, where it is suggested that privatisation has clearly not worked and could have actually harmed the delivery of the service (see Chapter 5).

Much of the public versus private debate centres upon utilitarian arguments such as which organisation provides the most effective service and or at the cheapest cost. However, there is also a moral dimension to these arguments. Fundamentally, what it boils down to is whether or not you believe the state alone has the right to punish. For example, in 2009 the Israeli Supreme Court ruled that private prisons were unacceptable in all circumstances (Addae, 2019). According to the ruling – even if the empirical data were to demonstrate that the private institutions performed better – they should still be rejected because they violate human dignity. This is because imposition of punishment is integral to criminal law and represents the most acute exercise of legal coercion as well as protecting the fundamental rights and interests of citizens. Therefore, enacting and enforcing criminal law is an inalienable state responsibility, constitutionally concerned with protection of individual liberties, public interest and civil peace.

As the political philosopher Michael Sandel (2012) has argued, we need to think carefully about how markets operate, what the limits of the market are, and ensure that whilst the increasing penetration of public services by the private sector persists (as it seems likely it will) that issues of legitimacy and public interest are at the forefront of these discussions. He argues that we have drifted from having a market economy to being a market society (Sandel, 2012: 10). Whereas the former is a tool for organising productive activity, the latter becomes a way of life in which market values encroach into every aspect of public life. Sandel questions the morality of market economies that reduce public goods to mere commodities that can be bought and sold to the highest bidder. He warns that such a situation not only widens inequalities but ultimately corrupts the values of society because 'markets don't only allocate goods; they also express and promote certain attitudes towards the good being exchanged' (Sandel, 2012: 8).

Driven by the desire to reduce costs, many American states are becoming increasingly reliant on an *offender-funded probation model* overseen by for-profit companies that manage probation requirements, electronic monitoring, drug-testing and fine collection. It is a lucrative business as there is no cap on the amount of fees that private probation companies can charge individuals, even those convicted of minor offences such as driving without a licence or being drunk in a public place. According to Human Rights

Watch, rates for basic supervision range from $35 to $100 per month, where additional services such as Global Positioning System (GPS) monitoring or drug testing can cost upwards of $180 to $360 per month (Gambino, 2014). In some cases, probation fees can be more than twice those of the court-ordered financial penalties. Unsurprisingly, many of those placed on probation only do so because they cannot pay their court fines in the first place and become increasingly unable to afford the probation fees accrued to the private company. Within this context, probation is ultimately reduced to a concern with debt collection and boosting the coffers of companies providing so-called *pay only* probation. Whilst this extreme form of *ultra-privatisation* has not and is unlikely to pervade the English and Welsh probation services and there has been a partial retreat from privatisation by the government, the situation in some parts of the United States offers a dystopian vision of how far an unregulated market can corrode systems of justice. Consider the case of Thomas Barrett who stole a $2 beer, was fined $200 by the court and ended up owing more than $1,000 to Sentinel Offender Services, the company supervising his probation. He resorted to selling his own blood plasma twice a week to pay Sentinel, according to an account he gave to Human Rights Watch.

CONCLUSION

In this chapter we have identified three key developments which we believe have had a significant impact on shaping contemporary policies and practices in both custodial and community settings. They reveal how kinder, gentler narratives of reform can obscure agendas of social control and challenge us to question the ways we replicate the status quo when pursuing change. We considered the expansion of social control, backed up by surveillance-based technologies drawing on the insights provided by Foucault, Cohen and others. We noted how these disciplinary techniques provided the potential for new forms of government and subsequently encroached into everyday life in many contemporary societies. We argued that rather than acting as an alternative to imprisonment, so-called community punishments have in fact supplemented and reinforced the dominant systems leading to both *mass incarceration* and *mass supervision*. We then explored the accompanying emphasis on risk as a contemporary feature of prison and probation work. We considered the drivers behind this trend and looked at the efficacy of some of the key practice initiatives which have emerged from it and its impact on traditional notions of the purposes of rehabilitation. Finally, we discussed the trend of outsourcing of public goods and the privatisation agenda, which has been a feature of criminal justice policy in England and Wales for the past 50 years or so. Again, we looked at the drivers behind this and argued that discussions surrounding the efficacy of privatisation had to be grounded in ethical considerations.

recommended reading

If you would like to engage in further reading, you may find the following resources particularly useful:

Shenwar, M. and Law, V. (2020) *Prison by Any Other Name: The Harmful Consequences of Popular Reforms*. New York: The New Press.

The authors of this text provide a powerful argument that the expansion of cost-effective substitutes for imprisonment have actually widened the net, weaving in new strands of punishment and control, and bringing new populations, who would not otherwise have been subject to imprisonment, under physical control by the state.

Norris, C. and Wilson, D. (2017) *Surveillance, Crime and Social Control*. Abingdon: Routledge.

This edited collection brings together a range of contributions that have informed debate and scholarship on the relationship between surveillance, crime and social control. The volume covers issues including surveillance, CCTV, technology and crime control and the future of surveillance.

Daems, T. and Vander Beken, T. (2018) *Privatising Punishment in Europe*. Abingdon: Routledge.

Bringing together scholars from across Europe and beyond, this book maps and describes trends of privatising punishment throughout Europe, paying attention both to prisons and community sanctions.

references

Addae, A.E., (2019) Challenging the constitutionality of private prisons: Insights from Israel. *William & Mary Journal of Race, Gender and Social Justice*, 25(3), 527–553.

Aebi, M., Delgrande, N. and Marguet, Y. (2015) Have community sanctions and measures widened the net of European criminal justice systems? *Punishment & Society*, 17(5), 575–97.

Bates, A. Macrae, R., Williams, D. and Webb, C. (2011) Ever-increasing circles: A descriptive study of Hampshire and Thames Valley Circles of Support and Accountability 2002–2009. *Journal of Sexual Aggression*, 18, 355–73.

Beck, U. (1992) *Risk Society: Towards a New Modernity*. London: Sage.

Bell, E. (2011) *Criminal Justice and Neoliberalism*. London: Palgrave Macmillan.

Bottoms, A. (1995) The philosophy and politics of punishment and sentencing. In C. Clarkson and R. Morgan (eds) *The Politics of Sentencing Reform*. Oxford: Clarendon Press, pp. 17–50.

Bryant, S., Peck, M. and Lovbakke, J. (2015) *Reoffending Analysis of MAPPA Eligible Offenders*. London: Ministry of Justice.

Canton, R. (2017) *Why Punish? An Introduction to the Philosophy of Punishment*. London: Palgrave Macmillan.

Canton, R. and Dominey, J. (2018) *Probation*. Abingdon: Routledge.

Christie, N. (2015) *Crime Control as Industry*. Abingdon: Routledge.

Clarke, M., Broen, S. and Võllm, B. (2017) Circles of Support and Accountability for sex offenders: A systematic review of outcomes. *Sexual Abuse*, 29(5), 446–78.

Cohen, S. (1985) *Visions of Social Control: Crime, Punishment and Classification*. Cambridge: Polity Press.

Craissati, J. (2019) *The Rehabilitation of Sexual Offenders: Complexity, Risk and Desistance*. Abingdon: Routledge.

Dearden, L. (2019) Former Serco directors charged with fraud over electronic tagging of criminals. *Independent*. Available at: www.independent.co.uk/news/uk/crime/serco-criminal-tagging-electronic-monitoring-fraud-prosecution-crime-sfo-a9248901.html (last accessed 31 July 2022).

Edwards, W. and Hensley, C. (2001) Contextualizing sex offender management legislation and policy. Evaluating the problem of latent consequences in community notification laws. *International Journal of Offender Therapy and Comparative Criminology*, 45, 83–101.

Feeley, M. and Simon, J. (1992) The new penology: Notes on the emerging strategy of corrections and its implications. *Criminology*, 30(4), 449–74.

Foucault, M. (1977) *Discipline and Punish: The Birth of the Prison*. London: Penguin.

Gambino, L. (2014) Thrown into jail for being poor: The booming for-profit probation industry. *The Guardian*. Available at: www.theguardian.com/money/2014/mar/02/poor-for-profit-probation-prison-georgia (last accessed 19 April 2019).

Garland, D. (1985) *Punishment and Welfare: A History of Penal Strategies*. Aldershot: Gower.

Garland, D. (2001) *The Culture of Control: Crime and Social Order in Contemporary Society*. Oxford: Oxford University Press.

Hanvey, S. (2011) But does it work? Evaluation and evidence. In S. Hanvey, T. Philpot and C. Wilson (eds) *A Community-Based Approach to the Reduction of Sexual Offending: Circles of Support and Accountability*. London: Jessica Kingsley, pp. 150–65.

Harrison, K. (2011) *Dangerousness, Risk and the Governance of Serious Sexual and Violent Offenders*. Abingdon: Routledge.

HM Inspectorate of Probation (2018) The quality of public protection work (probation services). Research and Analysis Bulletin 2018/02.

Kemshall, H. (2020) A critical review of risk assessment policy and practice since the 1990s, and the contribution of risk practice to contemporary rehabilitation of offenders. In P. Ugwudike, H. Graham, F. McNeill, P. Raynor, F.S. Taxman and C. Trotter (eds) *The*

Routledge Companion to Rehabilitative Work in Criminal Justice. Abingdon, Oxon: Routledge, pp. 220–32.

Kewley, S. and Brereton, S. (2022) Public protection: Examining the impact of strengthened public protection policy on probation practice. In L. Burke, N. Carr, E. Cluley, S. Collett, and McNeill, F. (eds) *Reimagining Probation Practice.* Abingdon, Oxon: Routledge, pp. 112–131.

Lobanov-Rostovsky, C. (2015) Adult sex offender management. Available at: www.smart.gov/pdfs/AdultSexOffenderManagement.pdf (last accessed 14 August 2021).

Marshall, D. and Thomas, T. (2015) Polygraphs and sex offenders: The truth is out there. *Probation Journal,* 62(2), 128–39.

Marshall, W.L. (2010) The role of attachments, intimacy, and loneliness in the etiology and maintenance of sexual offending. *Sexual and Marital Therapy,* 25, 73–85.

Mathiesen, T. (1983) The future of control systems – The case of Norway. In D. Garland and P. Young (eds) *The Power to Punish.* London: Heinemann.

McCarten, K. and Kemshall, H. (2008) The potential role of recovery capital in stopping sexual offending: Lessons from Circles of Support and Accountability to enrich practice. *Irish Probation Journal,* 17, 87–106.

McNeill, F. (2019) *Pervasive Punishment: Making Sense of Mass Supervision.* Bingley: Emerald Publishing.

McNeill, F. and Weaver, B. (2010) *Changing Lives? Desistance Research and Offender Management.* Glasgow: Scottish Centre for Crime and Justice Research.

McWilliams, W. (1983) The Mission to the English Police Courts 1876–1936. *Howard Journal of Criminal Justice,* 22: 129–147.

Miller, R.J. (2014) Devolving the carceral state: Race, prisoner re-entry and the micro-politics of urban poverty management. *Punishment and Society,* 16(30): 305–35.

Ministry of Justice (2021) Serious further offences 2021 bulletin. Available at: https://assets.publishing.service.gov.uk/government/uploads/system/uploads/attachment_data/file/1028666/Serious_Further_Offences_bulletin_2021_Final.pdf (last accessed 17 May 2022).

Muir, R. (2012) After the G4S debacle, it's time to re-think the role of the private sector. *New Statesman,* 17 July.

NOMS (2016) *Public Protection Manual.* 2016 Edition. Available at: https://assets.publishing.service.gov.uk/government/uploads/system/uploads/attachment_data/file/911340/psi-18-2016-pi-17-2016-public-protection-manual.pdf (last accessed 31 July 2022).

Prescott, J. and Rockoff, J. (2011) Do sex offender registration and notification laws affect criminal behaviour? *Journal of Law and Economics,* 54, 161–206.

Raynor, P. and Robinson, G. (2009) *Rehabilitation, Crime and Justice.* Houndmills: Palgrave Macmillan.

Robinson, G. and McNeill, F. (2010) The dynamics of compliance with community supervision. In F. McNeill, P. Raynor and C. Trotter C (eds) *Offender Supervision: New Directions in Theory, Research and Practice.* Willan. pp. 367–384.

Rose, N. and Miller, P. (1992) Political power beyond the state: Problematics of government. *British Journal of Sociology*, 43, 172–205.

Sandel, M. (2012) *What Money Can't Buy: The Moral Limits of Markets*. London: Penguin.

Schenwar, M. and Law, V. (2020) *Prison by Any Other Name: The Harmful Consequences of Popular Reforms*. New York: The New Press.

Simon, J. (2007) *Governing through Crime: How the War on Crime Transformed American Democracy and Created a Culture of Fear*. Oxford: Oxford University Press.

Sparks, R. (2010) David Garland. In K. Haywards, S. Maruna and J. Mooney, J. (eds) *Fifty Key Thinkers in Criminology*. Abingdon: Routledge, pp. 290–6.

Thomas, T. (2009) The sex offender register: some observations on the time periods for registration. *Howard Journal of Crime and Justice*, 48(3), 257–66.

Vanstone, M. (2004) *Supervising Offenders in the Community: A History of Probation Theory and Practice*. Aldershot: Ashgate.

Waquant, L. (2009) *Punishing the Poor: The Neoliberal Government of Social Insecurity*. Durham: Duke University Press.

Ward, T. and Maruna, S. (2007) *Rehabilitation*. Abingdon: Routledge.

Wilson, R.J., McWhinnie, A., Picheca, J.E., Prinzo, M. and Cortoni, F. (2007) Circles of Support and Accountability: engaging community volunteers in the management of high-risk sexual offenders. *The Howard Journal of Criminal Justice*, 46(1), 1–15.

2

UNDERSTANDING CONTEMPORARY PENOLOGY

MODELS AND APPROACHES

IN THIS CHAPTER, YOU WILL EXPLORE

1. The key components of the Risk-Needs-Responsivity (RNR) model of offender rehabilitation

2. The various theoretical explanations that have been developed to explain the desistance 'journey', examining how and why people move away from offending and towards an improved social position

3. Strengths-based approaches that attempt to countenance an over-emphasis on risk and provide a more holistic approach to assessing and working with individuals in prison and probation settings.

INTRODUCTION

Many criminological endeavours, some of which we discussed in the previous chapter, have traditionally focused on helping us understand what causes offending, although in recent years there has been increasing interest in the process whereby individuals cease offending and alongside this the approaches required to support and sustain them in doing so. Since the mid-1990s, claims for what works with those who offend have been promoted as providing an evidence-based theoretical coherence for probation practice (Canton and Dominey, 2018). However, according to Ward and Maruna (2007: 28), the emphasis on *what works* has neglected the issue of *how it works*. In this chapter we therefore consider a number of models and approaches that seek to enhance the change process by assessing the level of motivation, identifying potential areas of resistance and developing strategies to combat this, clarifying roles and responsibilities in the change process, and providing a rationale for allocating resources where they are most needed. In doing so, we want you to move beyond taken for granted assumptions which prison and probation work are sometimes subject to and how they are incorporated into the work of penal agents. As Ward and Maruna (2007: 33) note, 'without a rehabilitation theory, practitioners and clients will be unaware of the broad aims of an intervention and their relationship to the causes of offending'. It is of course difficult to separate such models, and the theories that underpin them, from human values and interests and, 'given that these can legitimately vary, the concerns of different groups often may result in the formulation of diverse problems and therefore solutions' (Ward and Maruna, 2007: 31).

KEY QUESTIONS TO CONSIDER WHEN READING THIS CHAPTER

1. How can probation practitioners best support the process of desistance?

2. How compatible are the current dominant models of offender management?

3. Are risk and strengths-based approaches compatible?

THE RISK-NEED-RESPONSIVITY (RNR) MODEL

The Risk-Need-Responsivity (RNR) model is largely accepted as being the leading model of assessment and treatment in the world. First developed by psychologists Don Andrews and Jim Bonta in the early 1990s it provides an empirically derived theory about the causes of criminal behaviour and suggests a framework for correctional intervention in terms of *who* should be treated (i.e., which individuals), *what* should be *treated* (i.e., which sorts of factors, flaws issues, or problems associated with their offending) and *how* to intervene (McNeill and Graham, 2020: 14). RNR is a structured treatment model in the sense that it consists of *core* principles (see below), along with overarching principles (such as respect for the person and the importance of evidence) and organisational principles in terms of workers and management (Bonta and Andrews, 2017). The principles underpinning the RNR model suggest that matching treatment to an individual's level of risk is the key to treatment success (Blasko et al., 2020: 1077). According to the RNR model, those at the highest risk of reoffending should receive the most intensive interventions; these interventions should target dynamic criminogenic needs (i.e. those amenable to change) and tailored to meet the needs of the individual under supervision. The three core RNR principles are:

- *Risk* is about *whom* to target, based upon an individual's likelihood of reoffending. This is important because interventions should match the likelihood of reoffending – rehabilitative interventions should be offered to moderate and high-risk cases, with low-risk cases receiving minimal intervention.

- *Need* is about *what* should be done – identified criminogenic needs should be the focus of targeted interventions, rather than other needs which are not related to offending behaviour.

- *Responsivity* is about *how* the work should be delivered, covering both general and specific responsivity. While general responsivity promotes the use of cognitive social learning methods to influence behaviour, specific responsivity provides that interventions should be tailored to, amongst other things, the strengths of the individual. Supervision skills are an aspect of responsivity. (HM Inspectorate of Probation, 2021).

Offending-related or criminogenic needs are those dynamic factors which independently contribute to or are supportive of offending. Studies have examined which factors are linked to reoffending, whether changes in these factors lead to changes in reoffending, and whether this holds true when considering the associations between such factors. A review of the current literature has identified the following eight core risk/need factors (see Figure 2.1).

Impulsivity	to thinking of consequences and managing emotions
Pro-criminal attitudes	to a non-criminal identity
Pro-criminal associates	to friends and social group not involved in crime
Poor family relationships	to supportive and caring relationships
Lack of work	to increased employability and satisfying employment
Drug misuse	to safe use or sobriety
Alcohol misuse	to sensible drinking or sobriety
Poor use of leisure time	to satisfying (non-criminal) activities

Figure 2.1   Addressing offending-related needs

(*Source*: HM Inspectorate of Probation, 2021, www.justiceinspectorates.gov.uk/hmiprobation/research/the-evidence-base-probation/models-and-principles/the-rnr-model)

Risk factors are also commonly conceptualised as *static* or *dynamic* risk factors. Static factors are risk variables that cannot change, such as previous offence history, previous custodial sentences or sex. Stable dynamic risk factors are risk variables that tend to be stable over time but are amenable to change, and acute dynamic risk factors are factors that change and fluctuate from one situation to another. Practitioners are required to assess both the risk of future offending and the risk of serious harm. The latter includes the relative likelihood that an offence will occur and the relative impact of the offence in terms of what might happen, to whom, under what circumstances and why. Some offences, such as shoplifting, might have relatively little impact but are most common whereas others, such as homicide are rare but have maximum impact (National Offender Management Service, 2016). Risk factors broadly fall within the following four domains (Ward and Maruna, 2007: 46):

1. *Dispositional factors* such as psychopathic or antisocial personality characteristics, cognitive variables, and demographic data.

2. *Historical factors* such as adverse developmental history, prior history of crime and violence, prior hospitalization, and poor treatment compliance.

3. *Contextual antecedents* to violence such as criminogenic needs (risk factors of criminal behaviour), deviant social networks, and lack of positive social supports.

4. *Clinical factors* such as psychological disorders, poor level of functioning, and substance abuse.

Applying the core RNR principles has been found to be associated with reductions in reoffending. Looking across studies, adherence to all three principles has been found to result in a 17 per cent positive difference in average recidivism between treated and non-treated individuals when delivered in residential/custodial settings, and a 35 per cent difference when delivered in community settings (HM Inspectorate of Probation, 2021). In contrast, recidivism increased when there was a failure to adhere to any of the RNR principles, i.e., if treatment targeted non-criminogenic needs of low-risk individuals using non-cognitive-behavioural techniques. (HM Inspectorate of Probation, 2021). Despite the empirical base of the RNR model, it has been criticised for over-emphasising risk factors and securing behavioural compliance with the law, at the expense of helping people to meet their basic human needs and build on their personal strengths (McNeill and Graham, 2020: 15). Ward and Maruna (2007) argue that focusing only on risk and criminogenic needs could be counterproductive as non-criminogenic needs are often a precursor to addressing criminality, and individuals need to be receptive and attentive to interventions and may not be so if they believe their basic needs have not been effectively addressed. Theories of change such as those emerging from the literature on desistance and the Good Lives Model attempt to redress this imbalance.

DESISTANCE

The process by which people come to cease and sustain cessation of offending behaviour, with or without intervention by criminal justice agencies. (McNeill and Weaver, 2007: 2)

There is no single definition of desistance but perhaps in its simplest terms the above definition by McNeill and Weaver gives us a good insight into how desistance is framed. Desistance research has developed over recent decades, and the collated evidence (HM Inspectorate of Probation, 2021) suggests that people are more likely to desist when they have strong ties to family and community, employment that fulfils them, recognition of their worth from others, feelings of hope and self-efficacy, and a sense of meaning and purpose in their lives. Several key principles have been identified for supporting desistance: being realistic about the complexity and difficulty of the process; building and sustaining hope; recognising and developing people's strengths; respecting and fostering agency (or self-determination); working with and through relationships (both personal and professional); recognising and celebrating progress; individualising support for change; developing social as well as human capital (HM Inspectorate of Probation, 2021).

Of course, we speak of a desistance process but in reality there are many and varied pathways away from criminality. The relationship between theories of desistance from crime and rehabilitation are far from straightforward but, in simple terms, whereas models of rehabilitation tend to start with the question of how best to intervene to produce change (see Chapter 4) desistance theory starts with trying to describe and understand the process of change itself. This distinction is important, not least because there is plenty of evidence that most desistance happens without rehabilitative interventions. Just as criminologists have recognised that some involvement in offending is normal in adolescence in the sense that the crime figures suggest that most of us do it, so they have come to recognise that spontaneous desistance is also a normal process in that most people stop offending without someone attempting to help them to stop.

However, just because in many cases desistance happens without being engineered by the state's penal agents does not mean that assistance is not needed. Increasing attention within desistance studies has therefore been paid to the implications for operational delivery. The term *assisted desistance* (King, 2013) has been used to describe the role that probation (and other agencies) can play, recognising that individuals can be supported to desist from crime. The following service delivery principles have been identified as supporting desistance processes (HM Inspectorate of Probation, 2021):

- Since the process of giving up crime is different for each person, delivery needs to be properly individualised and their individuality *respected.*

- Service users are most influenced to change by those whose advice they respect and whose support they value. Personal and professional relationships are key to change and so *building positive relationships* is important.

- Desistance is related to the external/social aspects of a person's life as well as to internal/psychological factors. Giving up crime requires new networks of support and opportunities in local communities, so we need to *recognise the significance of social context.*

- Promoting a range of protective factors and taking a strengths-based approach should be part of the supervision process. For example, strong and supportive family and intimate relationships can support individuals in their desistance journey and so we need to *recognise and develop people's strengths.*

Although desistance is essentially an individual process it is supported by social actors, relationships and contexts – and it can be just as easily undermined by them. Many people within the criminal justice system will have long-established patterns of criminal behaviour – sometimes going back to childhood – and so as with any type of behavioural change it is unlikely to be straightforward and will encapsulate a range of emotions including hope, fear and disappointment.

Most empirical measures of desistance focus on whether the person has stopped offending or not. For example, reoffending is often conceptualised in terms of the effectiveness of probation in terms of whether or not the person has committed a further offence within two years of committing their original offence. Some desistance theorists argue that to simply focus on the endpoints of non-offending ignores the processes by which this state is achieved. Moreover, there is an important difference between someone merely not offending for a period and coming through a process of change to identify himself or herself as a *non-offender*. As such, a distinction is often made in desistance literature between primary, secondary and tertiary desistance. *Primary desistance* refers to any lull or crime-free gap in the course of a criminal career whereas *secondary desistance* is the assumption of the identity of a *non-offender* or a changed person. In addition, *tertiary*

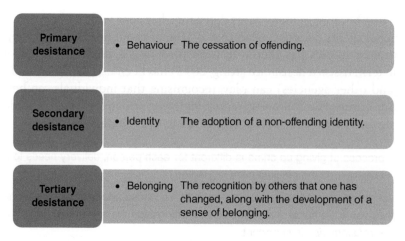

Figure 2.2 Three stages of desistance

(*Source*: HM Inspectorate of Probation 2021), www.justiceinspectorates.gov.uk/hmiprobation/research/the-evidence-base-probation/models-and-principles/desistance)

desistance suggests that since identity is socially constructed and negotiated, securing long-term change depends not just on how one sees oneself but also on how one is seen by others, and on how one sees one's place in society (see Figure 2.2). Nugent and Schinkel (2016) have refined and relabelled these three forms or aspects as *act, identity* and *relational* desistance.

The main theories that underpin our understanding of the desistance process can be broadly categorised as individual, structural or interactionist. Of these, individual (or what is also sometimes called ontogenic) theories of desistance have the longest history and are based on established links between age and certain criminal behaviours. As we mentioned earlier, it is argued that at some point most people will stop offending and that this is a natural process, which is linked to growing older and the sense of becoming more mature. The key task for criminal justice interventions therefore is to speed up this natural process as quickly as possible. Research studies consistently indicate a sharp increase in the arrest rate in the early teenage years, which peaks in the late teens or early adult years before decreasing over the remaining age distribution. This tends to be a consistent trend across all societies. Maturational reform theories attribute these changes to the physical, mental and biological changes that accompany the maturation process. While individual/ontogenic theories are useful, there are methodological and value-laden problems (Weaver, 2019). First, they assume that all human choice is equal and free, but in reality, we see the inequalities, barriers and constraints of marginalised communities across criminal justice systems and wider global communities. Second, specific crime types appear to have differing trajectories (e.g. sexual offending and white-collar crime). Thus, the operationalisation of the desistance process is more complex than individual/agentic theories first propose.

Structural (or sociogenic) theories of desistance stress the association between desistance and circumstances external to the individual but including the individual's reaction to and interaction with those circumstances. Such theories stress the significance of family ties, employment or education, for example, in explaining changes in criminal behaviour across the life course. These ties create a stake in conformity. Social control theorists argue that deviance arises from weak social bonds and that distance is facilitated where bonds to external factors such as a spouse or a career are developed or strengthened. Social bonds include significant relationships, responsibilities and having a stake in conformity. However, it is important to stress that they are not confined solely to the formal institutions of marriage or employment. Most social theorists recognise that key life events such as marriage or unemployment are likely (although not necessarily) to be correlated with causes of desistance. Such findings imply that desistance cannot be attributed solely to social attachments acting as external forces. What matters, rather, is what meaning the individual gives to these developments, and their impact on the informal social controls that reduce opportunities and motivations to offend.

Narrative (or interactionist) theories of desistance combine both individual and structural explanations. In considering the dynamics of desistance they tend to start with the individual's own account of their experiences of the desistance process. These approaches emphasise the significance of subjective changes in self and identity, reflected in changing motivations, greater concerns for others or more consideration of the future consequences of their actions. Desistance theorists are increasingly focusing on changes of personal cognition, self-identity and self-concept which might precede or coincide with changes in social bonds. These so-called *turning point* events may have a different impact depending on the person's level of motivation, their readiness to reform or how they interpret the meanings of such events. This understanding implies that desistance is not an event (like being cured of a disease) but a process and that (because of the subjectivities involved) the process is inescapably individualised.

SAMPSON AND LAUB: AGE-GRADED THEORY OF INFORMAL CONTROL

One of the earliest and most influential desistance theories was the age-graded theory of informal social control developed by Sampson and Laub (1993). Sampson and Laub's approach highlights the importance of the bond between the individual and society. Sampson and Laub argue that an individual's engagement in crime is more likely when this bond is weakened or broken. Over and above this, various formal and informal social institutions help to form and cement the bond between the individual and society. For example, for children of school age, the school, the family and peer groups influence the nature of the bond between them and their wider communities. For older people, employment, marriage and parenthood operate in a similar way. These institutions and the relationships between individuals that they encourage help the formation of social bonds which in turn creates informal social control (in that those individuals will not wish to be thought of negatively by those people important to them, and, realising this, will refrain from offending). Sampson and Laub argue that whilst continuity in an individual's life is to be expected (and can be observed), key events and turning points can trigger changes in an individual's bond to society and hence can influence patterns of offending/avoidance of offending. In addition, because many relationships – such as those formed through marriage, parenting, or via employment – endure over time, so these accumulate resources, such as emotional support between marriage partners, and help sustain conventional goals and conformity. Whatever one makes of these critiques, Sampson and Laub's work does run the risk of presenting desistance as something which happens because of other social processes, with little input from the desisters themselves.

GIODIONO ET AL.: COGNITIVE SHIFTS AND HOOKS FOR CHANGE

Rather than assuming that changes in offending careers are related to objective changes such as employment or marriage as Sampson and Laub do, Giordiono et al. (2002) focus on cognitive shifts, that is, changes in outlook and thinking, as the main drivers of desistance. They found that amongst those they interviewed the desistance process involved four phases:

1. A general cognitive openness to change

2. An exposure and reaction to hooks for change or turning points

3. Envisioning an appealing and conventional replacement self

4. A transformation in the way the actor views deviant behaviour.

In this model of cognitive transformation, life events can only aid the cessation of offending if the individual is receptive to their desistance potential. By being open to change people can take advantage of particular *hooks* that they may encounter that lead them away from offending. It is perhaps for this reason that motivation has become such an important factor in probation work. Put simply, 'the more motivated the offender is to change, the more likely it is that efforts to help will be a success' (Farrall, 2020: 67). Robinson (2011: 202) identifies the following features of motivational work:

- Being clear about the supervisory role, including purpose and expectations of supervision, the appropriate use of authority, and the role of enforcement

- Pro-social modelling and reinforcement, involving clear expectations about required values and behaviours and their reinforcement through the use of rewards. Challenge and confrontation of undesirable behaviours and discouragement of pro-criminal attitudes and values

- Negotiated problem solving, clear objective setting, monitoring and accountability of the offender's progress

- Honest, empathetic relationship with an emphasis on persistence and belief in the offender's capacity to change.

MARUNA: MAKING GOOD – DESISTERS, PERSISTERS AND REDEMPTION SCRIPTS

Shadd Maruna's study (2005) of the criminal histories of a group of people in the Liverpool area was groundbreaking in that it was one of the first attempts that asked the person themselves what had made them stop offending or not. Amongst those interviewed

Maruna identified two groups he termed *persisters* and *desisters*. Desisters in his study believed they could control their futures in some way while persisters continued to hold a sense of being doomed or fated to their situation. Desisters wanted to give something back to society. According to Maruna, involvement in what he terms generative activities, such as helping others, mentoring, doing volunteer work, are critical. However, he also argues that society's reaction in supporting and reinforcing the development of fledgling prosocial identities is also an important influence on the process of desistance. Desistance then is tied up in a process by which those who have offended come to see themselves as essentially *good* people who (often through little fault of their own) acted in *bad ways*. Rather than something to be ashamed of, these previous bad ways are employed as a means for re-making sense of their lives and as a basis for contributing to society. To desist from crime, those individuals in Maruna's study needed to develop a coherent, prosocial identity for themselves. They did so through what Maruna terms redemption scripts, typically:

I was essentially good but came from a poor background. I got drawn into drugs and crime as a way of escaping my background, but over time this became a trap. However, with the help of [a good person] who could see the good in me I was able to change and am now the person I ought to have been.

BOTTOMS AND SHAPLAND: SEVEN-STEP PROCESS OF DESISTANCE

Bottoms and Shapland (2011), in an important contribution to desistance theory, produced a seven-step process of desistance. Crucially, they note that neither the dispositions nor the potential of individuals, nor their social positions and resources, are static. Rather, they can change over time, producing interaction effects in the broader process of change. Their model (2011) suggests that various *triggers* produce in active criminality the desire to *wish to change*, which leads to them *beginning to think about themselves and their surroundings differently*. This in turn leads the would-be desister into *taking action towards* desistance, which leads on to *attempts at maintenance*. If the would-be desister continues along the route to desistance they will *find reinforcers* to desistance which lead eventually to a *crime-free identity as a non-offender*. It is understandable that many people do so unsure of their motivation and prospects, and uncertain that the venture is worthwhile. When this ambivalence meets the harsh realities of the journey and the demands that it makes, relapse becomes likely. The model of desistance formulated by Bottoms and Shapland recognises this in its cyclical design; indeed, most of the desisters in their study required several cycles through the process to achieve desistance. In Bottoms and Shapland's (2011) model, the end of the journey comes when sufficient reinforcement of change allows the person to exit with a reformed, *crime-free* identity.

MCNEILL: A DESISTANCE PARADIGM FOR OFFENDER MANAGEMENT AND FOUR FORMS OF REHABILITATION

In his proposed desistance paradigm for offender management, Fergus McNeill (2006) argued that the field of corrections needs its own 'Copernican Correction'. McNeill is referring to the fact that up until the 16th century it was believed that the earth was the centre of the universe and that all the other planets in the solar system revolved around us. This was turned on its head by the Polish astronomer Nicolaus Copernicus who established that Earth was a planet that orbited the sun. In a similar way, McNeill contends that supervision and support services revolve around the individual change process, rather than requiring the individual's life to revolve around programmes and interventions. Moreover, he suggested a shift away from seeing the person under supervision as the target of the intervention (the *thing* to be fixed) to seeing the broken relationships between individuals, communities and the state as the breach in the social fabric (or breach of the social contract) that requires repair. Importantly, this casts correctional agencies less as agents of 'coercive correction' and more as mediators of social conflicts. The objective becomes not the correction of the deviant so much as the restoration of the citizen to a position where they can both honour the obligations and enjoy the rights of citizenship. In another key contribution to desistance literature, McNeill developed what he termed the four forms of rehabilitation – personal, legal, social and moral.

McNeill contends that traditional rehabilitative efforts have been primarily concerned with what he terms *personal rehabilitation*. This is principally concerned with promoting positive individual-level change in the person being supervised. It focuses on helping people develop the capabilities they need to achieve their legitimate goals and realise their aspirations so that they no longer need to pursue these goals through criminal activity. It is based on an acknowledgement that change will happen gradually and setbacks are likely, so the practitioner has a key role in preparing individuals for the journey from crime. When people, or systems, speak of rehabilitation they often have in mind those rehabilitative interventions aimed at supporting an individual to change something about themselves so that the likelihood of offending is reduced. Offending behaviour programmes, for example, typically seek to make good on these sorts of deficits by tackling the criminogenic needs associated with offending, and especially repeat offending. Of course, such an approach can be criticised for treating symptoms as causes in recasting social injustices as personal failings. Simply attempting to correct the individual does nothing to remedy the structural causes of crime. Indeed, some criminologists, such as Pat Carlen, argue that rehabilitation has never been adopted in practice as intended and instead functions to legitimise the state's power to punish.

In this respect, offender behaviour programmes and other interventions seek to support and may be part of personal rehabilitation, but they are not of themselves rehabilitation. In simple terms, this is because the assistance needed is not just a process of personal development; it is a social and political project that affects and is affected by a person's legal standing. Change at the individual level can never be in itself enough to deliver social justice (Burke et al., 2018). Fundamental to this is ensuring that our formal systems do not impede personal rehabilitation. This leads us to *legal rehabilitation,* which is about securing a person's return to full citizenship status, with all the attendant rights and responsibilities. It is also about removing the stigma of criminal conviction. Justice would suggest that once a person has served their sentence and paid their dues to society then that is the end of it. There should be no punishment beyond the sentence. However, we know that the stigma of being involved in the criminal justice system goes on after a sentence has been served in terms of access to housing and health needs and access to employment. Legal rehabilitation is about removing this stigma and ensuring that the rehabilitated person can access the opportunities and benefits of legitimate society. However, throughout the world we have complex systems of disqualification of people whose debts are settled.

There is some evidence that for many people desistance is about personal redemption, not necessarily in the spiritual or theological sense but rather in the sense of finding a way to 'make good' on a troubled and troubling past by making a positive contribution to society (Maruna, 2005). Moral rehabilitation requires the person who has committed a crime to demonstrate acceptance of the mutual obligations that citizens hold in common. This can be demonstrated practically by some form of reparation. Sometimes it requires mediation or restorative work with victims and/or their families. Whereas personal rehabilitation is largely private and focused on the individual, moral rehabilitation requires a dialogue, often with the local community and victims, about *how* to ensure people can rehabilitate. In practice, moral rehabilitation is difficult. Even if the individual settles their debt to the state (through serving a prison sentence or completing unpaid work) it does not necessarily mean their victim(s), or their families will feel that their debt has been settled or that they are willing to have them back into the community. In this respect, state-imposed punishment does not necessarily satisfy the needs of individuals or marginalised communities who themselves may feel threatened (Burke et al., 2018). These are the approaches that restorative justice often seeks to address and repair (see Chapter 13 for further discussion).

Social rehabilitation is a less formal process, linked to finding acceptance and belonging in a community because crucially it is these kinds of social ties that can sustain positive changes long after supervision has ended. This implies a need to build relationships with family, friends and contacts who can help sustain a positive lifestyle. Drawing on research and theory into social capital, these connections include:

- *Social bonds*, usually with similar people connected to us through, for example, ethnic, national or religious identity
- *Social bridges*, with members of other communities
- *Social links*, with institutions, including local and central government services. (Albertson, 2021: 12)

These *means and markers* indicate the extent to which a person is integrated, but they also highlight the opportunities and resources that should assist people to integrate in other ways.

The study of social capital has developed as an area of great interest to researchers, government agencies, and community and welfare organisations. According to Albertson (2021: 12), probation practitioners have a key role in assisting those on probation by signposting them 'to opportunities to build their social capital in the wider community context, which largely sit outside of the criminal justice system'. The notion of social capital was developed by authors such as Robert Granfield and William Cloud (2001) who applied the concept of capital to recovery-orientated scholarship. They devised the term *recovery capital* to describe the breadth and depth of internal and external resources that an individual can draw upon to initiate and sustain recovery from substance use (Granfield and Cloud, 1999). Since then, academics such as White (2008) and Best and Laudet (2010) have developed this concept to describe observed changes in substance users' resilience and robustness of social and emotional circumstances in long-term recovery. Granfield and Cloud (1999) suggest that the concept of recovery capital can be refined as four interrelated forms: social, physical, human and cultural.

1. *Social capital* is affected by the environmental context in which an individual is embedded (Cloud and Granfield, 2008) and comes about through changes in relations among persons that facilitate action (Coleman, 1988). Cloud and Granfield (2008) suggest that membership in a social group confers resources and reciprocal obligations, which an individual can use to improve their life. Social capital is an important component of the recovery process as it affects an individual's options, resources, information and available support (Best and Laudet, 2010; Cloud and Granfield, 2008). For instance, when substance users have access to social capital, expectations from family and friends can serve as a valuable resource, whether it is emotional support or access to opportunities that help to facilitate recovery from substance use.

2. *Physical capital* includes savings, property, investments and other financial assets (Granfield and Cloud, 2001). Individuals who are considered to be financially stable possess physical capital (Granfield and Cloud, 2001). Substance users who have a moderate level of physical capital have more recovery options than those without financial resources (Granfield and Cloud, 1999, 2001) as they may be able to take leave of abstinence from their job or take an extended holiday to address their substance use. They may also have the ability to temporarily or permanently relocate if they decide that a geographical move is needed in order to recover from substance use.

3. *Human capital* covers a wide range of human attributes that provide an individual with the means to function in society (Best and Laudet, 2010; Granfield and Cloud, 1999). It is created by changes in persons that bring about skills and capabilities that make them able to act in new ways (Coleman, 1988). Human capital includes skills such as problem solving; self-esteem and interpersonal skills; educational achievements; physical, emotional and mental health;

aspirations; and personal resources such as commitment and responsibility that will help an individual to manage everyday life (Daddow and Broome, 2010).

4. *Cultural capital* refers to an individual's attitudes, values, beliefs, dispositions, perceptions and appreciations that derive from membership of a particular social or cultural group (Bourdieu, 1986). It refers to an individual's ability to act in accordance with culturally defined norms, values and expectations. Individuals who use substances but have a stake in societal conformity are said to have a distinct advantage over those who have been socialised to reject them (Granfield and Cloud, 2001). The quality and quantity of recovery capital that an individual has is both a cause and a consequence of recovery from substance use as it can hold substantial implications for the options available to the individual when attempts to desist from substance use are made (Granfield and Cloud, 2001).

Justice capital was originally developed as a measure of the neurodevelopmental resources that allow individuals to communicate, understand and be engaged with fairly and equitably (Best and Hamilton, 2020). It has since been extended to include aspects of the environment or institution that create the conditions for those fair and equitable exchanges to happen. In closed institutions like prisons or detention centres, it is the capacity to prevent abuse, discrimination and isolation as well as the ability to nurture human flourishing that is the institutional marker of justice capital. At an institutional level, justice capital is the extent of belief in reintegration and rehabilitation for all and the embodiment of that belief in activities and relationships that actively promote positive change. Where individual and institutional components of justice capital come together, there is a fundamental belief in the possibility of sustainable positive change and a sense that the institution can act as a turning point in addiction, mental health and crime careers by providing opportunities, relationships and pathways to inspire hope and positive engagement from a diverse and heterogeneous group of people (Ibid).

Justice capital does not merely reside inside individuals but between people, creating a radius of trust and a ripple effect that benefits not only those who are directly involved in the criminal justice system, but also their families, and the communities in which they are located. Justice capital is a unifying concept that lays the foundations for measurement and mapping of strengths whether in closed institutions or in a community setting. This is critical in changing our approach from a deficits model based on failure and risk towards innovation, strength, and hope. Secondly, the idea of justice capital is based on growth and strength and its application challenges the stain of irreversibility that conviction and institutionalisation inflict. Building justice capital in prisons (and other closed institutions) inherently builds bridges into the community based on strengths and relationships that challenge stigmatisation and exclusion. Justice capital is the metric of its capacity to catalyse positive changes for all (Best and Hamilton, 2020). The acronym CHIME (connectedness, hope, identity, meaning and empowerment) was initially developed in relation to the key components of effective recovery-oriented services within mental health services and interventions (Leamy et al. 2011). This has been translated into a Chime in Action model in which positive social connection is the critical starting point for the initiation of recovery (Best and Hamilton 2020). There are five elements to the Chime in Action model:

1. *Connectedness* involving peer support and social groups

2. *Hope and optimism* involving the motivation to change, hope and positive thinking

3. *Identity* in the sense of establishing a more positive sense of self and overcoming stigma

4. *Meaning* in the sense of securing meaningful social roles and goals

5. *Empowerment* in terms of taking control of one's life, accepting personal responsibility and focusing on one's strengths.

Positive social support drives the belief that change is possible, generating a sense of hope that energises attempts to manage change. This in turn generates the capacity to engage in meaningful activities (Best et al., 2011; Cano et al., 2017) that creates a sense of empowerment (linked to self-esteem and self-efficacy), which in turn helps to build a positive sense of identity. This creates a virtuous circle of positive social support and positive identity predicated on active participation and engagement in activities that promote and support recovery (Best, 2019).

Although each of the forms of rehabilitation we have discussed helps us to understand the various aspects of the desistance process, they are in reality interdependent and as Canton (2018: 260) points out, it suggests a wider focus of probation work than individual change alone:

> **Probation agencies have a role in helping ex-offenders to exercise their legal rights in relation to disclosure of their past offending (legal rehabilitation), in supporting resettlement and reintegration by enabling people to have fair access to resources (social rehabilitation) and perhaps in encouraging society to accept its responsibilities to deal with ex-offenders on an appropriate moral basis that does not reduce them to the worst things they ever did (moral rehabilitation).**

KEMSHALL: A BLENDED APPROACH TO RISK MANAGEMENT AND DESISTANCE

Hazel Kemshall (2021) has recently contended that all risk work is ultimately a balance between risk and rights, protection and integration, desistance supportive work and control, with the appropriate balance tailored to the individual service user. The art of professional practice is the skill to weigh up such balancing acts in a transparent, defensible and evidential way. A blended approach to risk management would according to Kemshall (2021: 5) utilise the following approaches for supporting desistance.

- *Using supportive authority*. Effective risk management benefits from the use of supportive authority in which supervisors are prepared to exercise appropriate authority to set expectations and encourage positive choices, censure risky behaviours and negative conduct, and signal disapproval or apply legitimate sanctions.

- *Reframing choices*. Whilst we may view such behaviours as risky, the individual may see them as rewarding or as intrinsically part of their habituated behaviours and self-identity. Central to effective risk management is the sound reframing of the cost–benefits of risky behaviour and the commitment of service users to this reframing, with constant reinforcement from the supervisor.

- *Building strengths and mitigating the 'pains of desistance'*. According to Kemshall (2021: 7) 'practitioners should not underestimate the importance of personal support, praise, and simply walking alongside the service user during this difficult journey'.

- *Appropriately using social capital and recovery capital*. Many of those caught up in the criminal justice system experience negative social capital in the form of stigma and rejection. Many will have used, and may continue to use, criminally based social capital. Enabling access to, and sustaining use of, positive social capital has thus been seen as intrinsic to the desistance process.

- *Enhancing resilience and combating fatalism*. Hope and agency have been seen as key elements of the desistance process. Enhancing coping and resilience to failure is also important and given the challenges of the self-risk management and desistance journey, practitioners should give this considerable attention. Practical skill building and the enhancement of recovery capital can assist individuals to successfully manage situations of adversity without reoffending and recovery capital can promote resilience.

THE GOOD LIVES MODEL

Rehabilitation as a practice has become so focused on lowering risk and increasing community safety that it is easy to overlook a rather basic truth: prisoners and probationers want a better life, not simply the promise of a less harmful one. (Ward and Maruna, 2007: 141)

The Good Lives Model (GLM) is perhaps 'the most systematically developed theory in the strengths-based domain' (Ward and Maruna, 2007: 24). It has been most extensively used in working with those convicted of sexual offences although it was designed to apply to all types of criminal behaviour. The Good Lives Model is psychologically based and in many respects acts as a counter to the risk-based models of assessment that dominate current relative practices in most countries. Maruna and Ward argue for a more holistic approach to assessment that not only considers the risks and needs of the individual but also attempts to consolidate their strengths and potential. According to Maruna and Ward, the common aspirations of most of those who commit offences are like the aspirations of the rest of us in that they want things such as secure relationships and stable income but they do not always or are not always able to achieve these through legitimate means. In understanding the aetiology of offending, the Good Lives Model draws on strain theory (Merton, 1938) to suggest that there are two basic routes to offending – direct and indirect. The direct route refers to situations where the individual seeks certain types of goods through criminal activity. The indirect route refers to situations where the pursuit of a certain good has consequences that increase the pressure to offend – for example, where the use of alcohol to relieve emotional pressure leads to a loss of control in particular circumstances. In the Good Lives Model, criminogenic needs are best understood as internal or external obstacles to the acquisition of primary human goods.

Maruna and Ward argue that individuals are more than the sum of their criminal records; they have expertise and strengths, which can benefit society and should be promoted. Many have had adverse developmental experiences and will lack the opportunities and support necessary to develop a coherent life plan. Consequently, they may lack skills and capabilities that they need to achieve a fulfilling life. Rehabilitation endeavours should therefore equip individuals with the knowledge, skills, opportunities and resources necessary to satisfy their life values in ways that do not harm others. In this respect they should focus on an individual's strengths rather than their risks/deficiencies. A major aim of rehabilitative work under the Good Lives Model is to help the person develop a life plan that involves ways of effectively securing what it terms 'primary human goods' and a sense of fulfilment without harming others. Ward and Maruna (2007: 109) define this sense of fulfilment as a 'satisfying lifestyle that extends over a number of domains and a significant period of time' rather than the 'hedonistic state of pleasure'. These primary human goods include, for example, life, knowledge, excellence and play and work, agency or autonomy, inner peace, friendship, community, spirituality, happiness and creativity. Because primary human goods are plural, there are many possible sources of motivation for human behaviour. The Good Lives Model views human beings as comprising a range of interconnected biological, social, cultural and psychological systems, and are interdependent to a significant degree. This means that they can only flourish 'within a community that provides emotional support, material resources, education and even the means of survival' (Ward and Maruna 2007: 117).

It therefore follows that supervision and treatment or intervention should focus positively on equipping people with the skills necessary to secure primary goods in socially acceptable and personally meaningful ways. By virtue of its focus on human goods or good outcomes this approach provides an explicit avenue by which to motivate individuals subject to supervision. In practice, the practitioner must balance the promotion of personal goods (for the individual) with the reduction of risk (for society). Too strong a focus on personal goods may produce a happy but dangerous individual; equally, too strong a focus on risk may produce a dangerously defiant or disengaged one. The practitioner has to create a human relationship in which the individual is valued and respected and through which interventions can be properly tailored in line with particular life plans and their associated risk factors. So, although as with RNR, interventions should be structured and systematic, they should also be shaped to suit the person in question. The language used by the practitioner and their organisation should be 'future-oriented, optimistic and approach goal focused' (Ward and Maruna, 2007: 127) in order to foster motivation. In the process of assessment, Ward and Maruna (2007) suggest that as well as addressing risk, needs and responsivity, practitioners should also assess the individual's priorities – their own goals, life priorities and their aims for the intervention. The authors identify a number of considerations, which they state need to be considered when applying the Good Lives Model to a treatment intervention (Ward and Maruna, 2007: 127–8):

> **Prisoners and probationers as whole individuals are more than the sum of their criminal record. They have expertise and a variety of strengths that can benefit society. Interventions should promote and facilitate these contributions whenever possible.**

At the same time, many prisoners and probationers are likely to have experienced adversarial developmental experiences and have lacked the opportunities and support necessary to achieve a coherent life plan. Consequently, such individuals lack many of the essential skills and capabilities necessary to achieve a fulfilling life.

Criminal actions frequently represent attempts to achieve desired goals but where the skills or capabilities necessary to achieve them are not possessed (direct route). Alternatively, offending can arise from an attempt to relieve the sense of incompetence, conflict or dissatisfaction that arises from not achieving valued human goods (indirect route).

1. Prisoners and probationers as whole individuals are more than the sum of their criminal record. They have expertise and a variety of strengths that can benefit society. Interventions should promote and facilitate these contributions whenever possible.

2. At the same time, many prisoners and probationers are likely to have experienced adversarial developmental experiences and have lacked the opportunities and support necessary to achieve a coherent life plan.

3. Consequently, such individuals lack many of the essential skills and capabilities necessary to achieve a fulfilling life.

4. Criminal actions frequently represent attempts to achieve desired goals but where the skills or capabilities necessary to achieve them are not possessed (direct route). Alternatively,

offending can arise from an attempt to relieve the sense of incompetence, conflict or dissatisfaction that arises from not achieving valued human goods (indirect route).

5. The absence of certain human goods seems to be more strongly associated with offending: self-efficacy/sense of agency, inner peace, personal dignity/social esteem, generative roles and relationships, and social relatedness.

6. The risk of offending may be reduced by assisting individuals to develop the skills and capabilities necessary to achieve the full range of human goods.

7. Intervention is therefore seen as an activity that should add to an individual's repertoire of personal functioning, rather than as an activity that simply removes a problem or is devoted to managing problems, as if a lifetime of grossly restricting one's activity is the only way to avoid offending.

CONCLUSION

Each of the models and approaches that we have outlined in this chapter provides a different perspective on what brings about the changes necessary for moving towards a non-offending lifestyle, but in many respects they are complementary and there is no single model that can adequately explain the complexities involved. The desistance paradigm, for example, deliberately forefronts processes of change rather than modes of intervention; it begins not with what the system or the worker does with the person, but with what the person is experiencing. However, practice under the desistance paradigm would certainly include intervention to meet needs and reduce risks as in the RNR model and certainly to develop strengths in line with the Good Lives Model. Critically, such interventions would not be concerned solely with the prevention of further offending but would be equally concerned with constructively addressing the harms caused by crime by encouraging the person to make good through the restorative processes we discuss later in this text.

recommended reading

If you would like to engage in further reading, you may find the following resources particularly useful:

McNeill, F., Raynor, P. and Trotter, C. (eds) (2010) *Offender Supervision. New Directions in Theory, Research and Practice*. Cullompton: Willan.

This edited collection brings together leading researchers to describe and analyse internationally significant theoretical and empirical work on offender supervision, and to address the policy and practice implications of this work. The book draws out the lessons that can be learned not just from studying 'what works?' but from exploring how and why particular practices support desistance from crime.

Ugwudike, P., Raynor, P. and Annison, J. (2019) *Evidence-Based Skills in Criminal Justice: International Research on Supporting Rehabilitation and Desistance*. Bristol: Policy Press.

This book brings together international research on skills and practices in probation and youth justice, while exploring the wider contexts that affect their implementation in the public, private and voluntary sectors. It also covers effective approaches to working with diverse groups such as ethnic minority service users, women and young people.

Best, D. and Colman, C. (eds) (2020) *Strengths-Based Approaches to Crime and Substance Use: From Drugs and Crime to Desistance and Recovery*. Abingdon: Routledge.

This edited collection explores the theoretical relationships between desistance and recovery approaches and the potential of a combined approach to assist individuals to pursue meaningful lives as well as less harmful ones.

references

Albertson, K. (2021) *Social Capital Building Supporting the Desistance Process*. HM Inspectorate of Probation, Academic Insights 2021/06. Available at: www.justiceinspectorates.gov.uk/hmiprobation/wp-content/uploads/sites/5/2021/06/Academic-Insights-Albertson-KM-design2-RM.pdf (last accessed 14 August 2021).

Best, D. (2019) *A Model for Resettlement Based on the Principles of Desistance and Recovery*. HM Inspectorate of Probation, Academic Insights 2019/03. Available at: www.justiceinspectorates.gov.uk/hmiprobation/wp-content/uploads/sites/5/2020/09/Academic-Insights-A-model-for-resettlement-based-on-the-principles-of-desistance-and-recovery.pdf (last accessed 14 August 2021).

Best, D. and Hamilton, S. (2020) Justice capital: from the darkness into the light. *The Power to Persuade*. Blog Post. Available at: www.powertopersuade.org.au/blog/recovery-capital-in-prisons (last accessed on 16 June 2020).

Best, D. and Laudet, W. (2010) Recovery capital as prospective predictor of sustained recovery, life satisfaction and stress among former poly-substance users. *Substance Use and Misuse*, 4, 27–54.

Best, D., Gow, J., Taylor, A., Knox, A. and White, W. (2011) Recovery from heroin or alcohol dependence: A qualitative account of the recovery experience in Glasgow. *Journal of Drug Issues*, 11(1), 359–78.

Blasko, B.L., Souza, K.A., Via, B. and Taxman, F.S. (2020) Performance measure in community corrections: Measuring effective supervision practices with existing agency data. In P. Ugwudike, H. Graham, F. McNeill, P. Raynor, F.S. Taxman and C. Trotter (eds) *The Routledge Companion to Rehabilitative Work in Criminal Justice*. Abingdon, Oxon: Routledge, pp. 1068–83.

Bonta, J. and Andrews, D.A. (2017) *The Psychology of Criminal Conduct*. (6th edn). Abingdon: Routledge.

Bottoms, A.E. and Shapland, J. (2011) Steps towards desistance among male young adult recidivists. In S. Farrall, M. Hough, S. Maruna and R. Sparks (eds) *Escape Routes: Contemporary Perspectives on Life after Punishment*. London: Routledge.

Bourdieu, P. (1986) The forms of capital. In J. Richardson (ed.) *Handbook of Theory and Research for the Sociology of Education*. New York: Greenwood, pp. 241–58.

Burke, L., Collett, S. and McNeill, F. (2018) *Reimagining Rehabilitation: Beyond the Individual*. Abingdon: Routledge.

Cano, I., Best, D., Edwards, M. and Lehman, J. (2017) Recovery capital pathways: Modelling the components of recovery wellbeing. *Drug and Alcohol Dependence*, 181, 11–19.

Canton, R. (2018) Probation and the philosophy of punishment. *Probation Journal*, 65(3): 252–68.

Canton, R. and Dominey, J. (2018) *Probation*. Abingdon: Routledge.

Cloud, W. and Granfield, R. (2008) Conceptualizing recovery capital: Expansion of a theoretical framework. *Substance Use and Misuse*, 43, 1971–86.

Coleman, J. (1988) Social capital in the creation of human capital. *The American Journal of Sociology*, 94, 95–120.

Daddow, R. and Broome, S. (2010) *Whole Person Recovery: A User-Centred Systems Approach to Problem Drug Use*. RSA Projects. Available at: www.drugsandalcohol.ie/14526/1/RSA-Whole-Person-Recovery-report.pdf (last accessed 29 June 2022).

Farrall, S. (2020) The long-term impacts of probation supervision. In D. Best and C. Colman (eds) *Strengths-Based Approaches to Crime and Substance Use: From Drugs and Crime to Desistance and Recovery*. Abingdon: Routledge.

Giordano, P.C., Cernkovich, S.A. and Rudolph, J.L. (2002) Gender, crime and desistance: Toward a theory of cognitive transformation. *American Journal of Sociology*, 107, 990–1064.

Granfield, R. and Cloud, W. (1999) *Coming Clean. Overcoming Addiction without Treatment*. London: New York University Press.

Granfield, R. and Cloud, W. (2001) Social context and natural recovery: The role of social capital in the resolution of drug-associated problems. *Journal of Substance Use and Misuse*, 36(11), 1543–70.

HM Inspectorate of Probation (2021) *Desistance – General Practice Principles*. Manchester: HM Inspectorate of Probation.

Kemshall, H. (2021) *Risk and Desistance: A Blended Approach to Risk Management. HM Inspectorate of Probation*, Academic Insights 2021/07. Available at: www.justiceinspectorates.gov.uk/hmiprobation/wp-content/uploads/sites/5/2021/06/Academic-Insights-Kemshall.pdf (last accessed 14 August 2021).

King, S. (2013) Assisted desistance and experiences of probation supervision. *Probation Journal*, 60(2), 136–51.

Leamy, M., Bird, V., Le Boutillier, C., Williams, J. and Slade, M. (2011) A conceptual framework for personal recovery in mental health: Systematic review and narrative synthesis. *British Journal of Psychiatry*, 199(6), 445–52.

Maruna, S. (2005) *Making Good: How Ex-convicts Reform and Rebuild Their Lives.* Washington D.C.: American Psychological Association.

McNeill, F. (2006) A desistance paradigm for offender management. *Criminology and Criminal Justice*, 6(1): 39–62.

McNeill F. and Weaver B. (2007) Giving up crime: Directions for policy. Glasgow: The Scottish Centre for Crime and Justice. Available at: https://strathprints.strath.ac.uk/36733/1/Giving_Up_Crime_tcm8_2569.pdf (last accessed 29 June 2022).

McNeill, F. and Graham, H. (2020) Conceptualizing rehabilitation: Four forms, two models, one process and a plethora of challenges. In P. Ugwudike, H. Graham, F. McNeill, P. Raynor, F.S. Taxman and C. Trotter (eds) *The Routledge Companion to Rehabilitative Work in Criminal Justice*. Abingdon, Oxon: Routledge, 1068–83.

Merton, R.K. (1938) Social structure and anomie. *American Sociological Review*, 3(5): 672–82.

National Offender Management Service (2016) *Public Protection Manual 2016 Edition*. London: National Offender Management Service.

Nugent, B. and Schinkel, M. (2016) The pains of desistance. *Criminology & Criminal Justice*, 16(5): 568–84.

Robinson, A. (2011) *Foundations for Offender Management: Theory, Law and Policy for Contemporary Practice*. Bristol: Policy Press.

Sampson, R.J. and Laub, J. (1993) *Crime in the Making: Pathways and Turning Points through Life*. Cambridge, MA: Harvard University Press.

Ward, T. and Maruna, S. (2007) *Rehabilitation*. Abingdon: Routledge.

Weaver, B. (2019) Understanding desistance: A critical review of theories of desistance. *Psychology, Crime and Law*, 25(2), 1–8.

White, W. (2008) The mobilization of community resources to support long term addiction recovery. *Journal of Substance Abuse Treatment*, 36, 146–58.

3
THEORISING PRISONS AND IMPRISONMENT

IN THIS CHAPTER, YOU WILL EXPLORE

1. The extent to which imprisonment can be justified and considered purposeful in the 21st century

2. The evolution and development of the modern-day prison in England and Wales

3. Efforts to justify imprisonment as a legitimate response to the failings of a wider socio-economic system that creates and subsequently leads to poverty, social inequality and crime.

INTRODUCTION

This chapter will consider the extent to which imprisonment is justified and purposeful in the 21st century. In doing so, the discussion will encourage you to critically engage with the evolution of prisons and concept of imprisonment more broadly. This is an important starting point for anyone with an interest in prisons (and indeed punishment more generally) because understanding how imprisonment has evolved over time will allow you to critically engage with both past and present attempts to justify the prison place. With a particular focus on prisons in England and Wales, this chapter will explore how the modern-day prison has evolved since its inception and examine how and why imprisonment occupies such a dominant position in contemporary penal imaginaries. Alongside this, the discussion will critically engage with long-standing justifications of imprisonment such as retribution, deterrence and rehabilitation. In doing so you will be encouraged to think beyond attempts to rationalise imprisonment and consider, in further detail, who goes to prison and why. This will contribute towards your understanding of imprisonment as well as the failings of a wider socio-economic system that leads to poverty, social inequality and crime.

THE EVOLUTION OF PRISONS AND IMPRISONMENT

Exploring the history and development of imprisonment is an important endeavour for anyone with an interest in penology because the prison place provides a physical manifestation of a society's belief about the necessary requirements of both punishment and justice. Through a summative discussion of the history and development of prisons in England and Wales this section will help you to explore how the aims and ambitions of imprisonment have diversified over time to ensure that the prison, as an institution, has evolved into a cornerstone of the criminal justice system and indeed modern-day society. Alongside this, you will be encouraged to explore why an institution that repetitively fails to meet its own aims and ambitions continues to thrive in a contemporary justice system and engage with taken for granted ideas about how we, as a society, respond to a minority of people who break the law.

Since the beginning of modern civilisation almost every society has used prisons of some kind to remove people who break the rules of their community. It is commonly held that the first prisons (of sorts) were in southern Mesopotamia (a region now home to modern-day Iraq, Kuwait, Turkey and Syria) during the reign of King Ur-Nammu around 2000 BCE. During this time, imprisonment was not considered to be a punishment per se and as a result it was often used as a temporary stop gap before a person was suitably punished. This may have included, for example, the death penalty or a life of slavery. It is important to note that definitions of suitable punishment vary over time (and place) and as such are usually influenced by the values, attitudes and belief systems of a society. For example, although little is known about prisons in ancient Egypt, it is suggested that they were an important component of Egyptian society as they upheld principles of justice of that time, including but not limited to a citizen's right to feel secure. Though punishment could be harsh and severe, people were imprisoned for the good of society until they could be educated and converted into a law-abiding person who would, upon their release, benefit wider society.

In ancient Rome, imprisonment was not a sentence under Roman statutory law. Although some people would spend a lot of time in prison, there was no such thing as being sentenced to prison. As enslavement was commonplace, most people who ended up in prison were sold as slaves or utilised by the Roman government as gladiators who would typically fight for the public in popular games held in large purpose-built arenas, such as the Colosseum in Rome. Although considered a glamorous profession, gladiators were slaves, had previously been slaves and/or were imprisoned. Furthermore, as gladiators were usually expected to fight to the death, they typically had a short life expectancy. During this time, conditions of imprisonment varied widely from misery and humiliation to comfort and luxury. This was because prison sentences for people considered to be of high status and/or wealthy were largely non-existent, with those in privileged socio-economic positions facing house arrest or banishment rather than imprisonment. Although the poor often avoided prolonged periods in prison, this was because they were usually swiftly sentenced to death. For those who were held in prison, records show that they were unhygienic, poorly ventilated, overcrowded and typically underground.

Moving forward to the Middle Ages in England and Wales, imprisonment was not a typical nor a widespread punishment. As a result, there was no formal prison system as we understand it today. Rather, people awaiting trial or punishment would be held in a tower or dungeon of a castle, unless they were a noble person, wealthy or influential member of society. This was until Henry II (King of England from 1154 until his death in 1189) initiated a series of legal reforms that gave the monarchy more control over the administration of punishment and justice. As part of his Assize of Clarendon (1166) he commanded the construction of prisons where the accused would remain while judges debated their fate. First built in 1188, Newgate was used as a prison for approximately 700 years and held people who had committed a variety of crimes, from theft to murder. Its construction was influenced by the concept of architecture terrible, an architectural style that highlights the oppressive nature of buildings through architectural details such as small windows and overt symbolism such as carved chains over entrances, to create a sense of deterrence and instil fear into all who pass by.

Prior to the 17th century, villages and towns throughout England and Wales relied on small gaols (old English word for jail), lockups and cages to punish people who had broken the law and deter potential lawbreakers. As there were no national standards, rules or regulations the gaoler (who was ultimately in charge of these institutions) would decide how the establishment would operate on a day-to-day basis. In the main, county goals were based on the notion of deterrence and viewed as an opportunity to profit from punishment (see below for a more detailed account of deterrence). This meant that people held in these institutions were charged a fee on admission and discharge for food and lodgings. As exposure to expense, disease and physical hardship were viewed as necessary conditions of imprisonment, people held in county gaols were subject to disease, starvation and eventually death. That said, things began to change in 1601 after the introduction of the Poor Law as each English county was required to provide houses of correction for those who had been convicted of petty crime or refused to work.

Houses of correction were designed to combat idleness amongst those in prison (historically idleness was considered a contributing factor to people's economic position) through punishment, hard labour and discipline. By being forced to work whilst subject to solitude, order and fasting, it was believed that people in prison would form good habits and a working ethos that would help to facilitate their return to the wider community and labour market. At the time, it was suggested that houses of correction were more progressive than county gaols as they provided a more humane version of custody that afforded a sense of reformation rather than simply detention. But in reality, houses of correction were little more than factories that produced commodities at a low cost due to the availability of forced, cheap labour.

Over time county gaols and houses of correction occupied the same premises and were supervised by the same gaoler. These joint institutions subsequently became known as prisons. As a direct response to the growing number of people sentenced to prison, as well as an increase in the use of long-term imprisonment and inability to transport people overseas, parliament passed the 1776 Hulks Act to increase prison capacity. This meant that in addition to prisons, people could now be imprisoned in hulks (boats that were afloat but could not go to sea) and required to undertake hard labour in dockyards and/or on riverbanks. People sent to prison hulks were required to engage in exhausting manual labour and were fed little other than bread, coarse or substandard food, water and/or small amounts of beer. Alongside malnutrition, poor sanitation and cramped conditions meant that disease and infection spread quickly amongst those on board prison hulks and as a result the mortality rate was particularly high.

Although overseen by local justices of the peace, prison hulks were managed by private contractors. The first contract was awarded to Duncan Campbell, a former transportation contractor, and in August 1776, a former transportation ship was moored in the River Thames. This became the first of many prison hulks to appear across the country. Like many prisons today, hulks held either males or females. Whilst there was a prison hulk for women (HMS Dunkirk, moored at Portsmouth between 1784 and 1791) as most females were deemed unfit to carry out the manual labour required by the Hulks Act they were typically sent to houses of correction instead. Children as young as eight were also held in prison hulks alongside their adult counterparts and it was not until 1825 that a hulk (HMS Euryalus) was designed to exclusively hold young boys. That is not to say that the living conditions were any better or indeed kinder to young people. On the contrary, it was not uncommon for boys (younger than 14) to be kept below deck for 23 hours per day and forced to do manual labour.

As prisons such as Millbank were established (opened in 1821), fewer people were sent to hulks until the Act expired in 1857. During the 19th century the government became more involved in the ownership and administration of prisons across the country which subsequently gave way to a more robust effort to collect personal information from people held in penal institutions. The Home Office and Prison Commission: Prison

Records 1770–1951 contains a register of people in prison during this time with photograph albums, minute books and visitors' logs. The Prison Registers (Millbank, Parkhurst and Pentonville) 1847–1866 holds information about each person's age, marital status, children, ability to read or write, trade, when and where convicted, sentence, previous offences and so forth. Similar information is held on the Register of Prisoners in County Prisons 1838–1875 and Millbank Prison Register 1816–1826 which also includes information on people's health and character whilst in prison. To date, not all categories of information have been transcribed and licensing conditions restrict what data is available to the public. That said, you can access a lot of the information held in these records by visiting the National Archives.

Public interest in prison conditions and the treatment of people in prison grew during the latter part of the 18th century. John Howard (1726–1790), a philanthropist and social reformer most known for his description of prison regimes in the 18th century, provided part of the drive for a fundamental reform of the English prison system. In his 1777 report *The State of the Prisons in England and Wales*, Howard highlighted how people in prison were not separated by sex or type of crime. Jailers were often corrupt and people in prison were dying of illness and/or disease. Too few people were employed to make prisons secure and safe, and many people remained in prison beyond their release date as they could not afford release fees (Howard, 2013). As a result, Howard went on to suggest that people in prison should be kept in solitary confinement to prevent the spread of negative influences and provide time to reflect on wrongdoing. This was based on the belief that prisons could be places of reform.

Using imprisonment as the pivot of punishment was embodied in the Penitentiary Act 1779, which supported the use of regular labour, solitary confinement, religious instruction, self-reflection, Christian principles and practices of moral duty. Howard recommended a system of classification to limit the spread of moral contamination between young people in prison for the first time and older, more experienced residents. The idea of categorisation persists today but has moved beyond ideas about moral contamination towards risk identification and management (see Chapter 5 for further discussion). The Penitentiary Act 1779 introduced the idea of state prisons for the first time. This was a significant development in penal history as it marked the first direct involvement of central government in prison administration. Although the ambitions of the Penitentiary Act 1779 were scaled down, it did facilitate the construction of two penitentiaries in London: HMP Pentonville and HMP Parkhurst. Over the course of the 1780s and 1790s, 60 new penal institutions were built, and numerous existing prisons were reformed based on the offerings of the Penitentiary Act. Under the stipulations of the Act, people found guilty of all but the most serious offences could be ordered to solitary imprisonment accompanied by well-regulated labour and religious instruction not merely to deter others from the commission of similar crimes but also to reform the individuals in question (Hardman, 2007).

Many new prisons were built with individual cells to accommodate two new regimes that were designed to reform people during their time in custody: the separate system and the silent system. In separate system prisons, people were isolated from each other, kept alone in cells for weeks at a time and forced to work on machines such as the crank which served no purpose other than to exhaust and punish people in prison who would be required to turn the crank handle up to 15,000 times a day. When leaving their cells, people in prison were made to wear a mask and ordered to maintain silence. No communication was permitted to avoid corruption and provide an opportunity for continuous self-examination and reflection. During allocated exercise time, people in prison would hold onto a rope several meters from the next person to prevent communication. In prisons with silent systems, people were forced to undertake repetitive tasks in complete silence, sleep on hard beds and eat basic food such as bread and water. These physically demanding punishments were harsh, brutal and rooted in a philosophy of deterrence and less eligibility. In sum, less eligibility holds the view that the 'level of prison conditions should always compare unfavourably to the material living standards of the labouring poor' (Sparks, 1996:74).

In 1816 the first national penitentiary opened in Millbank, London. Based on a separate system of solitary confinement, Millbank Prison could accommodate up to one thousand people – many of whom were serious lawbreakers from across the country. By the 1840s there was growing concern about the severity of prison regimes and its effect on the mental health of people in prison. As a result, association time (time allowed out of one's prison cell to mix with other people serving a custodial sentence) was introduced as long periods of separation were now deemed unsafe.

Elizabeth Fry (1780–1845) was an English philanthropist who, like Howard, became involved in issues of penal reform. Commonly known for exposing the appalling living conditions in women's prisons as well as her efforts to improve them, Fry called for the state to look at the needs of women in prison. In 1817 she established the Association for the Improvement of Female Prisoners in Newgate prison, the first of many ladies' societies for promoting the reformation of females in prison. In doing so, Fry introduced lady visitors to female prison establishments as she believed that by associating with pure, high standing and holy women, females serving a custodial sentence would somehow be spiritually uplifted. Bible classes and employment opportunities such as needlework and knitting were central to the new daily routine for women, with begging, swearing and gambling prohibited. Though problematic, this approach was indicative of attempts to improve living conditions in prison whilst promoting moral reform through discipline and compassion.

Campaigns that took place during the 18th and 19th centuries began to change people's attitudes towards prison, increasingly defined as a place of reform and rehabilitation. Continued pressure from penal reformers such as Howard and Fry subsequently led to the 1823 Gaols Act, which stated that prisons should be made secure, jailers should be paid a fair wage, females should be kept separately from their male counterparts, doctors and chaplains should visit prisons, and attempts should be made to reform people serving a custodial sentence. By the end of the 19th century, prison regimes had moved away from attempts to reform people serving a custodial sentence through separation or silence in favour of hard labour, hard fare and hard board (see the 1865 Prisons Act). In 1894 a departmental committee under the leadership of Herbert Gladstone was established to report on the conditions of the penal system. The subsequent publication of the Gladstone Report (1895, cited in Scott, 2008) went some way to question beliefs about imprisonment at the time, suggesting that people should be better people when they left prison through regimes of deterrence and reform. The Prison Act of 1898 went some way to advocate reformation as the key role of prison, and in many ways set the tone for prison policy today, leading to the dilution of the silent and separate system, the abolition of hard labour and establishing the idea that prison work should be productive. Although seemingly positive, such shifts in penological thinking provide another, more discreet way in which the state gained control over the masses at a time when different work and social habits were required to support the new industrial marketplace (Wilson, 2014).

During the early 1900s there were further changes to the prison system such as attempts to establish after-care facilities, improve educational provisions and diet. The Prison Act 1948 abolished arcane ideas about hard labour and penal servitude and the 1949 English Prison Rules introduced, for the first time, the idea that the primary purpose of prison was to support people to lead a good and useful life. The reformation of prisons seemingly coincided with a growth in the use of imprisonment after World War II (1939–1945). In 1908, the prison population was just over 22,000 – a record level that would not be exceeded until 1952 (UK Parliament, 2021), after which the number of people sent to prison steadily rose to 49,000 by 1988 (Ibid). The rise in numbers from the early 1990s has occurred despite there being no significant increase in the number of people being sentenced in court. Rather, the increase can be attributed to a plethora of changes that allowed courts in England and Wales to consider previous convictions when passing sentence, the introduction of automatic life sentences for some sexual and violent crimes, as well as an increase in the use of short custodial sentences for anti-social crimes (UK Parliament, 2021).

CONCERNS OVER SECURITY

Until the early 1960s security in prison was not considered especially important. However, a growing long-term prison population combined with an increasing number of people convicted of serious crimes contributed to the emergence of a crisis of containment that put issues in and around security firmly on the penal agenda (Cavadino and Dignan, 1992). Such concerns were compounded by a significant increase in the number of attempted and actual escapes by people serving a custodial sentence, including notorious individuals such as Charles Wilson who escaped from Winson Green Prison in 1964 in just under three minutes, Ronnie Biggs, who escaped from HMP Wandsworth in 1965, just 15 months into his custodial sentence, and George Blake who escaped from HMP Wormwood Scrubs in 1966.

As a result, a committee under the leadership of Lord Mountbatten was established to examine why the escapes had taken place and to make recommendations to improve prison security. The Mountbatten Report suggested that the problem lay in the insufficiently secure accommodation for a small number of very high-risk people, together with overly secure regimes for the rest of the prison population (Newburn, 2003). The Mountbatten Committee recommended that a system for categorising people in prison should be introduced, separating those requiring the highest possible degree of security from those who could be reasonably trusted to serve their sentence. In theory, the policy of concentration would not only ensure that people considered to require high security were kept in secure settings but that security could be somewhat relaxed in other establishments.

In 1968, a subcommittee of the Advisory Council on the Penal System was established to consider what regime would be appropriate for those who pose the highest risk. The committee rejected the policy of concentration on the basis that providing adequate work and recreational facilities in establishments for such a small number of people would be problematic and transferring people in prison who became unsettled or unsettled others would not be feasible. In response, the subcommittee suggested a policy of dispersal whereby people deemed to require high-security measures would be dispersed amongst selected training prisons with upgraded security measures (see Chapter 5 for further discussion). This, according to Scraton et al. (1991: 110) 'led directly to a major intensification in the levels of security and control experienced by prisoners as well as a significant increase in the number of prison officers employed to manage the system'. The Thatcherism of the late 1970s further transformed the prison system into a 'pawn' in a political battleground (Menis, 2018: 484). This new era of imprisonment, typically associated with managerialism and penal populism, brought into sharp focus how the failings of the prison system 'cannot be attributed any longer solely to its nature' (Ibid), drawing our attention more than ever before to the fact that the prison place has transformed into a highly politicised entity, with a confused and indeed confusing sense of purpose. To illustrate this point, we will now turn our attention to the infamous Strangeways riots, which unfolded in England during the 1990s.

Strangeways (now HMP Manchester) opened in 1868 as a local prison designed to hold people sentenced to custody from the surrounding area, those on remand or serving custodial sentences of less than five years. The infamous riot began on 1 April 1990 when people serving a custodial sentence took control of the chapel and ended on 25 April 1990 when the final five protesters were removed from the prison rooftop. In the months leading up to the riot, the prison was described as intolerable given that it was overcrowded, unsanitary and inhumane. During the disturbance, the prison was gutted and subsequent repairs cost more than £55 million. A person serving a custodial sentence was killed during the riot; 147 prison officers and 47 residents also received serious injuries.

The riot at Strangeways quickly sparked a series of copycat disturbances in prisons across England, Scotland and Wales that resulted in the British government announcing a public inquiry into the riots headed by Lord Woolf. Central to Woolf's understanding of the disturbances was the recognition that there was no single cause of the riot and no simple solution or action, which would prevent future rioting in prisons. Rather, Woolf suggested that security, control and justice are equally important and must be balanced if a prison system is to be stable. The Woolf report indicated how in the case of Strangeways, an overemphasis on security gave insufficient weight to justice and often led to inappropriate control measures. As such, he recommended that a contract be drawn up between prisons and those held within them to clarify what people serving a custodial sentence should expect to receive from the prison and how the institution expects everyone to behave in return (Day et al., 2015).

Such proposals formed the basis of the Incentives and Earned Privileges (IEP) scheme which was introduced in 1995 across prisons in England and Wales. Each person in prison is given an IEP status (basic, entry, standard or enhanced) based on their behaviour. When an individual enters prison, they are given an entry level status. As such, they are, for example, not allowed to wear their own clothes, are expected to demonstrate good behaviour and attend all required induction courses. After 14 days, people with an entry level status will be promoted to standard status if they are adequately abiding by the prison rules and regulations. In most prisons in England and Wales standard status will allow people to wear their own clothes (for example). After a further three months, individuals with standard status can apply for enhanced status if they are behaving to a consistently high standard and engaging well with specified activities and/or interventions which will afford access to extra privileges such as more domestic visits, an in-cell television, personal cash and so on. The main criterion for promotion is good and compliant behaviour, as well as willingness to help other people serving a custodial sentence. Since its introduction the IEP scheme has gone on to become a key tool in prison management given that good behaviour can be rewarded and bad behaviour/failure to comply with prison rules and regulations can be punished through basic level status, which permits access to limited activities and resources that are typically stipulated by law.

Although heralded as historically significant, the Woolf report was not that innovative as many of the recommendations were based on the concept of humane containment, first mentioned in the 1969 Home Office White Paper *People in Prison*. Furthermore, the Woolf report also failed to recognise the deeply problematic nature of punishment and imprisonment more broadly and/or examine the intractable and inherent problems reflecting the deep malaise in the prison estate (Scott, 2020). Whilst the Strangeways riot provided a unique moment in time to learn from the mistakes of our past, just over

25 years later Lord Woolf himself believes that 'we've allowed ourselves to go backwards and we're back where we were at the time of Strangeways' (Williams, 2015: para. 13). Despite Woolf's recommendation to use imprisonment as a last resort, England and Wales continues to have the highest rate of imprisonment in Western Europe (Prison Reform Trust, 2019) with numbers predicted to increase from just over 79,000 in November 2021 to approximately 97,500 by July 2025 (Ministry of Justice, 2021). This forecast provides an alarming insight into the use of imprisonment in England and Wales, particularly when considered alongside contemporary failings of the prison system to keep people safe and well during a global health pandemic (COVID-19):

> **At the start of the pandemic, ministers in England and Wales were told that up to 3,500 prisoners might die because our overcrowded, dilapidated prisons represented such a fertile environment for disease to spread. Despite that horrific prospect, they chose not to organise a major early release programme as they were advised. Though prisoners and prison staff have sadly died, those predicted numbers have not materialised, but to achieve that outcome prisoners have spent almost an entire year largely confined to their cells and for the most part denied face to face contact with their loved ones. (Dawson, 2021: 4, cited in Prison Reform Trust, 2021)**

By exploring the evolution of prisons in England and Wales it becomes clear that answers to fundamental questions such as 'what do prisons do?', 'what are prisons for?' and 'what does imprisonment achieve?' are far from straightforward. To further help you to consider these questions, the next part of the chapter will introduce you to four long-standing justifications of imprisonment which include (but are not limited to) deterrence, incapacitation, just deserts and rehabilitation. As you read through next section, you may find it useful to consider the material in relation to what you already know about *who* goes to prison (see Chapter 5 for further discussion) and *why* (see Chapter 11 for further discussion).

JUSTIFYING IMPRISONMENT

In the 1920s, Alexander Paterson, the then prison commissioner declared that 'people come to prison as punishment not for punishment' (Ruck, 1951: 23 cited in Moore, 2008: para. 3). This is an important statement for any budding penologist as it clearly, albeit briefly, outlines how a prison sentence is a punishment in its own right and as such, punishment (of any kind) is not required or necessary when someone is imprisoned. Understanding the meaning and intention behind this quotation is important as imprisonment is one of the most 'significant powers available to the state' (Gauke, 2018: para. 4). Although sentencing has become harsher, and more people are exposed to the prison place as well as the collateral consequences of imprisonment, we are still unable to unequivocally justify why some lawbreakers are repeatedly sent to prison. To illustrate this point, let us now explore a series of theoretical frameworks that have attempted to justify the role and function of the prison place in modern times.

Deterrence

I said at Blackpool that prison works – and it does. First, it deters many people from crime. If the sanction of prison were not available, who can possibly doubt that many more would be tempted to commit crimes? Secondly, while they are in prison, criminals cannot commit further crimes against the public. That can have a real and quantifiable effect. Our research into a sample of burglars given community service orders in 1987 suggested that, had they been in prison for a year, we could have prevented between three and 13 crimes per burglar. (Howard, 1993: para 7)

Put simply, deterrence suggests that people are deterred from crime by the threat of punishment. The object of deterrence is to make consequences harsh enough so that the public will fear receiving a similar punishment and will consequently be dissuaded from engaging in similar behaviour. Whilst such sentiments underpin the above quotation, and indeed much of the speech delivered by Michael Howard (leader of the Conservative party from November 2003 to December 2005) during his 'does prison work?' address to the Conservative party conference in 1993, they are subject to intense debate and critique. But before we critically engage with the offerings of deterrence, let us now consider the concept in more detail.

Deterrence can be specific (or individual), which refers to the direct effect of punishment on the future behaviour of people who experience it, or general, which refers to the preventative effect of the threat of punishment on the general population. Individual deterrence calls for punishment to have a direct impact on a person whereas principles of general deterrence are applied to a wider community as a method of social control, focused on teaching the public a lesson. Developed by 18th century philosophers such as Jeremy Bentham and Cesare Beccaria, deterrence theory suggests that crime results from a rational calculation of the costs and benefits of criminal activity. In other words, people will commit crimes when the benefits outweigh the costs (Spohn, 2007). Therefore, according to the principles of deterrence, punishing people who have broken the law will serve as an example to the rest of the community and deter other people from committing crime. But if this is the case why does crime persist, and why are reoffending rates so high? From January to March 2020 in England and Wales alone, the proven reoffending rate for adults released from a custodial sentence of less than 12 months was 57.5% (Ministry of Justice, 2022). This, alongside official projections about the prison population in England and Wales (see Figure 3.1 below), raises a series of fundamental questions about the concept of deterrence in both theory and practice

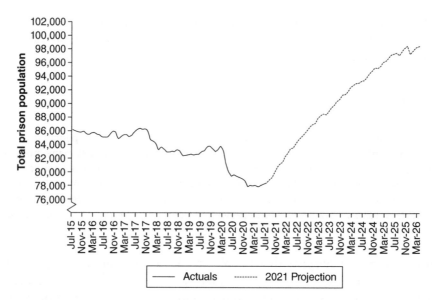

Figure 3.1 Total prison population projection for England and Wales (July 2021 to March 2026)

(*Source*: Ministry of Justice (2021) *Prison Population Projections 2021 to 2026, England and Wales*. Available at: https://assets.publishing.service.gov.uk/government/uploads/system/uploads/attachment_data/file/1035682/ Prison_Population_Projections_2021_to_2026.pdf (last accessed 25 July 2022)

Generally speaking, the concept of deterrence rests upon three separate but interconnected elements: *certainty, severity* and *immediacy*. Certainty refers to the probability of legal sanctions. Thus, by increasing the certainty of punishment, potential lawbreakers may be deterred by the risk of apprehension. The second concept, severity, refers to the onerousness of the legal sanction imposed. In other words, the severity of punishment will influence behaviour if potential lawbreakers weigh up the consequences of their actions and conclude that the risk of punishment is too severe. The third and final concept, immediacy, refers to the lapse in time between the crime and its punishment. In its simplest form, this means that lawbreakers need to associate the punishment with the violation of the law so punishment must occur within a short space of time after the offence is committed. Gibbs (1975) suggests that these concepts are important for deterrence theorists as they underpin commonly held assumptions about deterrence which suggest:

- The greater the actual certainty, swiftness and severity of punishment, the greater the perceived certainty, swiftness and severity of punishment

- The greater the perceived certainty, swiftness, and severity of punishment, the less the crime

- The greater the actual certainty, swiftness and severity of punishment, the less the crime.

AN INTRODUCTION TO PENOLOGY

Theorists such as Beccaria and Bentham assume that there is a strong positive relationship between actual punishments and perceived punishments. However, as Kleck (2018) notes, public policies that are designed to reduce crime by increasing the deterrent effect of punishment are unlikely to succeed because they are not likely, in general, to increase prospective lawbreakers' perceptions of the risks of committing crime. That said, deterrence theorists believe that if punishment is severe, certain and swift, a rational person will measure the gains (benefits) and losses (costs) before engaging in crime and will be deterred from breaking the law if the loss is greater than the gain. But what does the term rational person mean, and who defines what rationality looks like when what is considered rational to one individual may be considered completely irrational to another person who has a different value system, financial pressures and social ties.

For classical philosophers, the concept of certainty is more effective in preventing crime than severity of punishment. The idea of deterrence remains a key intellectual foundation for western criminal justice systems today even though such ideals create more frequent and harsher punishments, assume prison is a deterrent and lawbreakers are rational cost–benefit calculators who consider the consequences of their behaviour before deciding to commit a crime. Deterrence theory also fails to acknowledge how for some people, in some instances, lawbreaking is driven by socio-economic factors such as unemployment, poverty, limited educational attainment, substance use, poor mental health and so on, rather than rationality and calculation. When thinking about the notion of deterrence we must also consider the dynamics of a modern criminal justice system. When only 9 per cent of crimes end with suspects being charged or summonsed in England and Wales, the overall deterrent effect of the certainty of punishment is reduced (Home Office, 2018). Alongside this, it is important to recognise how enhancing the severity of punishment will have little impact on people who do not believe they will be apprehended for their actions. Thus, when considering the notion of deterrence, it is important to consider the role and impact of both threat and credibility.

Incapacitation

Incapacitation refers to the restriction of an individual's freedoms and liberties so that they do not have the capacity to commit further crime(s). Since the inception of prisons, imprisonment has been justified as a means of removing individuals who have broken the law from society (Bhati, 2007), the idea being that a lawbreaker will be sent to prison to protect society and prevent further criminal activity. Imprisonment is, however, not the only form of incapacitation. Before we move on, it is important to recognise that incapacitation can also be used to describe and justify community sanctions and measures that restrict an individual's liberties and freedoms within the community, such as home detention curfews (HDCs). Zimring and Hawkins (1995: 158) suggest that the 'capacity to control rather than influence is the most important reason for the great and persistent popularity of incapacitation as a penal method'. The utilisation of incapacitation to justify imprisonment is not only the most obvious and least contentious but the most publicly appealing given its simplicity and apathetic goal.

Although incapacitation cannot rectify crimes that have already taken place, it does attempt (in theory at least) to prevent crimes from being committed. *Selective incapacitation* is a strategy that seeks to protect the public and save resources by imprisoning only those who pose the greatest threat to society. This is calculated through an assessment of a lawbreaker's crimes and likelihood of future lawbreaking. The goal of selective incapacitation is to reduce crime and create a more efficient use of prison space. Attempts to put into practice the idea of selective incapacitation can be found in the Criminal Justice Acts of 1967 and 1991, which advocate the use of extended sentences for the most persistent lawbreakers whose previous convictions suggest that that they pose a genuine risk to society. Such endeavours must however be treated with caution as the vague terminology underpinning the Criminal Justice Act 1967 meant that the ambitions of selective incapacitation were lost in translation, with 16 per cent of extended sentences passed between 1974 and 1976 relating primarily to property offences as opposed to violent or sexual offences (Dingwall, 1998). A more recent example of such disproportionality can be found in the, now defunct, Indeterminate Public Protection (IPP) sentence which was first introduced in England and Wales on 4 April 2005 through the Criminal Justice Act (CJA) 2003.

The test for an IPP sentence was that a person was over 18, had been assessed as dangerous and had committed a sexual or violent offence where the maximum penalty was at least ten years (see Chapter 1 for a more detailed discussion of risk and dangerousness). Assessment was, however, notoriously difficult, made worse by the fact that when the Act was first enacted, it contained a presumption of dangerousness where the person in question had been convicted of one of the relevant offences and the court felt that it was reasonable to conclude that they were dangerous. Bearing this in mind, and the fact that specified relevant offences involved several minor offences, it is not surprising that judges were forced to impose life sentences in unsuitable cases. Although judges (in some cases) were able to impose lower minimum tariffs, as they were still indeterminate sentences, release would only occur when the individual could prove to the parole board that it was no longer necessary for them to be detained in custody on the grounds of public protection. The most common way in which a person could prove this was through completion of accredited offending behaviour programmes (OBPs). However, due to the insufficient provision of OBPs, many people in prison were unable to evidence within their minimum terms that they had shown a reduction in their risk (see Chapter 9 for further discussion of OBPs). In addition, data from the Prison Service's Safer Custody Group illustrates how people serving an IPP sentence have raised incidents of self-harm (37 per cent) in comparison to other people serving a custodial sentence (23 per cent) (see Figure 3.2). This, according to HM Inspectorate of Prisons and Probation (2008), is consistent with their complex needs, uncertainty about length of time in custody and frustration with regard to their ability to progress through the system (Ibid).

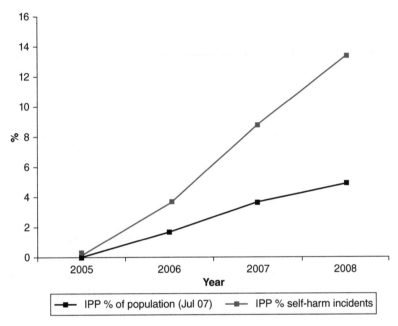

Figure 3.2 IPP population and self-harm incidents in England and Wales

Source: HM Chief Inspector of Prisons and Probation (2008) *The indeterminate sentence for public protection. A thematic review.* Available at: www.justiceinspectorates.gov.uk/probation/wp-content/uploads/sites/5/2014/03/hmip_ipp_thematic-rps.pdf (last accessed on 25 July 2022)

The Criminal Justice and Immigration Act 2008 went some way to limit the application of IPP sentences by tightening the eligibility criteria, which subsequently required that a person be convicted of a serious, specified offence meriting a determinate sentence of at least four years (effectively a minimum two-year tariff). Though a step in the right direction, the non-retrospective application of the Act means that those sentenced prior to 2008 with short tariffs remain in custody serving disproportionately long sentences. Jacobson and Hough (2010) suggest this is because the parole board is overstretched and as a result there can be lengthy delays for oral hearings. Parole board decisions tend to be risk averse and OBPs (completion of which is considered essential for release) are limited in availability, scope and effectiveness, with many of those serving an IPP sentence regularly refused a place on OBPs. It is also inherently difficult to demonstrate reduced risk in custodial settings when one has been deemed dangerous by the courts.

As such, the IPP sentence can be seen as the epitome of the move towards a risk-based penal strategy based primarily on the future risk an individual is predicted to present, rather than the crime for which they have been convicted (Ashworth, 2010: 422 citied in Howard League for Penal Reform, 2013). Despite efforts to amend the sentence, just seven years after its inception it was abolished by the Legal Aid Sentencing and Punishment of Offenders Act (2012) following heavy criticism. However, as such amendments are not retrospective, thousands of people in prison and beyond remain subject to this deeply problematic sentence. To date, there are more than 1,700 people in prison serving an IPP sentence without a release date (UK Parliament, 2021a), 96 per cent of whom have completed their minimum term and more than 500 held in prison more than ten years longer than the tariff they were given (Ibid).

In its most basic sense, incapacitation is a flawed concept that lacks ambition given that its goal is achieved simply by placing a person in prison (Scott, 2008). When we consider this, alongside the inherent problems which surround imprisonment, its collateral consequences and reoffending rates, we must consider to what extent the concept of incapacitation is defendable in contemporary society. Parallel to this, it is important to question the oversimplistic version of imprisonment offered by incapacitation which overlooks how people in prison can, and indeed do, commit further criminal offences during their custodial sentence. Alongside this, it is also important to consider how incapacitation can be applied unfairly and indeed unjustly to justify imprisonment of those who are deemed sufficiently dangerous (see Chapter 11 for further discussion).

Retribution

Retribution has a long history in law and philosophy found in the *lex talionis* of early Roman law and the *eye for an eye* precept in the Old Testament. You may hear the phrase *an eye for an eye* when attempts are made to justify punishment and imprisonment based on retributive ideals. But, contrary to popular belief, *lex talionis* (which means law of the same kind) is not about retribution. Rather, it is about restoration and balance. Thus, according to retributive ideals, punishment can be justified as it is a way of restoring the status quo that was disrupted by the lawbreaker. Rawls (1971) suggests that it is morally fitting that a person who does wrong should suffer in proportion to their guilt, with the severity of the punishment dependent on the depravity of their acts. But how punishment performs this function remains a matter of controversy, particularly as societies tend to deprive lawbreakers of human resources, time and/or money which, for most people, have little to no relation to the harm caused by their original actions.

The doctrine of proportionality, originally advocated by Italian criminologist Cesare Beccaria, who viewed the harsh punishments of his day as disproportionate to many of the crimes committed, seeks to limit arbitrary and capricious punishment to ensure that lawbreakers are being punished according to their just desert. In theory, proportionality goes some way towards achieving a balanced approach to punishment and justice as it requires a court to consider various and often-competing interests in formulating a sentence commensurate with offence seriousness and culpability. However, the idea that there should be a proportional relationship between a crime and punishment is difficult, if not impossible, to achieve. This is particularly so as we live in an inherently unequal society with systems of punishment heavily focused on working-class crimes that typically deprive people of their liberty, autonomy, human resource and finances, which (in most cases) have little to no relation to the harm caused by the crime committed.

In more recent years, retribution has been popularised through the term just deserts, which represents the idea of fair and appropriate punishment related to the severity of the crime committed. Although retribution seems to be the main motivation underpinning punitive attitudes towards sentencing, there is some confusion in the literature in terms of what retribution means. Gerber and Jackson (2013) distinguish between *retribution as revenge*, which focuses on a desire to punish lawbreakers to retaliate against a past wrong and make the person in question suffer, and *retribution as just deserts*, which details a preference to restore justice through proportional compensation. Garber and Jackson (2013) go on to highlight how these distinct dimensions of retribution not only have different ideological and motivational beginnings but different consequences in terms of how we treat and respond to those who have broken the law. For instance, retribution as revenge is associated with the motivation to enforce boundaries with those who have broken the law as well as an ideological preference for power and dominance as well as support of harsh punishment. Retribution as just deserts is, however, motivated by a restorative function (see Chapter 13 for a more detailed discussion).

Retribution, from a just deserts perspective, responds to a lawbreaker's behaviour in a way that respects their choice to engage in unlawful behaviour and defines crime as conduct that disturbs relationships within the community. As such, the goal of retribution is to reconcile these relationships by making a lawbreaker pay for the disturbance, harm and hurt caused by their behaviour. Whilst this may seem more progressive than retribution as revenge, implementing appropriate responses to lawbreaking is still largely determined by the theory of punishment to which a society subscribes as well as perceptions about the right way to punish people who break the law. The long-standing over-reliance on imprisonment , despite its inherent harms and collateral consequences, raises fundamental questions about a society's ability and indeed willingness to prioritise appropriate responses to lawbreaking over punitive measures that please the masses and create an illusion that something is 'being done' about crime (see Chapter 13 for a further discussion). Figure 3.3 below separates the sentenced prison population in England and Wales by offence type (correct as of March 2022). In doing so, it provides an opportunity for you to critically engage with the extent to which imprisonment is utilised as an appropriate response across a variety of offence types.

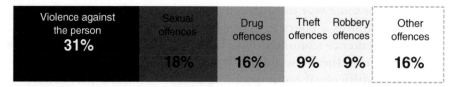

Figure 3.3 Prison population in England and Wales by offence type. Percentages have been rounded so may not add up to 100 per cent

Source: HM Government (2022) *Prisons Data*. Available at: https://data.justice.gov.uk/prisons (last accessed 25 July 2022)

Rehabilitation

We will consider the justifications for rehabilitation more fully in Chapter 4 but before doing so let us now focus on the rehabilitative potential of prisons. This is important because 'at first glance, the rehabilitation of those in custody might appear to be a laudable and desirable goal, but ultimately an unachievable one' (Jewkes and Gooch, 2020: 153). This is particularly clear when we look at the evidence base, which highlights how reoffending rates for those released from prison remain stubbornly high, custodial sentences increase the likelihood of future offending (Bales and Piquero, 2012) and for some people (especially women) with a history of trauma and poor mental health who have 'suffered poverty, homelessness and domestic abuse, prison might be a place of refuge and respite rather than rehabilitation' (Cain, 2016, cited in Jewkes and Gooch, 2020: 153).

Since the inception of the Penitentiary Act 1779, which made the rehabilitation of people in prison a function of all custodial establishments, efforts to help those serving a custodial sentence have taken place, in varying forms and to differing degrees, across the prison estate. Whilst in the past rehabilitative efforts may have been directed at reforming the character of people in prison through silence, isolation, labour, punishment and medical interventions, its contemporary focus (according to official discourse) now rests on helping people during their custodial sentence so that they can return to society as functioning, law-abiding members of the community, which in turn prevents (or at the very least reduces) further lawbreaking. This ambition is reflected in HM Prison Service's statement of purpose: 'we keep those sentenced to prison in custody, helping them lead law-abiding and useful lives both while they are in prison and after they are released' (HM Prison Service, 2022: para, 1). As well as political discourse:

> **Prison provides offenders with the opportunity to reflect on, and take responsibility for, their crimes and prepare them for a law-abiding life when they are released. It is only by prioritising rehabilitation that we can reduce reoffending and, in turn, the number of future victims of crime. (Gauke, 2018: para. 8)**

This ambition can also be seen in a rapidly unfolding desire to promote a *rehabilitative culture* in prisons across England and Wales whereby prisons work towards the provision of rehabilitative opportunities for people in their care that contributes 'to the prison being safe, decent, hopeful and supportive of change, progression and to helping someone desist from crime' (Mann et al., 2018: 04). Chapter 11 details more fully how the prison service attempts to work alongside people during their time in prison, but for the purpose of this section it is important to note that rehabilitative opportunities in custodial settings vary from therapeutic interventions to address the psychological causes of criminal behaviour, to educational, vocational and employment opportunities, drug treatment and healthcare services to prepare people for release and reintegration into the wider community. In more recent times we have witnessed art-based interventions grow in scope and popularity due to their proven positive impact on engagement, motivation and the provision of opportunities for people to develop new skills, as well as discover new ways of behaving and relating to others (National Criminal Justice Arts Alliance, 2016). Although such developments are promising, it is important to recognise that the availability and accessibility of rehabilitative opportunities vary enormously between prisons and people serving a custodial sentence (with some individuals not eligible for certain opportunities due to their index offence and/or length of time left to serve, for example).

In 2002, the Social Exclusion Unit published a report called *Reducing Re-offending by Ex-prisoners*, which identified nine factors that influence reoffending: education, employment, drug and alcohol use, mental and physical health, attitudes and self-control, institutionalisation and life skills, housing, financial support and debt, and family networks. These factors were later transformed, *in the Reducing Re-offending National Action Plan*, into seven pathways which aimed to guide service provision and promote partnership working with third sector organisations to achieve the best results possible (Home Office, 2004). Although not dissimilar to the nine factors identified by the Social Exclusion Unit in 2002, the seven pathways include accommodation; education, training, and employment; health; drugs and alcohol; finance; benefit and debt; children and families, and attitudes, thinking and behaviour. Whilst insightful, we must remember that imprisonment may, in reality, make the factors associated with reoffending worse. This is because a third of people in prison will lose their home while in custody. Two-thirds will lose their employment. Over a fifth face increased financial problems as a direct result of custody and more than two-fifths lose contact with their family, with many experiencing a deterioration in their mental and physical health, life and thinking skills and substance use (Social Exclusion Unit, 2002). Thus, despite attempts to help people during their time in prison, by aggravating the factors associated with reoffending, prison sentences are counterproductive, eroding rather than enriching rehabilitation.

The seven pathways to reduce reoffending go some way to capture the vast, multifaceted nature of rehabilitation, recognising the role of both the individual and society in one's journey away from criminal activity. Despite such insight, rehabilitative initiatives are typically based on and influenced by a desire to target criminogenic need and lower risk factors on an individual level (see Chapter 2 for a more detailed discussion). Though such endeavours are important, politicising individual lawbreakers as agents of rehabilitation whilst simultaneously absolving the state of any responsibility and/or wrongdoing does little more than reinforce the status quo for those who fall into the criminal justice system ripe for re-moralisation, reconstruction, reform and rehabilitation.

Although it has been suggested that rehabilitation is a more humane objective of imprisonment, particularly when compared to concepts such as deterrence and incapacitation, we must critically engage with the design, delivery and effectiveness of ongoing penal policies and practices, in the name of rehabilitation, that are still firmly focused on poor, working-class lawbreakers. As Carlen (2012: para. 2) suggests, 'it is not surprising that it has always seemed easier (and cheaper) to attempt rehabilitation of the lawbreaking poor than to consider how best to respond to press mendacity, political malfeasance and corporate recklessness and greed'.

CONCLUSION

Prior to the 1970s, rehabilitation was widely accepted as a legitimate goal of imprisonment, with prisons serving as places of reform and reformation whereby people serving a custodial sentence could be rehabilitated in preparation for their return to the wider community. However, this changed during the 1970s because of a dramatic shift in the balance between punishment and rehabilitation. Rising crime rates and prison overcrowding contributed to disillusion with the effectiveness of prison-based rehabilitative opportunities and OBPs were hit particularly hard (see Chapter 9 for further discussion). This growing scepticism was compounded by the work of Martinson (1974: 49) who, after a review of 231 studies of prison rehabilitative programmes, concluded that 'education (...) or psychotherapy at its best, cannot overcome, or even appreciably reduce, the powerful tendency for offenders to continue in criminal behaviour'. Although Martinson recounted his conclusions in 1974, he has become synonymous with the term *nothing works*. Despite efforts to withdraw his findings, the idea that nothing works had serious implications for the rehabilitative potential of prisons for years to come, so much so, that by the early 1980s scholars such as Anthony Bottoms were discussing the collapse of the rehabilitative ideal (see Chapter 2 for further discussion). This subsequently had a profound impact on the day-to-day operation of prisons, and opportunities for people within them, now described as human ware-houses, with deterrence and incapacitation at the forefront of penal policy and practice once again.

> A great mass of academic and social research has produced arguments on both sides as to whether more prison produces less crime. My judgement is that there is no simple and con-clusive answer. You can't actually prove it either way. I am sure that prison is the necessary punishment for many serious offenders. But does ever more prison for ever more offenders always produce better results for the public? (...) Just banging up more and more people for longer without actively seeking to change them is, in my opinion, what you would expect of Victorian England (...) It is time we focused on what is right for today's communities. (Clarke, 2010: para. 49)

Whilst it is important to engage with efforts to understand the theoretical underpin-nings of prisons and imprisonment more broadly, recognising how such endeavours do not take place within a vacuum is just as important because 'politically, it has proven difficult for governments to take action to reduce the number of inmates, even at times of severe pressure on prison capacity' (UK Parliament, 2021: para. 5). Under-standing the politicised nature of imprisonment in England and Wales is an import-ant endeavour for anyone with an interest in penology as it highlights how and why age-old justifications of imprisonment are routinely called upon, despite their limita-tions in theory and practice, to legitimise the prison place in contemporary society. As such, the authors contend that rather than asking, 'Does prison work?' (because this is clearly irrelevant given that prisons still exist despite their inherent failings), we should consider whether prisons are useful, to whom and in what ways. In his book *Prison on Trial*, Mathiesen offers a more critical interpretation of imprisonment which outlines how prisons have an *expurgatory function* through the provision of an insti-tution within which a proportion of the 'unproductive population of late capitalist societies could be housed, controlled and conveniently forgotten' (Mathiesen, 1974: 142). It has a *power-draining function* that places people in a situation whereby they 'remain unproductive, non-contributors to the system containing them' (Mathiesen, 1974: 142); a *diversion function* which distracts and diverts attention away from the socially dangerous acts committed by those in power; and a *symbolic function* which illustrates how people who are sent to prison are stigmatised and marginalised from their law-abiding counterparts.

Before moving on to the next chapter, take some time to consider the functions of imprisonment as described by Mathiesen alongside contemporary attempts to justify who goes to prison and for what purpose. In doing so, you may wish to con-sider what this tells you about the prison place and why we, as a society, continue to invest in a failing institution that struggles to define, in theory and practice, its aims and ambitions.

recommended reading

If you would like to engage in further reading, you may find the following resources particularly useful:

Barton, A. and Brown, A. (2012) Dark tourism and the modern prison. *Prison Service Journal*, 199, 44–9.

This paper examines the prison place as a site of 'dark tourism' through an analysis of the ways in which, and reasons why, former prisons have become popular tourist destinations. In doing so, the paper examines how prison tourism can facilitate the construction of dominant narratives around the politics of punishment that leave little space for critical scrutiny or challenge.

Davis, A. (2003) *Are Prisons Obsolete?* New York: Seven Stories Press.

This book provides an insightful introduction to prison abolitionism that will help you to think beyond the idea of prisons and imprisonment.

Scott, D. (ed.) (2013) *Why Prison?* Cambridge Studies in Law and Society. Cambridge: Cambridge University Press.

This edited collection brings together critical scholars who engage with the question why prison through a careful analysis of the theory, policy and practice which underpins both the design and delivery of imprisonment.

references

Bales, D.B. and Piquero, A.T. (2012) Assessing the impact of imprisonment on recidivism. *Journal of Experimental Criminology*, 8(1), 71–101.

Bhati, A. (2007) Estimating the number of crimes averted by incapacitation: an information theoretic approach. *Journal of Quantitative Criminology*, 23, 355–75.

Carlen, P. (2012) Against rehabilitation for reparative justice. Speech. London: Centre for Crime and Justice Studies. Available at: www.crimeandjustice.org.uk/resources/against-rehabilitation-reparative-justice (last accessed 29 June 2022).

Cavadino, M. and Dignan, J. (1992) *The Penal System: An Introduction*. London: Sage.

Clarke, K. (2010) The government's vision for criminal justice reform. Speech. London: Centre for Crime and Justice Studies. Available at: www.crimeandjustice.org.uk/resources/governments-vision-criminal-justice-reform (last accessed 29 June 2022).

Day, M., Hewson, A. and Spiropoulos, C. (2015) Strangeways 25 *Years On: Achieving Fairness and Justice in our Prisons. Prison Reform Trust.* Available at: https://prisonreformtrust.org.uk/publication/strangeways-25-years-on-achieving-fairness-and-justice-in-our-prisons (last accessed 29 June 2022).

Dingwall, G. (1998) Selective incapacitation after the Criminal Justice Act 1991: A proportional response to protecting the public? *The Howard Journal of Crime and Justice,* 37(2), 177–87.

Gauke, D. (2018) Prison reform speech. Available at: www.gov.uk/government/speeches/prisons-reform-speech (last accessed 29 June 2022).

Gerber, M. and Jackson, J. (2013) Retribution as revenge and retribution as just deserts. *Social Justice Research,* 26, 61–80.

Gibbs, J.P. (1975) *Crime, Punishment, and Deterrence.* New York: Elsevier.

Hardman, P. (2007) The origins of late eighteenth-century prison reform in England. PhD thesis. Available at: https://core.ac.uk/download/pdf/40065064.pdf (last accessed 29 June 2022).

HM Chief Inspector of Prisons and HM Chief Inspector of Probation (2008) *The Indeterminate Sentence for Public Protection: A Thematic Review.* Available at: www.justiceinspectorates.gov.uk/probation/wp-content/uploads/sites/5/2014/03/hmip_ipp_thematic-rps.pdf (last accessed 29 June 2022).

HM Prison Service (2022) About us. Available at: www.gov.uk/government/organisations/hm-prison-service/about (last accessed 29 June 2022).

Home Office (2004) *Reducing Reoffending: National Action Plan.* Available at: www.nicco.org.uk/userfiles/downloads/024%20-%20Reducing%20Reoffending%20Action%20Plan%202004.pdf (last accessed 29 June 2022).

Home Office (2018) *Crime Outcomes in England and Wales: Year Ending March 2018.* Statistical Bulletin HOSB 10/18. Available at: https://assets.publishing.service.gov.uk/government/uploads/system/uploads/attachment_data/file/729127/crime-outcomes-hosb1018.pdf (last accessed 29 June 2022).

Howard, J. (1993) Parliamentary business. Available at: https://publications.parliament.uk/pa/cm199394/cmhansrd/1993-11-23/Debate-2.html (last accessed 29 June 2022).

Howard, J. (2013) The State of the Prisons in England and Wales: With Preliminary Observations and an Account of Some Foreign Prisons. Cambridge: Cambridge University Press.

Howard League for Penal Reform (2013) The never-ending story: Indeterminate sentencing and the prison regime. Research briefing. Available at: https://howardleague.org/wp-content/uploads/2016/05/never-ending-story-IPP.pdf (last accessed 29 June 2022).

Jacobson, J. and Hough, M. (2010) *Unjust Deserts: Imprisonment for Public Protection.* Prison Reform Trust. Available at: www.ojp.gov/ncjrs/virtual-library/abstracts/unjust-deserts-imprisonment-public-protection (last accessed 29 June 2022).

Jewkes, Y. and Gooch, K. (2020) The rehabilitative prison: An oxymoron or an opportunity to radically reform the way we do punishment?' In P. Ugwudike, H. Graham, F. McNeil,

P. Raynor, F. Taxman and C. Trotter (2020) *The Routledge Companion to Rehabilitative Work in Criminal Justice*. Oxford: Routledge, pp. 153–66.

Kleck, G. (2018) Deterrence: Actual versus perceived risk of punishment. In G. Bruinsma and D. Weisburd (eds) *Encyclopaedia of Criminology and Criminal Justice*. New York: Springer. https://doi.org/10.1007/978-1-4614-5690-2_408

Martinson, R. (1974) What works? Questions and answers about prison reform. *The Public Interest*, 35, 22–54.

Mathiesen, T. (1974) *The Politics of Abolitionism*. London: Martin Robertson.

Mann, R., Howard, F., and Tew, J. (2018) What is a rehabilitative prison culture? *Prison Service Journal*, 235, 3–10. Available at: www.crimeandjustice.org.uk/sites/crimeandjustice.org.uk/files/PSJ%20235%20January%202018.pdf (last accessed 25 July 2022).

Menis, S. (2018) The crisis of penal populism: Prison legitimacy and its effects on women's prisons in the UK. *Forensic Research & Criminology International Journal*, 6(6), 484–9.

Ministry of Justice (2021) *Prison Population Projections 2021 to 2026, England and Wales*. Available at: https://assets.publishing.service.gov.uk/government/uploads/system/uploads/attachment_data/file/1035682/Prison_Population_Projections_2021_to_2026.pdf (last accessed 29 June 2022).

Ministry of Justice (2022) Proven reoffending statistics: January to March 2020. Available at: www.gov.uk/government/statistics/proven-reoffending-statistics-january-to-march-2020/proven-reoffending-statistics-january-to-march-2020 (last accessed 29 June 2022).

Moore, J. (2008) Prison – More than detention. *Criminal Justice Matters*. 102. Available at: www.crimeandjustice.org.uk/publications/cjm/article/prison-more-detention (last accessed 29 June 2022).

National Criminal Justice Arts Alliance (2016) *Arts, Culture and Innovation in Criminal Justice Settings: A Guide for Commissioners*. Available at: www.artsincriminaljustice.org.uk/wp-content/uploads/2016/07/CommissioningGuide_FINAL.pdf (last accessed 29 June 2022).

Newburn, T. (2003) *Crime and Criminal Justice Policy*. Harlow: Pearson Longman.

Prison Reform Trust (2019) *Prison: The Facts*. Bromley Briefings Summer 2019. Available at: https://prisonreformtrust.org.uk/publication/prison-the-facts-summer-2019 (last accessed 29 June 2022).

Prison Reform Trust (2021) *Bromley Briefings Prison Factfile*. Winter 2021. Available at: https://prisonreformtrust.org.uk/wp-content/uploads/2022/01/Bromley_Briefings_winter_2021.pdf (last accessed 29 June 2022).

Rawls, J. (1971) *A Theory of Justice*. Cambridge, MA: Harvard University Press.

Scott, D. (2008) *Penology*. London: Sage.

Scott, D. (2020) Remembering and forgetting the Woolf Report. Blog post. Available at: www.open.ac.uk/researchcentres/herc/blog/remembering-and-forgetting-woolf-report (last accessed 29 June 2022).

Scraton, P., Sim, J. and Skidmore, P. (1991) *Prisons under Protest*. Buckingham: Open University Press.

Social Exclusion Unit (2002) *Reducing Re-offending by Ex-Prisoners*. Available at: www.bristol.ac.uk/poverty/downloads/keyofficialdocuments/Reducing%20Reoffending.pdf (last accessed 30 June 2022).

Sparks, R. (1996) Penal 'austerity': the doctrine of less eligibility reborn? In R. Matthews and P. Francis (eds) *Prisons 2000. An International Perspective on the Current State of Affairs and Future of Imprisonment*. London: Palgrave Macmillan pp. 74–93.

Spohn, C. (2007) The deterrent effect of imprisonment and offenders' stakes in conformity. *Criminal Justice Policy Review*, 18(1), 31–50.

UK Parliament (2021) Reforming prisons, reforming prisoners. Available at: www.parliament.uk/business/publications/research/olympic-britain/crime-and-defence/reforming-prisons-reforming-prisoners (last accessed 30 June 2022).

UK Parliament (2021a) Justice Committee launches an enquiry into IPP sentences. Available at: https://committees.parliament.uk/committee/102/justice-committee/news/157647/justice-committee-launches-inquiry-into-ipp-sentences/#:~:text=However%2C%20there%20are%20still%20more,the%20tariff%20they%20were%20given (last accessed 30 June 2022).

Williams, S. (2015) Strangeways riot: Lord Woolf calls for new UK jail inquiry. Available at: www.bbc.co.uk/news/uk-england-manchester-31737055 (last accessed 30 June 2022).

Wilson, D. (2014) *Pain and Retribution: A Short History of British Prisons 1066 to the Present*. London: Reaktion Books.

Zimring, F. and Hawkins, G. (1995) *Incapacitation: Penal Confinement and the Restraint of Crime*. New York: Oxford University Press.

4

THEORISING PROBATION AND REHABILITATION

┌─── **IN THIS CHAPTER, YOU WILL EXPLORE** ───┐

1. The contested nature of rehabilitation and the different theoretical perspectives that help us understand and make sense of this concept

2. The justifications and criticisms of rehabilitation as a method of state punishment

3. How the delivery of rehabilitative practices has changed over time in response to wider social, political and economic factors

4. The challenges facing probation in the wake of the failure of the Transforming Rehabilitation (TR) reforms and the return of probation work to the public sector.

INTRODUCTION

If there is something that is indisputable about the idea of rehabilitation, then it is undoubtedly its disputability. (Kanduc, 1996: 149)

In the previous chapter you were introduced to the main justifications for the infliction of state punishment through the use of imprisonment. In some respects, those sanctions delivered in the community, such as probation, have required less justification as they have been promoted as more humane alternatives to imprisonment. The Council of Europe defines community sanctions and measures as a means of maintaining an individual in the community whilst restricting their liberty through the imposition of conditions and/or obligations designated in law (Council of Europe, 1992, Appendix: para. 1). It perhaps goes without saying then that there needs to be some justification for restricting an individual's liberty whether it be in custody or in the community or else it would be a basic infringement of their personal freedoms. We therefore begin this chapter by exploring how rehabilitation has evolved both as a concept and a practice and discuss its contested nature. Traditionally community sanctions and measures and the role of probation in implementing them have been justified in terms of their reformative and rehabilitative potential. However, such notions can only be understood within their historical and ideological context. As we highlighted in relation to imprisonment in the previous chapter, the history and development of probation in England and Wales has also been shaped by broader ambitions and social contexts. So, as in the previous chapter, as you read this chapter, we encourage you to reflect on what you see as the main purpose of probation work and why it has seemingly failed to displace the dominance of imprisonment in contemporary penal imaginaries.

KEY QUESTIONS TO CONSIDER WHEN READING THIS CHAPTER

1. When we talk about rehabilitation what exactly is it that we are trying to achieve?
2. Is it the role of the state to rehabilitate individuals?
3. What is the role of the Probation Service in achieving the aims of rehabilitation?

WHAT IS REHABILITATION?

Nowadays, we tend to discuss rehabilitation in terms of community corrections and community-based responses to support individuals within the criminal justice system, but historically the penitentiary, as a site of confinement, was perhaps the first practical expression of the reformative power of religious contemplation and penance through hard labour leading to what the French philosopher Michel Foucault (1977) described as *coercive soul-transformation* (see Chapter 2 for further discussion). In recent years the rehabilitative endeavour has become more of a means of achieving other system aims such as reducing reoffending and protecting the public rather than an end or *good* within itself. It is important therefore that we examine the justifications for rehabilitation and how they have been affected by broader societal developments regarding the imposition of state-sanctioned punishment as well as considering some of the contemporary challenges in implementation.

According to Durnescu et al. (2016) most Anglophone probation studies tend to focus on rehabilitation, either directly or indirectly, as both a penal ideal and as a practice. Rehabilitation and particularly claims for its effectiveness are however undoubtedly contentious. Take for example the following statement from the former Director General of the Prison Service that received high-profile coverage in the national press.

Stop fretting about rehabilitation. Politely discourage those who will urge you to believe that they have a six-week to six-month course which can undo the damage of a lifetime. The next time someone tells you they have a quick scheme which can transform lives – transform is the word of which you should be particularly suspicious – politely explain that life isn't that simple. (Sir Martin Narey, quoted in Taylor, 2019)

Of course, the issue here is what is meant by rehabilitation. In the past, the discourse of rehabilitation has been used to justify everything from political re-programming to castration to aversion therapy to education to family contact to the provision of housing and work (Burke and Collett, 2014). It is therefore not surprising that the public are somewhat unsure as to what the term means. In the above quote, Martin Narey seems to be implying that attending a 'six-week to six-month course or programme' constitutes rehabilitation but as we discussed in Chapter 2 in relation to the process of desistance, rehabilitation is a much broader concept than one of bringing about personal change through a specific form of intervention. In this chapter therefore we consider the theories underpinning this concept, how it has adapted over time to meet wider societal expectations and some of the contemporary challenges involved in its delivery. A key starting point in this task will be to discuss exactly what is meant and understood by the term *rehabilitation*.

The concept of rehabilitation was first conceived in French law in the second half of the 17th century as a means of *undoing* or ending a criminal conviction. According to this legal model of rehabilitation the principal objective of rehabilitation is to restore the state of citizenship. This process of restoration involves adopting the rights and obligations of *normal* citizens. The rehabilitated person is perceived as having paid the penalty for their offence and as subsequently showing a commitment to *going straight*. Deleting a person's criminal record (once they have served their sentence) serves to *de-label* the individual as an 'offender' and enable them to shed a negative identity and assume a positive, non-criminal one (McNeill, 2012). Essentially it referred to the endpoint or outcome of a process that involved settling the putative debt implicit in the commission of an offence. As such, the legal model of rehabilitation views the rehabilitated person as deserving of a return to the community of law-abiding citizens and restoration to the status and entitlements of full citizenship. The Rehabilitation of Offenders Act 1974 enshrined this principle in law in England and Wales. Subject to certain caveats, concerning the type and severity of the offence, sentences become spent after a period of time although, as we saw in Chapter 2 in our discussion of desistance, in reality the stigma of criminalisation can extend way beyond the completion of the sentence.

In Britain and elsewhere the history of attempts to rehabilitate people has been linked with the emergence and development of positivist criminology and the view of offending behaviour as determined (to a greater or lesser extent) by factors which lie outside the individual's control (such as poverty, mental illness or attitudes learned from antisocial/pro-criminal peers or family members). From this perspective it follows that whilst an individual might bear some responsibility for their offending, they can claim some mitigation for their behaviour and it might be possible to prevent reoffending if the underlying factors which led them to offend – such as the harmful aspects of their behaviour and triggers to offending – are tackled or confronted. Consequently, it follows that they ought to be treated or helped, and by implication there should be action by the state to support this process, much like someone suffering from a physical illness, in an attempt to remove the causes of their offending (Raynor and Robinson, 2009). There is also the assumption that experts with relevant training will guide the individualised treatment needed. It is also reformative in that it seeks to bring about a change in behaviour or desirable state. It was this set of assumptions which animated the so-called 'treatment model' which dominated the way in which people were dealt with in the mid-20th century (see 'The changing faces of probation and rehabilitation' below). It was also seen as a more progressive alternative to retributive punishment. Of course, even if the aim of rehabilitation is well intentioned in the sense that it is trying to help or support the individual, in a penal sense, it still involves doing things to them (whether that involves their reporting to a probation officer or attending a treatment programme or undertaking unpaid work) and therefore it requires justification.

JUSTIFYING REHABILITATIVE PUNISHMENT

The Criminal Justice Act 2003 made it a requirement that every community order must include *at least one requirement imposed for the purposes of punishment* and this has been reinforced in subsequent legislation. The rationale for such a move appears to be based on the perennial perception that the public lacks confidence in community sentences. This view persists despite research finding little evidence that the public want community sentences to be unproductively harsh (Maruna and King, 2008). Indeed, adding punishment purely for the sake of general deterrence and increasing public confidence has shown to have limited positive effects. Moreover, as Robinson and Ugwudike (2012) point out, equating *toughness* with *legitimacy* is extremely problematic. Making community orders overly harsh and punitive in a misguided attempt to match the damaging impact of imprisonment can undermine notions of legitimacy and jeopardise compliance and desistance.

Certainly, the idea of rehabilitative punishment is not uncontested. For some theorists, rehabilitation is conceptually divorced from punishment in that it is not understood as an objective or quality of a positive process of punishment but rather as an antidote to punishment, or more precisely, the potentially harmful effects of punishment. In many European jurisdictions the idea of punitive community sanctions is an anathema. Indeed, implicit in the notion of probation is the avoidance of state punishment and for much of its history in this country, it was used *instead* of punishment. Recent attempts to promote rehabilitation's punitive credentials have been evident in the attempts to rebrand community-based sanctions as *punishments in the community* providing a cheap and credible alternative to custody for those committing less serious offences. According to this view, just as retributive punishment may be deserved, so the offender deserves not to be unduly damaged by the experience of punishment. Any damage inflicted on the individual in the process of punishing them ought to be offset or mitigated by rehabilitative measures. This is often referred to as *rights-based rehabilitation* and it is guided by four key principles: the assertion of the duty of the state to provide for rehabilitation; the establishment of proportional limits on the intrusions opposed; the principle of maximising choice and voluntarism in the process; and a commitment to using prison as a measure of last resort (Lewis, 2005).

If we accept the view that to a large extent those who offend are victims of forces beyond their control, we can clearly justify the argument that they therefore merit whatever help might be available to prevent further offending and facilitate a *normal life* – much in the same way that we would justify the provision of physiotherapy to a person with a broken limb. We can take this argument further. If we accept that crime is caused, at least in part, by social deprivation (e.g. poverty) or other problems which society has failed to address (e.g. mental illness) such that the individual's capacity to avoid crime has been compromised, then it is possible to argue that society has an *obligation* to intervene or help the person out of the situation they find themselves in. Put another way, we might argue that the individual has a right to receive help to avoid further offending. This is one version of *rights-based* or *state-obligated* rehabilitation.

Rotman (1990) argues that just as the state has a right to punish the offender for their wrongdoing, so the individual has the right not to be *dehabilitated* by the effects of punishment. In other words, the individual should not be in a worse position (economically, socially, psychologically, etc.) after a period of punishment. By seeking to reduce reoffending and to reduce crime, rehabilitative approaches seek to promote society's right to safety constructively and to protect individuals from victimisation. In this respect, rehabilitation also reflects *utilitarian* arguments. Utilitarianism is a philosophy which originates in the work of the English philosopher Jeremey Bentham and was subsequently developed by John Stuart Mill. Utilitarians argue that an action is ethically or morally right if it produces the greatest happiness for the greatest number, that is the best overall consequence. Unlike retribution, which sees punishment as an end in and of itself, rehabilitation is like incapacitation and deterrence in that it aims to benefit society through reduced reoffending. However, it is different from these other perspectives in that it is the only one that implicitly attempts to bring about a change in the individual and an improvement in their circumstances.

Raynor and Robinson (2009a: 21) distinguish between an optimistic and guarded version of rehabilitation with utilitarian thinking. The optimistic version of rehabilitation claims that rehabilitation contributes to the common good because society as a whole benefits from dealing with offenders in such a way as to reduce their offending. A more guarded claim for justifying rehabilitation is that even if we cannot be completely confident in our ability to change people for the better, we can at least avoid unnecessary harm resulting from excessive or damaging penalties. Current models of rehabilitation – particularly those based on social learning theory and often delivered through offender behaviour programmes – aim to empower individuals to take more control of their lives and behaviour and to make more prosocial choices by helping them to learn necessary skills such as listening, communication, problem solving and self-control. Such approaches recognise problems in relation to resources and opportunities but see little point in improving access to them without also ensuring that people have or develop the necessary skills to benefit from them. It might of course be argued that we could more effectively protect society from crime and victimisation by locking up those who offend in large numbers and keeping them there indefinitely. This is not, however, a wholesale answer to the problem of crime for most people. For one thing it would raise important questions about justice and proportionality. For another, incapacitation would be a very expensive solution and of course at some point the vast majority would have to be released.

CONCERNS WITH REHABILITATIVE PUNISHMENT

As we have noted, rehabilitation has largely been viewed as a progressive and more humanitarian approach than those located in more retributive forms of sentencing, but this does not mean that it has been without criticism. The first concern with rehabilitative punishment is around the question of justice. Proponents of retributive sentencing argue that the purpose of punishment is to signal disapproval of the individual's wrongdoing and to clearly condemn their criminal actions. We would still have to punish someone who has committed a serious crime even if they were truly repentant and promised never to commit another crime because their actions deserve it. Censure is important because unless the criminal justice system fails to punish those who have violated society's rules then it will send out the wrong signal and fail to show society that it takes its own rules – and the breach of them – seriously. Consider the following quote which argues that punishing criminals can actually be more merciful than rehabilitation:

> When we argue about what is effective, instead of what is right, we grant the State the authority to prevent and to cure, and in so doing, we grant it a more expansive role than it previously had. The State becomes a doctor who diagnoses, treats, and pronounces a cure, but in a prison, unlike in a hospital, the patient has no right to refuse or discontinue the treatment. Before the rise of rehabilitation, we permitted the State to punish strictly in proportion to the crime committed. Once the punishment was paid, the State had no further right over the prisoner, unlike now. (Hammill, 2016: para. 9)

From this perspective sentencing individuals with a view to rehabilitation is problematic on the grounds that it can lead to disproportionate sentences. Proponents of retributive justice and desert-based sentencing argue that allowing sentencing decisions to be influenced by a desire to change or rehabilitate individuals invites extended periods of punishment which go beyond what is deserved (in respect of the seriousness of the crime committed).

As Canton (2017: 123) notes, 'among the most serious misgivings about rehabilitation has been the way in which the nature and duration of the intervention could come to depend not on the seriousness of the offence but on the endeavour to change the offender'. Rehabilitation is seen as potentially problematic when it is used to decide whether or not someone should be released from prison. How can prison staff, probation officers or psychologists tell if a person has reformed or will probably not offend again? Evidence has shown that discretion can result in unfair, incorrect and even discriminatory practices. This is sometimes called 'back-end sentencing' because the person is sentenced once in court but in reality they are also sentenced again out of court because the final date for their release depends on the judgement of probation officers or prison staff. In a contemporary sense, similar arguments have been put forward against the disproportionate use of indeterminate public protection sentences.

Secondly, retributivists argue that crime is the result of choices made by the individual rather than a disease or illness. Therefore, the criminal justice system must condemn those choices when they violate society's rules. To claim that criminals are a product of their circumstances is therefore to deny free will and individual choice. Instead, retributivism recognises the individual's status as a moral actor who should take responsibility for their actions rather than make excuses for them. As Canton (2009:13) points out, 'community supervision can raise human rights questions of its own'. A third criticism then concerns the application of potentially unethical practices in the name of rehabilitation. A wide variety of practices have been claimed from the treadmill and crank to extended periods of solitary confinement to psycho surgical and medical interventions. The history of rehabilitation includes the use of drugs to chemically castrate those convicted of committing sexual offences, to tranquillise dangerous individuals and to arouse pain and fear in the context of aversion therapy. The dangers of the inappropriate use of rehabilitation are graphically described in the novel *A Clockwork Orange* by Antony Burgess (1972). The central protagonist is Alex, a member of a violent youth gang. Following the murder of an elderly woman Alex is sentenced to 14 year's imprisonment. Whilst in prison he is subjected an extreme form of aversion therapy that makes him ill if he thinks about violent acts. Alex's rehabilitation is deemed a success by the authorities but a prison chaplain who befriends Alex questions the ethics of removing an individual's fee-will even if it is for the greater good of society.

The boy has no real choice, has he? Self-interest, the fear of physical pain, drove him to that grotesque act of self-abasement. Its insincerity was clearly to be seen. He ceases to be a wrongdoer. He ceases also to be a creature capable of moral choice. (Burgess 2013: 143)

A Clockwork Orange is a fictional work, but it nonetheless captures the darker and potentially abusive side of rehabilitation even when it is well intentioned. Alan Turing, the World War II codebreaker who in 1952 was prosecuted for homosexual acts which were at that time illegal in England and treated with chemical castration as an alternative to prison. Before moving on, consider the following question: Is it morally right to use *aversion therapy* or *chemical castration* in the name of rehabilitation? Is it right to infringe an individual's human rights if it is for the greater good or the protection of others?

This leads us to the issue of *coercion*. Though it might be said that all punishment is coercive, coercion seems to be a particular problem for correctional rehabilitation, since it seeks to change the individual rather than simply to restrain, confine or otherwise punish them. That suggests a particular form of intrusion into the inner world, even the identity of the subject, in respect of which coercion raises particular moral problems. Rotman (1990: 8) distinguishes between models of rehabilitation as a technology designed to mould the individual and encourage conformity to some predesigned pattern of thoughts and behaviour and those which are client centred and, importantly, voluntary. For Rotman, rehabilitation is not something which should ever be imposed on the individual and attempts to rehabilitate individuals should be subject to their consent and should invite the active participation of people in their own process of rehabilitation. Coercing individuals – as part of a court order – to attend rehabilitative programmes is increasingly regarded as an acceptable course of action, particularly for those who are considered to present a high risk of harm to the public. Typically, interventions offered to these groups are coercive not in the sense that the individual has no choice but to cooperate, but rather in the sense that there are likely to be negative consequences for non-participation. This might mean, for example, less likelihood of securing parole or early release from custody or, in the case of community-based sentences, a return to court for re-sentencing if the individual fails to comply with a treatment programme ordered by the court.

Another issue here is whether or not relatively scarce rehabilitative resources should be reserved for those who are motivated to change. Those who argue against coercing individuals into treatment do so on the grounds that if a person voluntarily enters treatment they are likely to be much more motivated and their intentions genuine. Experienced individuals will know how to play the system and say the right things in the knowledge that this will enhance the chances of a favourable parole application or early release. Others argue that coercion is not necessarily unethical, and it depends on whether the professionals involved exercise coercion in an ethical or abusive way, and the impact of coercion on programme effectiveness. Although a person may be forced to undertake the rehabilitative component of a court sentence, they may not feel they are being coerced, particularly if they accept that rehabilitation is a legitimate or welcome course of action. Alternatively, a person who perceives their entry into a rehabilitative programme as the result of coercion may well change their opinion as the programme progresses if they begin to perceive the intervention in more positive terms and their internal motivation increases. Another criticism of rehabilitation – whether voluntary or coerced – points to the problems inherent in offering rehabilitative resources and *help* to those who commit a crime, whilst such assistance remains unavailable to others in society who have not offended but may be experiencing some of the same personal problems and social/economic disadvantages. Where this occurs, rehabilitation offends the principle of *less eligibility* which was another concept formulated by Jeremy Bentham in the late 18th century. First, he argues that improved opportunities should be part of a general social policy agenda, such that socially disadvantaged *non-offenders* ought to enjoy the same access to appropriate sources of help. His second argument is that rehabilitation should offer opportunities to offenders rather than confer opportunities on them. Raynor and Robinson (2009: 13) point out, in practice there are limits to the principle of eligibility in that many correctional interventions are based on assessments of the likelihood of the individual responding positively to them. Nor does it mean that all those who commit crimes are regarded equally in terms of whether their offences are spent or not. For example, the Rehabilitation of Offenders Act 1974 does not apply to all sentences and some sentences never become spent.

THE CHANGING FACES OF PROBATION AND REHABILITATION

Ever since community sanctions made their way into the criminal justice system, the 'methods of treatment' have evolved in line with a range of influencing factors, including the prevailing political climate and policy or public sensibilities, as well as the current state of knowledge in the field. (Geiran and Durnescu, 2019: 21)

In this section we consider the changing nature of rehabilitation through the lens of the development of the Probation Service as the agency with the primary responsibility for delivering rehabilitative services to adults within the criminal justice system in England and Wales. As Canton and Dominey (2018) note, we should think of probation development as involving a number of partial and overlapping accounts rather than a single history. Although grounded in structures of local service delivery and systems of local accountability, probation has historically had a strong sense of its own identity as a national system of offender rehabilitation. This partly reflects its operational base within national criminal justice legislation (particularly sentencing powers) and the role of the *probation officer* as an *officer of the court* (McWilliams, 1983).

1876–1930s: saving souls through divine grace

The concept of probation in the sense of a suspension of sentence of imprisonment – or being given a second chance – can be traced back to mediaeval times and the legal provision of recognisance. However, the Probation Service has its contemporary roots in the late 19th century donation given by Frederick Rayner – a Hertfordshire magistrate who became increasingly concerned with what he saw as the revolving door between the court and the prison for those committing petty and minor offences – to the Church of England Temperance Society to appoint a police court missionary, the forerunner of the modern probation officer. The term *police court* refers to what we now know as the magistrates' court and the term *missionary* refers to the religious underpinnings of this endeavour. The early police court missionaries were generally low paid and so their motivations were based on their own sense of religious duty. Saving the souls of others was seen as a means of gaining redemption in the next world (McWilliams, 1983). Traditional histories of probation tend to portray these early movements as signs of a progressive and more humane criminal justice developments. However, a more revisionist reading of them has suggested that the growth of probation – and its official support by the state – was as much motivated by concerns regarding the behaviours of the itinerant working classes who were flooding into the industrialised urban conurbations and whose drunkenness and petty crime posed a threat to the so-called respectable classes (Vanstone, 2004). This was one reason why those who were subject to early probation were required to take the pledge that they would abstain from alcohol consumption. According to Robinson (2016: 32) the 'founding narrative' of probation work in England and Wales was a reformative one, 'albeit fairly strictly limited to the "deserving" and potentially "corrigible" among the offending population, deemed worthy of a chance to avoid, or (in the case of ex-prisoners) receive help to mitigate, the moral and social damage caused by imprisonment'.

1930s–1970s: casework and the treatment model

Over time the Probation Service became more professionalised and in the early part of 20th century it was brought under state control, although the police court missionaries continued for about 30 years to work alongside the newly formed probation officers. McWilliams (1986) describes the early development of probation as being based on a transformation from 'a service devoted to the saving of souls through divine grace to an agency concerned with the scientific assessment and treatment of offenders' (McWilliams, 1986: 241). Drawing on the emerging sciences in the early 20th century – such as psychology, physiology and psychiatry, which enabled the classification of types of behaviour – the probation officer's role became less about saving souls and more about providing a professional service to the courts. The role of the probation officer was to diagnose what the problem was and then advise the court on appropriate treatment. This gave rise to what became known as casework as part of the medical model that saw crime as a disease. As Tidmarsh (2022) notes, 'The words "advise, assist and befriend" (Jarvis, 1972: 16) were inscribed within the Probation of Offenders Act 1907, constituting an ideology of service premised on working with offenders'.

Gradually religious ideals were supplanted by medical and therapeutic models of rehabilitation characterised by their clinical, individualised and treatment-orientated practices. These ideas fitted well with the penal–welfare complex that emerged in the early 20th century with its emphasis on collective security and the provision of a safety net for the most disadvantaged through universal social benefits under the umbrella of the welfare state. Throughout most of the 20th century and particularly with the creation of the welfare state after the Second World War, probation flourished as rehabilitation was seen as the primary and most progressive form of approach to dealing with criminality. Consequently, in the 20th century the ascendancy of penal-welfarism (which asserted rehabilitation over punitive measures where possible) provided the organising principle, intellectual framework and value base that bound together the criminal justice system and made sense of it for practitioners (Garland, 2001). Central was the role of the professional worker providing expert judgement based upon the accumulated experience of social work and a growing body of theory from the social sciences.

1970s: 'nothing works' and the collapse of the rehabilitative ideal

However, from the 1970s, as the power of professionals in clinical settings came under critical scrutiny, their role too was challenged, both on the grounds of efficacy and morality. This resulted in the reformulation of rehabilitative practices 'not as a sort of quasi-medical treatment for criminality but as the re-education of the poorly socialised' (McNeil, 2012: 7). The challenge to clinical notions of rehabilitation came from across the political spectrum and not necessarily from the usual contemporary suspects such as the media. Rehabilitation, specifically in the form of the treatment model, was particularly criticised by left-wing civil libertarians because it was adjudged to interfere too much in the lives of individuals and seemed to operate unquestioningly in the interests of the state, consciously or unconsciously propagating its prevailing ideology. The ideological underpinning of the rehabilitative endeavour was also criticised for ignoring the social context of crime and by implication presenting criminal behaviour as a *social disease* that could be treated in much the same way as a physical ailment. According to Canton (2017: 121) 'A telling criticism of rehabilitation as practised … is its tendency to reinterpret social injustices as personal failings and to focus on changing people rather than the circumstances in which they find themselves.'

However, the critical issues were not simply about social and economic disadvantage but also about how far delinquent or criminal behaviour was symptomatic of individual pathology. Theoretical perspectives such as labelling theory in turn articulated the view that interventions could make matters worse by reinforcing deviant behaviour. *Due process* lawyers drew attention to the problems of injustice which stemmed from indeterminate sentencing and questioned whether unreliable predictors of future behaviour – based on the unsubstantiated claims of professional wisdom – should continue to influence sentencing. Instead, it was argued that rehabilitation should be provided within the context of a determinate sentence, the length of which should be proportionate to the seriousness of the offence. The law-and-order lobby, on the other hand, argued that rehabilitation was soft on crime and put the needs of the perpetrator before those of the victim (Murray, 1990). Finally, rising crime rates during the post-war period and the absence of empirical evidence about the impact of rehabilitative measures also appeared to suggest that treatment was failing to reduce criminal activity.

Robert Martinson's work in 1974 heralded the era of *nothing works* although the term was never used by Martinson himself and it is debatable whether such a belief in the rehabilitative potential of probation work was widely felt by front-line practitioners (Vanstone, 2004). This led to a recasting of probation's function as being one of providing an alternative to custody. Those welfare discourses and techniques that previously provided the rationale for rehabilitative work ultimately lost their political and cultural purchase. As a result, a key feature of the contemporary reform and modernisation agenda has been the search by politicians and policy makers for a new or more explicit identity for probation. This fitted in with the government's wider reform and modernisation agenda to search out efficiency and effectiveness in supposedly improving public services. From the mid-1990s this has been couched within the language of reducing reoffending.

1980s: 'punishment in the community'

The election of the Margaret Thatcher-led government in 1979 – on a strong law and order platform – reinforced the criticisms of rehabilitation that had gained momentum in the 1970s. However, whilst the Thatcher government wanted to present itself as being strong on crime (which in the public imagination tends to be equated with sending more people to prison) it was faced with the problem that as a result of wide-scale industrial action and civil disorder in the 1980s, the economy was in a state of recession. The government therefore needed to cut back on criminal justice spending and of course prison is the most expensive sanction in the criminal justice system. Thatcher's response to this conundrum was to redefine probation to make it appear tougher with the aim of presenting it as a more credible alternative to imprisonment, with the Probation Service becoming a deliverer of punishments in the community. For David Garland (2001) the replacement of the broader project of penal-welfarism with more intrusive forms of social control and surveillance can be located in the social, economic and political drivers of late modernity. Rehabilitation, with its emphasis on the collective, did not resonate or was unable to respond to increasing insecurity amongst the middle-classes and their distrust of professional penal expertise.

Surprisingly for a party that prided itself on its law and order credentials, the Thatcher government continued to invest significantly in the Probation Service; its funding increased during the Thatcher years and it also produced a number of liberal policies around criminal justice which culminated in the 1991 Criminal Justice Act. This act was based on the belief that imprisonment only served to make bad people worse, in the words of the opening paragraph of the Act. However, the murder of James Bulger brought about another change in probation's fortunes. Panic about crime and particularly serious crime among young people created what Anthony Bottoms (1995) calls a climate of *popular punitiveness*, suggesting that the public wanted more and stiffer sentences and the politicians had to react to this. This led to a competition between the main political parties as to who could present themselves as being the toughest in addressing the crime problem. As a result, the prison population started to increase again. This became known as the period of *prison works* in the sense that even if prison didn't rehabilitate, it was still worth sending people to prison because it gave the community a rest from the criminal behaviours of hardcore and persistent criminals.

It is fair to say that probation's prospects in the 1990s looked bleak. Probation's traditional affiliation with social work was seen as evidence of it being soft on crime and so in the 1990s it was forced to break away from social work into separate training arrangements designed to focus much more on its criminal justice credentials. However, at the same time significant research was emerging from North America which was challenging the nothing works mantra and claimed that properly targeted, delivered and evaluated rehabilitative programmes could actually work for some people. This gave rise to the Risk-Need-Responsivity (RNR) model of rehabilitative intervention which we discussed in Chapter 2.

1997–2010: renaissance of rehabilitation, evidence-based practice, managerialism

The election of Tony Blair as Prime Minister in 1997 in what became known as New Labour, marked another change. In opposition Labour had promoted the notion of being tough on crime and tough on the causes of crime. Although in retrospect it could be argued that it was much more focused on the former, it did invest substantially in rehabilitative programmes in an attempt to establish the evidence base for what became known as 'What works'. As its tenure developed the Labour government became increasingly obsessed with driving up standards in public service through the imposition of targets, audits and other performance-related mechanisms, which increasingly took away the discretion of frontline workers such as probation officers (Burke and Collett, 2014). The reconfiguration of probation practice along apparent *what works* lines was subsequently characterised by a creeping emphasis on managerialism, centralised control and a performance culture based upon national standards for supervision and targets set by central government. The priority given to risk management and public protection and a move towards accredited programmes as part of What works initiative, also further served to diminish the practitioner's voice in probation policy and practice. According to Nellis (2007) it also meant that probation's *humanistic sensibilities* were somewhat eroded in the process.

In order to ensure that probation work was being undertaken consistently – and therefore could be measured in terms of its effectiveness – the Labour government abolished the 54 probation areas and created a National Probation Service. However, in 2003, just three years later – before the new organisation could really find its feet – the Labour government decided to reorganise probation yet again and created the National Offender Management Service, which brought together prisons and probation into a single organisation, which it claimed would provide a more seamless approach to delivering rehabilitative services. Many commentators in probation feel that this was in effect a takeover by the prison service, with many of the managers from the Prison Service seconded into the highest positions in the new organisation, and as such probation lost its distinctive voice in the criminal justice system.

2010 – early 2020s: Outsourcing, risk and commodification

The financial crash of 2008 effectively ended the New Labour government, and two years later it was replaced by a coalition of the Conservatives and Liberal Democrats. Faced with a downturn in the economy, the coalition government presented the economic crisis caused by the financial crash as requiring curtailment of the public purse and rolling back public spending, which it claimed had gotten out of control under New Labour. In 2010, the coalition government launched what became known as its *rehabilitation revolution*. This envisaged a much greater role for the private and voluntary sectors in the provision of probation services. Within the overall discourse of offender management, probation supervision can be seen as what Deering argues is mainly concerned with 'assessing and managing risks, enhancing offenders' motivation to attend accredited programmes, gate-keeping access to services to address certain criminogenic needs and enforcing orders rigorously' (2011: 452). Those individuals assessed as lower risk would be allocated to non-specialist probation staff with larger caseloads and through the commissioning and outsourcing of services ultimately be supervised by a range of voluntary or private sector providers. It was envisaged that around 70 per cent of probation work could be outsourced to the private and voluntary sector on a contracted basis, although in reality this figure turned out to be much more like 50 per cent.

This culminated in the Transforming Rehabilitation (TR) reforms (Ministry of Justice, 2013), which split the Probation Service into two. A new National Probation Service was created that would remain in the public sector but would deal solely with individuals who posed the highest risks, with medium- and low-risk individuals being assigned to one of the 21 community rehabilitation companies, which were mainly owned and managed by private companies. The intended reforms were summarised by the government in the following way:

- for the first time in recent history, new statutory rehabilitation extended to all 50,000 of the most prolific group – offenders sentenced to less than 12 months in custody;

- a fundamental change to the way we organise the prison estate, in order to put in place an unprecedented nationwide 'through the prison gate' resettlement service, meaning most offenders are given continuous support by one provider from custody into the community;

- opening up the market to a diverse range of new rehabilitation providers, so that we get the best out of the public, voluntary and private sectors, at the local as well as national level;

- new payment incentives for market providers to focus relentlessly on reforming offenders, giving providers flexibility to do what works and freedom from bureaucracy, but only paying them in full for real reductions in reoffending;

- a new national public sector probation service, working to protect the public and building upon the expertise and professionalism which are already in place. (Ministry of Justice, 2013: 6–7)

Despite widespread criticisms from a range of bodies within and outside government, academics and the Probation Service itself that the proposals were untested and risked an unnecessary fragmentation of the Probation Service, the government ploughed ahead. Following a series of damning reports by the Justice Secretary and particularly Her Majesty's Inspector of Probation, who described the TR reforms as 'irredeemably flawed' (HM Inspectorate of Probation, 2019) the government announced its intention to cancel the probation contracts with the private sector early and in 2020 it announced that all case management functions would be brought back under public control. In February 2021, the Ministry of Justice published the final version of its Target Operating Model for Probation Services in England and Wales (HM Prison and Probation Service, 2021). These changes are discussed in more detail in Chapter 6.

The Justice Secretary's announcement marked a remarkable reversal of direction for a party which had for over 30 years promoted the market as the most effective way to deliver public services. All of this begs the question: why did it go so wrong? Were the reforms 'irredeemably flawed' or was the failure merely a case of poor and rushed implementation? The TR reforms were undoubtedly controversial and faced opposition from most within the sector (Burke and Collet, 2014; Deering and Feilzer, 2015). They were introduced too fast and without sufficient planning or research into the costing and implementation of what were new and highly complex organisational and relational models of service delivery that relied on new and untested suppliers. As a result, the reforms created a disjointed and complex system that hindered rather than assisted rehabilitation, with confusing accountability, decision making and service delivery responsibilities. Moreover, inaccurate modelling of how much work, and therefore profit, would go to the private sector and third sector organisations meant that in practice the hoped-for innovation from these sectors did not materialise as they struggled to deliver core services within the funding available. We will consider the impact of these changes on probation staff in Chapter 8.

CONTEMPORARY CHALLENGES

Like all organisations, an obvious challenge that probation and those involved in the delivery of rehabilitative services are currently facing is how to deal with the repercussions of COVID-19. In response to the pandemic, probation has had to adopt an exceptional delivery model which has moved the service away from what were mainly face-to-face interactions with individuals on supervision and as a result most contacts now are made either in the form of telephone calls or other virtual interactions. For high-risk individuals, the Probation Service has had to make doorstep visits, and those subject to unpaid work and accredited programmes have been unable to complete the requirements of their sentences as before (Justice Select Committee, 2020).

It will be interesting to see how this change in the way that practitioners interact with those under their supervision are maintained when the situation returns to normal – whatever that normal might look like. At present, however, there is a significant backlog of cases that need to be dealt with by the courts. These are likely to filter through eventually and probation will have to deal with this (Justice Select Committee, 2020). It certainly looks likely that for the further foreseeable future probation will be continually working with high caseloads and reduced resources at the same time as undergoing major restructuring.

Bringing together the existing NPS staff with those in the CRCs will not be easy or straightforward. There are currently at least eight different operating models, and variations in approach also exist between the NPS regions (House of Commons Justice Committee, 2021). Research following the creation of the CRCs suggested that the split within probation created a considerable amount of resentment among staff and had resulted in a high turnover amongst the workforce as many experienced staff left (Deering and Feilzer, 2015; Robinson et al., 2016). There was also a feeling that probation had become a two-tier service, with the NPS doing the real probation work and many within the CRC understandably resented this. There is considerable work to be done therefore to rebuild trust and heal rifts within the profession. At the same time, there is much to learn and retain from the CRCs, which developed innovations such as support hubs, co-location with statutory and voluntary partners, and service-user involvement.

21	Number of existing CRC contract package areas
7	Number of parent organisations currently delivering CRC probation services
12	Number of new probation regions in England and Wales under the unified model
54	Number of organisations involved in the transition programme (employing individuals who will be assigned to either the new unified probation service or the Dynamic Framework)
16,333	Estimated workforce of new unified mode
9,533	Number of staff currently employed by the National Probation Service
7,500	Approximate number of CRC posts (full-time equivalent) who will be assigned to either the new unified probation service or the Dynamic Framework
223,000	Estimated unified caseload on day one of transition[2]
112,723	Estimated caseload that will transfer from CRCs to the unified service
11	Number of different types of support to be commissioned under the Dynamic Framework
118	Number of contracts/lots to be awarded for employment, training and education; accommodation; wellbeing; and women's services

Figure 4.1   Transition to unified probation model

(*Source* HM Inspectorate of Probation 2021: 7. Available at: www.justiceinspectorates.gov.uk/hmiprobation/
research/the-evidence-base-probation/models-and-principles/desistance (last accessed 6 November 2022))

Uniting these two separate organisations into a single entity will therefore be challenging (see Figure 4.1). The future roles and responsibilities of those with a sentence management role carry more certainty than for other staff, particularly those in corporate and resettlement functions. The majority of staff responsible for delivering accredited programmes and rehabilitation activity requirements (RARs) will transfer into specialist interventions teams in the new structure. However, other staff will transfer to Dynamic Framework providers, for example those providing some outsourced Through the Gate support services. CRC staff will need refresher training, or to be inducted, in working with those convicted of committing sexual offences, MAPPA cases and foreign nationals. NPS staff will need to (re)learn the challenging work of managing low- and medium-risk of serious harm cases, where post-sentence discovery often reveals chaotic lifestyles, multiple needs and deeper problems such as domestic abuse and child safeguarding concerns. Also, the NPS is now located within the civil service and is therefore subject to civil service rules. A concern is that this will stifle innovation and that probation will become purely a risk management organisation in the narrowest of terms. The regional structure of the new organisation will also be a challenge in terms of how responsive it is to local needs – the development of probation has traditionally been at the local level, but this will clearly be much more difficult under the new arrangements.

Another major challenge facing probation will be building confidence with external stakeholders and the wider public. Recent high-profile cases – such as that of Joseph McCann (see Chapter 2 for further discussion) who committed a series of horrendous crimes whilst on supervision – have been subject to wide-scale negative press reporting and have undoubtedly harmed public perceptions of probation work, even though such cases are thankfully very rare. A key part of this will also be regaining the confidence of sentencers. Since 2010 the number of community sentences passed by the courts has consistently fallen, which suggests a lack of confidence in the recent probation arrangements (Centre for Justice Innovation, 2019). This is particularly stark for women in the criminal justice system. Since 2010 the number of women sentenced to imprisonment has doubled whereas those sentenced to community sentences has halved.

CONCLUSION

In some quarters rehabilitation has become somewhat tainted, but as this chapter has shown, the concept has nevertheless displayed qualities of endurance and adaptability. According to Gwen Robinson (2008), this is because it has been able to adapt to prevailing, and sometimes conflicting, meta-narratives. In this respect, rehabilitation, and by implication the Probation Service, has been largely successful in repositioning itself within the dominant contemporary policy and practice discourses of managerialism and risk. However, it is important to note that these developments did not occur in a straightforward linear process and that many new practices and initiatives existed alongside more traditional rehabilitative methods. Nevertheless, these changes have fundamentally changed the nature of rehabilitation in contemporary society. Today it could be argued that rehabilitation is seen less of an objective (or goal) in its own right but instead a mechanism for achieving wider objectives of crime reduction and public protection. Despite this, the concept of rehabilitation has remained an incredibly durable one. According to Robinson, this transformative process has been a successful appeal to three dominant narratives which she characterises as utilitarian, managerial and expressive. *Utilitarian* narratives measure the success of rehabilitative work in terms of a reduction of reoffending. *Managerial* narratives see community sanctions as a means of exerting control over those for whom custody is judged unnecessary or too expensive. Expressive narratives involve the communication of censure and responsibilities of the individual who has offended.

It could be argued therefore that the concept of rehabilitation has been one of the most significant developments underpinning contemporary criminal justice systems and it is thus important to understand the different justifications that have been presented to explain it. These, as we have seen, can be both practical and symbolic in that they can be about attempting to change an individual's behaviour or moral values and restoring their reputation and status as a citizen. In this chapter we have explored how ideas surrounding rehabilitation have developed over time and been subject to changes brought about by wider social, political and economic influences. Unlike retributive sanctions, rehabilitation forces us to consider the reasons why individuals find themselves caught up in the criminal justice system and at its best it supports individuals in achieving positive changes in their lives rather than merely punishing them. Because it is premised on collaborative relationships, it also conveys the message that society also has an obligation to help those who fall short of the standards of behaviour it has set. However, it is not easy to justify the provision of help and support to those who have committed criminal acts when the needs of other groups in society are not met. Rehabilitation is both cheaper and less harmful to the individual than incapacitation and has been seen in many societies as an alternative to imprisonment. This has led to the development of a range of rehabilitative sanctions and measures aimed at reducing the use of short-term prison sentences although, as we saw in Chapter 1, rather than displacing the prison it has led to the emergence of *mass supervision* alongside an ever-expanding prison population. As we have discussed in this chapter, the infliction of unethical and dubious practices on some individuals has been justified in the name of rehabilitation so we need to consider carefully how it is used and what it is trying to achieve.

recommended reading

If you would like to engage in further reading, you may find the following resources particularly useful:

Canton, R. (2017) *Why Punish?* London: Red Globe Press.

This is an excellent overview of the origins, meanings and purposes of punishment. Chapter 6, 'Rehabilitation and desistance', provides an authoritative account of many of the contemporary debates around rehabilitation.

Ward, T. and Maruna, S. (2007) *Rehabilitation*. Abingdon: Routledge.

This text provides a succinct summary and critique of offender rehabilitation and provides a comprehensive evaluation of both the Risk-Needs-Responsivity Model and the Good Lives Model that we discuss further in Chapter 11.

Raynor, P. and Robinson, G. (2009) *Rehabilitation, Crime and Justice*. Basingstoke: Palgrave Macmillan.

This text examines the history, theory and practice of rehabilitation and shows how penal policy and practice have been influenced by differing views of the value and effectiveness of rehabilitation, ranging from early optimism to 'nothing works' and more recent attempts to develop evidence-based practice.

Robinson, G. and Crow, I. (2009) *Offender Rehabilitation: Theory, Research and Practice*. London: Sage.

This comprehensive text explains all the key themes in the development and practice of offender rehabilitation from both a theoretical and historical context.

references

Bottoms, A. E. (1995) The philosophy and politics of punishment and sentencing. In C. Clarkson and R. Morgan (eds) *The Politics of Sentencing Reform*. Oxford: Clarendon Press.

Burgess, A. (2013) *A Clockwork Orange*. London: Penguin Classics.

Burke, L. and Collett, S. (2014) *Delivering Rehabilitation: The Politics, Governance and Control of Probation*. London: Routledge.

Canton, R. (2009) Nonsense upon stilts? Human rights, the ethics of punishment and the values of probation. *British Journal of Community Justice*, 7(1), 5–22.

Canton, R. (2017) *Why Punish?* London: Red Globe Press.

Canton, R. and Dominey, J. (2018) *Probation* (2nd edn). Abingdon: Routledge.

Centre for Justice Innovation (2018) Renewing trust: How can we improve the relationship between probation and the courts. Available at: https://justiceinnovation.org/sites/default/files/media/documents/2019-02/cji-renewing-trust_2018-d-sw_1.pdf (last accessed 31 July 2022).

Council of Europe (1992) Recommendation No. R (92) 16 of the Committee of Ministers to Member States on the European rules on community sanctions and measures. Available at: https://rm.coe.int/16804d5ec6 (last accessed 30 June 2022).

Deering, J. (2011) *Probation Practice and the New Penology: Practitioner Reflections*. Farnham: Ashgate.

Deering, J. and Feilzer, M. (2015) *Is Transforming Rehabilitation the end of the Rehabilitative Ideal?* Bristol: Policy Press.

Durnescu, I., McNeill, F., and Butter, R. (2016) Introduction: Questions, questions, questions. In McNeill, F., Durnescu, I and Butter, R. (eds) *Probation*. London: Palgrave Macmillan, pp. 1–7.

Foucault, M. (1977) *Discipline and Punish*. London: Allen Lane.

Garland, D. (2001) *The Culture of Control*. Oxford: Oxford University Press.

Geiran, V. and Durnescu, I. (2019) *Implementing Community Sanctions and Measures. Council of Europe Guidelines*. Available at: https://rm.coe.int/implementing-community-sanctions-and-measures/1680995098 (last accessed 2 July 2021).

Hammill, R. (2016) Why punishing criminals can be more merciful than rehabilitation. *The Federalist*. Available at: https://thefederalist.com/2016/11/21/punishing-criminals-can-merciful-rehabilitation (last accessed 31 March 2021).

House of Commons Justice Committee (2021) *The Future of the Probation Service*. https://committees.parliament.uk/publications/5602/documents/66142/default/ (last accessed 31 July 2022).

HM Inspectorate of Probation (2021) *A Thematic Review of Work to Prepare for the Unification of Probation Services*. Available at: www.justiceinspectorates.gov.uk/hmiprobation/wp-content/uploads/sites/5/2021/05/Transition-inspection-report-v1.0-.doc.pdf (last accessed 3 November 2021).

HM Prison and Probation Service (2021) *The Target Operating Model for Probation Services in England and Wales: Probation Reform Programme*. London: HM Prison and Probation Service.

Justice Select Committee (2020) *Coronavirus (COVID-19): The Impact on Probation Systems*. London: House of Commons.

Kanduc, Z. (1996) The idea of rehabilitation: A criminological view. *UDK* 343.9 Available at: https://hrcak.srce.hr/file/138607 (last accessed 30 June 2022).

Lewis, S. (2005) Rehabilitation: Headline or footnote in the new penal policy? *Probation Journal*, 52(92), 119–35.

Martinson, R. (1974) What works? Questions and answers about prison reform. *The Public Interest*, 35, 22–54.

Maruna, S. and King, A. (2008) Selling the public on probation: Beyond the bib. *Probation Journal*, 55(4): 337–51.

McNeill, F. (2012) Four forms of supervision: Towards an interdisciplinary perspective. *Legal and Criminological Psychology*, 17(1), 18–36.

McWilliams, W. (1983) The mission to the English police courts 1876–1936. *Howard Journal*, 23(3), 129–47.

McWilliams, W. (1986) The English probation system and the diagnostic ideal. *Howard Journal*, 25(4), 241–60.

Ministry of Justice (2013) *Transforming Rehabilitation: A Revolution in the Way We Manage Offenders*. London: Ministry of Justice.

Murray, C. (1990) *The Emerging British Underclass*. London: Institute of Economic Affairs.

Nellis, M. (2007) Humanising justice: The English probation service up until 1997. In L. Gelsthorpe and R. Morgan (eds) *Handbook of Probation*. Cullompton: Willan, pp. 25–59.

Raynor, P. (2014) Consent to probation in England and Wales: How it was abolished and why it matters. *European Journal of Probation*, 6(3), 296–307.

Raynor, P. and Robinson, G. (2009) Why help offenders? Arguments for rehabilitation as a penal strategy. *European Journal of Probation*, 1(1), 3–20.

Raynor, P. and Robinson, G. (2009a) *Rehabilitation, Crime and Justice*. Houndmills: Palgrave Macmillan.

Robinson, G. (2008) Late-modern rehabilitation: the evolution of a penal strategy. *Punishment & Society*, 10(4), 429–45.

Robinson, G. (2016) The Cinderella complex: Punishment, society and community sanctions. *Punishment & Society*, 18(1), 95–112.

Robinson, G. and Ugwudike, P. (2012) Investing in 'toughness': Probation, enforcement and legitimacy. *The Howard Journal of Crime and Justice*, 51(3), 300–16.

Robinson, G., Burke, L. and Millings, M. (2016) Criminal justice identities in transition: The case of devolved probation services in England and Wales. *British Journal of Criminology*, 56(1), 161–78.

Rotman, E. (1990) *Beyond Punishment: A New View of the Rehabilitation of Criminal Offenders*. New York: Greenwood Press.

Taylor, D. (2019) Prisoner rehabilitation does not work, says former prisons boss. *The Guardian*, 29 October. Available at: www.theguardian.com/society/2019/oct/29/prisoner-rehabilitation-does-not-work-says-former-prisons-boss (last accessed 30 June 2022).

Tidmarsh, M. (2022) *Professionalism in Probation: Making Sense of Marketisation* Abingdon: Routledge.

Vanstone, M. (2004) *Supervising Offenders in the Community: A History of Probation Theory and Practice*. Aldershot: Ashgate.

5

ORGANISATION AND STRUCTURE OF PRISONS

IN THIS CHAPTER, YOU WILL EXPLORE

1. How the Prison Service in England and Wales is organised and structured

2. The varying functions of prisons across England and Wales

3. How to critically engage with the role and function of regulatory bodies such as HM Inspectorate of Prisons, Independent Monitoring Boards and Prisons and Probation Ombudsman.

INTRODUCTION

This is the first of four chapters in the *design and delivery* section of the book, which is intended to help you apply the knowledge that you have gained from the foundations section to the real world. Whilst the focus of this chapter is the organisation and structure of prisons in England and Wales, when combined with the offerings of Chapters 6 to 8, this section provides an opportunity for you to critically engage with the extent to which the aims and ambitions of the theoretical offerings detailed across Chapters 1 to 4 can be realised at the coal face of service delivery. In doing so, you are encouraged to consider the usefulness of such perspectives, models and approaches within and across contemporary sites of punishment as well as their ability to alleviate vulnerability, inequality and marginality.

Whilst there is much debate and controversy about the aims, ambitions and effectiveness of imprisonment (see Chapter 3 for further discussion), less attention has been invested in discussions about the day-to-day organisation and structure of prisons, even though no two penal institutions are the same. With a particular focus on prisons in England and Wales, this chapter will encourage you to critically engage with the organisation and structure of custodial environments through a consideration of the extent to which these long-standing institutions can meet their own aims and ambitions. To understand how prisons in England and Wales operate, we must first explore the prison landscape, taking into consideration who is held in the prison system, why and at what price. Appreciating who resides in prison is an important component of your studies as this will help you to understand how the prison system is organised and structured to keep people safe and secure during their time in custody.

We will then explore the sentencing framework, how it influences who goes to prison and on what grounds. You will be encouraged to think about the space between the rhetoric of policy and the reality of practice. Through a detailed discussion of age, sex and security categorisation, we will explore how prisons in England and Wales are organised into a structured system of punishment. You will not only be encouraged to consider how the day-to-day design of prisons reflects ideas about their purpose and function but whether they are able to meet the increasingly diverse needs of people within them (see Chapter 11 for a more detailed discussion). Finally, the chapter will discuss the role of regulatory bodies such as HM Inspectorate of Prisons, Independent Monitoring Boards, and the Prisons and Probation Ombudsman, which will help you to understand how and to what extent the prison system is accountable for its actions.

KEY QUESTIONS TO CONSIDER WHEN READING THIS CHAPTER

1. Are prisons able to meet their aims and objectives?

2. To what extent are custodial sentences reserved for the most serious offences?

3. Are prisons an example of evidence-based practice or politics-based evidence?

THE PENAL LANDSCAPE IN ENGLAND AND WALES

At the time of writing there were 121 prisons in England and Wales, 108 of them public sector prisons and 13 private sector prisons (Ministry of Justice, 2022). Most of these institutions hold men (99), 11 hold women, 10 hold young people and one acts as a public sector immigration removal centre (see Figure 5.1 below). Even though there is no correlation between levels of crime and the prison population, England and Wales have witnessed a 74 per cent increase in the prison population in the last 30 years, which is projected to rise by a further 20, 000 people by 2026 (Prison Reform Trust, 2021). This is an astonishing figure and is particularly concerning when considered alongside the

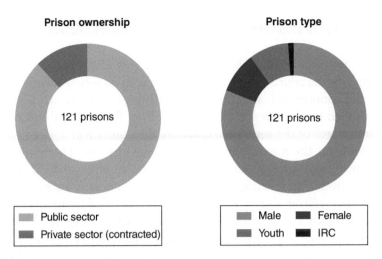

Figure 5.1 Prison ownership and type

Source: HM Government (2022) Prisons data. Available at: https://data.justice.gov.uk/prisons (last accessed 25 July 2022)

controversies which surround imprisonment (see Chapter 3 for further discussion) and the continued use of prisons despite their inherent failings (see Chapter 11 for further discussion).

As of the 31 December 2021, there were 79,092 people serving a custodial sentence, of whom 75,881 were male and 3,211 were female (Ibid). Whilst most people serving a custodial sentence are between the ages of 30 and 39 (25,794), there has been a steady increase in the number of people over the age of 70 serving a custodial sentence (1,693). The reasons will be discussed further in Chapter 11 and the demographics of people serving a custodial sentence in England and Wales will be discussed in detail in Chapters 9 and 11. The contents of this textbook will therefore help you to develop an informed insight into how prisons are organised and to what extent they can meet the needs of a heterogeneous group of people held in their care for increasingly long periods of time.

Official data show how approximately 30 per cent of the prison population have been convicted of an offence that includes violence towards a person, 19 per cent have been convicted of a sexually motivated crime, 16 per cent of drug-related offences, 9 per cent of theft, a further 9 per cent robbery and 16 per cent of other offences (Ministry of Justice, 2022). In 2021, the average length of prison sentence for all offences in England and Wales was 18.6 months compared to 11.4 months in 2000 (Ministry of Justice, 2021). Now that you have a brief insight into why people are serving a custodial sentence, let us now consider how people end up in the prison system through an exploration of the sentencing framework.

HOW DOES IMPRISONMENT FIT INTO THE SENTENCING FRAMEWORK?

According to the Sentencing Council (2021: para 1), a custodial sentence is the most severe sentence available to the courts that is reserved for the most serious offences and imposed when the 'offence committed is so serious that neither a fine alone nor a community sentence can be justified for the offence' (section 152(2) of the Criminal Justice Act 2003).

The type and length of the sentence passed by the courts will depend on the seriousness of the crime and the maximum penalty allowed by law. There are four types of custodial sentence: suspended sentence, determinate sentence, extended sentence and life sentence. A sentence of less than six months (from a magistrate's court) or between 14 days and two years (from a crown court) can be suspended for up to two years. When a person is issued with a suspended sentence they will be expected to comply with requirements, such as unpaid work, set by the court. Failure to comply with set requirements and/or a further conviction for another crime during the suspension period will typically result in the person serving a prison sentence for the original crime as well as the new offence.

A determinate sentence is the most common type of prison sentence. The court will set a fixed length of time that a person is required to spend in prison. Release will vary depending on the length of sentence passed. For example, people sentenced to 12 months or more will spend half of their sentence in prison and half in the community on licence. In 2019, 76,000 people were given a determinate sentence, which represents 6 per cent of total sentences passed during this time (Sentencing Guidelines, 2022).

Extended sentences were introduced to provide extra protection to the public in cases where someone is found guilty of a specified crime and/or is deemed to be a significant risk to the public. The judge will decide how long a person should stay in prison and will fix an extended licence period of up to eight years. Rather than being released automatically at the half point of the sentence, people serving an extended sentence may be released after serving two-thirds of their sentence if the parole board deems them suitable for release. In 2019, 700 people were given an extended prison sentence (Sentencing Guidelines, 2022). This represents just 1 per cent of people sentenced to immediate custody.

When a life sentence is passed, a person will be subject to that sentence for the rest of their life. A judge must specify the minimum term a person must spend in prison before they are eligible to apply for parole. A whole life order will, however, require a person to spend the rest of their life in custody. As of June 2020, there were 63 people serving a whole life sentence in England and Wales, with a further three being treated in secure hospitals (Sentencing Guidelines, 2022). In addition, if a person is convicted of committing more than one crime, they will typically be given a sentence for each of their crimes. The sentences can be served concurrently (at the same time) or consecutively (one after the other). It is the responsibility of the judge to tell an individual not only what sentences have been passed, but how they should be served.

Once a person is sentenced to custody, efforts are made to ensure that they are allocated to a suitable prison establishment. This is a complex task that is fraught with difficulty given the array of competing interests that are involved in the process, risk factors, needs and vulnerabilities amongst people sentenced to custody. To illustrate the multiplex nature of this task, this section will focus on age, sex and security categorisation and show how difficult it is to ensure that people are housed in suitable (and indeed safe) conditions during their time in prison.

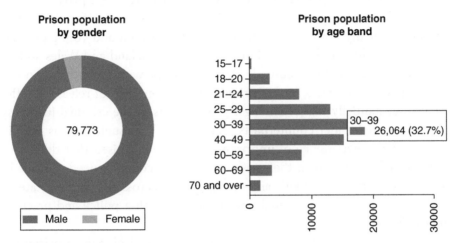

Figure 5.3 Prison population by gender and age band

Source: HM Government (2022) *Prisons data*. Available at: https://data.justice.gov.uk/prisons (last accessed 25 July 2022)

Age

The cases of children (aged between 10 and 17) who commit a crime may be processed through a youth court system rather than an adult court system. Youth courts are less formal than their adult counterparts and are closed to members of the public (unless they have explicit permission to attend). There are many different pathways for children and young people whose cases are processed through the youth court system. Some will be free to return to the wider community to undertake community-based interventions and programmes. Others may be required to undertake a period of detention depending on the nature and severity of the crime committed and/or the degree to which they are considered to pose a threat to society and/or themselves. In the United Kingdom children can be detained in secure children's homes, secure training centres and young offender institutions.

Secure children's homes are operated by local councils and designed for children aged between 10 and 14. They can house between eight and 40 children and provide 30 hours of education and training per week, following a school-like timetable. Secure training centres are operated by private companies that should provide 30 hours of education and training per week. They are designed for children and young people up to 17 years of age and can house between 50 and 80 people. Young offender institutions are operated by both the prison service and private companies. They cater for young people aged 15 to 21, with those under 18 held in different buildings, and typically house between 60 and 400 children and young people.

Despite a fall in the number of children in custody, England and Wales still has the highest imprisonment rate for children in Western Europe with more than two-thirds of children going on to commit a further crime within 12 months of release. Reoffending rates are also substantially higher amongst young adults in the criminal justice system in comparison to their older counterparts (Nacro, 2021). Though there is little insight into young women's experience of imprisonment, it is recognised that they are a particularly vulnerable group given their wide-ranging and complex needs. This is further compounded as the number of girls and young women across the secure estate continues to fall as they become increasingly overlooked at both a policy and practice level (Goodfellow, 2019).

Although Chapter 11 will discuss in detail the needs of an ageing prison population, as we also considering age in this context, it is important to assess how (if at all) older people can be suitably accommodated in prison. An inquiry by the Justice Select Committee in 2013 found that in too many cases older people in prison were being held in establishments that could not meet their basic needs, were not being provided with essential social care and were being released back into the community without adequate support (Age UK, 2019: para. 2). A further report in 2018 found that older people in prison are not being provided with accessible accommodation, appropriate support or age-specific programmes, which resulted in increased physical isolation and marginalisation (HM Inspectorate of Prisons and Care Quality Commission, 2018). Whilst efforts have been made to improve prison accommodation for older people in prison (see Chapter 11 for examples), there is a long road to travel before this fast-growing penal population can experience suitable accommodation during their custodial sentence.

Sex

Since the inception of imprisonment, the needs of women serving a custodial sentence have been little more than an afterthought in penal policy and practice. Until the beginning of the 19th century, when houses of correction introduced separate cell blocks and exercise areas for women, men and women would typically serve a custodial sentence side by side. Women, in some cases, were allowed to bring dependent children with them into prison whilst they served their sentence. That said, in contemporary times, the separation of women and men in custodial environments is now included in the United Nations Standard Minimum Rules for the Treatment of Prisoners (UNODC, 2020) as well as the Prison Rules 1999 (see Section 12). Alongside this, the United Nations Standard Minimum Rules for the Treatment of Prisoners suggest that young females (between 18 and 20 years of age) should be housed separately from adult women whilst in prison (UNODC, 2020). Despite such insights there are no young offender institutions in England and Wales that exclusively accommodate young adult women. As a result, young adult women are integrated, in varying ways and to varying degrees, into adult establishments, many of which have integrated young offender institution facilities.

In addition to the establishments already discussed there are mixed-sex prisons that separately accommodate both males and females during their custodial sentence. HMP Peterborough, located in Cambridgeshire, is the only purpose-built private prison for adult men and women (including young women) in the United Kingdom. A recent inspection by HM Inspector of Prisons (2021: 03) found 'the prison treated the women respectfully, although there was evidence to suggest that there was much more to do to embed an approach that considered more fully the trauma many women had experienced, and which is so often linked to their offending' (see Chapter 9 for further discussion of trauma-informed work in custodial settings). Though not a particularly popular option in the UK, mixed-sex prisons are commonplace in other countries. Legislation in Denmark, for example, does not dictate that people must be placed in separate penal institutions. Despite guidance in well-recognised and respected documents such as nited Nations Standard Minimum Rules for the Treatment of Prisoners (UNODC, 2020), Denmark prioritises a principle of normalisation whereby 'as far as possible life inside prison should reflect life outside prison' (Mathiasse, 2017: 387).

The public sector equality duty requires public services, including those delivered by the private sector, to consider how their policies and/or decisions affect people who are protected under the Equality Act 2010. This means that prisons must assess and meet the specific needs of both women and men in their care. The *Women's Policy Framework*, implemented in 2018, sets out the Ministry of Justice's expectations for the design and delivery of services working with women in custody and community settings. The Framework requires staff to be aware of gender-specific issues that affect women and respond appropriately to ensure that their needs are met. Such endeavours are supported by the *Guidance on Working with Women in Custody and Community* which outlines how practitioners working with women in custody and the wider community can deliver services that 'capture and reflect best practice' to 'empower women to engage in their own rehabilitation' (Ministry of Justice, 2018: 07).

Despite such endeavours, as women occupy such a small space in the criminal justice landscape, they are easily overlooked in criminal justice policy, planning and service delivery. Across the UK, approximately 12,000 women are imprisoned each year. This equates to approximately 5 per cent of the overall prison population. To date, the female prison estate is distributed sporadically throughout the UK. There are no female prisons in Wales, just one in Scotland (HMP Corton Vale) and 12 in England. As a result, females can be sent to an establishment that is a considerable distance from their home, families and friends which subsequently means that they are more prone to social isolation.

Punitive practices, such as imprisonment, continue to take place even though most women in prison have been convicted of non-violent crimes that are, in the main, led by a need to survive. A blog by Scott and Gosling (2015: para 3) suggests that women in prison have been 'failed by society rather than present[ing] a danger to our society'. This is largely because women in prison tend to come from impoverished and socially excluded backgrounds and have been victims of horrendous life circumstances, such as sexual abuse as children and domestic abuse as adults. Such poignant observations are even more alarming when you look at the rate of imprisonment amongst women on a global scale. A study conducted by the Australian Institute for Health and Welfare (2020) found that between 2000 and 2016, the female prison population increased by 53 per cent, growing at twice the rate of the total prison population and more than twice the rate of the general population.

In 2018, the Ministry of Justice published a *Female Offender Strategy* to outline the government's commitment to reduce the imprisonment of vulnerable women who could be better supported in the community. The strategy aims to reduce the number of women entering the criminal justice system, increase the use of community sentences, reduce short custodial sentences and deliver a better experience for those in custody, claiming to be 'committed to doing all we can to protect and support the most vulnerable in our society' (Ministry of Justice, 2018: 3). Whilst the strategy reflects a long-standing need for a gender specific approach to respond to the vulnerabilities of women in the criminal justice system it 'lacks clarity and offers little assurance that the direction taken will result in actual change and positive reform' (Booth et al., 2018: 1). Fewer than four years later, the publication of a briefing paper *Focus on Women's Prisons*, based on five inspections of women's prisons in the space of six months, illustrates a series of persistent weaknesses with regard to attempts to ensure women are suitably accommodated in penal environments (HM Inspectorate of Prisons, 2022).

SECURITY CATEGORISATION

People who are sent to custody are assigned a security category so that they can be assigned to an appropriate prison. As a result, prisons in England and Wales are categorised according to their security ranking and predominant function. There are four security rankings: categories A, B, C and D. Category A prisons house people serving a custodial sentence who, if they were to escape, would pose the most threat to the public, police or national security. Category B prisons are typically local prisons or training prisons. Category C prisons should, in theory, provide opportunities for people serving a custodial sentence to develop life skills so that they can work and (re)settle back into the wider community upon release. Those who can be reasonably trusted not to escape are housed in Category D, or open, prisons. Category A, B and C prisons are known as closed prisons as they are designed to hold people who are trusted not to try to escape. In England and Wales, adult male prisons are further divided into the following predominant functions: training prisons, local prisons, high security prisons and open prisons, each of which will be discussed shortly.

During the 1960s, several notorious and high-profile people escaped from prisons across the UK. Charles Wilson, a member of the Great Train Robbery gang, escaped from prison in 1964 just four months into his 30-year sentence for his part in the theft of £2.6 million from a Royal Mail train in 1963. Soon after, in 1965, Ronnie Biggs, one of the leaders of the Great Train Robbery gang, escaped from HMP Wandsworth by scaling a 30-foot wall with three other people serving a custodial sentence, just 15 months into his 30-year sentence. He went on to spend the next 36 years on the run until 2001 when he surrendered to the police. In 1966, George Blake – a spy with Britain's Secret Intelligence Service (MI6) and double agent for the Soviet Union – escaped from HMP Wormwood Scrubs, London.

Prior to these infamous escapes, prison security was not considered particularly important (see Chapter 5 for further discussion). But this was all set to change as the Mountbatten Committee, chaired by Earl Mountbatten, was established in October 1966 to explore prison escapes and security, and provide recommendations on how to improve security arrangements in prisons across the country. Alongside escapes and security, the Mountbatten Committee looked at issues such as staff morale, prison management and central government control, prison-based social work, family involvement and prison regimes. In December 1966, the Mountbatten Report was published. In 52 recommendations, it proposed a significant upgrade to physical security across the prison estate.

The Mountbatten Committee proposed that all males serving a custodial sentence should be classified into four security categories according to their security risk, escape risk and danger to the public. Category A included people serving a custodial sentence who would pose the most threat to the public, the police or national security should they escape. Mountbatten recommended that people considered to be Category A should be housed together in a new, purpose-built, escape-proof prison called HMP Vectis on the Isle of Wight. Category B included people serving a custodial sentence who did not need to be held in the highest security conditions, but the potential for escape should be made very difficult. Category C included those who could not be trusted in open conditions but were considered unlikely to make a determined escape attempt and Category D included those who could be trusted in open prison conditions.

Allocating a security category to every person serving a custodial sentence has since been used to assess people in prison according to the level of security deemed necessary to safely hold them in custody (see Rule 7 of the Prison Rules 1999). This process is linked to and based on the concept of individualised risk assessments (UNODC, 2020). In a prison setting, an individualised risk assessment involves a systematic analysis of a person using assessment tools, available documentation, interviews and observations to determine a person's risks (including risk of self-harm and suicide, risk to other people, risk of escape and risk to the public in the event of an escape). It also includes an analysis of factors that should be addressed to reduce or manage those risks. Individualised risk assessments are important in custodial establishments as they (in theory at least) recognise that stand-alone factors such as the crimes people are convicted of 'are not necessarily the best proxies for estimating the risk that a prisoner may pose in a prison setting or to the community and, therefore, are not suitable stand-alone determinants of classification, categorisation and allocation decisions' (UNODC, 2020: 03) (see Chapter 1 for a further discussion of risk and risk management).

The Advisory Council on the Penal System, a subcommittee chaired by Professor Leon Radzinowicz, accepted Mountbatten's recommendation to categorise people serving a custodial sentence but rejected his policy of concentration. This was due to a concern that it would be impossible to provide an orderly, constructive regime in an Alcatraz-style prison such as HMP Vectis. Rather, the subcommittee recommended a policy of dispersal whereby people considered to be security Category A could be dispersed across several secure locations in the prison system, with all people deemed to be security Category A further divided into one of three escape risk classifications.

1. *Standard escape risk.* This person would be highly dangerous if at large in the community but there is no specific information or intelligence to suggest there is a threat of escape.

2. *High escape risk.* This person would be highly dangerous if at large in the community. One or more of the following factors are present and suggest that the person may pose a raised escape risk: access to finances, resources and/or associates that could assist an escape attempt; position in an organised crime group; nature of current/previous lawbreaking; links to terrorist networks; previous escape(s) from custody.

3. *Exceptional escape risk.* The criteria for high escape risk apply here as well as credible information and/or intelligence (either internal to the prison or from external agencies) that would suggest that an escape attempt is being planned and the threat is such that the individual requires conditions of heightened security to mitigate this risk.

(National Offender Management Service, 2016)

In England and Wales, prisons that are designed to make escape impossible are known as high security prisons. In the UK there are eight high security prisons: HMP Belmarsh, HMP Frankland, HMP Full Sutton, HMP Long Lartin, HMP Manchester, HMP Wakefield, HMP Whitemoor and HMP Woodhill, five of which are dispersal prisons (HMP Frankland, HMP Full Sutton, HMP Long Lartin, HMP Wakefield, HMP Whitemoor). The remaining three operate as local prisons with the ability to hold people who have security Category A status. These local prisons provide a key role in the high-security estate as they are equipped to hold people on remand as well as those awaiting allocation who would otherwise be housed in dispersal prisons. You will find out more about the role and function of local prisons as you progress through this chapter.

Arguments for and against the dispersal system have been ongoing since its inception. Broadly speaking, the policy of dispersal aims to ensure that one prison is not overburdened by people with a security category A status, with those deemed to be category A accommodated within a larger prison population. Though seemingly more progressive than a policy of concentration, when translated into practice the policy of dispersal becomes costly to both the prison system and those held within them. This is largely because all people serving custodial sentences in dispersal prisons are subject to heightened risk and security measures to accommodate a small number of people considered to be high-risk. As a result, control and surveillance are prioritised at the expense of other objectives such as work, training and education.

Security categorisation is a risk management process that aims to ensure those who are sentenced to custody are assigned the lowest security category appropriate to managing their risk of escape or absconding, harm to the public, further crimes in prison, violent or other behaviour that impacts the safety of those in prison and/or control issues that disrupt the security and good order of the prison (Ministry of Justice, 2020). Together with other factors such as length of sentence, security categorisation will determine the type of prison a person is allocated to. This, however, is not a one-off process. When someone is sentenced to custody they will be assessed and reassessed during their time in prison. For example, if a person is sentenced to between one and four years, they will be assessed every six months. If the sentence is more than four years, they will be assessed every year until the last two years of their sentence when they will be assessed every six months.

In addition, people serving a custodial sentence can be re-categorised if an incident has occurred or new information has emerged that may have an impact on their level of risk. If a person's risk is raised or lowered because of re-categorisation, prison staff can take action to transfer them to a more appropriate prison. If someone serving a custodial sentence is not happy with their re-categorisation, they can appeal the decision via the prison complaint system. Prison staff are then, in theory, required to justify their decision and provide reasoning for their categorisation. Re-categorisation has, for many years, proved to be a controversial issue. Although the Prison Service Instruction (PSI 40/2011, section 5.1) states that 'an individual's security category must not be adjusted to achieve a better match with available spaces within the estate', the Prison Officers Association (POA) have alleged for some time that the re-categorisation process is flawed, with people serving custodial sentences being 'inappropriately downgraded' to fill spaces in open prisons and ease overcrowding (Grimwood, 2015: 6).

Women serving a custodial sentence are subject to a different security categorisation process than their male counterparts. In England and Wales, women serving a custodial sentence are considered suitable for either open or closed conditions. Women who are held in closed conditions do not require the highest security conditions but present too high a risk for open conditions. Women who are considered low risk can be held in open conditions if they can be reasonably trusted to live in open conditions. Although there are two other categories for women serving a custodial sentence (Category A status and restricted status) very few women are given this status due to the nature of their definition and crimes typically committed by females.

- *Category A* status can be given to females serving a custodial sentence whose escape would be highly dangerous to the public, police or the security of the state and for whom the aim must be to make escape impossible.
- *Restricted status* can be given to a young female or adult female (convicted or on remand) whose escape would present a serious risk to the public and who are required to be held in designated secure accommodation.

Effective security categorisation is fundamental to risk management and ensuring good order is maintained in prisons. It supports the duty of HMPPS to implement the sentences of the courts, protect the public and provide a safe, secure and ordered custodial environment (HM Government, 2020). That said, security categorisation is not without its limitations. For example, the fundamental aim of security categorisation is to place people in prison with the correct (but lowest possible) level of security based on their risk of dangerousness and/or likelihood of escape. Though there have been few escapes by people with security Category A status, such occurrences persist. In addition, evidence suggests that people in prison have not only been inappropriately de-classified to alleviate prison overcrowding (Grimwood, 2015) but in many cases over-classified and subject to regimes that are more restrictive than required (Penal Reform International, 2015). This is not to say that the security categorisation system is ineffective, nor is it a claim that such endeavours have alone prevented escapes in recent times. Rather, this is an attempt to critically examine the concept of security categorisation in theory and practice to enhance your criminological imagination and ability to question the penological status quo.

TYPE AND FUNCTION OF PRISON

In addition to age, sex and security categorisation, prisons are further divided according to type and function. For this discussion, the term type will be used to differentiate between state and private prisons. The difference between the two will be discussed in further detail below. The term function will be used to differentiate prisons in England and Wales based on their roles, responsibilities and purpose within the prison system.

Private prisons

A series of changes such as the nationalisation of custodial establishments during the late 1800s and early 1900s gave way to the birth of the modern-day prison in England and Wales. Although principles of privatisation can be traced throughout the history of imprisonment (see Chapter 3 for a more detailed discussion), from charging people rent for their bed and board, to the use of manual labour of people in prison to generate revenue, interest in and commitment to private prisons did not (re)surface until the late 1980s (see Chapter 2 for a more detailed discussion). This appetite was accelerated by the Criminal Justice Act 1991 and its provision to allow the management of any prison to be contracted out to whomever the Home Secretary considers appropriate. As a result, the prison service in England and Wales has been divided into state-owned and run prisons, commonly referred to as public sector prisons, and private prisons that have either been purpose built by a private company or acquired from the state, with private companies required to manage and oversee the day-to-day operation of these institutions.

The ability to privatise prisons was pursued to respond to problems associated with overcrowding as well as the financial burdens of imprisonment. It is, however, important to note that efforts to privatise punishment are controversial. Advocates of privatisation suggest that private prisons reduce public spending, offer a more business-like approach to prison management, put less pressure on the government to maintain prison establishments and provide opportunities for prisons to become more autonomous, innovative and responsive to the needs of those within them. However, the ethics of private companies to profit from the pain and punishment of others is questionable. As conversations about profit margins, accountability and contestability dominate the penal landscape, endeavours to protect human rights and respond to the needs of people serving custodial sentences fall by the wayside (see Chapter 11 for a more detailed discussion).

Alongside this, it is important to note how providing opportunities for private companies to profit from punishment contributes to further pressure for penal expansion. Put simply, more people in prison equals more money for investors. Additionally, prison privatisation has been described as a smokescreen that permits the fragmentation of state responsibility and accountability for prisons and indeed those within them. Due to commercial confidentiality, key financial and operational details of contracts drawn up between private companies and the government are not available for public scrutiny, which makes it difficult for Parliament to hold companies to account. Despite ongoing concerns, the role of private prisons is substantial, housing approximately 15 per cent of the total prison population in England and Wales.

The privatisation of prisons is not a phenomenon exclusive to England and Wales. At least 11 countries across North America, South America, Europe, Africa and Oceania are engaged in some level of prison privatisation (Mason, 2013). Private prisons in the United States held 115,428 people in 2019, which represents 8 per cent of the total state and federal prison population (The Sentencing Project, 2020). Since 2000 the number of people housed in private prisons across America has increased 32 per cent compared to an overall rise in the prison population of 3 per cent (Ibid). It is also important to note that the role of the private sector in custodial environments extends far beyond the parameters of our discussion so far. The most usual form of penal privatisation (across the globe) is the contracting out, or outsourcing, of specific aspects of service delivery such as but not limited to medical and mental health services, education and training opportunities, food supplies and drug treatment. Outsourcing specific aspects of penal service delivery is not something that is specific to privately operated prisons and takes place across both state prisons and private prisons.

Training prisons

Training prisons can hold a variety of people over the age of 21 serving a range of sentences from short sentences to life imprisonment. Their primary purpose is to provide a variety of vocational courses and training facilities across a wide number of areas such as bricklaying, plastering and industrial cleaning. Some Category C training prisons are also known as resettlement prisons. This is because they hold people serving a short prison sentence, typically between 12 months and four years, and work alongside resettlement providers to prepare those serving a custodial sentence for release. HMP Berwyn is a Category C, adult male prison in Wrexham, Wales. It is also known as a training prison for young adult and adult men with a resettlement function . The prison also has a remand facility for 200 unsentenced adult men and young adult men.

Local prisons

Most people will start their custodial sentence in a local prison. This is because local prisons tend to accommodate men, women and young adults who are remanded in custody before trial, or after sentencing are sent direct from the courts. Local prisons provide a holding purpose as they house people who have been given a custodial sentence who are awaiting initial assessments, classification and allocation to another establishment to serve their sentence. HMP Manchester, formerly known as Strangeways, is a high-security men's public prison in the north-west of England. It is a local prison that holds people who have been remanded into custody from courts in the Manchester area as well as those who have been classified centrally as Category A.

High-security prisons

There are eight prisons considered to be high-security establishments. In England and Wales, there are two types of high-security prisons: core local prisons and dispersal prisons. Core local prisons hold people who are awaiting trial, sentence or allocation to another prison (Beard, 2021). Dispersal prisons are high-security training prisons for people who have been sentenced to a long-term custodial sentence. They are usually Category A or B. HMP Wakefield is a Category A men's prison located in West Yorkshire, England. Designated a dispersal prison in 1966, HMP Wakefield is the oldest of the dispersal prisons in operation across England and Wales. The Close Supervision Centre in HMP Wakefield provides a psychologically informed structured environment in which the most dangerous, difficult and disruptive people are managed through a robust care and management approach. The aim of the Close Supervision Centre is to assess, monitor and reduce risk so that the individual can progress along the appropriate care pathway, which may include an eventual return to mainstream prison, access to treatment or referral to a specialist service such as a secure hospital.

Open prisons

Open prisons accommodate people serving a custodial sentence who have been given a Category D status as they are considered to present little to no danger to the public should they escape (Beard, 2021). People in open prisons tend to include those who have served a long sentence and are working their way down the security categories as they prepare for release into the wider community, as well as those who have committed non-violent crimes such as fraud. Open prisons tend to have limited physical security with no perimeter wall around them and to be situated in rural areas. HMP Kirkham is a Category D men's prison located in Kirkham, Lancashire.

In 2004, it became the first prison for adult males in England to trial the intermittent custody scheme (ICS) introduced through the Criminal Justice Act 2003 (Penfold et al., 2006). The scheme was intended to punish people who had received a custodial sentence but did not present a risk to the public or require immediate, full-time custody. The scheme saw some people held at Kirkham from Monday to Friday (released at weekends) whilst others were released during the week and held on a Saturday and Sunday in prison, with the aim of allowing people sentenced to short custodial sentences to remain in employment, housing and maintain family ties during their sentence. Although ICSs were viewed as a useful sentence as they allowed judges to pass a custodial sentence whilst avoiding disproportionate damage, they were abandoned in 2006.

Additional functions and features

Alongside their predominant function, many prisons across England and Wales have additional functions and features. For example, HMP Garth is a Category B training prison in Lancashire, England that accepts men serving four years or more. In addition to the provision of educational, training and vocational opportunities, the prison is home to the Beacon Unit which is an innovative prison-based assessment and treatment service for people with at least two years left in prison (but less than 20 years) who demonstrate significant personality-related needs. The service forms part of the National Personality Disorder Strategy for people in prison and is delivered in conjunction with Mersey Care National Health Service Foundation Trust (specialist mental health provider). The Beacon Unit aims to improve the psychological well-being of men in their care through the provision of a trauma, attachment and biopsychosocial understanding of personality development and disorder (see Chapter 9 for further insight into trauma-informed care).

A further example is HMP Grendon. HMP Grendon is a Category B men's prison located in Buckinghamshire, England. The prison is operated by HMPS and is jointly managed with HMP Spring Hall, situated next to Grendon. HMP Grendon is the only therapeutic community (TC) prison in the United Kingdom based on treatment principles that originated in the Henderson Hospital, London. HMP Grendon provides group therapy and structured community living where people serving a custodial sentence are encouraged to have shared responsibility for day-to-day decision making and problem solving. Group-based therapy is designed to promote positive interpersonal relationships, personal responsibility and social participation whilst simultaneously addressing a range of unmet needs amongst those serving a custodial sentence. It is one of the most researched prison establishments in the world, establishing standards for good relationships between those who live and work in custodial environments, as well as low levels of violence and self-harm.

Taking a moment to think about how penal institutions are organised and structured provides a useful insight into a society's priorities, attitudes and values that contribute to our understanding and attempts to rationalise why people go to prison. Whilst it is important to understand macro attempts to organise a vacuous system of imprisonment, it is just as important to consider micro attempts from those who live and work in these environments to organise prison life (see Chapter 7 for further discussion). A recent publication by Schliehe and Crewe (2021: 1) on cell-sharing in prison illustrates this point: 'the politics involved in cell-sharing reach into the most personal parts of prisoners' lives and are highly determinate of their experiences of imprisonment'. Such sentiments will be further explored in Chapters 9 and 11.

GOVERNANCE AND ACCOUNTABILITY

To ensure that prisons in England and Wales are held to account for their actions as well as the events that take place within them, they are subject to a plethora of legal frameworks and governance processes on international, national and local levels, requiring them to act legally, lawfully and morally. Given the scope and complexity of this arena, the discussion that follows will provide you with a summative account of some of the most influential guidelines and robust attempts to ensure that the prison place provides suitable accommodation and experiences for *all* people in their care. To open the section, the discussion will explore the European Prison Rules (which set out standards for the management of prisons and treatment of people in prison) and The Prison Rules 1999 (which is an important piece of legislation which governs how prisons are run). Following on from this, the discussion will explore the role and impact of prison inspection and monitoring bodies such as HM Inspectorate of Prisons, Independent Monitoring Boards and the Prisons and Probation Ombudsman that are required to ensure relevant frameworks are applied correctly and consistently at the coal face of service delivery.

European Prison Rules

The European Prison Rules were created by the Council of Europe, a leading human rights organisation including 46 member states (27 of which are members of the European Union). Established in 1949, the Council of Europe is one of the oldest and biggest European organisations, which unifies member states to promote principles of human rights. All members of the Council of Europe have signed up to the European Convention on Human Rights, a treaty designed to protect human rights, democracy and the rule of law. In 1973 the Council of Europe created the European Prison Rules which were later reformulated in 1987, 2006 and 2020 to reflect developments in penal policy, sentencing practice and the overall management of prisons in Europe. The

European Prison Rules are based on the United Nations Standard Minimum Rules for the Treatment of Prisoners. Although they are not legally binding, they provide recognised standards on good principles and practices in custodial settings.

The European Prison Rules were created under article 15b of the Statute of the Council of Europe taking in the European Convention on Human Rights and case law from the European Court of Human Rights, as well as standards developed by the European Committee for the Prevention of Torture and Inhumane or Degrading Treatment or Punishment. Alongside, the United Nations has created the Minimum Standard Rules for the Treatment of Prisoners which state that 'all prisons shall be subject to regular government inspection and independent monitoring' (Rule 9, Council of Europe, 2006: 7). While the establishment of prison inspection and monitoring bodies is a requirement for all Council of Europe member states, no single model for such bodies exists across Europe. This means that there is little consistency in the application of such principles and associated practices across member states.

The Prison Rules 1999

The Act of Parliament which specifies the legal rules that apply in prisons is the Prison Act 1952. Section 47(1) of the Act states that the Secretary of State 'may make rules for the regulation and management of prisons (...) and for the classification, treatment, employment, discipline and control of persons required to be detained therein' (see Loucks, 2000). The Prison Act 1952 is still a significant piece of legislation as The Prison Rules 1999 are made under the authority of this Act. The Prison Rules 1999 is an important piece of legislation as it governs how prisons are run, including, for example, regulations on aspects of prison life such as (but not limited to): religion, medical attention, physical welfare and work, education, communication, removal and search of property, prison officers and people accessing prisons. Whilst The Prison Rules 1999 apply to every prison, the governing governor may have local rules as well (we will discuss the role of the governing governor in more detail in Chapter 7).

Although The Prison Rules 1999 provides a useful legal framework that goes some way to organise and structure penal environments, a great deal of discretion is left to prison authorities. As a result, the Prison Service regularly issues documents, rules and regulations to guide the application of these Rules. Following recommendation 60 in the Woodcock Report (1994, cited in Loucks, 2000), which called for the simplification and consolidation of such guidance, prison service orders (PSOs) and prison service instructions (PSIs) were created. PSOs are permanent directions which replaced a mixture of standing orders, circular instructions, instructions to governors and manuals containing mandatory requirements. People serving a custodial sentence should have access to them through prison libraries as should members of the public, unless the PSOs have a protective marking. PSIs, on the other hand, are short-term directions which include a mandatory element. Since 2009 only PSIs have been issued which means that the prison service is now regulated by PSOs issued before 2000 which have not been withdrawn or amended and PSIs after 2009 which are yet to expire.

Governmental inspection and independent monitoring

92 Prisons shall be inspected regularly by a governmental agency in order to assess whether they are administered in accordance with the requirements of national and international law, and the provisions of these rules.

93.1 The conditions of detention and the treatment of prisoners shall be monitored by an independent body or bodies whose findings shall be made public.

93.2 Such independent monitoring body or bodies shall be encouraged to co-operate with those international agencies that are legally entitled to visit prisons.

(Rule 9, part VI of the European Prison Rules, citied in Council of Europe, 2006: 32)

Throughout the UK, prison inspectors and monitoring bodies are required to undertake a variety of functions from auditing and examining budgets to financial and strategic planning, to assessment of compliance with national and international law governing how and in what ways people serving a custodial sentence should be treated. As such, the discussion will now explore the role and function of HM Inspectorate of Prisons, Independent Monitoring Boards and the Prisons and Probation Ombudsman. In doing so, you may find it useful to consider the degree to which such organisations are able to have an impact within a highly politicised system of punishment.

HM Inspectorate of Prisons

HM Inspectorate of Prisons for England and Wales is an independent inspectorate which reports on conditions for and treatment of those in prison, young offender institutions, secure training centres, immigration removal centres, police and court custody suites, customs custody facilities and military detention (HM Inspectorate of Prisons, 2020). The work of HM Inspectorate of Prisons is underpinned by independence, impartiality and integrity, respect for human rights, diversity and equality of outcomes for all, as well as a belief in the capacity of both individuals and organisations to change and improve. A chief inspector reports directly to the Secretary of State for Justice on conditions for and treatment of those in custody. Six inspection teams work under the chief inspector, with each team inspecting a specific type of establishment or service. Alongside inspection teams, HM Inspectorate of Prisons employs a research team, editorial and administrative staff.

Custodial environments in England and Wales are inspected by HM Inspectorate of Prisons at least once every five years (depending on the population in custody and the level of risk). Some inspections are classed as an announced inspection as the prison is informed before HM Inspectorate of Prisons visit. Most inspections are, however, unannounced which means HM Inspectorate of Prisons does not notify establishments prior to their arrival. Inspectors assess prisons based on a series of broad thematic judgements known as healthy establishment tests, influenced and informed by international human rights standards. Although the tests vary slightly according to the establishment, they have all been developed from HM Inspectorate of Prisons' four tests of a healthy prison: *safety, respect, purposeful activity* and *rehabilitation,* and release planning (HM Inspectorate of Prisons, 2020).

Prison inspections usually take place over two weeks, during which HM Inspectorate of Prisons collects information from those who live and work there, visitors as well as others who have in interest in the establishment under inspection. Broadly speaking there are three types of inspections: full inspections, full follow-up inspections (inspectors assess progress made and undertake an in-depth analysis of the establishment), and short follow-up inspections (inspectors focus on progress made and note any additional areas of concern). The purpose of each inspection is to judge the quality of outcomes for people in custody against each area of the healthy prison test. There are four possible outcomes of an inspection:

- *Good*. There is no evidence that outcomes for people serving a custodial sentence are adversely affected in any significant areas.

- *Reasonably good.* There is evidence of adverse outcomes for people serving a custodial sentence in a small number of areas. There are no significant concerns and procedures to safeguard outcomes are in place.

- *Not sufficiently good.* There is evidence of outcomes for people serving a custodial sentence being adversely affected in many areas. If left unattended, issues are likely to become a serious concern.

- *Poor.* There is evidence that outcomes are seriously affected by current practice. Remedial action is required to ensure adequate treatment of and/or conditions for people in prison.

(HM Chief Inspector of Prisons, 2017)

Once the inspection is complete, HM Inspectorate of Prisons state their key concerns and make recommendations to help prisons improve. Though they are unable to close prisons, they can raise an urgent notification with the Secretary of State for Justice. In addition, since April 2019, HM Inspectorate of Prisons has introduced Independent Reviews of Progress for prisons deemed to be failing and/or unsafe. Independent Reviews of Progress are designed to assess and evidence how far prisons have implemented their recommendations from previous inspections and identify barriers to change. Prisons that are subject to the urgent notification protocol will be considered a priority under the Independent Reviews of Progress model. Independent Reviews of Progress are not inspections and do not result in new judgements against the healthy prisons test. Rather, a prison's progress is assessed against recommendations made during the previous inspection and one of four judgements is made: no meaningful progress, insufficient progress, reasonable progress, or satisfactory progress. Independent Reviews of Progress are announced in advance and usually take place between eight and 12 months after the original inspection. They last for approximately two days and are undertaken by a team of inspectors who publish their findings approximately 25 days after their visit to the establishment.

The Independent Reviews of Progress may seem plausible, given the attempt to hold prisons accountable for their failings and efforts to rectify emerging issues behind the prison walls, but little has changed. If you look at the recently published Independent Reviews of Progress for HMP Pentonville in London, you will see little improvement:

'Unfortunately, our findings at the end of this IRP, more than nine months after the inspection, were a cause for continued concern. The prison had made good progress in only one of the 15 key concerns and recommendations, and reasonable progress against only a further three. There had been no meaningful progress against six key concerns and recommendations, and insufficient progress against the remaining five.' (HM Inspectorate of Prisons, 2020: 11)

This is not an isolated occurrence. Both HM Inspectorate of Prisons and countless official inquiries have routinely identified failings of the prison service over many years, yet they persist. The systematic non-implementation of recommendations by HM Inspectorate of Prisons and/or official inquiries have devastating consequences for people serving a custodial sentence, which can result in the loss of life and self-harm. Such occurrences not only disproportionately affect people with protected characteristics but compound social inequality and deprivation amongst people serving a custodial sentence (for further discussion see Chapter 11).

Independent Monitoring Boards

The Prison Act 1952 requires the Secretary of State for Justice and the Home Secretary to appoint independent boards to monitor prisons and places of detention. Independent Monitoring Boards play a crucial role in the independent oversight of prisons and immigration detention. Members of the Independent Monitoring Board are appointed by government ministers and granted unrestricted access to these establishments as well as those within them. They are allowed to make frequent visits to custodial establishments and have access to official records – except for healthcare records, staff personnel records and certain classified information about the establishment. They are part of the United Kingdom's National Preventive Mechanism set up under the United Nations Optional Protocol for the Convention against Torture to prevent inhumane treatment in places of detention that operate out of sight of the public.

The Independent Monitoring Boards focus on safety (including violence and self-harm, safeguarding and use of force), humane treatment (including segregation, equality, and accommodation), health and well-being (including primary care, mental health, exercise and drug and alcohol treatment), as well as progression and release (including education, training, offender management and preparations for release). All their findings are provided to those who are responsible for managing the establishment and published in annual reports. Independent Monitoring Boards in establishments that hold children and young people under the age of 18 make a separate assessment of the provision and availability of education. The work of the Independent Monitoring Boards complements that of HM Inspectorate of Prisons as well as the Prisons and Probation Ombudsman.

Prisons and Probation Ombudsman (PPO)

The Prisons and Probation Ombudsman carries out independent investigations into complaints and deaths in custody. It has three main duties: (1) to investigate complaints made by people in prison, those under probation supervision and immigration detainees, (2) to investigate the death of people in prison, approved premises and immigration detainees due to any cause, (3) to investigate deaths of those who have recently been released from prison or immigration detention using their discretionary powers. The purpose of these investigations is to understand what happened, to correct any injustices and identify learning. Such endeavours are not only aimed at building accountability within and between custodial establishments but are an attempt to enhance the procedural fairness experienced by people serving a custodial sentence.

Common law recognises procedural fairness, or the existence of due process, as a key principle of just decision making. Fairness requires regularity, predictability and certainty from authorities when dealing with members of the public. When legislation provides power to authorities, there is an assumption that it will be exercised fairly. But what is fair depends on the context of the decision. In a prison context, the term procedural justice refers to the degree to which someone perceives people in authority to apply processes or make decisions about them in a fair and just way (HM Government, 2019). Research suggests that people in prison with a more positive perception of procedural justice exhibit lower levels of prison rule breaking and misconduct, better emotional well-being and mental health, as well as lower rates of future lawbreaking (Ibid).

The Strangeways riot (see Chapter 3 for further discussion) provides a perfect example of how people in prison may disengage with authority figures and prison regimes if they do not feel their treatment, living conditions and experiences are procedurally just.

When thinking about what can be done to promote procedural justice in prison settings, the government notes the importance of the following practices: personalise contact, for example, using a person's first name; offer opportunities to ask questions; explain how processes work and why they are in place; allow people to have their say; explain reasons behind decisions, and encourage people and their efforts. Though promising, we must critically engage with such endeavours as the prison system has a long history of non-implementation of recommendations, whether from official inquiries, HM Inspectorate of Prisons, Independent Monitoring Board or Prisons and Probation Ombudsman reports. This not only has devastating consequences for those living and working in custodial environments but raises significant questions about the ways in which contemporary prisons are governed and held to account.

recommended reading

If you would like to engage in further reading, you may find the following resources particularly useful:

Aitken, D. (2021) Investigating prison suicides: The politics of independent oversight. *Punishment and Society*, https://doi.org/10.1177%2F1462474521993002

This article examines the arrangements in place to investigate prison suicides in England and Wales, focusing on inquiries by the Prisons and Probation Ombudsman and coroners' inquests whilst raising important questions about the politics of punishment.

Ludici, A. (2021) Can a prison be self-managed? A study of the informal organisation of a Bolivian prison. *Crime, Law and Social Change*, 76, 195–213.

This article explores the unique features and general organisation of Bolivian prisons, including the presence of wives and children, self-management of activities within the prison as well as opportunities for people serving a custodial sentence to take part in various activities.

Roffee, J. (2017) Accountability and oversight of state functions: Use of volunteers to monitor equality and diversity in prisons in England and Wales. *Sage Open*, 7(1).

This article explores the strengths and limitations of volunteers with regard to efforts to ensure the prison place remains accountable for its actions within prisons across England and Wales.

references

Age UK (2019) Older prisoners (England and Wales). Available at: www.ageuk.org.uk/globalassets/age-uk/documents/policy-positions/care-and-support/ppp_older_prisoners_en_wa.pdf (last accessed 30 June 2022).

Australian Institute of Health and Welfare (2020) The health and welfare of women in Australian prisons. Available at: www.aihw.gov.au/getmedia/32d3a8dc-eb84-4a3b-90dc-79a1aba0efc6/aihw-phe-281.pdf.aspx?inline=true (last accessed 30 June 2022).

Beard, J. (2021) The prison estate. Briefing Paper. House of Commons. Available at: https://researchbriefings.files.parliament.uk/documents/SN05646/SN05646.pdf (last accessed 27 July 2022).

Booth, N., Masson, I. and Baldwin, N. (2018) Promises, promises: Can the female offender strategy deliver? *Probation Journal*, pp. 1–10. Available at: https://dora.dmu.ac.uk/bitstream/handle/2086/16962/Comment%20piece%20-%20final%20version%20PDF.pdf?sequence=1 (last accessed 30 June 2022).

Council of Europe (2006) *European Prison Rules*. Available at: https://rm.coe.int/european-prison-rules-978-92-871-5982-3/16806ab9ae (last accessed 30 June 2022).

Goodfellow, P. (2019) Girls in custody – Outnumbered, locked up and overlooked. Blog post. Available at: www.russellwebster.com/goodfellow (last accessed 30 June 2022).

Grimwood, G. (2015) *Categorisation of Prisoners in the UK*. Available at: https://research-briefings.files.parliament.uk/documents/CBP-7437/CBP-7437.pdf (last accessed 30 June 2022).

HM Government (2019) Procedural justice. Available at: www.gov.uk/guidance/procedural-justice (last accessed 30 June 2022).

HM Government (2020) Security categorisation policy framework. Available at: www.gov.uk/government/publications/security-categorisation-policy-framework (last accessed 30 June 2022).

HM Inspectorate of Prisons (2020) Our expectations. Available at: www.justiceinspectorates.gov.uk/hmiprisons/our-expectations (last accessed 30 June 2022).

HM Chief Inspector of Prisons (2017) HM Chief Inspector of Prisons for England and Wales. Available at: www.justiceinspectorates.gov.uk/hmiprisons/wp-content/uploads/sites/4/2017/07/HMIP-AR_2016-17_CONTENT_11-07-17-WEB.pdf (last accessed 27 July 2022).

HM Chief Inspector of Prisons (2021) Report on an independent review of progress at HMP Pentonville. Available at: www.justiceinspectorates.gov.uk/hmiprisons/wp-content/uploads/sites/4/2020/03/Pentonvilleweb-IRP-2020.pdf (last accessed 27 July 2022).

HM Inspectorate of Prisons (2022) *Focus on Women's Prisons: A Briefing Paper from HM Inspectorate of Prisons*. Available at: www.justiceinspectorates.gov.uk/hmiprisons/wp-content/uploads/sites/4/2022/02/Womens-briefing-paper.pdf (last accessed 30 June 2022).

HM Inspectorate of Prisons and Care Quality Commission (2018) *Social Care in Prisons in England and Wales: A Thematic Report*. Available at: www.justiceinspectorates.gov.uk/hmiprisons/wp-content/uploads/sites/4/2018/10/Social-care-thematic-2018-web.pdf (last accessed 30 June 2022).

Penfold, C., Hunder, G. and Hough, M. (2006) *The Intermittent Custody Scheme: A Descriptive Study*. Home Office Online Report 23/06. Available at: http://file:///C:/Users/sschgosl/Downloads/The_intermittent_custody_pilot_a_descriptive_study%20(1).pdf

Loucks, N. (2000) *Prison Rules: A Working Guide*. Available at: www.prisonreformtrust.org.uk/wp-content/themes/chd/old_files/Documents/prisonrulesworkingguide.pdf (last accessed 30 June 2022).

Mason, C. (2013) *International Growth Trends in Prison Privatization*. Available at: https://www.sentencingproject.org/publications/international-growth-trends-in-prison-privatization (last accessed 30 June 2022).

Mathiasse, C. (2017) Being a woman in mixed gender prisons. In P. Smith and T. Ugelvik (eds) *Scandinavian Penal History, Culture and Prison Practice*. London: Palgrave, pp. 377–404.

Ministry of Justice (2018) *Female Offender Strategy*. Available at: www.gov.uk/government/publications/female-offender-strategy (last accessed 30 June 2022).

Ministry of Justice (2020) Safety in custody: Quarterly update to December 2019. Available at: www.gov.uk/government/statistics/safety-in-custody-quarterly-update-to-december-2019 (last accessed 30 June 2022).

Ministry of Justice (2021) Criminal Justice System statistics quarterly update year ending 2020. Available at: www-statista-com.eu1.proxy.openathens.net/statistics/1100628/prison-sentence-length-in-england-and-wales-over-time

Ministry of Justice (2022) Prisons data. Available at: https://data.justice.gov.uk/prisons (last accessed 30 June 2022).

Nacro (2021) Youth Justice facts and figures. Available at: www.beyondyouthcustody.net/about/facts-and-stats (last accessed 30 June 2022).

National Health Service (2017) Safeguarding adults. Available at: www.england.nhs.uk/wp-content/uploads/2017/02/adult-pocket-guide.pdf (last accessed 29 July 2022)

National Offender Management Service (2016) *Category A Function: The Review of Security Category – Category A/Restricted Status Prisoners (PSI 08/2013)*. Available at: https://assets.publishing.service.gov.uk/government/uploads/system/uploads/attachment_data/file/910233/PSI-08-2013-The-Review-of-Security-Category-Category-A-Restricted-Status-Prisoners-Revised-June-2016.pdf (last accessed 27 July 2022).

Penal Reform International (2015) *Balancing Security and Dignity in Prisons: A Framework for Preventive Monitoring*. Available at: https://cdn.penalreform.org/wp-content/uploads/2016/01/security-dignity-2nd-ed-v6.pdf (last accessed 30 June 2022).

Prison Reform Trust (2021) *Prison: The Facts*. Bromley Briefings Summer 2021. Available at: https://prisonreformtrust.org.uk/wp-content/uploads/2022/01/Prison_the_facts_2021.pdf (last accessed 30 June 2022).

Schliehe, A. and Crewe, B. (2021) Top bunk, bottom bunk: Cell-sharing in prisons. *The British Journal of Criminology*, 62(2), 484–500.

Scott, D. and Gosling, H. (2015) A radical and ambitious approach to women who break the law. Blog post. Available at: www.crimeandjustice.org.uk/resources/radical-and-ambitious-approach-women-who-break-law (last accessed 30 June 2022).

Sentencing Council (2021) Custodial sentences. Available at: www.sentencingcouncil.org.uk/sentencing-and-the-council/types-of-sentence/custodial-sentences (last accessed 30 June 2022).

Sentencing Guidelines (2022) Determinate prison sentences. Available at: www.sentencing-council.org.uk/sentencing-and-the-council/types-of-sentence/determinate-prison-sentences/#:~:text=In%202019%2C%2076%2C000%20offenders%20were,total%20immediate%20custodial%20sentence%20outcomes (last accessed 30 June 2022).

The Sentencing Project (2013) *Private Prisons in the United States*. Available at: www.sentencingproject.org/publications/private-prisons-united-states (last accessed 30 June 2022).

United Nations Office on Drugs and Crime (UNODC) (2020) *Handbook on Classification of Prisoners*. Available at: www.unodc.org/documents/dohadeclaration/Prisons/HandBookPrisonerClassification/20-01921_Classification_of_Prisoners_Ebook.pdf (last accessed 30 June 2022).

6

ORGANISATION AND STRUCTURE OF PROBATION

```
╔════════════ IN THIS CHAPTER, YOU WILL EXPLORE ════════════╗

  1.  How community sentences are defined, legislated and fit into the sentencing framework,
      including mechanisms of accountability and governance in probation work

  2.  The composition of the probation workforce and those subject to its oversight and
      supervision

  3.  The organisational structures for the delivery of the probation service in England and
      Wales and the proposed reorganisation as part of the current probation reforms.

╚═══════════════════════════════════════════════════════════╝
```

INTRODUCTION

As with prisons, which we discussed in the previous chapter, organisational change and restructuring have often been used as mechanisms to influence the aims, ambitions and effectiveness of probation. This chapter therefore encourages you to critically engage with the organisation and structure of contemporary probation in England and Wales taking into account who is on probation, the demographics of the workforce and how its work sits within the sentencing framework. As in the previous chapter, we will discuss the role of regulatory bodies such as HM Inspectorate of Prisons, the Independent Monitoring Boards and the Prisons and Probation Ombudsman, which will help you to understand how and to what extent probation is accountable. We begin our discussion with an exploration of the meaning and purpose of probation.

> ... probation is not a 'thing' to be taken or left but a set of ideas and possibilities to be used creatively and strategically to solve local problems of criminal justice ... [It is] a framework into which locally feasible and desirable solutions may be fitted into. (Harris, 1995: 207)

> There is not a unified notion of what constitutes probation but there are clear indications that almost all probation systems and practices tend to adjust and match developments of time and place in terms of culture, economics, politics and criminal justice philosophies while preserving some key features of its origin and, in virtually all cases, the professional identity and orientation of probation officers. (Klaus, 1998)

As the above quotes suggest, it is difficult to pinpoint precisely what probation work is. The word probation is derived from the Latin term *probatio* meaning a period of testing or proving oneself (House of Common Justice Committee, 2021: 5). When we commence employment, for example, there is often a probationary period during which the individual is able to demonstrate their capability and capacities for the role. In a criminal justice sense, it clearly involves a period of time, either following sentence or a period of imprisonment, in which the individual is expected to demonstrate their motivation and capacity to refrain from offending. However, in professional, academic and public discourses the term is often used ambiguously and can be interpreted as referring to specific organisational/bureaucratic features, a set of values for conducting the supervision of individuals or groups or indeed as a (now defunct) sentence of the court. Durnescu (2008) identified four main types of probation services priorities according to their expressed purposes and mission statements:

1. Promoting the use of community sanctions and measures
2. Assisting judicial decision making
3. Rehabilitation/public protection
4. Punishment or enforcement according to their expressed purposes and mission statements.

Shapland et al. (2012) added three more, focused on the individual's welfare, on victims' interests and on reparation. This is important because what a probation service sees as its purpose will be reflected in measuring the success of its work. Of course, each of these purposes may be pursued in quite different ways, and several of them may be pursued in tandem. The priority given to each of its purposes is likely to vary over time, reflecting changes in penal philosophy. Those who are placed on probation and the offences they commit may also vary from country to country.

As we saw in Chapter 4, our contemporary understandings of what constitutes probation emerged from a number of disparate ideas and initiatives in the 19th century and is implicitly tied up with the sentencing aims of rehabilitation, punishment, deterrence and reparation. As set out in law, probation services have multiple aims, including working with individuals under supervision to help bring about positive changes in their lifestyles, protecting the public through reducing the risk of further offending, addressing the harm caused by the original offence through highlighting the effects of crime on victims, and facilitating appropriate punishment (HM Prison and Probation Service, 2021). These aims are not mutually exclusive and sometimes perhaps conflict. For example, recalling a person to prison might not be perceived by the individual as bringing about a positive change in their lifestyle but it might be necessary in the interests of public protection.

The aims of probation work must also respond to the needs of a range of different stakeholders including, but not exclusively, the individual being supervised, their victims and the wider community. The Target Operating Model (HM Prison and Probation Service, 2021) produced as part of the probation reform programme, provides a model of Assess, Protect and Change to describe how probation work aims to respond to each of these constituencies (see Figure 6.1). *Assess* involves accurately assessing the individual's risks and needs considering any protected characteristics or specific considerations. *Protect* is about managing an individual's risks and needs in conjunction with other relevant agencies and taking appropriate enforcement actions when required. *Change* is about empowering and motivating individuals to make lasting changes by building positive relationships to support their integration into the community.

Probation work is organised and delivered around a number of key tasks that can be undertaken prior to sentence, as part of a court order or following release from a period of imprisonment. Ultimately, probation is responsible for ensuring that the requirements of the court order are met and that appropriate action is taken if they are not complied with. It does this through a range of interventions (see Chapter 10) which it delivers either itself or through referral to a range of external providers.

KEY QUESTIONS TO CONSIDER WHEN READING THIS CHAPTER ARE

1. Is probation able to meet its aims and objectives?

2. Should probation be reserved for those who pose a risk, either to themselves or the wider community?

3. Should probation be publicly funded?

HOW DOES PROBATION FIT INTO THE SENTENCING FRAMEWORK?

The Criminal Justice Act 2003 and Offender Rehabilitation Act 2014 replaced existing court orders with two main sentences:

1. *Community Order* – replaced all pre-Criminal Justice Act community sentences for adults. Under this order, a number of possible requirements must be added, such as supervision, unpaid work and drug treatment

2. *Suspended Sentence Order (SSO) with requirements attached* – this new order was introduced for offences which pass the custody threshold. One or more of the same set of possible requirements must be added to this order.

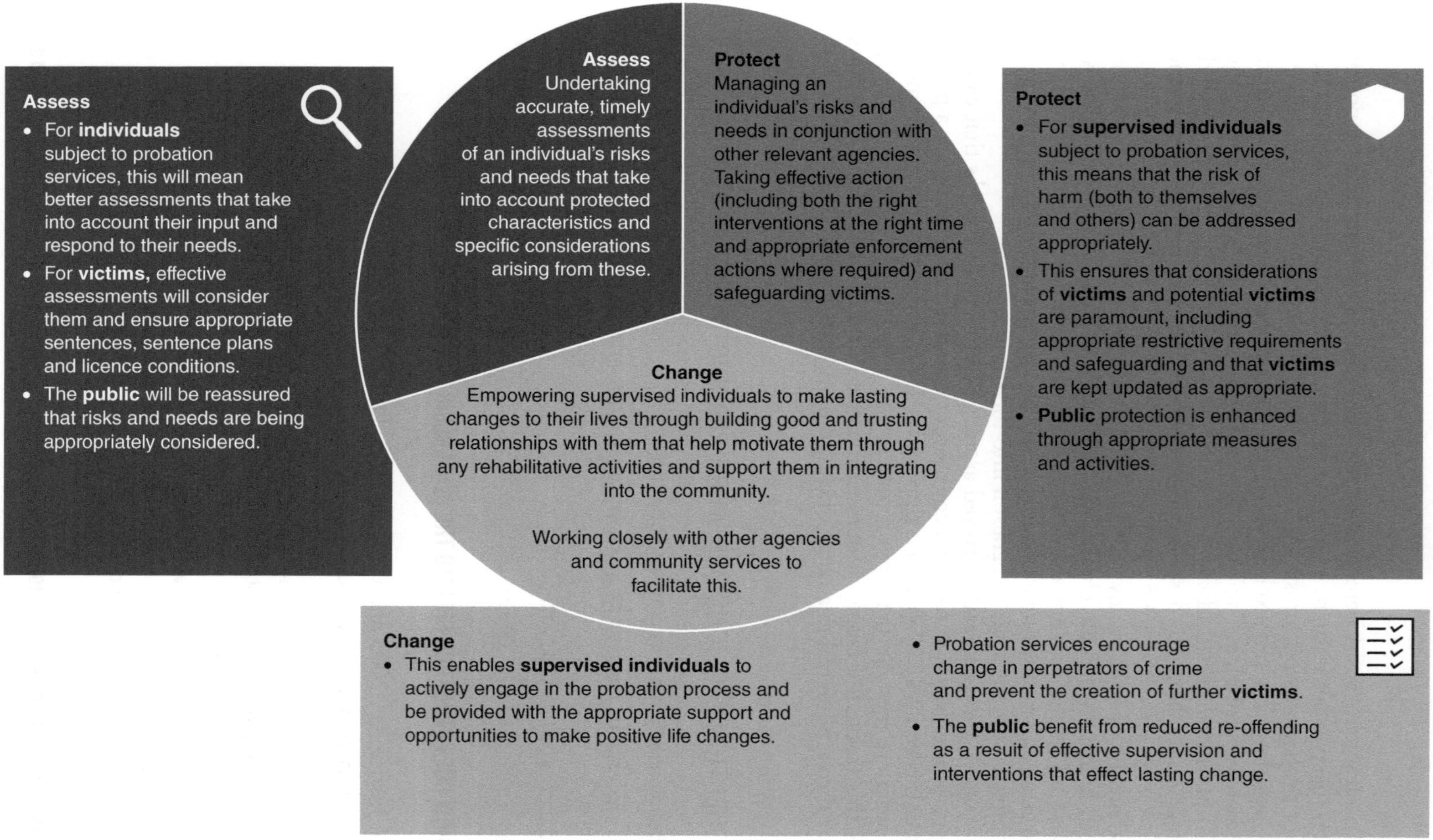

Assess

- For **individuals** subject to probation services, this will mean better assessments that take into account their input and respond to their needs.
- For **victims**, effective assessments will consider them and ensure appropriate sentences, sentence plans and licence conditions.
- The **public** will be reassured that risks and needs are being appropriately considered.

Protect

- For **supervised individuals** subject to probation services, this means that the risk of harm (both to themselves and others) can be addressed appropriately.
- This ensures that considerations of **victims** and potential **victims** are paramount, including appropriate restrictive requirements and safeguarding and that **victims** are kept updated as appropriate.
- **Public** protection is enhanced through appropriate measures and activities.

Assess

Undertaking accurate, timely assessments of an individual's risks and needs that take into account protected characteristics and specific considerations arising from these.

Protect

Managing an individual's risks and needs in conjunction with other relevant agencies. Taking effective action (including both the right interventions at the right time and appropriate enforcement actions where required) and safeguarding victims.

Change

Empowering supervised individuals to make lasting changes to their lives through building good and trusting relationships with them that help motivate them through any rehabilitative activities and support them in integrating into the community.

Working closely with other agencies and community services to facilitate this.

Change

- This enables **supervised individuals** to actively engage in the probation process and be provided with the appropriate support and opportunities to make positive life changes.

- Probation services encourage change in perpetrators of crime and prevent the creation of further **victims**.
- The **public** benefit from reduced re-offending as a result of effective supervision and interventions that effect lasting change.

Figure 6.1 Probation's role to assess, protect and change

(*Source* HM Prison and Probation Service 2021: 7, Available at: https://assets.publishing.service.gov.uk/government/uploads/system/uploads/attachment_data/file/1061047/MOJ7350_HMPPS_Probation_Reform_Programme_TOM_Accessible_English_LR.pdf (last accessed 7 October 2022))

The seriousness of the offence should be the initial factor in determining which requirements to include in a community order (Criminal Justice Act 1991). A community sentence should only be considered when an offence is considered *serious enough* (Criminal Justice Act 2003, section 148) but not *so serious* that only custody can be justified (Criminal Justice Act 2003, section 152). Offence-specific guidelines produced by the Sentencing Council (2016) refer to three sentencing levels – *low, medium,* and *high* – within the community order band, based on the seriousness of the offence. In general, only one requirement will be appropriate in the case of low sentencing levels that only just cross the community order threshold or where the seriousness of the offence or previous convictions means that a discharge or fine is inappropriate. More intensive supervision combining two or more requirements may be appropriate for those offences that only just fall below the custody threshold, or where the custody threshold is crossed but a community order is deemed more appropriate.

Those under supervision must comply with the order of the court or the terms of release from prison on licence. This can include attending regular meetings with probation workers and following other rules – for example, residing at an agreed address or obeying a curfew (to protect the public) or completing other activities designed to reduce the likelihood of them reoffending. For example, courts can order that an individual undertakes a drug or alcohol treatment requirement if satisfied that the individual is dependent on or misuses drugs. Treatment requirements are often delivered in partnership with locally commissioned substance misuse services. There are 12 requirements that can form part of a community order.

1. *Supervision.* This requires the person to attend regular appointments with probation. The goal is to change the person's attitude and behaviour in a bid to stop them reoffending.

2. *Unpaid work.* This can range from 40 to 300 hours, to benefit the local community.

3. Curfew. This stipulates that the individual must remain in an agreed location for specified hours. Curfews are usually electronically monitored via tagging.

4. *Programmes.* These are designed to address and change a perpetrator's behaviour. Programmes are accredited and have been created to tackle attitudes and patterns of behaviour that contribute to offending.

5. *Drug rehabilitation requirement* (DRR). This requires the person to have treatment to address their drug misuse. The DRR can take between six months and three years to complete, and they must provide samples for testing when required.

6. *Alcohol treatment.* In cases where offenders have a drink dependency that causes them to commit a crime, they can be ordered by the court to complete alcohol treatment. This is a tailored programme aiming to reduce dependency on alcohol and can also last between six months and three years.

7. *Attendance centre*. This requires the person to visit the attendance centre for between 12 and 36 hours and is only available for those under 25.

8. *Rehabilitation activity requirement* (RAR). This requires the person to comply with any instructions given by the responsible officer to attend appointments with them (or another person) so as to carry out work to promote their rehabilitation and desistance.

9. *Residence*. The person must reside at a specified address for up to three years, such as an approved premises or a private address.

10. *Mental health treatment*. This is only to be applied with the consent of a person with a conviction and is issued with direction from a doctor or physiologist.

11. *Exclusion*. The person is excluded from entering a particular place or location for a period of up to two years, such as specific shops, properties or streets.

12. *Prohibited activity*. The person must not participate in stipulated activities for a certain period (up to three years), such as not attending a football match.

The requirements will be influenced by a range of factors including the stated purposes of the sentence, the risk of reoffending and the individual's ability to comply. At least one requirement must be imposed for the purpose of punishment and/or a fine imposed in addition to the community order unless there are exceptional circumstances which relate to the offence or the person that would make it unjust in all the circumstances to do so. Thirty-nine per cent of individuals serving a community sentence and 40 per cent serving a suspended sentence are subject to a rehabilitation activity requirement. Unpaid work is the next most common provision. Accredited programmes and treatment orders are much less common (HM Inspectorate of Probation, 2019: 49).

HOW MANY PEOPLE ARE ON PROBATION SUPERVISION?

As of September 2020, there were 222,657 individuals supervised by the Probation Service in England and Wales. The total caseload of people supervised before or after release from prison at the end of September 2020 was 137,035, representing a decrease of 7 per cent compared to the end of September 2019. Offender management statistics (Ministry of Justice, 2020) reveal that the probation caseload fell year on year from 2010 until 2014, reflecting decreases in general crime levels, and subsequently the numbers coming to courts and being sentenced. Caseloads began rising again in 2015 following the Transforming Rehabilitation (TR) reforms, including the introduction of the Offender Rehabilitation Act (ORA), which brought almost all those leaving custody into post-release supervision (see Chapter 10). This considerably increased the number of post-release service users managed by probation in the community, climbing from just under 40,000 on 31 March 2015 to 68,863 on 31 March 2020, a rise of 74 per cent. Overall, the number of service users receiving pre- and post-release supervision has risen by 39 per cent since 2010. Changes have also been seen in relation to the types of cases being supervised. During this period, community sentences in the probation case-load declined by 27 per cent, reflecting the popularity of the suspended sentence order which, while delivered by probation services in the community, is a custodial sentence. These orders have proved popular at the expense of community orders. Those currently supervised under community orders have declined by 31 per cent since 2008, whereas SSOs have remained relatively stable (see Figure 6.2).

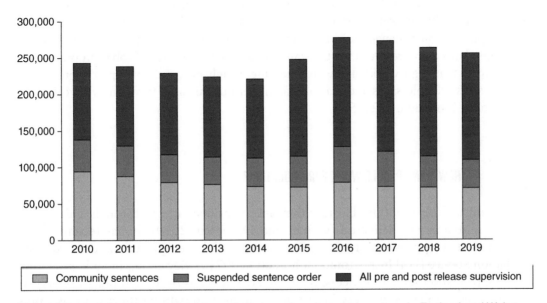

Figure 6.2   Individuals supervised by probation services by sentence type in England and Wales, 2010–2019

(*Source*: HM Inspectorate of Probation 2021: 11, Available at: www.justiceinspectorates.gov.uk/hmiprobation/wp-content/uploads/sites/5/2021/03/Caseloads-and-Workloads-RAB-LL-designed-RM-amends-Mar-21.pdf (last accessed 7 October 2022))

The result of the TR reforms (discussed in Chapter 4) combined with offending and sentencing trends have left probation services with a caseload of service users who have more complex needs, more entrenched offending attitudes, behaviours and lifestyles, and often higher levels of risk than before the ORA was implemented (HM Inspectorate of Probation, 2021: 7). Within the UK, there is no legislation or guidance specifying the ideal or maximum caseload size to be held by a probation worker so it is difficult to put a precise number on what a probation caseload should be. This is because there are too many interconnected variables in relation to case complexity, such as the administrative support available, and the interventions and services that can be accessed. The most recent Council of Europe Annual Penal Statistics found that 'the ratio of probationers per individual staff member varied from 4.7 in Norway to 240 in Greece with an average (median) ratio of 33 cases' (HM Inspectorate of Probation 2021: 7).

However, a recent inspection into probation caseloads, workloads and staffing levels (HM Inspectorate of Probation, 2021: 4) found that when probation practitioners hold a caseload of 50 or more, they are less likely to deliver high-quality work meeting the aims of rehabilitation and public protection. Less than half (46 per cent) of probation practitioners believed they had a manageable workload, while just over half (54 per cent) considered that team workloads were actively managed. Probation officers were less positive about their workload than probation services officers, and those working in community rehabilitation companies (CRCs) were less positive than their NPS counterparts. Senior managers in both the CRCs and the NPS agreed that workloads were unbalanced and resulted in stress and anxiety for many staff. Probation practitioners claimed that high workloads were exacting a high personal toll upon them in the form of stress, sleeplessness and fear of making serious mistakes through overwork (HM Inspector of Probation, 2021: 5).

HOW MANY PEOPLE WORK FOR PROBATION?

Probation staff are important because they are the primary means through which community sentences are delivered (Geiran and Durnescu, 2019). It has recently been estimated that approximately 16,333 workers will be employed in the reunified Probation Service (HM Inspectorate of Probation 2021a). Key grades include probation officers, probation services officers, (collectively known as probation practitioners), as well as senior probation officers. Staff training to be a probation officer work as a probation services officer (PSO), so a proportion of the probation services officers in post will be working towards the professional probation officer qualification. The demographic of the probation workforce has changed significantly in recent years. Whereas men comprised the majority of the service in the post-war period, women now account for approximately 70 per cent of staff (Kirton and Guillaume, 2015). There has also been a sustained growth in the number of (unqualified) probation service officers relative to (qualified) probation officers, with the former comprising approximately 50 per cent of staff by 2012 (Mair, 2016). Probation service officers were introduced as *ancillaries* in the 1970s to assist probation officers in their role, managing generic cases and performing specialist functions like unpaid work. Their training is much shorter, has less academic rigour and is subject to local fluctuations (Gale, 2012). Against a backdrop of rising caseloads, however, the probation service officers' role has gradually expanded to encompass tasks typically performed by probation officers (Tidmarsh, 2020: 104).

Low staffing levels have historically been problematic for probation services. HM Inspectorate of Probation conducted an inspection on the central functions supporting the National Probation Service in January 2020, which found that 60 per cent of probation officers in the NPS were carrying a workload over the 100 per cent target level and some much more. This reflects an ongoing and, in some areas, critical shortage of probation officers. The new operational model for probation (HM Prison and Probation Service, 2021) includes a new *Probation Workforce Programme* committed to increasing the recruitment of probation offices to have a minimum of 1,000 new probation officers in training. HMPPS is also committed to enhancing qualification routes by improving the existing Professional Qualification in Probation (PQiP) and testing an accelerated progression pathway from probation services officer to probation officer launched in 2020/21 (House of Commons Justice Committee, 2021). These measures will not solve the significant shortages of experienced employees that will still be apparent at the point of transition. In her evidence to the House of Commons Justice Committee, the Director General of Probation and Wales admitted that the additional recruitment is designed to bring caseloads down by 20 per cent on average but that it was unlikely to get significantly ahead of demand until 2024–2025 (House of Commons Justice Committee, 2021: 37).

HOW IS THE PROBATION SERVICE ORGANISED AND MANAGED?

As we saw in Chapter 5, probation has existed as a statutory organisation in England and Wales since 1907, operating as a set of area-based services interacting at arms length with central government. It became the National Probation Service in 2001 but in 2004 was subsumed into the newly formed National Offender Management Service following a review by Patrick Carter (2003) who had been asked by the government to explore ways of achieving a better balance between the prison population in England and Wales and the resources available for the correctional services. In May 2007, the correctional services element of the Home Office was moved to join the former Department of Constitutional Affairs in the newly created Ministry of Justice (MoJ). In January 2008, the Secretary of State for Justice announced major organisational reform which resulted in the Director-General of Her Majesty's Prison becoming the chief executive of NOMS and assuming responsibility for the NPS and HM Prison Service and management of contracts for private sector operation of prisons and prisoner escorting. Following this, the chief executive post was reclassified as director-general and NOMS was designated as an executive agency within the Ministry of Justice. In 2017, the then Secretary of State for Justice confirmed that NOMS would be replaced by HMPPS. The NPS delivers services under a service level agreement with Her Majesty's Prison and Probation Service (HMPPS). As outlined in Chapter 5, since 2014 probation services have been divided into the National Probation Service (NPS) and community rehabilitation companies (CRCs). Following the failure of the TR reforms, all responsibility for sentence management will move to the The Probation Service, which will be split into 12 regions across England and one for Wales with boundaries aligned to those of the police force and local authority areas. The National Probation Service will undertake all sentence management functions, advice to court, victim support and delivery of definable interventions (unpaid work, accredited programmes and structured interventions). Northern Ireland will continue to have its own probation service, whilst in Scotland criminal justice social workers are managed within the social work departments of local authorities.

An HMPPS regional probation director will oversee each region to provide strategic leadership in line with the overarching strategic direction of the HMPPS and be responsible for the overall delivery and commissioning of probation services. In England, they will report into the wider HMPPS structure and be line managed by the chief probation officer. In Wales, the regional probation director will report into the executive director for HMPPS in Wales who has responsibility for all probation services and prisons in Wales. Leadership in both England and Wales will be ultimately brought together under the director general for probation (HM Prison and Probation Service, 2021: 140). Each regional probation director in England and Wales will be supported by a senior leadership team that brings together responsibility for operational and intervention delivery, commissioning and contract management of specialist rehabilitative and resettlement support and operational support services that support front-line delivery (HM Prison and Probation Service, 2021: 140). Within the regions, operational delivery has been reorganised into 108 probation delivery units (PDU), each managed by a head of PDU with the most complex PDUs supported by a deputy head. The boundaries of the PDUs have been developed to align with upper tier and unitary local authority boundaries. At this level, teams will undertake supervision of all individuals and ensure that public sector local responsibilities (such as victim liaison and local adult and child safeguarding responsibilities) are discharged.

The new model of probation was implemented in June 2021 although it was not intended to be fully embedded until 2022 onwards. A Target Operating Model (HM Prison and Probation Service 2021) for unified probation delivery was published in February 2021 to provide clarity on how all elements of probation work are to be delivered and set out longer-term ambitions to reform and transform probation services by 2024. The Target Operating Model makes clear that it is not an expectation that all of the operating model will be fully functional from the end of June 2021, but rather that it will be implemented over the course of the next few years in a three- stage approach described as 'installed, stabilised and transformed'. New national probation standards were published in conjunction with the Target Operating Model and are mandated for use from day one of the unified service. The new standards are focused on outcomes, rather than process or input, and concentrate on how staff work with service users in the community and those serving custodial sentences. The aim of the standards is to drive up levels of quality and consistency during the period of transition and stabilisation (HM Inspectorate of Probation 2021b: 18).

New national standards for probation work were published alongside the Target Operating Model. These include face-to-face monthly meetings for supervised individuals and the probation practitioner. This is the absolute minimum and cases should be managed at levels appropriate to risk and need (HM Inspectorate of Probation, 2021b: 63). Post-sentence supervision cases will be excluded from the minimum monthly face-to-face contact requirement, given that its sole focus is rehabilitation. Where cases are assessed as low risk and rehabilitative needs have been addressed, a process will be put in place whereby the probation practitioner may refer to their line manager for suspension of face-to-face contact with oversight undertaken by telephone contact (HM Inspectorate of Probation, 2021b: 64).

GOVERNANCE AND ACCOUNTABILITY

HM Inspectorate of Probation

As a public service, probation has to be accountable in terms of both the services it delivers and meeting performance measures set by government. There are a number of mechanisms used to ensure this such as standards, service level agreements, good practice guidance, probation instructions and external inspections. HM Inspectorate of Probation has been an important commentator on contemporary probation practice and its former chief inspector, Dame Glenys Stacey, was a critical voice in highlighting the shortfalls of the TR reforms and encouraging the government to reverse the policy. Founded in 1936, HM Inspectorate of Probation was put on a statutory basis by the Criminal Justice Act 1991. The Criminal Justice and Court Services Act 2000 provided the Secretary of State with further powers to appoint inspectors and to provide them in turn with the powers of inspection. HM Chief Inspector of Probation's responsibilities are set out in section 7 of the Criminal Justice and Court Services Act 2000, as amended by the Offender Management Act (2007), section 12(3)(a). This requires the Chief Inspector to inspect (section 1) and report to the Secretary of State (section 3) on the arrangements for the provision of probation services.

The Inspectorate's main functions are to assess the effectiveness of probation work, identify and disseminate best practice, challenge poor performance and make recommendations as to improvements needed. Each probation provider is inspected annually and inspections are announced well in advance so that the inspectors, in conjunction with the service being inspected, can identify a sample of cases to be inspected, collate evidence and schedule the inspection. During the fieldwork a team of inspectors will visit probation offices and meet with probation staff and sometimes service users also.

The case files of those selected are examined and information provided to the lead inspector who will compile a report on completion of the inspection. After the report is published, probation services are required to liaise with HMPPS to agree a draft action plan that addresses the recommendations made.

All services are rated overall as *Outstanding, Good, Requires improvement* or *Inadequate* as well as being rated at the level of individual standards. The Inspectorate also provides thematic reports on specific aspects of probation practice. For example, the Inspectorate has recently reviewed the preparations made for the unification of probation services, race equality in probation and the impact of the exceptional delivery model introduced by probation in response to the COVID-19 pandemic. Following a thematic review of serious further offences committed by individuals who had recently been under the supervision of probation at the time of the offence (HM Inspectorate of Probation, 2020), the Secretary of State asked the Inspectorate to take on a new quality assurance process. As a result, the Inspectorate will examine and rate a sample (approximately 20 per cent) of serious further offences and convene multi-agency learning panels to bring together agencies involved in specific cases to improve practice and strengthen partnership working. However, as Badachha et al. (2022) observe, although the inspectorate undoubtedly plays an important role within probation work given its ability to influence probation policy and practice, there is limited evidence as to whether it actually changes things on the ground.

Her Majesty's Prisons and Probation Ombudsman

In 2001 Her Majesty's Prisons Ombudsman's remit was extended to include complaints from those under probation supervision. The office was renamed the Prisons and Probation Ombudsman to reflect this change. A further extension in 2006 incorporated complaints from those in immigration detention centres. The Prisons and Probation Ombudsman (PPO) is appointed by and reports directly to the Secretary of State for Justice. The Ombudsman's office is wholly independent of the services within its remit, which include those provided by Her Majesty's Prison and Probation Service (HMPPS), the National Probation Service for England and Wales, the Youth Justice Board for England and Wales, and those local authorities with secure children's homes. It is also operationally independent of, but sponsored by, the Ministry of Justice (MoJ). The Prisons and Probation Ombudsman's main investigative duties relating to probation work include investigating complaints made by individuals under probation supervision, deaths of residents in approved premises and the postholder also has discretionary powers to investigate deaths of recently released prisoners or detainees. In 2019/20 the Prisons and Probation Ombudsman received 4,686 complaints of which 294 were about probation services.

The number of deaths of people on probation caseloads has increased steadily in the eight years from 2010 and self-inflicted deaths are overrepresented in the probation caseload. This rate is even higher among women (Phillips, 2020: 66). There were 955 deaths of people on the probation caseload in the year 2017/18 with around one-third being self-inflicted (one-third of deaths were as a result of a 'natural' cause and the remaining third are recorded as unknown cause) (Ministry of Justice, 2018). There were 17 deaths of residents living in probation approved premises (Prisons and Probation Ombudsman, 2020). Pluck and Brooker (2014) found that in one probation area of England more than 30 per cent of probation service users reported having attempted suicide at some time in their life (Borrill et al., 2017: 7). People on probation are 8.67 times more likely to die by suicide than people in the general population and 1.42 times more likely to die by suicide than people in prison (Phillips et al., 2018).

A study by Borrill et al. (2016) found that probation individuals who died by suicide often experienced multiple interrelated stressors in the lead-up to their deaths, making it unsurprising that they had begun to struggle to meet the legal requirements of their sentences. However, in comparison with prisons, service users in the community who took their own lives were not considered to pose a high risk of reoffending or causing serious harm to others (although a number of index offences were categorised as violent) (Borrill et al., 2017: 14). Warning and breach processes could be a potential stressor for suicidal action when coupled with other personal or situational vulnerabilities (Borrill et al., 2017: 16). Some individuals also had a range of different requirements associated with their sentence, which involved appointments with a range of different organisations or individuals. In several cases, last minute changes to appointments appeared to reveal how an apparently small change in supervision arrangements could have a knock-on effect on other commitments in service users' lives, sometimes contributing to already heightened stress (Borrill et al. 2017: 15). The findings highlighted the importance of consistency in staff when forming positive relationships with probation service users, as a change in relationships or routines may contribute to distress. This finding highlights the protective role that the supervisory relationship can play in both assessing and managing the risk of suicide in vulnerable service users (Borrill et al. 2017: 16).

The European Probation Rules

The European Probation Rules were developed by the Council of Europe and are grounded in the European Convention on Human Rights (Canton, 2019: 5). The rules set out basic principles for probation agencies and services, drawing out the implications for organisation, policy and practice. They cover the organisation of probation services, the tasks and responsibilities involved in probation work, the processes of supervision, work with victims of crime, complaints procedures, inspection and monitoring, research and evaluation, and relations with the media and the public. The rules are recommendations and nation states are not legally required to adhere to them, and as Canton (2019) observes, they are not as well known as they should be in England and Wales. The European Probation Rules have been criticised for failing to make a discernible difference in some countries, particularly those with well-established systems, but most countries have found them a useful benchmark for informing national standards and criteria for inspection (Canton, 2019).

WHAT IS INVOLVED IN PROBATION WORK?

When most people think of probation they think of a person sitting in a probation office talking to a probation officer. This is certainly true in the sense that the probation order has traditionally been seen as the most influential tool in probation's toolbox. However, what is less understood is the range of interventions delivered and the different settings in which what we could broadly define as probation work is undertaken. These are discussed in more detail in Chapter 10. Ultimately, probation practitioners work with individuals to rehabilitate and reduce their reoffending whilst at the same time protect the public from the harms of offending. Both of these approaches are incorporated into the concept of supervision. Supervision is the core responsibility of the probation practitioner, who oversees and is responsible for the effective delivery of the sentence of the court. The practitioner needs to build a positive relationship that can balance care with control to support desistance and prevent further victims of crime. The importance of this supervisor/supervisee relationship is a constant theme in probation research (see, for example, Burnett and McNeill, 2005; King, 2013; Rex, 1999). Commonalities that exist within many accounts of the relationship aspect of desistance interventions suggest that talking and listening are fundamental aspects of probation work, both as a method of dealing with particular problems and as a means of nurturing the relationship necessary to enable probationers to be receptive to more direct guidance (King, 2013: 138). Evidence points to the importance of the relational aspects of practice for outcomes such as desistance, compliance and legitimacy (McNeill and Weaver, 2010; Robinson and McNeill, 2008; Ugwudike, 2010).

Meeting the needs of those under supervision, promoting their social inclusion and enhancing community safety require a range of support provided by a number of agencies and so, understandably, collaborative working has become 'part of the cultural fabric of probation practice in England and Wales' (Robinson et al., 2014). Such work brings probation into contact with the public, private and voluntary sectors, the media and the public. The quality of joint work depends 'on a combination of effective administrative processes, adequate information technology, facilitating organisational cultures and amenable staff (Dominey, 2019: 289). According to Senior et al. (2016) the world of probation also operates in and around four major systems of social organisation – the correctional system, the social welfare system, the treatment system and the community.

The interactions between these four social systems will vary over time, place and jurisdiction and will invariably be subject to debate and disputes.

In the correctional world, probation has an important role in terms of enforcing court orders, risk management and public protection. In the social welfare world, it provides a brokerage role with a range of employment services and accommodation providers and the direct provision of approved premises. Brokerage entails recognising that aspects of change sometimes need to be supported by other organisations and by other people and that probation practitioners can use their skills to promote the engagement of others. In the treatment world, it delivers accredited programmes and signposts individuals to a range of non-accredited programmes. In the community, dealing with an individual court order takes place in the community where the individual resides and operates within the nexus of family and community relationships through which they engage (Bottoms, 2008). This can include restorative justice, community engagement and reparative measures such as unpaid work. In practice such systems overlap both in terms of their purposes and the spaces they occupy but also because of the multiple needs of many of those subject to probation supervision. However, navigating these different systems can be challenging and can 'contribute to isolating individuals who need access to multiple systems but for whom their lesser eligible status makes it problematic for them to get reasonable help' (Senior et al., 2016: 13). As Dominey (2019: 291) observes, the interplay between probation supervision and the wider community is complex. Whilst the community can be a source of resources and opportunities that can support desistance (see Chapter 2) probation practitioners can lack the time or the skill needed to engage with informal networks and develop social capital. In addition, communities which are fragile because of economic disadvantage, rapid social change and declining cohesion and trust offer fewer options for those already facing multiple disadvantages

SENTENCE MANAGEMENT AND DELIVERY

Supervision is a complex process because the needs of those being supervised are complex and even though many of those caught up in the criminal justice system experience common challenges and problems (such as drug dependency, unstable backgrounds and restricted opportunities), their journeys towards non-offending are individual to them. As Reed and Dominey (2020) note, this means that 'the shape of the supervisory relationship needs to be different on every occasion, reflecting the differences between the people involved and the shifting dynamics of motivation, need and power'. As such there is no single unified model that can be applied to all (Smith et al., 2018: 409) although HM Inspectorate has helpfully drawn the evidence on good practice from a range of research areas on desistance, supervision skills and procedural justice (HM Inspectorate of Probation, 2021a). These are: a) establish a positive trusting relationship, b) meet urgent needs, c) use structured supervision, d) work with the the service user to establish goals and solutions, e) build social capital, and f) build and maintain motivation.

Contemporary probation practice is based upon the ASPIRE model of case supervision (see Figure 6.3). ASPIRE stands for assessment, sentence planning, implementation, review and evaluation. This is a cyclical process reflecting the gradual, non-linear and multidimensional nature of desistance, which is often characterised by 'ambivalence and vacillation' (McNeill, 2009: 31), and so careful consideration needs to be given to how relapses are dealt with. Service users have highlighted the importance of each stage of the ASPIRE process involving real collaboration and co-production. The desistance literature also emphasises the need for assessment to pay attention to the individual's legitimate aspirations and to identify and develop personal strengths and skills and not just their offending behaviour.

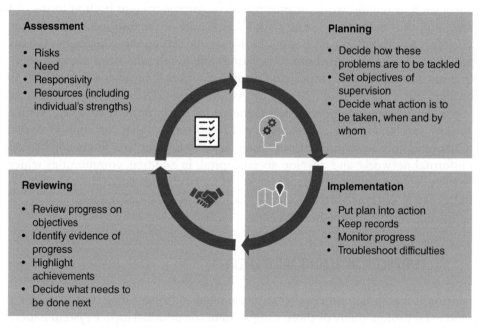

Figure 6.3 The ASPIRE model of case supervision

(*Source*: HM Inspectorate of Probation. Available at: www.justiceinspectorates.gov.uk/hmiprobation/effective-practice/case-supervision (last accessed 7 October 2022))

The first stage of the process involves preparation and information gathering. A diverse range of sources of information should be utilised, including court reports, previous records and, in appropriate cases, information gained from other agencies or people who know the service user. Establishing motivation is a key factor in enabling positive change.

AN INTRODUCTION TO PENOLOGY

However, motivation alone may not be sufficient and so a key role for practitioners is to help individuals identify potential and actual obstacles and develop the confidence and ability to take the necessary steps to overcome them. Traditionally, assessment used to be undertaken in a manner that depended on the skills, experience and *diagnostic* judgement of individual practitioners – an approach commonly referred to in the literature as *clinical* or *person-by-person* assessment. This approach relies on the practitioner's skills, experience and judgement, and whilst these are undoubtedly important, there is also the danger that they can lead to error and bias, stereotypical assumptions and discriminatory practices. The complexity of contemporary risk management has required a more systematic and rigorous approach. Assessment instruments that have been developed to guide the practitioner to identify certain variables or risk markers that are known to be correlated with offending and to explore the significance of a specified variety of associated needs are now widely used. The principle (and the arithmetic) are very much like those used by insurance companies to assess the risk that you will be involved in a motoring accident, which in turn sets the premium to be paid. There are a number of technical requirements for assessment tools – they should be reliable (consistent between assessors), valid (identifying the most relevant risks and needs), sensitive (to change), and predictive (of future reoffending) (HM Inspectorate of Probation, 2021c). There have been four broad historical waves of assessment types within probation practice (HM Inspectorate of Probation, 2021c):

- *First generation* (1900–1970s). Assessment was based upon unstructured practitioner judgement. The unstructured approach has been found to be of relatively poor predictive value, being subject to biases and inconsistency. As such, this approach can lead to poor planning and implementation of interventions

- *Second generation* (1970s–1990s). Assessment uses actuarial scales. These match the characteristics of an individual against an extensive database to determine the statistical likelihood of reconviction The actuarial approach is data driven and can perform well in terms of predictive validity. However, most actuarial approaches do not indicate the nature, severity and imminence of reoffending nor predict levels of risk after treatment.

- *Third generation* (1990s–2000s). Tools incorporate dynamic risk assessment. Factors amenable to change such as lifestyle, employment, accommodation, attitudes, cognitive deficits, self-regulation and behaviours are considered. This more holistic, personalised and analytical approach to assessment, alongside actuarial predictors, helps with sentence planning and selecting appropriate interventions.

- *Fourth generation* (current). Assessment tools are more systematic and comprehensive. They are explicitly founded upon the Risk-Need-Responsivity (RNR) principles. The tools integrate elements of case management, such as intervention planning and implementation along with monitoring and review. This approach typically involves targeting the criminogenic needs of individuals and treatment, which, for cognitive elements, often uses cognitive behavioural therapy. This can lead to modest reductions in reoffending, especially when interventions are rigorously implemented and combined with support in solving practical problems.

Nowadays, a plethora of assessment tools are available, reflecting the diversity of offending and service users. There are general assessment tools and specialist ones (such as for those convicted of sexual offences or domestic violence, for extremists or for individuals with various forms of mental illness or learning disability). There are also general psychological assessment tools in use in criminal justice settings. The main probation assessment tool currently in use in England and Wales is the Offender Assessment System (OASys), which was initially developed in 2001, building upon the What works evidence base. OASys provides a standardised assessment of the needs and risks of service users which, once identified, can be used to develop and deliver sentence plans. Within OASys, the following eight factors are scored as criminogenic needs: accommodation; education, training and employment; relationships; lifestyle; drugs misuse; alcohol misuse; thinking and behaviour; and attitudes.

There now seems to be a consensus that assessments based on actuarial methods are significantly more accurate than clinical ones (Andrews and Bonta, 2010). However, such tools and approaches have not been without criticism. Canton (2013: 72), for example, argues that assessment tools cannot hope to capture the indefinite ways in which people and their circumstances differ. Whilst they can help predict which *group* or *type* of person might reoffend they cannot identify which individuals within these populations will go on to reoffend (Kewley and Brereton (2022). Assessment instruments have been seen to be gendered and fail to accommodate diversity. As females' offending and crime-related needs are different from males', their pathways to desistance may not be assumed to be the same (Barr, 2019; Corston, 2007). Risk assessment cannot ever be an exact science. Whilst actuarial tools are significantly more accurate than clinical ones, they tend to be more successful at predicting reconviction than serious harm. This is because violent behaviour is often dependent on a range of circumstances and events that may be in themselves hard to predict. Professional relationships are therefore a large part of effective risk management. Supervision is not primarily a surveillance and crime control process, but a framework of support. Monitoring depends centrally on the maintenance of a relationship, with every effort being made to achieve cooperation, openness and trust.

A single sentence plan will be drawn up after a thorough assessment is made. Resources and interventions, commissioned and purchased by the regional director, are engaged, using a brokerage approach. As McNeill and Weaver (2010: 15) note, 'offender management services retain an important role in advocating for offenders so that they can access the social goods and resources which so often they have been denied'. Interventions are the activities and resources needed to deliver specific requirements as part of the sentence (see Chapter 10). In this respect, supervision provides the context in which the interventions fit and evidence suggests that supervision should help individuals 'overcome practical obstacles to desistance such as drug misuse. Intensive supervision programmes which emphasise control over support may not work, whilst those which combine support with sanctions are more successful' (HM Inspectorate of Probation, 2019: 30).

The planning process involves setting out what is to be done about the needs identified and how to develop and utilise the service user's personal strengths and skills. This involves 'the development and continuous review of strategies for change' (McNeill, 2009: 34). At the planning stage, practitioners need a good understanding of the resources and services available, with other agencies being involved where necessary to assist with the necessary joining up. The service user may have multiple complex needs and may require 'interventions that work in a variety of ways to address a variety of issues' (McNeill, 2009: 34). Plans should be drawn up in collaboration with the person being supervised. A person under supervision will, however, almost certainly disengage if they feel that a plan is not realistic or achievable. Plans may therefore need to be broken down into a smaller number of *steps* with realistic, short-term objectives that are specific and measurable, so that progress can be monitored as part of the reviewing process. Practitioners should thus make efforts to engage the service user as an active participant and help them to set goals. Where they may have misgivings about some of the plans proposed, especially when they include interventions designed to minimise the risk of harm to other people, this should be acknowledged and considered. Ideally the individual should be aware of the plans and should be actively involved in monitoring and managing their own risk. However, in some situations, aspects of the plan cannot appropriately be shared with the individual as they may deny the risk they present or may not wish to engage. In these circumstances, there should still be a proportionate, defensible and recorded plan to manage the risk.

There should be a strong and natural connection between planning and implementation, maintaining a personalised approach which fully engages the service user. Research studies indicate that desistance from crime is more likely where the delivery of services is consistent and integrated, and learning consolidated. In order to do this the practitioner must employ a range of both relationship and structuring skills. Helping the individual overcome practical obstacles to desistance may be a necessary first step in establishing stability so that work can be effectively undertaken to address additional needs (see discussion of recovery capital in Chapter 2). Practitioners need to maintain a balance between encouragement and *pushing*, with due regard to the individual's autonomy and agency. Wherever possible, practitioners should act as positive and motivating role models for those being supervised, use natural opportunities to demonstrate thinking and behavioural skills, and work with service users to seek out solutions through problem-solving advice. Attention should be given to promoting compliance. This includes both helping the person to recognise the positive changes and benefits from desistance and taking full account of personal circumstances that might make compliance more difficult, and working with the service user to overcome such difficulties. The consequences of non-compliance should be explained to the person. Instances of non-compliance and relapse should be dealt with in a proportionate, fair and transparent manner. After enforcement action, re-engaging constructively with the service user is vital to avoid a negative cycle of repeated failure to comply.

Reviewing progress towards objectives is another integral part of case supervision. Practitioners also need to take account of fresh information and unexpected events, recognising that a service user's risks, needs, protective factors and circumstances can change over time, and that lapses and relapses are not uncommon, particularly for those involved in persistent offending. Reviewing progress should be well informed, analytical and personalised. The process should be used to analyse new information (including information from other practitioners and agencies), verify changes in behaviour, adapt or change actions that are completed or no longer appropriate, and re-explore the full range of available resources. Any changes in risks, needs and strengths and/or new obstacles to compliance and engagement should be identified and discussed, with appropriate strategies developed. Progress and achievements should be recognised and celebrated (Maruna, 2011). Research findings from OASys and elsewhere indicate that reviewing assessments can improve prediction of reoffending by keeping dynamic risk factors up to date, providing an evidence-based mechanism for changes in the delivery of services for individual service users. As with the earlier stages of the ASPIRE process, the service user should be meaningfully involved wherever possible, reviewing plans in collaboration, re-evaluating goals and developing solutions, helping them to take further charge of their own lives.

COMPLIANCE AND ENFORCEMENT

Those subject to community sentences are *involuntary* (Trotter, 2006) in the sense that they are obliged to do so by the courts rather than they themselves freely seeking help and guidance. Community sentences also require them to keep appointments as instructed and to participate in (or refrain from) activities which they might otherwise choose not to do (Canton and Dominey, 2018). On the other hand, probation cannot achieve its intentions unless the individual attends and participates, and a failure to enforce requirements can undermine the validity of the sanction in the eyes of sentencers, politicians and the public. Moreover, studies suggest that there is a link between non-compliance and an increased risk of reoffending (Ugwudike and Phillips, 2020: 870). Probation practitioners must therefore enforce supervision requirements according to a statutory enforcement framework. This includes issuing warning letters for failure to comply and instigating breach proceedings through the courts within a clearly specified timeframe in line with national requirements at the time. As Geiran and Durnescu (2019) note, it is important to balance the competing issues of consistency and fairness with individual circumstances and needs. The combination of greater demands and more rigorous enforcement is therefore likely to entail more breach proceedings and, at least potentially, larger numbers of people sent to prison in response. Indeed, it has been estimated that around a quarter of those in prison are for failing to comply with their community sentence.

According to Canton and Dominey (2018) there are a number of factors that can affect an individual's willingness to change and these in turn can affect their motivation to engage with probation. Some behaviour is entrenched and difficult to change even when the risks and costs are well known (much addictive behaviour is of this type). Rewards are often immediate and costs far off and difficult to calculate. The person may lack the positive support and long-term rewards to maintain the change. The *incentive situation* of getting caught and imprisoned may not last and individuals may revert to problematic behaviours on release. They may not believe they can change or that they have the skills and resources to achieve this. However, as Geiran and Durnescu (2019) note, there is no absolute resistance and there is no absolute participation. In practice, the person's motivation to participate in the supervision process can be placed on a continuum from involuntary to voluntary participation. Moreover, this motivation is often fluid and therefore can change depending on some personal or social events in the life of the individual. Re-engaging constructively in a proportionate, fair and transparent manner with the person after non-compliance is therefore vital to avoid a negative cycle of repeated failure to comply.

Resistance can be seen as part and parcel of probation work and there have been attempts to help us understand why individuals comply. Anthony Bottoms (2013) identified several dimensions to compliance. He differentiated between what he termed 'instrumental compliance' (related to incentives and disincentives) and 'normative compliance' (related to beliefs and attachments). Normative compliance is closely tied to the concept of legitimacy. Research indicates that people are most likely to be engaged with and accepting of the outcomes of a process if they believe it to be both fair and legitimate and as McNeill (2009: 37) observes, 'the best developed approach to securing compliance will fail unless organisational arrangements exist that underpin the worker's legitimate authority'. Bottoms distinguishes constraint-based compliance (mechanisms that restrict the individual) and compliance based on habit and routine. However, as Canton and Dominey (2018) point out, in reality the different forms of compliance identified by Bottoms are mutually reinforcing. Employment, for example, makes a difference to habits and routines and lifestyles, but also brings informal social controls with both constraint and normative implications. This calls for what Bottoms (2013) describes as a creative mixing of constraint-based mechanisms to achieve compliance.

Robinson and McNeill (2008) developed Bottoms' model by distinguishing between short-term *formal* or technical compliance and more lasting *substantive* compliance. The former is the act of complying with the minimum requirements of a court order (i.e. attending appointments but not fully engaging with the objectives of the order). In contrast, substantive involves a positive attempt to change attitudes or improve circumstances. Models of change such as Risk-Needs-Responsivity, desistance and the Good Lives Model all aim to build substantive compliance in the sense that people refrain from offending because they come to see it to be wrong and to have no place in their self-identity (see Chapter 2).

Irwin-Rogers (2017) has recently developed a theoretical framework based on the concept of legitimacy, designed to promote a better understanding of the dynamics of supervisory relationships. The framework distinguishes between legitimacy based on procedures and legitimacy based on outcomes, arguing that supervisors are most likely to make a positive contribution to the achievement of these outcomes when they focus on establishing and maintaining a good level of procedure-based legitimacy. This is because procedure-based legitimacy facilitates constructive relationships, which, in turn, give supervisors many opportunities to work towards desirable outcomes, whereas poor quality relationships do not. 'The implications for policy and practice are clear: a narrow focus on outcomes is likely to be counterproductive. Instead, a focus should be placed on developing and implementing policies and practices that will enhance the procedure-based legitimacy of supervisors' (Irwin-Rogers 2017: 68).

As Canton and Dominey suggest, the challenge in practice is to make these different aspects of compliance work together. Contemporary enforcement policy has tended to limit itself by concentrating on the single, instrumental dimension of threat, even though there is little evidence that making probation tougher results in positive outcomes in terms of compliance. Ugwudike's (2008) study found that compliance primarily stemmed from the actions of practitioners in managing practical obstacles to attendance. Where individuals complied, they attributed it mostly to the positive benefits of the supervision provided rather than threats of recall.

CONCLUSION

In this chapter we initially considered the official purposes of probation and how they differ in different jurisdictions before outlining how this is conceptualised in the current probation reform programme in England and Wales. We then looked at how probation fits into the sentencing framework and the range of requirements that the courts can impose in community orders and recent trends in their usage. This led us to consider how probation is organised and managed and how many people work in the organisation. We outlined the new organisational structures introduced in 2021 following the failure of the TR policy. We also explored issues of accountability and governance focusing specifically on the role of HM Inspectorate of Probation and the Prisons and Probation Ombudsman in ensuring this. Of particular concern were the number of deaths of people under probation supervision, which we also covered in this section. We then looked at what probation work involves and how this is enacted in a range of different settings before focusing on sentence management and delivery and the nature of compliance and enforcement.

recommended reading

If you would like to engage in further reading, you may find the following resources particularly useful:

Gelsthorpe, L. and Morgan, R. (2007) *Handbook of Probation*. Cullompton: Willan.

Part 1 of this edited collection has a number of contributions that outline the story of probation in England and Wales prior to the Transforming Rehabilitation (TR) reforms.

McNeill, F. and Beyens, K. (2013) *Offender Supervision in Europe*. Basingstoke: Palgrave.

Drawing on the findings from a European research network spanning 20 countries, this book provides the first comprehensive review of research on offender supervision in Europe.

Vanstone, M. and Priestley, P. (2016) *Probation and Politics*. London: Palgrave Macmillan.

This book is a collection of essays by former probation practitioners who address the history of probation, its underlying values and working methods, and the way in which it has been systematically dismantled by successive political administrations. It makes a compelling case for the reinstatement of an evidence-based probation service as the primary criminal justice agency concerned with helping people who come before the courts to be contributing citizens.

references

Andrews, D.A. and Bonta, J. (2010) *The Psychology of Criminal Conduct* (5th edn), Abingdon, Oxon: Routledge.

Badachha, S., Moore, R. and Phillips, J. (2022) Reimagining probation practice indirectly: How the work of the inspectorate can support a reimagined probatiom. In L. Burke, N. Carr, E. Cluley, S. Collett and F. McNeill (eds) *Reimagining Probation Practice: Re-forming Rehabilitation in an Age of Penal Excess*. Abingdon: Routledge.

Barr, U. (2019) *Desisting Sisters: Gender Power and Desistance in the Criminal (In)Justice System*. Palgrave Macmillan.

Borrill, J., Cook, L. and A. Beck (2017) Suicide and supervision: Issues for probation practice. *Probation Journal*, 64(1), 6–19.

Bottoms, A. (2008) The community dimension of community penalties. *Howard Journal of Criminal Justice*, 47(2), 146–69.

Bottoms, A. (2013) Compliance and community penalties. In A. Bottoms, L. Gelsthorpe and S. Rex (eds) *Community Penalties*. Abingdon, Oxon: Routledge.

Burnett, R. and McNeill, F. (2005) The place of the officer–offender relationship in assisting offenders to desist from crime. *Probation Journal*, 52(3), 221–42.

Canton, R. (2013) The European Probation Rules: assessment and risk. *EuroVista*, 3(2), 68–88.

Canton, R. (2019) *European Probation Rules*. HM Inspectorate of Probation Academic Insights 2019/02. Manchester: HM Inspectorate of Probation.

Canton, R. and Dominey, J. (2018) *Probation*. (2nd edn). Abingdon, Oxon: Routledge.

Carter, P. (2003) *Managing Offenders, Reducing Crime: A New Approach*. London: Home Office.

Corston, J. (2007) *The Corston Report: A Review of Women with Particular Vulnerabilities in the Criminal Justice System*. London: Home Office. Available at: https://webarchive. nationalarchives.gov.uk/ukgwa/20130128112038/http://www.justice.gov.uk/publica-tions/docs/corston-report-march-2007.pdf (last accessed 30 June 2022).

Dominey, J. (2019) Probation supervision as a network of relationships: Aiming to be thick, not thin. *Probation Journal*, 66(3): 283–302.

Durnescu, I. (2008) An exploration of the purposes and outcomes of probation in Europe. *Probation Journal*, 55(3), 273–81.

Gale, J. (2012) Government reforms, performance management and the labour process: The case of officers in the UK probation service. *Work, Employment and Society*, 26(5), 822–38.

Geiran, V. and Durnescu, I. (2019) *Implementing Community Sanctions and Measures*. Council of Europe Guidelines. Available at: https://rm.coe.int/implementing-community-sanctions-and-measures/1680995098 (last accessed 2 July 2021).

Harris, R. (1995) Reflections on comparative probation. In K. Hamai, R. Ville, R. Harris, M. Hough and U. Zvekic (eds) *Probation Round the World: A Comparative Study*. London and New York: Routledge.

HM Inspectorate of Probation (2019) *Report of the Chief Inspector of Probation*. Manchester: HM Inspectorate of Probation.

HM Inspectorate of Probation (2020) *A Thematic Inspection of Serious Further Offences (SFO) Investigations and Review Processes*. Manchester: HM Inspectorate of Probation.

HM Inspectorate of Probation (2021) *Caseloads, Workloads and Staffing Levels in Probation Services*. Research & Analysis Bulletin 2021/02. Manchester: HM Inspectorate of Probation.

HM Inspectorate of Probation (2021a) *EEffective Practice Guide: Models and Principles*. Manchester: HM Inspectorate of Probation. Available at: www.justiceinspectorates.gov. uk/hmiprobation/research/the-evidence-base-probation/models-and-principles (last accessed 3 July 2021).

HM Inspectorate of Probation (2021b) *A Thematic Review of Work to Prepare for the Unification of Probation Services*. Manchester: HM Inspectorate of Probation.

HM Inspectorate of Probation (2021c) *Effective Practice Guide: Assessment*. **Error! Hyperlink reference not valid.** (last accessed 30 June 2022). Manchester: HM Inspectorate of Probation.

HM Prison and Probation Service (2021) *The Target Operating Model for Probation Services in England and Wales: Probation Reform Programme*. London: HM Prison and Probation Service.

House of Commons Justice Committee (2021) *The Future of the Probation Service: Eighteenth Report of Session 2019–21*. HC 285. House of Commons Justice Committee 2021.

Irwin-Rogers, K. (2017) Legitimacy on licence: Why and how it matters. *The Howard Journal of Crime and Justice*, 56(1), 53–71.

Kewley, S. and Brereton, S. (2022) Public protection. In L. Burke, N. Carr, E. Cluley, S. Collett and F. McNeill (eds) *Reimagining Probation Practice: Re-forming Rehabilitation in an Age of Penal Excess*. Abingdon: Routledge.

King, S. (2013) Assisted desistance and experiences of probation supervision. *Probation Journal*, 60(2), 136–51.

Kirton, G. and Guillaume, C. (2015) *Employment Relations and Working Conditions in Probation after Transforming Rehabilitation – with a Special Focus on Gender and Union Effects*. London: School of Business and Management, Queen Mary University.

Klaus, J.F. (1998) *Handbook on Probation Services: Guidelines for Probation Practitioners and Managers*. Rome/London: United Nations Interregional Crime and Justice Research Institute.

Mair, G. (2016) 'A difficult trip I think': The end days of the probation service in England and Wales? *European Journal of Probation*, 8(1), 3–15.

Maruna, S. (2011) Reentry as a rite of passage. *Punishment & Society*, 13(1), 3–28.

McNeill, F. (2009) *Towards Effective Practice in Offender Supervision*. Glasgow: The Scottish Centre for Crime & Justice Research.

McNeill, F. and Weaver, B. (2010) *Changing Lives? Desistance Research and Offender Management*. Report No 03/2010. Glasgow: The Scottish Centre for Crime and Justice Research.

Ministry of Justice (2018) *Deaths of Offenders in the Community: Annual Update to March 2018*. London: Ministry of Justice.

Phillips, J. (2020) What should happen after the death of a probationer? Learning from suicide investigations in prison. *Probation Journal*, 67(1), 65–70.

Ministry of Justice (2020) Offender management statistics bulletin, England and Wales. Available at: https://assets.publishing.service.gov.uk/government/uploads/system/uploads/attachment_data/file/882163/Offender_Management_Statistics_Quarterly_Q4_2019.pdf#:~:text=247%2C759%20offenders%20on%20probation%20at%20the%20end%20of,available%20and%20provides%20comparisons%20to%20the%20previous%20year. (last accessed 31 July 2022).

Phillips, J., Padfield, N. and Gelsthorpe, L. (2018) Suicide and community justice. *Health and Justice*, 6(19): 1-12.

Pluck, G. and Brooker, C. (2014) Epidemiological survey of suicide ideation and acts and other deliberate self-harm among offenders in the community under supervision of the Probation Service in England and Wales. *Criminal Behaviour & Mental Health*, 24(5), 358–64.

Prisons & Probation Ombudsman (2020) Annual Report 2019/20. Available at:. https://s3-eu-west-2.amazonaws.com/ppo-prod-storage-1g9rkhjhkjmgw/uploads/2020/11/6.6752_PPO_Prisons-and-Probation-Ombudsman-Annual-Report-2019_20_v8_WEB.pdf (last accessed 31 July 2022).

Reed, R. and Dominey, j. (2022) Individual interventions: Reimagining the one-to-one intervention at the heart of probation practice. In In L. Burke, N. Carr, E. Cluley, S. Collett and F. McNeill (eds) *Reimagining Probation Practice: Re-forming Rehabilitation in an Age of Penal Excess*. Abingdon: Routledge.

Rex, S. (1999) Desistance from offending: Experiences of probation. *The Howard Journal of Criminal Justice*, 38(4), 366–83.

Robinson, G. and McNeill, F. (2008) Exploring the dynamics of compliance with community penalties. *Theoretical Criminology*, 12(4), 431–49.

Robinson, G., Priede, C., Farrall, S., Shapland, J. and McNeill, F. (2014) Understanding 'quality' in probation practice: Frontline perspectives in England and Wales. *Criminology and Criminal Justice*, 14(2), 123–42.

Senior P., Ward, D., Burke, L., Knight, D., Teague, M., Chapman, T., Dominey, J., Phillips, J., Worrall, A. and Goodman, A. (2016) The essence of probation. *British Journal of Community Justice*, 14(1), 9–27.

Sentencing Council (2016) Imposition of community and custodial sentences: Definitive Guideline. Available at: www.sentencingcouncil.org.uk (last accessed 2 July 2021).

Shapland, J., Bottoms, A., Farrall, S., McNeill, F. Priede, C. and Robinson, G. (2012) *The Quality of Probation Supervision – A Literature Review*. Centre for Criminological Research University of Sheffield and University of Glasgow.

Smith, A., Heyes, K., Fox, C. and Harrison, J. (2018) The effectiveness of probation supervision towards reducing reoffending: A rapid evidence assessment. *Probation Journal*, 65(4), 407–28.

Tidmarsh, M. (2020) 'If the cap fits'? Probation staff and the changing nature of supervision in a community rehabilitation company. *Probation Journal*, 67(2), 98–117.

Trotter, C. (2006) *Working with Involuntary Clients: A Guide to Parctice* (2nd edn). London: Sage.

Ugwudike, P. (2008) Developing an effective mechanism for encouraging compliance with community penalties. PhD thesis. Swansea University.

Ugwudike, P. (2010) Compliance with community penalties: the importance of interactional dynamics. In F. McNeill., P. Raynor and C. Trotter (eds) *Offender Supervision: New Directions in Theory, Research and Practice*. Cullompton: Willan Publishing.

Ugwudike, P. and Phillips, J. (2020) Compliance during community-based penal supervision. In P. Ugwudike, H. Graham, F. McNeill, P. Raynor, F.S. Taxman and C. Trotter (eds) *The Routledge Companion to Rehabilitative Work in Criminal Justice*. Abingdon, Oxon: Routledge, pp. 870–81.

7
PRISON CULTURES

┌─── **IN THIS CHAPTER, YOU WILL EXPLORE** ───┐

1. Theoretical frameworks that attempt to explain how and why prison social structures exist

2. How people living, working and visiting prison establishments narrate their experience of prison

3. The extent to which the existing literature captures people's varying experiences of prisons and imprisonment.

INTRODUCTION

Scholars who have examined the microclimate of prisons have noted the presence of two separate but interconnected social structures, referred to in this chapter as occupational cultures and prison cultures. The term occupational culture refers to a distinctive pattern of thought and behaviour shared by members of the same occupation that is reflected in their language, values, attitudes, beliefs and customs. They are socially constructed patterns of shared thinking, feeling and behaving that are distinctly associated with particular occupations (Schein, 2010). Understanding the occupational culture of prison officers is an important component of your studies as it provides a lens through which you can see how they perceive 'their challenging and complex working world, and their place in it' (Garrihy, 2020: 128). On the other hand, the term prison culture is used to encapsulate the norms, values, beliefs and attitudes of those living in custodial settings. It is most typically drawn upon when attempts are made to explain how people navigate the prison place during their custodial sentence. Though insightful, it is contested, subject to debate and interpretation, given that people's circumstances and experience of prison vary. That said, understanding prison cultures provides an important insight into the day-to-day workings, and indeed failings, of custodial settings. Through an exploration of both occupational cultures and prison cultures, this chapter sheds light on the tensions and dilemmas which emerge as people living and working in custodial environments make sense of their obligations, roles and responsibilities. In doing so the discussion explores how official and unofficial processes contribute towards the creation and maintenance of occupational cultures and prison cultures amongst those living and working in penal settings. To conclude, the chapter will examine how and in what ways the prison place has an impact beyond the prison gates, on family members who have a loved one in prison. You will be encouraged to consider the ways in which the prison experience extends beyond those sentenced to imprisonment to family members, typically forgotten but subject to a hidden prison sentence.

KEY QUESTIONS TO CONSIDER WHEN READING THIS CHAPTER

1. To what extent is there a distinctive culture amongst people living and working in a custodial environment?

2. What impact does this have on the day-to-day organisation and operation of a prison?

3. How do people living, working and/or dealing with the collateral consequences of imprisonment navigate their experiences?

ORGANISATIONAL CULTURES

Liebling and Crewe (2014: 155) define organisational culture as 'a collective construction of social reality: shared habits of thought, attitude and language, consisting of "working rules" but also of emotional frameworks or sensibilities that might explain those working rules'. Put simply, it is the values shared by individuals within an organisation and how they manifest themselves in the practices of the organisation. It includes the working environment and the daily routines of practitioners within the organisation and how they make sense of their work and their reasons for doing it. Occupational culture is therefore a useful conceptual tool for analysing the values and beliefs held by prison officers (and probation workers) and how this binds them together. Organisational cultures can be a unifying force, particularly in periods of change because:

> **naturally, in these circumstances practitioners look to familiar roles, routines and shared language to bolster their sense of self, and consequently change in the norms around practice and culture tends to be gradual and perhaps uneven, prompted by new procedures, technology or the physical environment over time. (Robinson, 2013: 95)**

However, they can also be characterised by entrenched behaviour and attitudes, exclusionary practices and therefore become an obstacle to change. As such, any exploration of occupational culture raises several questions including: What is it and how does it come about? How does it shape notions of what personal qualities, values and skills are required to be an effective prison officer? How are these qualities and skills developed and sustained? How far does it shape the relationships and power relations between workers and their colleagues, those in their care, and their interactions with other agencies?

In his classic study of street-level bureaucrats, Lipsky (2010) describes the contribution of those involved in the delivery of public services in two related respects. Firstly, they exercise discretion in the decisions they take regarding those they interact with and secondly, their collective responses come to represent the public face of the agency they work for. Street level bureaucrats – such as prison officers and probation workers – are often committed to providing a good service and doing socially useful jobs but their working environment can sometimes make it difficult to offer the service they desire, or the service user wants and/or needs. When explaining the behaviour of street-level bureaucrats, it is important to understand the conditions under which they operate and the nature of their work. According to Erasmus (undated) street-level bureaucrats typically face the following key challenges: inadequate resources, an ever-growing demand for their services, vague or conflicting organisational expectations, performance measures and an involuntary clientele, each of which will now be explored in further detail.

Inadequate resources

The prison service has been subject to stringent cuts to their funding because of the austerity measures introduced by the coalition government in 2010. Over 7,000 prison officer posts were cut and many of those who left the service were experienced staff – replaced by less experienced workers. Inexperience or a lack of training may mean that front-line workers lack the personal resources required for their jobs, including the resources to deal with the often-stressful nature of their work. Furthermore, a growing focus on administrative tasks, such as filling out forms, can also limit the time they have for face-to-face work with people in their care.

An ever-growing demand for their services

At the same time as budgets have been cut, the demand for prison places has increased, even though overall levels of crime in England and Wales have been falling. Less crime does not necessarily mean less work for prison officers as people in the prison system often have complex needs and/or more entrenched patterns of criminal behaviour. If more services become available, they will be used. If the prison or probation services receive more money, there is a tendency that it will be used to offer additional services rather than easing the pressure on existing ones.

Vague or conflicting organisational expectations

The criminal justice system in England and Wales operates to reduce crime and reoffending; to punish lawbreakers; to protect the public; to provide victims with reparation; to increase public confidence, including victims and witnesses; and to ensure the system is fair and just. These goals can, in practice, be ambiguous, vague or conflicting. For example, prisons are required to prepare individuals for release but at the same time maintain security. Prison officers are expected to support and help individuals but at the same time monitor their behaviour and enforce the requirements of the Prison Rules (see Chapter 5 for a more detailed discussion). Managing these different expectations can therefore be extremely challenging.

Performance measures

Under the guise of managerialism, the adoption of market sector disciplines has been encouraged as a way of improving public service standards and increasing government control over what is delivered. This has involved redefining the relationship between public sector professionals and people who use their services to one of provider and consumer evaluated through quantitative measurements of performance and target-setting. It is often difficult or impossible to measure the extent to which the performance of a street-level bureaucrat contributes to achieving their agency's goals. For example, if there is a lack of clarity or conflict about goals, how can performance measurements be operationalised? Performance measurement is also complicated by the fact that street-level bureaucrats engage in complex interactions with other people. In a particular situation it may not be easy to know what the correct thing is to do, especially if there is more than one appropriate course of action. In addition, the information needed to make a proper evaluation may not be available. For example, if street-level bureaucrats operated a programme that had a 50 per cent success rate, how should that be interpreted? Is it good because they were targeting especially difficult clients or is it poor because they were focusing their efforts on an easy-to-reach target population? This was one of the features of the payment-by-results approach to commissioning services as part of the Transforming Rehabilitation (TR) reforms (see Chapter 4 for further discussion).

AN INTRODUCTION TO PENOLOGY

An involuntary clientele

Contemporary public services are expected to provide more choice for citizens through market-based mechanisms. However, individuals who are in prison do not voluntarily choose the service they are attending and often have little say in the services provided to them. This raises several challenges for prison officers in terms of how they exercise authority in working with individuals who may be unwilling or unmotivated to change or even recognise that they have a problem to be addressed. In response to these challenges, street-level bureaucrats sometimes develop patterns of practice, routines and interactions that help them to deal with the chronic shortage of resources and the often-high demand for their services. These patterns of practice will often accord with the policies of their employing organisations but sometimes create situations that are unintended by the agencies whose policies are being implemented and may even work against the objectives of such agencies and their policies.

CAPITAL, FIELD AND HABITUS

Pierre Bourdieu (1980) developed the concepts of capital, field and habitus to highlight how individuals make sense of their external environment because of socialisation and established practices. Bourdieu argued that cultural and social forms of capital are based on, but not necessarily determined by, the amount of economic capital possessed and subsequently shape how social hierarchies are reproduced. For Bourdieu capital takes different forms. Social capital refers to the networks of 'useful relationships that can secure material or symbolic profits' (Bourdieu, 1986: 249). However, rather than just presenting social capital as a fundamentally supportive network of social connections (which of course it can be) Bourdieu uses the concept to explain the realities of social inequality. Put simply, 'it's not what you know, it's who you know.' Bourdieu further divides cultural capital into three forms: *embodied* (the inculcation and assimilation of long-lasting dispositions of the mind and body), *objectified* (material objects that have cultural meaning) and *institutionalised* (recognition received from an institution).

The three forms of capital outlined above combine to produce an individual habitus which shapes the way that individuals perceive the social world around them. These dispositions are usually shared by people with similar backgrounds (such as social class, religion, nationality, ethnicity, education and profession) and are typically acquired through imitation and the way in which individuals are socialised, including their individual experience and opportunities. Bourdieu argued that the reproduction of the social structure results from the habitus of individuals and that these concepts are embedded in relations of power and are experienced differently by individuals within the organisation. Power is culturally and symbolically created and constantly re-legitimised through the interplay of agency and structure. It occurs through socialised norms or tendencies that guide behaviour and thinking. Habitus represents the individual's 'feel for the game' (Bourdieu, 1980: 52) in terms of their 'internal set of dispositions that shape perception, appreciation, and action' (Page, 2013: 152). These dispositions are both shaped by past events and in turn shape current practices; in this respect they are 'not fixed or permanent and can be changed under unexpected situations or over a long historical period' (Navarro, 2006: 16). Bourdieu employs the concept of *doxa* to explain the taken for granted assumptions, or common sense, behind the decisions we make.

The field refers to the formal rules that govern the organisation. It is the arena, or social context, in which a specific habitus is realised. Everyone is positioned within the field by their possession of different types of capital and the strategies they employ contribute to its reproduction. For Bourdieu (1980) tensions arise when individuals encounter and are challenged by different contexts and in this respect his theory 'can be used to explain how people can resist power and domination on one [field] and express complicity in another' (Moncrieffe, 2006: 37). Clearly, where there is a conflict between the organisational field and individual habitus (Bourdieu, 1977) there is the possibility that some workers will leave the organisation or display signs of low levels of resistance (Cheliotis, 2006).

Bourdieu has since been criticised for presenting a somewhat deterministic view of social capital that 'ultimately remains one in which things happen to people, rather than a world in which they can intervene in their individual and collective destinies' (Jenkins, 2002: 91). Edgar Schein (1992), on the other hand, sought to explain why people behave differently in various organisations and argued that the culture of an organisation affects how those who work for it see it and how they perform their roles and duties. He observed that culture is a form of learned behaviour that is constantly in the process of forming and learning. Over time basic assumptions become embedded and offer a shared system of meaning that is passed down to new employees framing what is deemed acceptable and unacceptable behaviour within the organisation.

Based on this observation, Schein introduced the organisational culture model. According to Schein culture can be analysed at several different levels. These levels range from tangible manifestations of what one can see and feel to deeply embedded, unconscious, assumptions. In between these levels are the various espoused beliefs, values, norms and rules of behaviour that workers within the organisation use as a way of understanding the culture of the organisation and presenting it to others. . The first and most visible level, centring on behaviour and artefacts, may tell us what an occupational group is doing but not necessarily why. These are the visible elements in the organisation and include the physical space and office design, but also involve social practices, leadership styles and work traditions. The next level of values may determine behaviour, but they are less observable and there may be a difference between stated and operating values.

Hofstede (1980) acknowledges that an individual's values may play a part in their attraction to working in an occupation but warns against overstating the influence of organisational cultures upon the individual's values which may already have been developed in other social contexts such as the family and school. The third level, where underlying assumptions develop out of values until they become taken for granted, is the deepest level of occupational culture. These are the sometimes-unconscious assumptions that have, over a period, become taken for granted as an organisationally acceptable way of perceiving the world. They can be the most difficult to relearn and change and although not always explicit they can be a powerful cultural determinant within the organisation.

Building on Schein's model, Johnson et al. (2011) identified six interrelated elements that make up what they termed the cultural web that shapes a work environment. These include stories, rituals and routines, symbols, organisational structure and control systems. Stories include past events and people that are discussed both inside and outside the organisation. Who and what the organisation chooses to immortalise says a great deal about what it values and perceives as good behaviour. Rituals and routines are the daily behaviours and actions of people that signal acceptable behaviour. This determines what is expected to happen in a situation and what is valued by management. Symbols are the visual representations of the organisation including logos, how plush the offices are as well as both formal and informal dress codes. Organisational structure includes both the structure defined by the organisational chart and the unwritten lines of power and influence that indicate whose contributions are the most valued. Control systems refer to the ways that the organisation is controlled. These include financial systems and rewards (including the way they are measured and distributed within the organisation). Power structures refer to pockets of real power in the organisation. This may involve one or two key senior executives, a whole group of executives, or even a department. These people have the greatest amount of influence on decisions, operations and strategic direction. Each of these elements can be important in shaping the occupational culture of prison work.

Stories are shared by workers as a means of socialisation of new recruits, setting boundaries in terms of acceptable/unacceptable behaviour and sometimes in the form of humour to take the sting out of difficult/upsetting situations. In policing this has become known as canteen culture (Waddington, 1999) and has its equivalence in prison in the officers' mess and in the probation tearoom (particularly prior to the advent of open plan offices). These can be incubators for developing both social solidarity among the workforce and prejudicial behaviours. Rituals and routines shape the daily existence within the prison. Myriad rules and regulations are used to govern every aspect of prison life in the total institution. Breaking the rules can incur sanctions for even minor infractions. Reception into prison is accompanied by a range of rituals that mark the individual's change from freedom to incarceration. The cultural symbols of the prison are evident in the uniforms worn, the keys, the prison walls, etc. Prisons have defined organisational structures that are both hierarchical in terms of power and accountability and largely based on a system of command and control that has its roots in the military. As previous chapters have detailed, prisons are under the control of HM Prison and Probation Service, which is part of the Ministry of Justice (see Chapter 3 for further discussion).

Although prisons have hierarchical structures and defined lines of accountability, the role and influence of front-line workers in terms of how they implement (and sometimes subvert) policy intentions cannot be underestimated in terms of the more informal power structures within both institutions. Distinctions have been drawn between organisational and occupational professionalism although to an extent both influence each other through the processes of selection and socialisation. *Professionalisation from above* (Graham, 2016) is based on accreditation and certification, involving hierarchical structures of responsibility and decision making, standardised work procedures and practices and an adherence to external regulation and accountability. Professionalisation in this sense 'aims to convince, cajole, or persuade practitioners to perform in ways that are deemed appropriate, effective and efficient to promote organisational objectives that are defined by government' (Brough et al., 2016: 72).

These forms of professionalism from above contrast with notions of *professionalism from within* (Graham, 2016). The latter is often characterised by the divergent views, experiences and roles of different subgroups and individuals within the organisation and how they relate to others in the field. These in turn are often backed up by an informal culture which also provides the means to alleviate stress, particularly during periods of change, through the support and camaraderie of fellow workers (Brough et al., 2016: 24). All these practical and organisational arrangements profoundly shape the culture of the agency as it is played out in the interactions between workers and the norms that develop around routine tasks. This is important because as Graham (2016: 67) points out, 'there is no point in conceptualising and analysing rehabilitation work merely as a technical and instrumental exercise if the workers involved make sense of it as a normative experience, incorporating affective labour and ideological dimensions'.

Such struggles have also been found in the social structures (more commonly known as prison cultures) amongst and between people serving a custodial sentence. Although the term social structure is difficult to define, it has become synonymous with attempts to explore and explain social arrangements and institutions such as family units, religion, education and systems of law and order that can be both the cause and consequence of action. From a sociological perspective, social structures consist of a stable arrangement of institutions that allow people in any given society to interact and live alongside each other. Within the context of prisons, scholars have noted the presence of two separate but interconnected social structures: the official social structure and the unofficial social structure which, when combined, go some way to create and indeed maintain a prison culture amongst people serving a custodial sentence.

In a prison context, official social structures consist of the rules, regulations, guidelines and processes that are underpinned by law, legislation and/or high-level policy directives (see Chapter 5 for further discussion). The official social structure is, in theory at least, designed to govern day-to-day activities that take place within custodial environments to maintain a proper balance between security, control and human rights. Allied with this is an unofficial social structure which contains a multitude of cultures and subcultures amongst people serving a custodial sentence that consists of values, norms, attitudes and behaviours that govern how people living in prison environments go about their day-to-day business. Although informal, the unofficial social structure is more powerful than official rules and regulations. The following section will discuss how and in what ways these social structures come together to create and maintain a prison culture.

PRISON CULTURES

For decades scholars have debated how and why social structures develop in prison amongst people serving a custodial sentence. Some suggest that cultures and subcultures develop as people adapt to the multiple and varied deprivations associated with imprisonment. This is commonly referred to as the deprivation model and will be explored in further detail as this chapter unfolds. Others suggest that cultures and subcultures are transported from the wider community into the prison environment – a perspective known as the importation model. Although different, both the model of deprivation and importation offer useful frameworks for understanding how and in what ways social structures develop and evolve within prison settings.

Deprivation model

Erving Goffman (1961) coined the term total institution to refer to a closed social system within which life is organised by strict norms, rules and schedules. In total institutions there is no individual autonomy. What happens in these institutions is determined by a single authority whose directives are carried out by staff who are required to enforce the rules. Total institutions are separate from the wider community in several ways and for different reasons. Examples include but are not limited to inpatient mental health facilities, military bases, boarding schools and prisons. Although participation in total institutions can be voluntary or involuntary, there is an expectation that once involved, people must follow the rules and adopt a new identity provided by the institution in question. In a penal context, entry into a prison involves being subject to a series of social and psychological attacks that not only undermine the sense of self but contribute towards the civic death of a person, considered to be one of the strongest condemnations of a society, due to the exclusion of people socially and politically from the society to which they belong.

Upon entering prison, people are stripped of their clothing and most of their personal possessions. They are examined, inspected, weighed, documented, classified and given a prison number. Routine assaults on an individual's sense of self and self-worth means imprisonment becomes painful, both physically and psychologically (Owen et al., 2017). In his seminal text *The Society of Captives: A Study of a Maximum-Security Prison* first published in 1958, Grahame Sykes highlights five deprivations that characterise prison life: deprivation of liberty, deprivation of goods and services, deprivation of heterosexual relationships, deprivation of autonomy and deprivation of security. The fundamental premise of imprisonment is to remove or restrict a person's liberty. This deprivation of liberty extends far beyond an individual's physical removal from society and permeates into their day-to-day experience of imprisonment which is subject to a wide range of control measures such as: being locked in a cell for prolonged periods of time, being strip searched, military-style formations in movement from one part of a prison to another, restrictions on visitations, sending and receiving mail and contact with the outside world.

The second pain of imprisonment is the deprivation of goods and services. This is largely due to that fact that in 'modern Western culture, material possessions are so large a part of the individual's concept of himself that to be stripped of them is to be attacked at the deepest layers of personality' (Sykes, 1958: 69). According to Sykes, the deprivation of heterosexual relationships and the 'involuntary celibacy' it represents is a 'figurative castration' which is both physically and psychologically 'serious' (Sykes, 1958: 70). The deprivation of autonomy highlights how people in prison are not only denied the ability to make choices for themselves, with regard to basic decisions such as when to sleep and eat, but access to personal information about themselves and their ongoing circumstances which can be withheld without full reason or explanation. Last, but by no means least, is the deprivation of security which details the prison place's ability to attack and subsequently erode a person's sense of security, physically, emotionally and psychologically.

These deprivations are commonly known as the *pains of imprisonment*. To modernise the work of Sykes, Crewe (2011) developed the concept with a particular focus on contemporary penal practice and how it has created new burdens and pains of imprisonment. These include but are not limited to the pains of uncertainty and indeterminacy. Although the 'tyranny of the indeterminate sentence' (Mitford, 1977: 92) has been discussed in detail in Chapter 5, its failings offer a useful contribution to the contemporary pains of imprisonment given the stress and anxiety experienced by people serving a custodial sentence caused by the uncertainty it creates about their future. This is in addition to the insecurities that result from a discretionary style of governance (Sparks et al., 1996). A further contemporary pain can be found in the *pains of psychological assessment*, which can define a person's future as well as significantly alter the present. Although such pains are primarily associated with people serving indeterminate sentences, they are also relevant to a much wider population, since a large proportion of people in prison undertake offending behaviour programmes and, consequently, go through a rigorous process of assessment to determine need and suitability (Crewe, 2011). The pains of self-government illustrates how tools such as mandatory drug tests and initiatives such as the incentives and earned privileges scheme reshape and relocate power, from prison authorities to individuals serving custodial sentences, as 'direct, personal oversight is not required for prisoners to be disciplined and made (relatively) compliant' (Crewe, 2011: 519). .

When thinking about the pains of imprisonment, it is important to recognise how such occurrences do not necessarily require any intervention from authorities as they are ingrained into the system. They are not necessarily intentional abuses of power, rather a side effect of penal policy. As a result, people serving a custodial sentence must adapt to the rigours of confinement, developing unique norms, values and social controls to adapt to the total institution. Sykes and Messinger (1960) suggest that people serving a custodial sentence develop an inmate code as a direct response to the pains of imprisonment, which holds the potential to influence interpersonal relationships between people living and working in custodial environments. The inmate code is an unwritten set of explicit values and norms that exist alongside the formal rules of the institution which assist in defining the way in which people serving a custodial sentence should behave. According to Sykes and Messinger (1960: 401–3) the inmate code includes words of caution such as 'Don't interfere with inmate interests' and 'Be loyal to your class of cons'; restrictions on arguments with other people serving a custodial sentence such as 'Play it cool and do your own time'; cautions to avoid the exploitation of others; rules about how to behave such as 'Don't be weak'; and guidelines regarding relationships with staff such as 'Don't be a sucker'.

Though contested, it has been suggested that such adaptations allow people to mitigate social isolation, compensate for a loss of autonomy, lessen the pains of imprisonment and resist the system. Clemmer (1940) coined the term *prisonisation* to illustrate how people serving a custodial sentence take on, to a greater or lesser degree, the folkways, morals, customs and general culture of a prison to protect their interests and mitigate the pains of imprisonment. Albeit in a female-specific context, Owen et al. (2017) highlight how people serving a custodial sentence develop prison capital – the skills, connections and knowledge needed to survive, endure and even thrive in prison. Prison capital fuels the creation and maintenance of social structures amongst people serving custodial sentences which contributes towards the (re)formulation of prison social systems that detail, albeit unofficially, accepted norms, values, attitudes and behaviours. Failure to adhere to the unofficial social system will ultimately leave people vulnerable, exposed and at risk (Owen et al., 2017).

As a result of prisonisation, people serving a custodial sentence, particularly those serving a long-term prison sentence, can become *institutionalised*. This is often described as a deliberate process whereby a person entering an institution is reprogrammed to accept and conform to strict controls that enable sizeable institutions to manage many people with minimum staff intervention. Crane (2019) describes institutionalisation as a chronic biopsychosocial state brought on by imprisonment and characterised by anxiety, depression, hypervigilance and a disabling combination of social withdrawal and/or aggression. The process of becoming institutionalised can have an impact on an individual's physical, mental and social well-being that may remain with them after release from prison. There is an infamous scene in the film *Shawshank Redemption* where Ellis 'Red' Redding (played by Morgan Freeman) describes the process of institutionalisation:

> He's just institutionalised (...) The man's been in here fifty years Heywood, fifty years. This is all he knows. In here he's an important man. He's an educated man. Outside he's nothin', just a used-up con with arthritis in both hands. Probably couldn't get a library card if he tried (...) Yanno what I'm tryna say (...) I'm tellin ya, these walls are funny. First you hate 'em, then you get used to 'em. Enough time passes, it gets so you depend on 'em. That's institutionalised (...) They send you here for life and that's exactly what they take. The part that counts anyway.

> (Darabont, F. (1994) The Shawshank Redemption. Columbia Pictures

Reflecting on this quotation, think about how coping strategies and responses to the prison environment, such as institutionalisation, have an impact on people both during and after a prison sentence. What do such occurrences tell us about the prison environment and impact of imprisonment both within and beyond the prison walls?

Importation model

The importation model suggests that prison cultures are influenced by factors external to the immediate context of the prison, as well as the immediate conditions of the prison. Advocates of the model suggest that people serving a custodial sentence import their characteristics and traits into the prison, bringing with them specific values, roles and behaviours from the outside world that reflect their previous lifestyle choices as well as other characteristics which influence, shape and direct how they conduct their lives in prison. For example, if an individual comes from an environment where violence is a normal response to the stresses and strains of everyday life, then according to the importation model they will continue with such responses when they are imprisoned. Thus, if the individual acts violently in prison, this should not be considered as a behaviour that is specific to the prison place as it has been imported from wider society.

Classic studies which explore the development and maintenance of prison cultures tend to focus on how people serving a custodial sentence are organised according to their crime, masculinity and criminal label. This has subsequently created a hyper-masculine interpretation of the prison place that contributes to an inaccurate representation of imprisonment and prisons more broadly, which further removes us from conversations about what prisons and the process of imprisonment means and indeed represent in the 21st century. That said, there are scholars such as David Maguire who have worked to dismantle long-standing preoccupations with hegemonic prison masculinities. Through a detailed analysis of men's experience of a vulnerable prisoner unit (VPU), Maguire highlights the dynamic, relational, fragile and spatial elements of masculinity amongst those who take on, to a greater or lesser degree, subordinated prison identities. In doing so, Maguire (2019: 1) suggests that such divergence:

> **offers researchers a new opportunity to shape and to inform policy debates on how, in extreme environments like the prison, alternative ways of 'being a man' might be opened up to those who have suffered at the most brutal end of prison hierarchies.**

As you work your way through this chapter, it is important to remember that people who occupy the prison place, whether as a member of staff or someone serving a custodial sentence, are not a homogeneous group of people who buy into a unifying culture (see Chapter 11 for further discussion). Although there is a consensus that those living and working in custodial environments are subject to a socialisation process (it is acknowledged that this could be official and/or unofficial), there remains some work to do before we, as a society, can claim to understand the divergent experiences of imprisonment. Taking this into consideration, the next section will explore the prison experience amongst two groups of people who are routinely forgotten in penological conversations about the prison place: prison officers and family members of people serving a custodial sentence. The first part of the section will explore the role and responsibilities of the prison officer. Although conversations about the prison officer have grown in breadth and depth in recent years, it remains an overlooked component of prison life – 'we never get recognised for anything unless something goes wrong' (Youle, 2020: para. 55) – despite providing a backbone to the prison service. The second part of the section will explore the impact of imprisonment beyond the prison gates, through an exploration of the literature in and around family members who have a significant other in prison.

Prison experiences

Prisons provide a highly structured and controlled environment which not only dictates how people living in prisons go about their day-to-day business but how prison practitioners and prison visitors go about theirs. However, one unanticipated situation can disrupt the equilibrium of a whole prison. Time spent living, working and indeed visiting prisons can create a wide-ranging set of challenges that can have an impact on people in varying ways. Some people are able to cope well with these challenges, while others are more severely affected. As such, when writing a textbook about the application of punitive measures across community and custodial environments, it is important to be aware of these challenges and how prison-related experiences (whether personal or professional) create lasting effects for everyone involved in some way with the prison place. As Chapters 9 and 11 will explore the prison experience of people serving a custodial sentence, this section will focus on the literature in and around the experience of prison officers and family members of people serving a custodial sentence.

Prison officers

In March 2022 there were 22,002 FTE band 3–5 prison officers in post in England and Wales (HM Prison and Probation Service, 2022), compared to 22, 536 in 2019 (HM Prison and Probation Service (2019). Official statistics note a current leaving rate of 14.5 per cent amongst prison officers (FTE band 3–5), with an increase of 5.4 per cent compared to the year ending 31 March 2021 (HM Prison and Probation Service, 2022). Data from public sector prisons shows that on 31 March 2020, 93 per cent of prison officers in England and Wales were white, while only 7 per cent were from Asian, Black, mixed and other ethnic groups (HM Government, 2021). Though not representative of staff in private sector prisons, the data highlights an over-representation of white prison officers in prisons across England and Wales. The impact will be discussed in further detail in Chapter 11. As of 30 September 2019, there were 16,040 male (average age of 41) and 6,387 female (average age of 36) prison officers in prisons across England and Wales (HM Government, 2019) which suggests an over-representation of middle-aged males in the prison service.

Since 2021, anyone applying to become a prison officer in England will work towards a level 3 Custody and Detention Professional Apprenticeship qualification (HM Government, 2020), which takes between 12 and 18 months to complete (HM Prison and Probation Service, 2022). Following a local induction in the applicant's 'home' prison (where they originally applied to work), they must undertake a foundation training programme that typically lasts eight weeks at a designated learning centre as close to the home prison as possible. Upon completion of the foundation training, trainee prison officers go back to their home prison to continue their training with regular support from an allocated mentor. The foundation training programme focuses on providing trainee prison officers with the skills and knowledge required to create a 'rehabilitative environment' as well as the 'tools and opportunities for people in custody to lead law-abiding lives upon release' (Ministry of Justice, 2021: para. 12).

The foundation training programme also provides an opportunity for trainee prison officers to learn first aid, food hygiene, health and safety, prison rules and regulations as well as de-escalation tactics. Once trainees complete the training programme and go back to their home prison, there are two further opportunities for short training (usually between 25 and 28 weeks, and 44 and 47 weeks) during their probationary period, at the end of which they are awarded a Level 3 professional apprenticeship in custody and detention. As prisons operate 24 hours a day, seven days a week prison officers are expected to work on some public and bank holidays, which are typically added to annual leave entitlements. Shifts usually follow regular hours, although the start and finish time may vary depending on the prison.

Though the provision of security is at the epicentre of the work conducted by prison officers, the role has evolved to include a wide variety of responsibilities and competing interests. As prison officers have the most day-to-day contact with people serving a custodial sentence, they invariably occupy an important role in terms of engaging people during their time in prison and reducing further lawbreaking. But capturing the role and function of the contemporary prison officer is a difficult if not impossible task. Whilst their role is varied, there are some key elements that all prison officers must be able to deal with. These include but are not limited to: supervising people serving a custodial sentence lawfully, safely and securely; performing security checks and search procedures; supervising visits and carrying out patrol duties; escorting people in prison to external appointments where required; advising and supporting people serving a custodial sentence, ensuring they have professional and/or specialist support if needed; responding to incidents; employing lawful physical control and restraint procedures; being aware of people's human rights and dignity; providing appropriate care and support; promoting anti-bullying and suicide prevention procedures; taking an active part in rehabilitation programmes; developing working relationships with other members of prison staff; preparing relevant reports and documents; maintaining prison records; and complying with national, local and institutional policy and legislation (Prospects, 2021).

Prison officers are expected to respond to and deal with a plethora of competing demands within a system that is under pressure alongside some of the 'most difficult and dangerous people in society, but also some of the saddest and most vulnerable' (Justice Committee, 2009: para. 30). Although research in and around the role of the prison officer has increased significantly in modern times, more insight is required into how roles, responsibilities, place of work and attitudes towards imprisonment influence the occupational culture amongst prison officers. Just like people serving a custodial sentence, prison officers are not a homogenous group of people who have the same attitudes, values and experiences of the prison place and those within it. To reiterate this point, let us now consider the work of Tait (2011) who, after conducting research in a male prison and a female prison, created five approaches to care amongst prison officers. These include but are not limited to true carer, limited carer, old school, conflicted and damaged.

Prison officers identified as true carers were confident, secure and highly engaged in their work. They developed relationships with people serving a custodial sentence with ease, providing support, reassurance and encouragement. This subsequently helped to maintain order. Limited carers were consistent in their approach, adhered to policies and practices on issues such as bullying and self-harm, but offered a pragmatic form of care. They were adept at defusing emotions and following requests from people living in custodial environments. Those considered old school possessed the confidence of experience and had long histories with many people serving a custodial sentence, but their care was contractual. For instance, old school carers would help people with their problems in return for compliance. Conflicted prison officers often conflated care with control. Care was often conditional, based on respect and focused on teaching people serving a custodial sentence to be *better* people. Damaged prison officers suffered a significant shift in their outlook following a sequence of traumatic events. Although limited in generalisability given the small sample size (45 prison officers in total) and focus on English prison officers, the findings highlight how both personal and institutional factors can shape the quality of care provided by prison officers.

The work of Tait (2011) is of particular interest for two reasons. Firstly, it provides a stark contrast to the idea that people in prison, whether they are working or living there, subscribe to an all-encompassing culture, highlighting instead how people's experiences – in this case prison officers – shape and mould their responses to the prison place, including those within it. Secondly, the findings illustrate how prison work can have a damaging effect on some people. In a later study that explored how those who work in prison are affected by and respond to self-harm amongst women in an English prison, Walker et al. (2017) found prison officers present a façade of coping to portray a sense that one is coping despite being deeply troubled by occurrences that take place in the workplace. When we consider the findings from this study, in relation to the perfect storm that has surrounded prisons in recent times, it is unsurprising to find that 'research suggests that up to 20 per cent of prison workers are suffering from some form of PTSD' with 'female prison workers, BME prison workers and more experienced staff' 'particularly likely to experience PTSD' (PTSD UK, 2022: para 9).

It is important to consider how and in what ways the role of the prison officer has diversified, and will continue to evolve, to accommodate unfolding penological issues of our time. For instance, we know that more people are dying in prison than ever before, whether from old age; poor health, suicide, self-inflicted death or murder. Allied with this, as we navigate the collateral consequences of a global health pandemic (COVID-19), we must consider whether, and to what extent, managing ill health and death is part of the job description for modern day prison officers. The discussion presented to you throughout this chapter is not intended to provide an in-depth account of the history and evolution of the prison officer's role. Rather, it is a vehicle to highlight some of the complexities which surround this all-encompassing role and an opportunity to consider the degree to which the presence of cultures and/or subcultures help or hinder those on the coal face of service delivery. This is an important effort for anyone with an interest in this area as we must recognise how personal attributes and professional socialisation processes, whereby people learn the craft of prison work, can shape and direct their approach to becoming and indeed being a prison officer (Arnold, 2016).

Family members of people serving a custodial sentence

When we think about people's experience of prisons and imprisonment our attention is naturally drawn to those who live and work in custodial environments. This is understandable given that they may be most affected by the prison place. Up to now, the discussion has focused on how people within custodial environments experience imprisonment. Although important, it is essential to acknowledge how and in what ways the pains of imprisonment extend beyond the prison gates to family members, friends and significant others of those serving a custodial sentence. Though existing research, which outlines the detrimental impact of prisons and imprisonment on family members, has grown in recent times we are yet to see a considered, joined-up conversation about the collateral consequences of imprisonment from a variety of perspectives including but not limited to those who live and work in, and visit, these institutions. Whilst there are initiatives developing across the prison estate to help alleviate some of the pains of imprisonment alongside more considered approaches to the design and layout of visiting rooms and visitors' centres (for example), there is more work to do.

When someone goes to prison, they will acquire a way to do time and serve their sentence. *Doing time* is a colloquial term used to describe how and in what ways people adapt to cope during their time in prison. As you now know, this is not the same for everyone. Although family members' experience is different from those serving a custodial sentence, Foster (2016) suggests that they too do time. A substantial characteristic of doing time for family members can be summed up in one word, waiting: 'Waiting for the visit; waiting for the court date; waiting for release; waiting for the letter; waiting for the phone call; waiting for things to go back to normal; waiting for things to get better' (Foster, 2016: 460). Alongside waiting, family members with a loved one in prison experience financial hardship which can be attributed to a decrease in income and increase in expenditure due to costly prison visits, phone calls and subsidiary money for their loved one during their custodial sentence. In addition, a recent report by Hextall (2022) illustrates how a parent's offence has a dramatic impact on the degree to which young people experience stigma and shame. This is particularly apparent amongst children of people who commit sexually motivated crimes who have been found to experience difficulties with regard to how they navigate adolescence, form their own sense of identity and sense of self. Although these children are more at risk of social exclusion and compromised emotional well-being, there are, at the time of writing, no government or social services available in England and Wales to respond to their needs (Ibid).

People serving a custodial sentence are entitled to social visits from friends and family members. Each prison tends to have different rules relating to visiting such as when you can visit, how often you can visit and how many visitors you can have at one time. Broadly speaking, in England and Wales, people on remand are allowed three one-hour visits per week and people who have been convicted are usually allowed at least two one-hour visits every four weeks. The number of and access to social visits may also be influenced by available facilities, staff shortages, prison lockdowns (think about the impact of COVID-19 on prison visits), relocation to other establishments, as well as the incentives and earned privileges status of people serving a custodial sentence. Although social visits are crucial, with the literature noting links between positive family ties and desistance, there are a varied and often complex array of issues which surround visiting a loved one in prison. In addition to the emotional turmoil a family member will experience before, during and after a visit, there are several obstacles a person must navigate before they get a chance to see their loved one.

After waiting three weeks for a phone call from the person you wish to visit, you now have all the information needed to book a visit. When they ring, you are asked to call the prison to book the visit. Others on the wing tell them that is how their family do it. Their phone credit runs out, so the call abruptly ends. You do not have a chance to ask any questions. You have not seen each other for four months and you know they are struggling. They are in a prison in your local area. You google the prison and look for a number to call. When you finally get through, they tell you to go online. A friend helps you to book the visit and you begin to think about what you will talk about. You don't drive and have a limited income, so you need to plan how to get there on public transport. You arrive at the prison; staff tell you that you are in the wrong place and direct you to a building over the road to wait with other visitors. You get there and people look at you. Someone asks if you need a locker for your belongings – you don't know who they are, but they tell you that they only take £1 coins, and you don't have one. You ask if you have time to go to a local shop for change. You get back, put your belongings into a locker and someone asks if you have your pound coins. You have never visited a prison before, and you have only just found out that you can only take coins into the visit room to buy refreshments. You go back to the shop to get some coins. You wait for processing to start. You show your identification and security checks begin. You wait for every other visitor to go through the same process as you. There has been an incident and you must wait while it is dealt with. You are escorted to a room. It's cold, damp and smells old, but you can see the person you have come to visit. Now you must wait your turn to go in and sit down. During the two-hour visit, you spend £9.80 on refreshments, and they tell you 'I'm sound' and little else. Conversation is hard over a plastic table in a noisy room.

Research highlights how many family members provide for their loved ones in prison to mitigate the pains of imprisonment. In shouldering a portion of the burden of doing time a person's everyday life is fundamentally altered. This process is known as 'secondary prisonisation' and is a phenomenon that is not exclusive to adults (Turanovic et al., 2012: 917). The imprisonment of a household member is one of the ten adverse childhood experiences (ACEs) that are proven to have a negative impact on a child's long-term health and well-being, school attainment and life experiences (Beresford, 2018; Kincaid et al., 2019) yet little is known about children who have a parent in prison. Estimates suggest that there are 312,000 children in England and Wales with a parent in prison (Kincaid et al., 2019). Children of Prisoners Europe estimate 800,000 children have a parent in prison on any given day in the European Union (COPE, 2016). This rises to 2.1 million when all Council of Europe countries are included (Ibid).

Although insightful, such estimates are the tip of the iceberg as research in this area is limited in terms of its efforts to capture the nuances which surround the experiences of children with a parent in prison. This is, to name just one example, because studies rarely distinguish which parent (mother or father) is serving a custodial sentence (Beresford, 2018). This is further compounded as even fewer studies attempt to draw direct comparisons between children's experience of having a mother in prison compared to a father (Beresford, 2018). Such distinctions are significant when you consider that only 5 per cent of children remain in their family home when a mother goes to prison (Ibid). It is also common for children with mothers in prison to be cared for by their grandparents (Beresford, 2018) who, as a result, find themselves providing a 'double duty' caring for their grandchildren in addition to their adult child whilst having limited resources and multiple needs themselves (Turanovic et al., 2012: 917). Although we know very little about the experiences of family members with a loved one in prison, it is an area of penological study and practice that is currently experiencing a significant amount of attention by academics, policy makers and practitioners alike. Whilst the term hidden sentence is offered to recognise and capture the experiences of family members with a loved one in prison, there is more work to do.

As you begin to think about the concept of a hidden sentence, it may be worthwhile revisiting Chapter 3 so that you can engage with this sentiment in a more critical fashion by considering how, and in what ways, imprisonment can be justified when innocent people are subject to a hidden sentence. In doing so you may also find it useful to consider how prison officers and their families negate the collateral consequences of prison work beyond the prison gates. This is an important exercise for anyone interested in understanding prison cultures in its broadest terms. Although prisons are highly emotive environments, often described as pressure cookers due to the emotionally charged nature of the institution, prison cultures, whether official or unofficial, do not permit the display of emotion – from practitioners or people serving a custodial sentence – for a variety of reasons. This means that people living and working in custodial environments undertake a form of emotional labour, a term used to describe the process of managing feelings and expressions, to fulfil the emotional requirements of a job, role or environment, to cope (or portray a sense of coping) with day-to-day pressures and strains.

When we think about the literature in and around this area of enquiry, whether from the perspective of those who live, work or visit the prison place, in relation to the concept of emotional labour, it becomes apparent that nobody escapes the abrasive properties of imprisonment. Recognising the presence of emotional labour amongst those who live or work in or visit custodial environments is an important endeavour for any aspiring scholar, policy maker or practitioner as it draws our attention to the ability of penal institutions to change, whether short, medium or long term, the emotional capacity and indeed capability of all involved. This not only has implications in terms of how these environments operate on a day-to-day basis, but how people cope with the realities of working or living in or visiting prisons. By putting emotional hardship at the epicentre of our studies, we may find ourselves in a stronger position to genuinely improve the theories, policies and processes that we seek to understand and apply in the name of justice.

recommended reading

If you would like to engage in further reading, you may find the following resources particularly useful:

Liebling, A., Johnsen, B., Schmidt, B., Rokkan, T., Beyens, K., Boone, M., Kox, M., and Vanhouche, A. (2021) Where two 'exceptional' prison cultures meet: Negotiating order in a transnational prison. *British Journal of Criminology*, 61(1), 41–60.

This paper explores learning from the Norgerhaven project – a Norwegian prison located in the Netherlands – that exposes many of the complexities of liberal penal power.

Foster, R. (2017) Exploring 'betwixt and between' in a prison visitors' centre and beyond. In D. Moran and A. Schliehe, A. (eds) *Carceral Spatiality*. Palgrave Studies in Prisons and Penology. London: Palgrave Macmillan.

This chapter demonstrates how family members, when visiting their loved ones in prison, occupy a liminal space in the prison place. Though technically 'outsiders' and legally free, they must adhere to the needs and demands of the institution which renders them in a position of being neither free nor 'prisoner' but somewhere in between.

Van Ginneken, E., Sutherland, A. and Mollemam, T. (2017) An ecological analysis of prison overcrowding and suicide rates in England and Wales 2000–2014. *International Journal of Law and Psychiatry*, 50, 76–82.

Using data from the Ministry of Justice for adult prisons in England and Wales from 2000 to 2014, this paper explores prison characteristics such as overcrowding, prison function, security level, population, size and turnover in relation to suicide rates amongst people serving a custodial sentence.

references

Arnold, H. (2016) The prison officer. In Y. Jewkes, B. Crewe and J. Bennett (eds) *Handbook on Prisons* (2nd edn). Abingdon: Routledge, pp. 265–83.

Beresford, S. (2018) What about me? The impact on children when mothers are involved in the criminal justice system. Prison Reform Trust. Available at: https://prisonreformtrust. org.uk/wp-content/uploads/2018/02/what-about-me.pdf (last accessed 30 June 2022).

Bourdieu P (1977) *Outline of a Theory of Practice*. Cambridge: Cambridge University Press.

Bourdieu, P. (1980) *The Logic of Practice*. Stanford, CA: Stanford University Press.

Bourdieu, P. (1986) 'The forms of capital.' In J.G. Richardson (ed.) *Handbook of Theory and Research for the Sociology of Capital*. New York: Greenwood Press, pp. 241–58.

Brough, P., Brown, J.M. and Biggs, A. (2016) *Improving Criminal Justice Workplaces: Translating Theory and Research into Evidence-Based Practice*. Abingdon: Routledge.

Cheliotis, L. (2006) How iron is the iron cage of new penology? The role of human agency in the implementation of criminal justice policy. *Punishment & Society*, 8(3), 313–40.

Clemmer, D. (1940) *The Prison Community*. New York: Holt, Rinehart & Winston.

COPE (2016) Data collection and children with imprisoned parents. Blog post. Available at: https://childrenofprisoners.eu/data-collection-and-children-with-imprisoned-parents (last accessed 30 June 2022).

Crane, J. (2019) Becoming institutionalised: Incarceration and 'slow death.' Blog post. Social Science Research Council. Available at: https://items.ssrc.org/insights/becoming-institution-alized-incarceration-and-slow-death/#:~:text=Crane's%20research%20finds%20that%20 imprisoned,term%20bodily%20and%20mental%20impact (last accessed 30 June 2022).

Crewe, B. (2011) Depth, weight, and tightness: Revising the pains of imprisonment. *Punishment and Society*, 13(5), 509-29.

Erasmus, E. (undated) Street level bureaucracy. Available at: https://hpsa-africa.org/images/Street_level_bureaucracy_final_for_web.pdf (last accessed 30 June 2022).

Foster, R (2016) 'Doing the wait': An exploration into the waiting experience of prisoners' families. *Time and Society*, 28(2), 459–77.

Garrihy, J. (2020) 'There are fourteen grey areas': 'Jailing', professionalism and legitimacy in prison officers' occupational cultures. *Irish Probation Journal*, 17, 128–50. Available at: www.pbni.org.uk/wp-content/uploads/2020/11/Joe-Garrihy.pdf (last accessed 30 June 2022).

Goffman, E. (1961) *Asylums: Essays on the Social Situations of Mental Patients and Other Inmates*. Oxfordshire: Transaction Publishers.

Graham, H. (2016) *Rehabilitation Work: Supporting Desistance and Recovery*. Abingdon: Routledge.

Hextall, R. (2022) *Invisible Harms and Hierarchies of Shame: The Distinct Challenges Faced by Children with a Parent in Prison for Sexual Offences. Children Heard and Seen*. Available at: https://childrenheardandseen.co.uk/wp-content/uploads/2022/01/Invisible-Harms-and-Hierarchies-of-Shame.pdf (last accessed 30 June 2022).

HM Government (2019) Prison officer breakdown by age and gender. Freedom of Information request. Available at: https://assets.publishing.service.gov.uk/government/uploads/system/uploads/attachment_data/file/862092/foi-191113015-prison-officer-breakdowns-age-gender-tables.ods (last accessed 30 June 2022).

HM Government (2020) Working in the prison and probation service. Blog post. Available at: https://prisonjobs.blog.gov.uk/ (last accessed 1 August 2022).

HM Government (2021) Prison officer workforce. Available at: www.ethnicity-facts-figures.service.gov.uk/workforce-and-business/workforce-diversity/prison-officer-workforce/latest (last accessed 30 June 2022).

HM Prison and Probation Service (2019) Her Majesty's Prisons and Probation (HMPPS) Workforce Statistics Bulletin, as at 30 September 2019. Available at: https://assets.publishing.service.gov.uk/government/uploads/system/uploads/attachment_data/file/847654/hmpps-workforce-statistics-september-2019.pdf (last accessed 27 July 2022).

HM Prison and Probation Service (2022) Her Majesty's Prisons and Probation workforce quarterly: March 2022. Available at: www.gov.uk/government/statistics/her-majestys-prison-and-probation-service-workforce-quarterly-march-2022/her-majestys-prison-and-probation-service-workforce-quarterly-march-2022 (last accessed 27 July 2022).

HM Prison and Probation Service (2022) Rewards and benefits. Available at: https://prisonandprobationjobs.gov.uk/prison-officer/rewards-and-benefits (last accessed 30 June 2022).

Hofstede, G. (1980) *Culture's Consequences: International Differences in Work-Related Values*. Beverly Hills, CA: Sage.

Jenkins, R. (2002) *Pierre Bourdieu*. London: Routledge.

Johnson, G., Whittington, R. and Scholes, K. (2011) *Exploring Strategy: Text and Cases* (9th edn). Harlow: Pearson.

Justice Committee (2009) Role of the prison officer. Available at: https://publications.parliament.uk/pa/cm200809/cmselect/cmjust/361/36104.htm (last accessed 30 June 2022).

Kincaid, S., Roberts, M. and Kane, E. (2019) *Children of Prisoners. Fixing a Broken System*. Available at: www.nicco.org.uk/userfiles/downloads/5c90a6395f6d8-children-of-prisoners-full-report-web-version.pdf (last accessed 30 June 2022).

Liebling, A. and Crewe, B. (2014) Staff–prisoner relationships, moral performance, and privatisation. In I. Durnescu and F. McNeill (eds) *Understanding Penal Practice*. New York: Routledge, pp. 153–66.

Lipsky (2010) *Street Level Bureaucracy: Dilemmas of the Individual in Public Service*. New York: Russell Sage Foundation.

Maguire, D. (2019) Vulnerable prisoner masculinities in an English prison. *Men and Masculinities*, 24(3), 501–18.

Ministry of Justice (2021) An introduction to POELT (Prison Officer Entry Level Training). Available at: https://prisonjobs.blog.gov.uk/2017/12/13/an-introduction-to-poelt-prison-officer-entry-level-training (last accessed 30 June 2022).

Mitford, J. (1977) *The American Prison Business*. Harmondsworth: Penguin.

Moncrieffe, J. (2006) The power of stigma: Encounters with 'street children' and 'restavecs' in Haiti. *IDS Bulletin*, 37(6), 34–46.

Navarro, Z. (2006) In search of cultural interpretation of power. *IDS Bulletin*, 37(6), 11–22.

Owen, B., Wells, J. and Pollock, J. (2017) *In Search of Safety: Confronting Inequality in Women's Imprisonment*. Berkeley, CA: University of California Press.

Page, J.A. (2013) Punishment and the penal field. In J. Simon and R. Sparks (eds) *The SAGE Handbook of Punishment and Society*. London: Sage, pp. 152–66.

Prospects (2021) Job profile: Prison officer. Available at: www.prospects.ac.uk/job-profiles/prison-officer (last accessed 30 June 2022).

PTSD UK (2022) PTSD in prison employees. Available at: www.ptsduk.org/ptsd-in-prison-employees/ (last accessed 27 July 2022)

Robinson, A. (2013) Transforming rehabilitation: Transforming the occupational identity of probation workers. *British Journal of Community Justice*, 11(2–3): 91–101.

Schein, E.H. (1992) *Organizational Culture and Leadership*. San Francisco: Jossey-Bass.

Schein, E.H. (2010) *Organizational Culture and Leadership* (4th edn) San Francisco: Jossey-Bass.

Sparks, R., Bottoms, A. and Hay, W. (1996) *Prisons and the Problem of Order*. Oxford: Clarendon.

Sykes, G. (1958) *The Society of Captives: A Study of a Maximum-Security Prison*. Princeton, N.J: Princeton University Press.

Sykes, G. and Messinger, S.L. (1960) The inmate social code. In N. Johnson, L. Savitz and M.E. Wolfgang (1962) *The Sociology of Punishment and Correction* (2nd edn). New York: John Wiley & Sons, pp. 401–8.

Tait, S. (2011) A typology of prison officer approaches to care. *European Journal of Criminology*, 8(6), 440–54.

Turanovic, J., Rodriguez, N. and Pratt, T. (2012) The collateral consequences of incarceration revisited: A qualitative analysis of the effects of caregivers of children of incarcerated parents. *Criminology*, 50(4), 913–59.

Waddington, P.A.J. (1999) Police (canteen) sub-culture: An appreciation. *British Journal of Criminology*, 39(2): 287–309.

Walker, T., Shaw, J., Hamilton, L., Turpin, C., Reid, C. and Abel, K. (2017) 'Coping with the job': Prison staff responding to self-harm in three English female prisons: A qualitative study. *Journal of Forensic Psychiatry and Psychology*, 28(6), 811–24.

Youle, E. (2020) This is what it is like to be a prison officer during the Coronavirus pandemic. *Huffington Post*. Available at: www.huffingtonpost.co.uk/entry/prison-guard-coronavirus_uk_5eac347dc5b6995f1400162b (last accessed 30 June 2022).

8
PROBATION CULTURES

┌──────── IN THIS CHAPTER, YOU WILL EXPLORE ────────┐

1. How the supervisory process is experienced from the perspectives of practitioners and those subject to supervision on both a practical and emotional level

2. What motivates individuals to become involved in this type of work, what training they receive, and how 'effectiveness' and 'quality' are defined on both a policy and practice level

3. The impact of recent reforms on the occupational culture of probation cultures.

INTRODUCTION

In the previous chapter you were introduced to the concept of occupational culture which we argued is an important component of understanding how penal agents make sense of their obligations, roles and responsibilities. We highlighted the tensions and dilemmas involved in such work and how practitioners resolve them in their daily interactions. Earlier, in Chapter 4, we outlined the broader structural and policy developments which have shaped probation practice. As we have noted though, how practitioners react to these changes and how they shape their daily encounters with those under their supervision is far from straightforward. For this reason, we now turn our attention to what matters to probation practitioners in terms of how they conceptualise and perceive *quality* in their work, what personal attributes they bring to these interactions, the skills they require and the training they receive, and the emotional dimensions involved. However, no account of this work would be complete without considering and understanding the views of those subject to such sanctions and so it is to this which we turn in the final section of this chapter.

WHAT DO WE KNOW ABOUT PROBATION CULTURE?

Although it has been in existence for over a century it is perhaps true to say that probation work has never attained the status of other organisations within the criminal justice system. Often characterised as interfering, well-intentioned (if somewhat naive) *do gooders*, probation staff have never had, nor sought, the symbolic status of other criminal justice professionals (Mair and Burke, 2013). With a few exceptions, probation workers are rarely portrayed in the crime dramas and documentaries that have become a staple of popular culture. As such probation remains something of a Cinderella service (Robinson, 2016) despite the fact that at any one time it is responsible for over three times as many individuals subject to penal sanctions than are in prison. It has been described as 'dirty work' (Mawby and Worrall 2013) in that it is socially necessary but lacks status or public trust. This cultural indifference to probation work (unless of course there is a serious case of further offending whilst under supervision) could perhaps be rooted in its lack of obvious symbolic representation compared to the uniformed police officer, the ritualised court setting or the 'iron bars, high walls or razor wire of the prison' (Maruna and King, 2008: 346). Yet this does not mean that the need to understand what motivates individuals to undertake this work, and the values and characteristics they present, is any less pressing. As Raynor and Vanstone (2018: 210) note: 'Working with troubled, often poor and disadvantaged people is demanding, stressful, risky, frustrating and emotionally draining. It needs a particular level of motivation and devotion.'

At its best good probation practice motivates people, it develops their capabilities and it seeks to secure opportunities for them to live better lives (Burke et al., 2019). Ultimately, probation practitioners work through direct engagement with people who have offended and who, in many cases, live at the margins of society in terms of their access to social and economic goods. Such relationships are mediated through the worker's own personality, values, knowledge and skills. For many probation workers it is more than just a job; it is a vocation. Probation work therefore has an inherently moral dimension because, as McNeill (2012) notes, it entails a dialogue that centres on the renegotiation of shared values and mutual reparation of the harms that individuals, communities and the state may have done to one another. Engaging with moral complexity is thus part and parcel of probation work but it does not take place in a vacuum and is subject to a range of competing and sometimes contradictory influences (Burke and Davies, 2011). Indeed, it could be argued that the policy failures that have been characteristic of contemporary practice might have been ameliorated somewhat if greater consideration had been paid to the role and influence of those tasked with their implementation.

It is important to acknowledge from the outset that there is not a single monolithic probation culture. Probation workers are involved in a range of different roles and settings and this will be reflected in their approach to their work. There can be differences between those working in urban and rural locations, different probation areas, and between offices in the same probation area (Mawby and Worrall, 2013: 350). Moreover, cultures can change over time and sometimes this will be reflected in generational differences. However, there is also evidence to suggest that despite the significant organisational changes to probation over several decades probation cultures co-exist and despite their differences share common values. These are underpinned by a belief in people to change and the importance of the relationship between probation worker and probationer in facilitating that change (Annison et al., 2008; Deering, 2010; Worrall and Mawby, 2014). They tend to conceptualise crime within structural causes that limit the choices available and leads some people to make bad choices in the form of offending rather than exercising rational free will (Deering, 2010). Grant (2016) developed the concept of the *durable penal agent* to argue that probation workers, of whatever generation, have particular values and principles that attract them to the work. These dispositions (formed before any decision was taken to enter the probation service) appear to enable them to persist in their work regardless of the policy turn. While probation's occupational culture has, in some ways, changed and adapted, in other respects it has proven to be remarkably resilient and practitioners appear to share common sets of values and principles regardless of how these subjective elements were forged.

Probation staff, and certainly those who have been in the service for several years, are accustomed to working within an organisation that is undergoing reform. Indeterminate change is the norm: it is a defining characteristic of their professional existence (Robinson and Burnett, 2007: 332). Studies into occupational cultures suggest that workers often continue to do what they have always done regardless of the employing organisation's change agenda and that their practices are not necessarily based on research evidence 'but rather are formed from gut-level, intuition, informal team socialization processes, training or a lack of training, learned behaviours, lacking resources, and so forth' (Rudes et al., 2014: 19). It therefore cannot be taken for granted that policy intentions will be adopted and operationalised as intended or that they will be either universally or uncritically accepted by staff. There may not only be significant differences between official accounts and how they are interpreted and acted out within the workplace but also between 'expressed beliefs and action' in terms of what individuals say and what they do '(Liebling et al., 2010: 157). Moreover, Ott (1989) acknowledges that organisations can also have subcultures that may sometimes coincide and sometimes conflict with the dominant occupational culture.

DOING PROBATION WORK

One of the most significant insights into the characteristics of contemporary probation culture and how probation workers construct their occupational identities was by Mawby and Worrall (2013). It involved interviews with 60 former and serving probation workers. Participants were asked about their reasons for joining the Probation Service,their daily routines and the work they undertook with individuals subject to probation interventions. They identified three *ideal cultural types* of probation worker:

- *Lifers*. These were mainly over 40 years of age and had spent most of their working lives working in probation. Many had either wanted to join probation from an early age or had been social work trained and they saw the job as a life-long vocation.

- *Second careerists*. In this group were individuals who had worked in unrelated or marginally related occupations. Some had studied as mature students and 'wanted to make a difference'.

- *Offender managers*. These people tended to be younger and had joined probation after the separation from social work training in the mid-1990s. They viewed their role differently from the other two groups in that it was dominated by computer-based risk assessment rather than face-to-face work; it did not involve any significant time visiting those they supervised at home or in the community; and inter-agency work was seen as a vital part of their work. Although this group wanted to work in the public sector, they had little investment in social work culture. They were nevertheless committed to their work and wanted to help people through their work.

Mawby and Worrall (2013) used the concept of *edgework* – activities that involve a form of *voluntary risk taking* – to explain how front-line probation staff mediate policies and guidelines with their established practices and values and within competing demands and resources. For example, this could involve deviating from national standards if there were circumstances in which the individual was unable to comply with the reporting requirements of their order. Edgework involves probation officers *putting their skills to the test* in ways which are sometimes tolerated by their organisation – even if they do not accord with official policies and guidelines – because there is a tacit recognition that such practices are desirable and achieve positive outcomes (Worrall and Mawby, 2013). Edgework can be exciting and empowering but there are serious consequences if the worker gets it wrong or miscalculates the risk, particularly if there is a serious further offence committed whilst under supervision. However, the authors are keen to point out that this is not about behaving recklessly or disregarding the organisation's objectives. Nor is it merely about a nostalgic return to a largely mythical golden age of probation when workers enjoyed largely unfettered autonomy and professional discretion. Rather, it is about putting their skills to the test for the good of the offender, victims, the public and the organisation (Mawby and Worrall, 2011, 2013). Worrall and Mawby identify four possible aspects of probation edgework.

- *Liking offenders and vicarious rule breaking*. Some probation workers not only liked the individuals under their supervision and were attracted to their behaviour but controlled this by working with them without crossing the boundary into illegality themselves.

- *Danger and threat of violence*. Although probation workers are not expected to put themselves in harm's way as police or prison officers do, they must still control difficult situations that can escalate into violence, harm or loss of professional face.

- *Fast and exciting*. Some probation workers appear to get an emotional charge from working in situations that could fall apart if they messed up.

- *Creativity and intensity of work*. Because probation work can be unpredictable it requires intellectual and emotional investment. By taking risks and being creative workers can feel that they are being true to themselves and making a difference. (Adapted from Worrall and Mawby, 2013)

In common with other studies highlighted in this chapter, Worrall and Mawby found that the relationship between the probation worker and those under their supervision was central to the objective of reducing reoffending. Workers differed though in their views about the purpose of the relationship, positioning themselves along a spectrum from *rehabilitation*, through *rehabilitation and risk assessment* to *risk assessment* and *offender management* (see also Durnescu, 2012). Lifers and second careerists tended towards the former positions, whereas offender managers tended towards the latter positions.

WHAT HAS BEEN THE EFFECT OF TRANSFORMING REHABILITATION ON THE CULTURE OF PROBATION WORK?

Most of the studies discussed so far were conducted before the implementation of the Transforming Rehabilitation (TR) reforms which, as discussed earlier, have had a profound impact on the organisation and delivery of probation services. In an online survey (1,300 responses) conducted just before the probation services were split, Deering and Feilzer (2015) found considerable opposition among probation workers to the proposed TR reforms. Many of those surveyed expressed 'anger, feelings of betrayal, and sadness about the destruction of the unified, public probation service' (Deering and Feilzer, 2015: 101). They feared that the erosion of traditional probation values brought about by the increasing emphasis on punishment, law enforcement and case management would be exacerbated under TR through the introduction of private and voluntary sector organisations into the *business* of probation.

Robinson et al. (2016) undertook research in a single community rehabilitation company to consider the impact on probation workers. Probation workers in the CRC expressed *hurt, anger, confusion* and *uncertainty*. One practitioner described it as *unwanted divorce* (Robinson et al., 2016: 167). Staff generally believed that the timescales for implementing the split had been unrealistic and that the failure to develop and test the changes had resulted in what some viewed as an indecent rush to prepare themselves for these two almost arbitrary organisations (Robinson et al., 2016). Respondents questioned the ethics of the new organisations, and like those whose views were canvassed in a similar study by Deering and Feilzer (2015), believed that although probation values had already come under pressure and been compromised before TR, this had been exacerbated by the structural split, producing a negative effect on all those involved. Robinson et al. (2016) highlighted a range of emotional costs involved in the restructuring of probation workers as they moved from a public to a privately owned organisation:

- *Separation and loss*. For some workers this involved a physical separation as they were re-allocated to a new building or office. There was also the pain of separation from service users with whom they had established working relationships but who had been transferred to the NPS due to their high-risk status. Many of those interviewed mentioned the physical loss of former colleagues to the NPS but there were also perceived losses relating to separation from the public sector which was seen to threaten the *probation ethos*.

- *Liminality and insecurity*. Probation workers in the CRC were operating in a temporary domain betwixt and between the old Probation Trusts and the new ownership. They were uncertain about their future terms and conditions of employment, and this added to their sense of insecurity.

- *Status anxiety*. Interviewees alluded to the idea of the NPS as the *elite* organisation, casting the CRC into the role of *second-class* probation.

- *Loyalty and trust*. The loyalties of many workers had become detached from the organisation in which they worked and, in this respect, former attachments and loyalties to the Probation Trust had not transferred unproblematically. Some of those interviewed expressed feelings of loyalty to the profession but not to the CRC. Practitioners implied a partial withdrawal of loyalty (i.e., *working to rule*) although whether this translated into practice was not clear.

- *Liberation and innovation*. The official rationale for the TR reforms included introducing more innovation into the system. Several participants voiced hopes of being liberated from bureaucracy, performance-related targets and national standards and saw the CRC as potentially a site for experimentation.

These studies seem to suggest that the part privatisation of the probation service under TR has had a significant impact on the culture and values of the organisation although its impact on the habitus of probation workers is less clear. According to Tidmarsh (2019: 3) 'the residue of humanitarian endeavour, therefore, persists within probation – although it is operationalised on a transformed landscape in which TR has intensified, if not initiated, the pressures of work'. There is some evidence that deepening cuts, precarious working environments and increasingly unmanageable caseloads amount to 'a pervasive form of systemic workplace harm, resulting in mental health issues, stress, and professional dissatisfaction' (Walker et al., 2019: 113). Conversely, it could be argued that the impact of TR is 'a continuation of a decades-long period in which probation's knowledge and modes of working have been diminished and downgraded' (Tidmarsh, 2020: 99).

HOW DO PROBATION PRACTITIONERS DEFINE QUALITY IN THEIR WORK?

Robinson (2020) notes that what constitutes quality is essentially subjective in the sense that it is often understood differently by different people. Understanding what matters to practitioners and how they construct notions of quality in their day-to-day practice has, however, according to Robinson, both theoretical and practical implications in that:

> **Firstly, it is of theoretical importance because it tells us a great deal about the contemporary culture or 'habitus' of practice in any given jurisdiction. In other words, *quality discourse* [emphasis in original] can serve as a sort of cultural barometer, capable of revealing commonly held assumptions (and, potentially, differences of opinion about what matters to the practitioner community). But practitioner perspectives on quality are also of practical significance, particularly for those who wish to change or improve practice. Constructions of quality are normative in the sense that they represent an 'ideal' of practice: that is, a vision or template of what practice ought to look like. (Robinson, 2020: 965)**

Shapland et al. (2012) undertook a review of the international literature on the quality of supervision. The researchers summarised their findings of what practitioners and service users saw as demonstrating quality in their interactions in a research summary produced by the Ministry of Justice (Shapland et al., 2012a: 1):

- Building genuine relationships that demonstrate *care* about the person being supervised, their desistance and their future – not just monitoring/surveillance

- Engaging offenders in identifying needs and setting goals for supervision, including a supervisory relationship which shows active listening by supervisors

- Supervisors who keep on trying to steer supervisees in a desisting direction through motivating them, encouraging them to solve problems and talking about problems

- An understanding of how desistance may occur, with thoughtful consideration of how relapse or breaches should be dealt with

- Attention to relevant practical obstacles to desistance, not just psychological issues

- Knowledge of and access to the resources of local services/provision, in order to help the supervisee deal with these practical obstacles

- Advocacy tailored to individual needs and capabilities, which may involve work by the supervisor, referral to others or signposting to others, depending on the supervisee's self-confidence and social capital.

The researchers were also commissioned by the National Offender Management Service (Shapland et al., 2012) to shed light on how probation workers understood quality in the context of one-to-one supervision in the community. The study adopted an appreciative inquiry approach developed by Liebling in the prison setting that focused on 'strengths, accomplishments, best practice and peak moments' (Liebling, 2004: 132). The research uncovered a considerable degree of consensus in the responses, although quality was not seen as comprising a single concept but included a number of factors which interact with and support the others. The researchers distilled the responses into several key themes. Probation workers, regardless of their role in the organisation, all saw *good working relationships* as crucial to delivering quality work. Good working relationships with those under their supervision were articulated in terms of 'building rapport; treating the offender respectfully; listening; being open and honest; following up on promised actions; taking time to get to know the person; being consistent; involving the offender in setting goals; establishing boundaries; and building trust' (Robinson, 2020: 960). Good relationships with other agencies were also viewed as important. Having enough *time* to work constructively with individuals was seen as important in achieving quality work. This wasn't just about the direct face-to face contact with individuals but also involved preparing and planning for supervision sessions and having the time to reflect and discuss cases with colleagues. Time was seen as a scarce resource within the organisation and many of those interviewed described having to *go the extra mile* to get things done (Robinson, 2020: 961). Those subject to probation supervision often present a range of emotional behaviours and practical problems. Workers therefore stressed the importance of *individualisation and flexibility* in responding to individuals' risks, needs and circumstances. To do this, relevant and up-to-date information about the individual and a knowledge of local resources was vital. Inflexible requirements regarding compliance and enforcement were not viewed as helpful in this respect.

In terms of the *goals and outcomes* of supervision, both the process and outcome were seen as important, and the latter was unlikely to be achieved in the absence of processes based upon a good working relationship. In terms of the *attributes, skills and values* it is not so much the merits of a specific technical approach that matter in securing outcomes but rather the qualities of the worker. The authors characterised these qualities as a combination of (largely soft/relational) skills, professional training (for qualified staff) and experiences accrued on the job, coupled with the values, personal experiences and qualities that participants brought to their work. Finally *support*, both formal and informal, from colleagues and managers was valued as a means of supporting quality work. Support from other agencies, both within and beyond the criminal justice system was particularly important for those working with more complex cases. Working with individuals was not seen as an exclusively one-to-one affair but needed to involve others with different abilities, resources and skills. The authors concluded that in this respect, collaborative working has become 'part of the normal cultural fabric of probation practice in England and Wales' (Shapland et al., 2014: 144).

Grant and McNeill (2015) subsequently adopted the methods deployed by Shapland et al. to explore the views of 25 Scottish criminal justice workers from one local authority area. Like their counterparts in England and Wales, the majority of Scottish criminal justice social workers described reciprocal, meaningful and trusting *relational processes* as the key to good quality work. However, they also expressed frustration at the lack of *resources* and time to achieve this. Perhaps unsurprisingly, given that criminal justice social workers in Scotland continue to be trained with a social work framework, practice was grounded in *social work values* (i.e. respecting the individual, promoting social inclusion and demonstrating anti-discriminatory practice). Social work values were seen as being far more influential in achieving quality supervision and often meant *going beyond national standards*. This involved 'degrees of resistance to, and resilience from, what they perceive as technocratic management styles' (Grant and McNeill, 2015: 1996). Even though Scotland operates a system of supervision distinct from that in England and Wales, there was a high degree of consistency in both jurisdictions in practitioners' perceptions of what constituted quality supervision. Quality in both studies emerged 'both as a lived experience and as a contextualised and constructed practice' (Grant and McNeill, 2015: 1999). In this respect, probation workers became 'cultural carriers' of probation (Clare, 2015: 50) regardless of the organisational structure they worked in. As Robinson (2020: 966) notes:

Attempts to change practice then are likely to fail unless they engage with these existing 'ideals' and succeed in either challenging them or persuading practitioners that new ways of working are consistent with their current understandings of what quality work is.

WHAT SKILLS ARE REQUIRED IN PROBATION WORK?

When we talk about 'using' skills, this does not usually mean selecting a skill from a behavioural repertoire like selecting the right spanner from a toolbox. What we are really talking about is skilled interviewing and interaction, and this is related to personal attributes and aptitudes. (Raynor, 2019: 8)

In his review of the research literature on skills and personal attributes of probation staff, Durnescu (2012) identified that what he termed *supportive skills* such as empathy, authenticity, reasonableness, good communication skills, an interest in people, a belief in the capacity for change were not only most valued by both practitioners and probationers alike but were also most likely to have a positive impact on further offending (2014: 189). These skills have also been referred to as *capital* elsewhere in the literature (see Chapter 2). Moreover, in their study of probation staff, Bonta and colleagues (2008) found that the amount of time spent discussing probationers' needs as opposed to the conditions of probation in their meetings was positively associated with a reduction in recidivism. Similarly, Petersilia and Turner's (1993) examination of intensive supervision programmes found that when they emphasised monitoring and surveillance at the expense of treatment and rehabilitation, failure rates were high and there was no effect on recidivism. Durnescu (2014) also identified other approaches, such an effective use of authority, role clarification and cognitive behavioural interventions, which though apparently less valued by probation staff and probationers also had a positive impact on reducing reoffending. Other skills or practices were less effective in terms of reducing reoffending but achieved different objectives such as, for example, securing compliance and building motivation.

The correlation between the role of practitioners in influencing the outcomes of individual supervision has been something a *black box* (Bonta et al., 2008) although recently a number of studies have sought to enhance our understanding of these processes. There has also been increasing international attention given to the skills involved in supervision and the methods that underpin the supervisory process. One of the earliest attempts to capture the skills utilised by workers was by Chris Trotter (1999) who developed a training programme that followed some of the elements of the responsivity principle. In this study, 30 probation officers were provided with five days of training on prosocial modelling, empathy and problem solving. After the initial training, 12 officers attended ongoing training sessions and applied the skills during supervision. The recidivism rate of 93 clients of the trained officers who continued their involvement in the ongoing training and applied these new skills was compared to 273 clients of officers who reverted to their routine supervision practices. The four-year reconviction rate was 53.8 per cent for the clients of the officers who continued to apply the skills taught in training as evidenced by file reviews. The rate for the clients of the officers who engaged in routine supervision practices was 64 per cent (Bourgon et al., 2011: 31).

One of the most developed approaches to evaluating the skills used by staff was that developed by Bonta et al. (2008). Using audiotapes of interviews, the researchers sought to assess the effects of a training programme – the Strategic Training Initiative in Community Supervision (STICS) – which was broadly based on principles of risk, needs and responsivity (RNR). This training programme included three days of training and ongoing clinical support activities (i.e. refresher courses, individual feedback and monthly meetings) with specific, practical and concrete RNR-based intervention techniques and skills. Officers trained in the STICS programme were instructed to assess and focus their efforts on the criminogenic needs of those under their supervision. These included positive relationship building and a structured approach to supervision, incorporating the use of cognitive–behavioural techniques; problem solving, decision making, consequential thinking and victim awareness (Bourgon et al., 2011). Their findings suggested that probation officers trained to use STICS were more effective in reducing reoffending than those who had not been trained and tended to have a more clearly defined structure of intervention, better relationship skills and employed more cognitive techniques. The amount of time workers spent discussing probationers' needs as opposed to the conditions of probation in their meetings was also positively associated with recidivism reductions in that the difference between the control group and the experimental group was 15 per cent (25.3 per cent for the experimental group and 40.5 per cent for the control group). This project has stimulated others to develop similar training programmes, for example Staff Training Aimed at Reducing Re-arrest (STARR) from Lowenkamp and colleagues at the United States Office of Probation and Pre-trial Services, and Effective Practices in Community Supervision (EPICS) from the Corrections Institute of the University of Cincinnati.

In England and Wales, the Skills for Effective Engagement and Development (SEED) training package was developed by the National Offender Management Service (NOMS) as part of its Offender Engagement Project (OEP). The overarching aim of the OEP was to reduce unnecessary prescription through process-based performance targets and national standards to enable practitioners to use their professional discretion and skills to reduce reoffending. It built on a pilot on professional judgement in Surrey and Sussex Probation Trust which showed that staff who were given more discretion in their work tended to have more purposeful and focused contact with those under their supervision (Rex and Hosking, 2013: 334). SEED is just one of the OEP projects and was targeted at practitioners and addresses how they relate to and work with those under their supervision. The initiative aimed to provide probation staff with additional training and continuous professional development in skills they could use in supervising individuals, particularly in one-to-one meetings. Like STICS, SEED was designed broadly in accordance with RNR principles, but it was also informed by emerging evidence about desistance from crime (Sorsby et al., 2017: 193). SEED focused on four key themes: *pro-social modelling, reflective supervision, observed practice* and *action learning*. The training consisted of three core training days and then three one-day quarterly follow-up training sessions.

Although the implementation of SEED was effectively derailed by the TR reforms, there were indications that practitioners valued it and overall reaction to the training was positive (Sorsby et al., 2013). Eighty-seven per cent thought it very important to their practice to continue to use the model and 70 per cent saw their time as more focused and three quarters mostly or always had a plan for supervision sessions (Rex and Hosking, 2013: 336). Practitioners reported that they were more focused and that they were undertaking more structured and better-quality work. The intervention was not perceived as overly prescriptive. Aspects of SEED that were particularly appreciated involved teams training together and discussing cases together between further training sessions. Interestingly, SEED was also appreciated specifically because the framework for supervision was based on empirical evidence (Sorsby et al., 2017: 211). Finally, although evidence of the impact of SEED training on supervisees' experience of supervision was limited, there were some indications that practitioners in the trained group were perceived as using a fuller range of SEED skills overall compared with those in the comparison group (Sorsby et al., 2017: 212). The Probation Service is, at the time of writing, rolling out a new supervision and line management framework under the umbrella of SEEDS 2. This includes a much greater focus on the emotional demands of probation work and includes provision for line managers to support staff with this side of their work (Phillips et al., 2020).

The Jersey Supervision Skills Study (JS3) is part of a long-term research partnership between criminologists in Swansea University and the Jersey Probation and After-Care Service (JPACS). The study commenced in 2007 and involved video-recording interviews by probation staff with those under probation supervision and an analysis of the interviews by researchers using a specially developed checklist (Raynor et al., 2009). The 63-item checklist covered nine skill clusters: interview set-up, non-verbal communication, verbal communication, effective use of authority, motivational interviewing, prosocial modelling, problem solving, cognitive restructuring and overall interview structure. The study aimed to compare staff who used a wide range of skills with those who used fewer skills, and to see if there were differences in outcomes. The average difference in reoffending rates when comparing outcomes for trained staff with those for untrained staff was 13 per cent. The largest difference was with supervision by more skilled staff, which resulted in a two-year follow-up reconviction rate of 26 per cent compared to 58 per cent among similar individuals supervised by less skilled staff. Some staff who had low average scores on the skills checklist were often scored more highly on some individual interviews suggesting 'that training for these staff would involve using their best skills in more of their work rather than trying to impart skills which they never used' (Raynor, 2020: 6).

The importance of these models of supervision is that they were not simply concerned with risk management or even a reductionist focus on offender compliance in accordance with the expectations of the court. Rather, they attempted to locate the individual under supervision within a wider professional and organisational context and thereby tailor supervision to the drivers of criminal behaviour and the degree to which the individual made progress (Toronjo and Taxman, 2018). This is critical because, as

Pereira and Trotter (2018) point out, research shows that supervision approaches that predominantly focus on formal compliance and performance management and that fail to balance the supervisory functions of accountability with education and support, limit the space for reflection and skills development by both supervisor and supervisee. Although they differ in the details of skill assessment and measurement, all these well-designed studies suggest that more skilled officers produce better results in terms of both reconviction and compliance (Trotter, 1996; Trotter and Evans, 2012).

EMOTIONS AND PROBATION WORK

Phillips et al. (2020) contend that the focus on the abilities of probation practitioners to *manage cases* has detracted from the emotional nature of such work. *Emotional labour* (Hochshild, 1983) is a term used to describe the ways in which workers either convey or supress their emotions in order to get the job done. Emotions such as happiness, humour and satisfaction are utilised by practitioners to 'foster good working relationships, encourage people to comply with the requirements of their orders and continue working to improve their lives (Phillips et al., 2020: 6). Sometimes they will be required to display *emotional neutrality* to disguise their true feelings when an individual is describing the circumstances relating to an offence (Westaby et al., 2019). Conversely, negative emotions such as anger, frustration and annoyance are used to convey disappointment that the individual has not done as well as expected or disapproval of their behaviour (Westaby et al., 2019). Drawing on the emotional labour literature Phillips et al. (2020: 5) identify three ways in which emotional labour is performed:

1. By *surface acting* which is where a worker simulates the emotions to be displayed in order to produce a desired emotional reaction in another person. This way of performing emotional labour results in the emotion that is being displayed differing from the one(s) being felt.

2. Through *deep acting* whereby a worker engages in the emotional display either directly or indirectly through the alignment of inner feelings with emotional labour expectations. This can be achieved by invoking those emotions either through experience or through a trained imagination. In this way the worker regulates their emotions in order to harmonise them with those expected by the organisation.

3. Workers may also express *genuine emotional responses*, aligning the worker's feelings with the emotional expectations of an organisation. Although such displays are more genuine, emotional labour is still required because the response will need regulating in order to be appropriately displayed.

Probation work involves a high degree of surface acting (i.e. the suppression of emotions) and research suggests that this can lead to burnout, stress and emotional exhaustion. However, it can be easier to cope with if the rules that govern the use of emotions are more explicit (Morris and Feldman, 1996). Employment requiring high levels of emotional labour can be stressful, but they can also bring high levels of job satisfaction (Phillips et al., 2020: 7). As we have noted, probation workers have to manage structural and organisational expectations as well as their own individual values and occupational cultures. The literature on *emotional literacy* (Knight, 2014) builds on this framework and includes the issue of how emotions are also key in motivating (or de-motivating) us in all aspects of our lives and work. Emotional literacy is defined as 'the ability to recognise, understand, handle and appropriately express emotions ... using your emotions to help yourself and others succeed' (Sharp, 2012). As we have noted already, probation workers work with individuals who can be challenging and regarded as undeserving and so have to manage the range of emotions this type of work can evoke. There is a danger that practitioners who feel the emotional impact of the work is ignored may become demotivated and less likely to want to engage in the sometimes messy worlds that probation work involves. Alternatively, they may continue to engage unsupported, but at risk of exhaustion and burnout. In the longer term, either of these ways of managing can lead to a reduction in performance and increased sickness absence. In 2018, HMPPS staff lost an average of 9.3 working days to sickness absence. The most common category of sickness absence in terms of days lost is mental and behavioural disorders, which includes stress-related absences. In the last year, 32.3 per cent of absences were for mental and behavioural disorders. This category was most prevalent for probation officers where 41.5 per cent of working days lost were attributed to mental and behavioural disorders. This can sometimes spill over into their personal and family lives. Research by Petrillo (2007) found that this was particularly true for female probation officers who were supervising high-risk individuals. Exposure to upsetting and harrowing material not only undermined their faith in humanity but also affected their relationships outside of work.

WHAT TRAINING DO PROBATION WORKERS RECEIVE?

The question of what sort of education should be provided to probation staff has attracted increased attention in many European countries over recent years (Carr, 2020). Probation traditionally borrowed knowledge and techniques from social work and this was reflected in the training arrangements. According to Durnescu (2012: 179), this 'enhanced the professional status of probation ... and helped probation officers to build up their legitimacy and public status'. The separation of probation training from social work in the mid-1990s (although it remains part of social work training in Scotland and Northern Ireland) was seen as one of the precursors of modernisation and as a means of presenting the service as a more effective and thus credible agency of criminal justice/enforcement. One of the forces behind the new award was a desire to change the staff profile of the probation service. In the mid 1990s, the then Home Secretary, Michael Howard, had talked about former members of the armed forces being encouraged to work in probation in order to deliver its status as a deliverer of 'punishment in the community. The Dews Report (Home Office, 1994) into the training of probation officers referred to an over-representation of young, unmarried women and Black people in the probation service. Ironically, there has been a feminisation of the Probation Service workforce since the 1990s (Annison, 2013). Unlike other parts of the criminal justice system like the police and prisons, over 70 per cent of the probation workforce are now women.

To become. a probation office you have to achieve The Professional Qualification in Probation (PQiP). This programme lasts 15 or 21 months depending on previous qualifications and is a mixture of workplace and online learning with the latter delivered by a contracted higher education provider. Training combines applied academic learning and practical skills development in order to equip the trainee with the necessary skills and knowledge. During training, trainees are employed as probation services officers (PSO). On successful completion of the programme, they are awarded a vocational qualification, the Diploma in Probation Practice, as well as an honours degree. What is distinctive about these later training developments is that they are aimed at probation *service* officers and not just those training to become qualified probation officers. This reflects a broader organisational change which has seen a significant increase in the deployment of probation service officers (PSOs) to deliver front-line services. Probation service officers were introduced as 'ancillaries' in the 1970s to assist probation officers in their role, managing generic cases but also performing specialist functions like unpaid work. Against the backdrop of rising caseloads, probation service officers' responsibilities have gradually expanded to encompass tasks typically performed by probation officers (Fitzgibbon and Lea, 2014).

In Scotland, criminal justice social workers carry out the work done by probation officers in England and you will need an undergraduate or postgraduate degree in social work approved by the Scottish Social Services Council. In Northern Ireland, probation officers are qualified social workers employed by the Probation Board for Northern Ireland. It is not a requirement to have worked with law breakers when applying for training (although obviously it helps and potential applicants are encouraged do voluntary work to support their academic qualifications if they do not have first-hand experience of probation work). Given probation works with people who have many problems and potentially present a range of challenging behaviours, the applicant's personal qualities are also very important because the success of probation depends upon the quality of the relationship between the worker and those under their supervision.

The current arrangements for delivering probation training in England and Wales are currently under review although the government has made a commitment to supporting a professional workforce through its Probation Workforce Strategy (HM Prisons and Probation Service, 2020). These plans will entail legally recognising probation as a regulated profession, which will involve creating a regulatory framework for establishing qualification requirements and practice standards, alongside a framework for continuous professional development and testing an accelerated progression pathway from probation services officer to probation officer which launched in 2020/21. Alongside this the strategy intends to establish a Curriculum Authority to ensure the provision of an evidence-based curriculum informed by experts. The plans include the potential recruitment of a minimum of a thousand new probation officers in training by January 2021. This appears to be a recognition of the need to invest in the probation workforce, particularly following the difficulties experienced as a result of the TR reforms (Carr, 2020). Significantly, the plans include the development of a *Cultural Code* which will be used as a tool to embed a unified, inclusive and diverse culture into all aspects of the workforce (HM Prisons and Probation Service, 2020: 10).

The Council of Europe (2019) has also issued *Guidelines Regarding Recruitment, Selection, Education, Training and Professional Development of Prison and Probation Staff* in recognition of the need to provide a set of standards that will apply to all Council of Europe member states. The guidelines outline a number of key principles relating to the recruitment, education and training, and professional development of prison and probation staff. In some countries prison and probation staff are employed by the same agency, and there are some areas of the guidelines that pertain to both. The guidelines also set out the educational entry standards that should apply for probation staff and further recommend that member states should develop a framework for continuous professional development (see Carr, 2020, for a more detailed discussion of these developments).

EXPERIENCING PROBATION AS A SERVICE USER

So far in this chapter we have focused on what matters to probation officers and what they value in their work. The other side of the coin is that probation workers are penal agents who exert control over other citizens. Therefore, any exploration of these interactions would be incomplete without also exploring the views of those subject to such sanctions. Sue Rex (2002) interviewed 60 individuals subject to probation supervision to explore what they valued in the process. Approximately a quarter of the sample were women and half were 30 years of age or over. Most of those interviewed considered probation to have assisted in the process of their desistance from offending. A commitment to supervision and to desist from criminality appeared to be generated by the personal and professional commitment shown by their probation officers whose reasonableness, fairness and encouragement seemed to engender a sense of personal loyalty (what they saw as a display of interest in their well-being). Providing encouragement and sustaining engagement were seen as the qualities most valued in a probation officer. Fifty-two (87 per cent) of those under supervision referred to the need for probation officers to demonstrate empathy, and 39 (65 per cent) commented that their supervisors' ability to listen, and to show interest and understanding, enabled them to talk (Rex, 2002: 372). Whilst the commitment, both personal and professional, shown by probation officers was vital in generating engagement and positive changes, it was accepted that this had to be balanced against a certain amount of professionalism and formality. Most of those interviewed acknowledged the more formal aspects of supervision 39 (65 per cent) and 35 (58 per cent) wanted to be treated with respect in the sense of not being judged or patronised (Rex, 2002: 371).

In terms of what they hoped to gain from supervision, those interviewed in Rex's study appeared to gain most from a problem-solving approach to the practical problems they faced (such as debts and accommodation) and helping them to develop better insight into their relationship difficulties or addictions. However, they did not expect the probation officer to necessarily *solve* their problems for them and there seemed to be an acceptance that this was something they had to do for themselves (Rex, 2002: 374). Effective supervision was very much framed as a negotiated process, but the findings suggested 'that probation officers may be hampered by their own tentativeness about engaging probationers fully in the making of plans to tackle the issues underlying their offending' (Rex, 2002: 380). Similar findings were found in a study by Farrall (2002). Although assistance in identifying employment opportunities and mending damaged family relationships appeared particularly important to those being supervised, paradoxically it was these areas that probation staff were most wary of intervening in. As a result, desistance could be attributed to specific interventions by the probation officer in only a few cases.

More positive findings regarding the experiences of probation supervision were recorded in the study by Mair and Mills (2009) into the impact of the community order and suspended sentence order which were introduced in 2003. Virtually all those interviewed expressed the view that their probation officer was easy to talk to, understanding and helpful with their problems (Mair and Mills, 2009: 37). Although the researchers acknowledge that their findings were based on a small snapshot study of a selective group and the methods employed may have resulted in a bias in favour of those who are compliant, supervision was generally seen positively as an opportunity to 'get things off your chest' (Mair and Mills, 2009: 32). The positive features of supervision highlighted by respondents generally related to receiving help and having someone to talk to. Some felt their probation officers had gone out of their way to help or had gone beyond what they had to do, particularly when brokering contact with support services. There appeared to be little resistance or concern about the surveillance or controlling role of a probation officer. Indeed, many implied that because they were aware of the boundaries in terms of compliance, their probation officer became more of a supportive guidance figure than the authoritarian law official some had expected. Although many of those interviewed by Mair and Mills appeared to have a 'good' relationship with their probation officer, the researchers found that in terms of what was actually occurring in supervision, 'on the surface, descriptions of supervision were often suggestive of a somewhat vague conversation rather than being explicitly task-focused' (Mair and Mills, 2009: 32). Although the individuals were seemingly complying with their orders, there was evidence of what Bottoms (2001) terms 'compliance based on habit and routine' in which the individual merely goes through the motions of compliance in an unreflective manner.

As Hayes (2018) points out, supervision can *help with desistance* through motivating and supporting the individual (although as we discussed in Chapter 2) this can also be provided by family and other non-penal actors). For individuals whose lives are chaotic and unstructured, probation supervision can provide *structure and order. The development of pro-social skills and attitudes* potentially made them better able to face the 'consequences of societal, communal, and economic responses to their conviction' (Hayes, 2018: 384). The final gain of probation supervision identified by Hayes was what he termed *at least it's not prison*. In this sense, regardless of the impositions of the community sanction, there was a sense of relief that it was not imprisonment. However, Hayes goes on to make the important point that 'Even where penal supervision does good, it also causes pain' (2018: 385).

Durnescu (2012) examined the experiences of 43 individuals on probation in Romania. Drawing on Sykes' (1958) classic study of the pains of imprisonment (see Chapter 5 for a further discussion), he identified the following types of deprivations and frustrations that he termed the *pains of probation*. Although these *pains* were not experienced by all those interviewed, Durnescu concluded that they were evident in the group as a whole. *Deprivation of autonomy* was one of the most frequently cited sources of anxiety and frustration. The requirement, imposed by the court, to attend regular appointments and inform probation of changes in circumstances contributed to a lack of agency amongst those interviewed. In this respect, they involved obligations which the individual would not necessarily otherwise agree to undertake (Hayes, 2018: 385). Some complained of having their employment opportunities restricted by the requirement to report to the probation office and had to *organise their daily routines around the sanction*. Supervision could also impinge on their *private and family lives* particularly when home visits were undertaken by the probation officer. Another important source of deprivation was that of *time*. Although the meetings with probation were often short (between 10 and 60 minutes) they often had to travel long distances to get there. This incurred *financial costs*, which in many cases they could not afford. The *stigmatisation effects of probation supervision* were raised by a number of respondents in terms of having to disclose their status to employers, family, etc. Supervision also involved a *forced return to the offence* which many found painful. Finally, the threat of being returned to court, and potentially imprisoned, if they did not comply with the sanction meant that they were living a life under *tremendous threat*. Although these pains were not experienced in a physical sense, they nevertheless 'cut deeply and are experienced in a variety of ways depending on the personal circumstances and histories of the participants' (Durnescu, 2010: 538). Hayes' (2015) English study involving nine individuals supervised within a single Probation Trust produced similar findings, identifying six clusters of pains:

1. *Pains of rehabilitation*, including shame about one's offending behaviour and mandatory lifestyle changes

2. *Deprivations of liberty*, in the sense of freedom, time and money

3. *Penal welfare issues*, associated with the loss of stability, family relationships, friendships, employment and employability, and other criminogenic factors as a result of one's conviction or punishment

4. *Pains inflicted by external agencies*, such as the welfare state or by charities

5. *Process pains* associated with perceived procedural unfairness, the pain of being a 'usual suspect' known to police, and the challenges inherent in the prosecution and conviction processes themselves

6. *Stigmatisation effects*, from family members, friends and strangers, and particularly potential employers.

These pains could be either unaffected, reduced or intensified by probation supervision. Hayes (2015: 95) notes that although the supervisory relationship alone was insufficient to enable individuals to escape these pains completely, when it worked well it did provide them with hope and a belief that they could overcome the problems they faced. The studies discussed here have some methodological limitations in that they are often based on small samples and are largely reliant on respondents' perceptions of events obtained mainly through interviews and questionnaires. Recent studies (Fitzgibbon, 2018; McNeill, 2018) have utilised more innovative methods, such as photography and song writing to enable individuals to capture their emotional experiences of being supervised. However, many of the studies discussed in this chapter suggest that although there appears to be some homogeneity of values and attitudes expressed by probation officers, this does not mean that the way in which they translate them into their working practices can be taken for granted. There is inevitably a diverse range of orientations among staff in terms of their reasons for joining probation, their attachment to the organisation, their job satisfaction, their attitudes to promotion, their working relationships with their colleagues and workers in other agencies, and how they perceive their role and those they supervise.

Research across Europe suggests that the experiences of supervision are very different in different countries, especially in relation to the extent that practical help is offered, but overall supervisees generally find it helpful (McNeill and Beyens, 2013). Respect and fairness from supervisors, good relationships between supervisors and supervisees in which they work *together* to address problems, and the provision of practical assistance all seem to help. This is consistent with other studies (Shapland et al., 2014: 141). To a large extent these sorts of factors influence the way people engage (or fail to engage) in changing their offending behaviour through supervision. While supervision has many diverse forms, they share an imminent, pervasive quality in which people are made subject to life-altering and freedom-limiting conditions and live under the constant threat of further (worse) sanctions being imposed should they be judged somehow to be 'failing'. Their status as semi-free citizens feels precarious. Being supervised in a fair and helpful way may make these pains easier to bear, but it does not remove them (McNeill and Beyens, 2013).

CONCLUSION

In our discussion at the start of this chapter, we have attempted to highlight the fact that probation culture is neither one dimensional nor unchanging. Throughout its history the probation service has had to balance society's expectations and in recent years has experienced unprecedented organisational changes brought about by the Transforming Rehabilitation (TR) reforms. These latest policy developments can be viewed as the culmination of managerially driven processes, risk management techniques, acute resource constraints and attempts to marketise the provision of rehabilitation. All of these factors may be influential in shaping supervisory encounters and approaches to probation work. However, considering the research conducted with probation workers into how they perceive these changes and what they view as important in their work, the overall impression is one of a group of workers still striving to utilise their professional skills and hold onto their humanitarian values, based on a belief in the individual's ability to change. This led us to a deeper consideration of how they define *quality* in their interactions with those under their supervision. Although notions of what constitutes quality in probation work is subjective, it has important theoretical and practical implications in that they both provide a template against which practitioners either adopt, adapt or resist new policy initiatives.

However, as important as practitioners' perspectives undoubtedly are, there needs to be an objective measure in terms of whether what they are doing is achieving desirable outcomes. We therefore considered several initiatives aimed at improving the skill sets among such workers which suggest that putting resources into staff development not only produces more skilled workers but also produces better outcomes. In addition to the skills that probation workers possess, the emotional aspects of their work, and the impact this can have on both their professional and private lives should receive greater acknowledgement. We also considered the training they receive. In the closing section of this chapter, we discussed the emerging research into the experiences of those subject to supervisory sanctions. The insights provided alert us both to the potential gains and to the limitations of probation supervision. In doing so they hopefully heighten our appreciation of the physical, psychological and financial demands that experiencing state-sanctioned punishments in the community has on individuals as well as those tasked with enforcing them.

recommended reading

If you would like to engage in further reading, you may find the following resources particularly helpful:

Deering, J. (2011) *Probation Practice and the New Penology: Practitioner Reflections*. Abingdon: Routledge.

Based on the author's empirical research, this book provides examples of 'real' practice through the lens of the modernisation of public services, managerialism and theories of organisational change.

Mawby R.C. and Worrall, A. (2014) *Doing Probation Work: Identity in a Criminal Justice Occupation*. Abingdon: Routledge.

This groundbreaking text focuses on the changes to the occupational culture of probation and the ways in which probation workers themselves view their roles.

Graham, H. (2018) *Rehabilitation Work: Supporting Desistance and Recovery*. Abingdon: Routledge.

This book provides a unique insight into what happens behind the closed doors of prisons, probation and parole offices, drug rehabs and recovery support services, drawing on the author's research in Australia.

Phillips, J., Waters, J., Westaby, C. and Fowler, A. (eds) (2020) *Emotional Labour in Criminal Justice and Criminology*. Abingdon: Routledge.

This edited collection explores ways in which workers in a range of criminal justice institutions as well as the voluntary sector manage their emotions in order to achieve the aims of their organisations and the subsequent impact of this on workers and service users.

references

Annison, J. (2013) Change and the Probation Service in England and Wales: A gendered lens. *European Journal of Probation*, 5(1), 44–64.

Annison, J., Eadie, T. and Knight, C. (2008) People first: Probation officer perspectives on probation work. *Probation Journal*, 55(3): 259–71.

Bonta, J., Rugge, T., Scott, T.L., Bourgon, and Yessine, A.K. (2008) Exploring the black box of community supervision. *Journal of Offender Rehabilitation*, 47(3), 248–70.

Bottoms, A.E. (2001) Compliance and community penalties. In Bottoms, A.E., Gelsthorpe, L. and Rex, S. (eds) *Community Penalties: Change and Challenges*, Cullompton: Willan.

Bourgon, G., Guiierrez, L. and Ashton, J. (2011) The evolution of community supervision practice: The transformation from case manager to change agent. *Irish Probation Journal*, 8, 28–48.

Burke, L. and Davies, K. (2011) Introducing the special edition on occupational culture and skills in probation practice. *European Journal of Probation*, 3(3): 1–13.

Burke, L., Collett, S. and McNeill, F. (2019) *Reimagining Rehabilitation: Beyond the Individual*. Abingdon: Routledge.

Carr, N. (2020) *Recruitment, Training and Professional Development of Probation Staff*. HM Inspectorate of Probation. Available at: www.justiceinspectorates.gov.uk/hmiprobation/wp-content/uploads/sites/5/2020/02/Academic-Insights-Carr-Final.pdf (last accessed 21 August 2021).

Clare, R. (2015) Maintaining professional practice: The role of the probation officer in community rehabilitation companies. *Probation Journal*, https://doi.org/10.1177%2F0264550514561776.

Council of Europe (2019) *Guidelines Regarding Recruitment, Selection, Education, Training and Professional Development of Prison and Probation Staff*. Available at: https://rm.coe.int/guidelines-training-staff/1680943aad (last accessed 19 February 2022).

Deering, J. (2010) Attitudes and beliefs of trainee probation officers: A 'new breed'? *Probation Journal*, 57(1): 9–26.

Deering, J. and Feilzer, M.Y. (2015) *Privatising Probation: Is Transforming Rehabilitation the End of the Probation ideal?* Bristol: Policy Press.

Durnescu, I. (2010) Pains of probation: Effective practice and human rights. *International Journal of Offender Therapy and Comparative Criminology*, 55(4): 530–545.

Durnescu, I. (2012) What matters most in probation supervision: Staff characteristics. Staff skills or programmes? *Criminology and Criminal Justice*, 12(2): 193–216.

Farrall, S. (2002) *Rethinking What Works with Offenders: Probation, Social Context and Desistance from Crime*. Cullompton: Willan.

Fitzgibbon, W. (2018) Photovoice and lived experiences of probation supervision: Using visual images to understand the experiences of service users. *Probation Quarterly*, December (10) 27–35.

Fitzgibbon, W. and Lea, J. (2014) Defending probation: Beyond privatisation and security. *European Journal of Probation*, 6(1), 24–41.

Grant, S. (2016) Constructing the durable penal agent: Tracing the development of habitus within English probation officers and Scottish criminal justice social workers. *British Journal of Criminal Justice*, 56(4): 750–68.

Grant, S. and McNeill, F. (2015) What matters in practice? Understanding 'quality' in the routine supervision of offenders in Scotland. *British Journal of Social Work*, 45: 1985–2002.

Hayes, D. (2015) The impact of supervision on the pains of community penalties in England and Wales: An exploratory study. *European Journal of Probation*, 7(2): 85–102.

Hayes, D. (2018) Experiencing penal supervision: a literature review. *Probation Journal*, 65(4): 378–93.

HM Prisons and Probation Service (2020) *Probation Workforce Strategy*. London: HM Prisons and Probation Service. Available at: https://assets.publishing.service.gov.uk/government/uploads/system/uploads/attachment_data/file/905417/probation-workforce-strategy-report.pdf (last accessed 21 August 2021).

Hochschild, A.R. (1983) *The Managed Heart: Commercialization of Human Feeling*. California: University of California Press.

Home Office (1994) *Review of Probation Officer Recruitment and Qualifying Training* (The Dews Report). London: Home Office.

Knight, C. (2014) *Emotional Literacy in Criminal Justice*. London: Palgrave Macmillan.

Liebling, A. (2004) *Prisons and Their Moral Performance*. Oxford: Oxford University Press.

Liebling, A., Price, D. and Shefer, G. (2010) *The Prison Officer*. Cullompton: Willan.

Mair, G. and Burke, L. (2013) *Redemption, Rehabilitation and Risk Management: A History of Probation*. Abingdon: Routledge.

Mair, G. and Mills, H. (2009) *The Community Order and the Suspended Sentence Order Three Years on: The Views and Experiences of Probation Officers and Offenders*. London: Centre for Crime and Justice.

Maruna, S. and King, A. (2008) Selling the public on probation: Beyond the bib. *Probation Journal*, 55(4): 337–51.

Mawby, R.C. and Worrall, A. (2011) *Probation Workers and Their Occupational Cultures*. University of Leicester and Keele University. Available at: https://sp.ukdataservice.ac.uk/doc/7086/mrdoc/pdf/7086probation_cultures_final_report.pdf (last accessed 30 June 2022).

Mawby, R. and Worrall, A. (2013) *Doing Probation Work: Identity in a Criminal Justice Occupation*. Abingdon, Oxon, Routledge.

McNeill, F. (2012) Four forms of 'offender' rehabilitation: Towards an interdisciplinary perspective. *Legal and Criminological Psychology*, 17(1), 18–36.

McNeill, F. (2018) *Pervasive Punishment: Making Sense of Mass Supervision*. Bingley: Emerald.

McNeill, F. and Beyens, K. (eds) (2013) *Offender Supervision in Europe*. Basingstoke: Palgrave.

Morris, J.A. and Feldman, D.C. (1996) The impact of emotional dissonance on psychological well-being: The importance of role internalisation as a mediating variable. *Management Research News*, 19(8): 19–28.

Ott, S.J. (1989) *The Organizational Culture*. Chicago, IL: Dorsey Press.

Pereira, C. and Trotter, C. (2018) Staff supervision in Youth Justice and its relationship to skill development: Findings from Australia. In P. Ugwudike, P. Raynor and J. Annison, J. (eds) *Evidence-Based Skills in Criminal Justice*. Bristol: Policy Press.

Petersilia, J. and Turner, S. (1993) *Evaluating Intensive Supervision Probation/Parole: Results of a Nationwide Experiment*. Washington D.C.: National Institute of Justice. Available at: www.ojp.gov/pdffiles1/Digitization/141637NCJRS.pdf (last accessed 20 August 2021).

Petrillo. M. (2007) Power struggle: Gender issues for female probation officers in the supervision of high risk offenders. *Probation Journal*, 54(4): 344–406.

Phillips, J., Westaby, C. and Fowler, A. (2020) *Emotional Labour in Probation*. HM Inspectorate of Probation academic insights. Manchester: HM Inspectorate of Probation. Available at: www.justiceinspectorates.gov.uk/hmiprobation/wp-content/uploads/sites/5/2020/04/Emotional-Labour-in-Probation.pdf (last accessed 20 August 2021).

Raynor, P. (2019) *Supervision Skills for Probation Practitioners*. HM Inspectorate of Probation: Academic Insights 2019/05. Available at: www.justiceinspectorates.gov.uk/hmiprobation/wp-content/uploads/sites/5/2019/08/Academic-Insights-Raynor.pdf (last accessed 20 August 2021).

Raynor, P. (2020) Probation for profit: Neoliberalism, magical thinking and evidence refusal. In P. Bean (ed.) *Criminal Justice and Privatisation*. Abingdon: Routledge.

Raynor, P. and Vanstone, M. (2018) What matters is what you do: The rediscovery of skills in probation practice. *European Journal of Probation*. 10(3), 199–214.

Raynor, P., Ugwudike, P. and Vanstone, M. (2009) *The Jersey Supervision Interview Checklist: Version 7C*. St. Helier: The Jersey Crime and Society Project.

Rex, S. (2002) Desistance from offending: Experiences of probation. *Howard Journal of Crime and Justice*, 38(4): 366–83.

Rex, S. and Hosking, N. (2013) A collaborative approach to developing probation practice: Skills for Effective Engagement, Development and Supervision (SEEDS). *Probation Journal*, (60)3: 332–38.

Robinson, G. (2016) The Cinderella complex: Punishment, society and community sanctions. *Punishment & Society*, 18(1): 95–112.

Robinson, G. (2020) How practitioners conceptualize quality: A UK perspective. In P. Ugwudike, H. Graham, F. McNeill, P. Raynor and F.S. Taxman (eds) *The Routledge Companion to Rehabilitative Work in Criminal Justice*. Abingdon: Routledge, pp. 958–67.

Robinson, G. and Burnett, R. (2007) Experiencing modernization: Frontline perspectives on the transition to a National Offender Management Service. *Probation Journal*, 54(4): 318–37.

Robinson, G., Burke, L. and Millings, M. (2016) Criminal justice identities in transition: The case of devolved probation services in England and Wales. *British Journal of Criminology*, 56: 161–78.

Rudes, D.S., Viglione, J. and Taxman, F. (2014) Professional identities in the United States' probation and parole. In I. Durnescu and F. McNeill (eds) *Understanding Penal Practices*. Abingdon: Routledge, pp. 11-30.

Shapland, J., Bottoms, A., Farrall, S., McNeill, F., Priede, C., Robinson, G. (2012) *The Quality of Probation Supervision – A Literature Review*. University of Sheffield: Centre for Criminological Research. Available at: www.sheffield.ac.uk/polopoly_fs/1.159010!/file/QualityofProbationSupervision.pdf (last accessed 20 August 2021).

Shapland, J., Bottoms, A., Farrall, S., McNeill, F., Priede, C., Robinson, G. (2012a) *The Quality of Probation Supervision – A Literature Review: Summary of Key Messages*. London: Ministry of Justice.

Shapland, J., Sorsby, A., Robinson, G., Priede, C., Farrall, S. and McNeill, F. (2014) What quality means to probation staff in England and Wales in relation to one-to-one supervision. In Durnescu, I. and McNeill, F. (eds) *Understanding Penal Practices*. Abingdon, Oxon: Routledge.

Sharp, P. (2001) Nurturing emotional literacy: a practical guide for teachers, parents and those in the caring professions. *Health Education*, 101(6): 292–4.

Sharp, P. (2012) *Nurturing Emotional Literacy: A Practical Guide for Teachers, Parents and Those in the Caring Professions*. Abingdon, Oxon: Routledge.

Sorsby, A., Shapland, J. and Durnescu, I. (2017) Promoting quality in probation supervision and policy transfer: Evaluating the SEED1 programme in Romania and England. In P. Ugwudike, P. Raynor and J. Annison (eds) *Evidence-Based Skills in Criminal Justice: International Research on Supporting Rehabilitation and Desistance*. Bristol: Policy Press, pp. 193–216.

Sorsby, A., Shapland, J., Farrall, S., McNeill, F., Priede, C. and Robinson, G. (2013) *Probation Staff Views of the Skills for Effective Engagement Development (SEED) Project*. University of Sheffield: Centre for Criminological Research. Available at: www.sheffield.ac.uk/polopoly_fs/1.293093!/file/probation-staff-views-seed.pdf (last accessed 20 August 2021).

Sykes, G. (1958) *The Society of Captives*. Princeton: Princeton University Press.

Tidmarsh, M. (2019) 'The right kind of person for the job'? Emotional labour and organizational professionalism in probation. *International Journal of Law, Crime and Justice*, 61, 100363.

Tidmarsh, M. (2020) 'If the cap fits?' Probation staff and the changing nature of supervision in a community rehabilitation company. *Probation Journal*, 67(2): 98–117.

Toronjo, H. and Taxman, F.S. (2018) Supervision face-to-face contacts: The emergence of an intervention. In P. Ugwudike, P. Raynor and J. Annison (eds) *Evidence-Based Skills in Criminal Justice*. Bristol: Policy Press.

Trotter, C. (1996) The impact of different supervision practices in community corrections. *Australian and New Zealand Journal of Criminology*, 28(2), 29-46.

Trotter, C. (1999) *Working with Involuntary Clients: A Guide to Practice*. London: Sage.

Trotter, C. and Evans, P. (2012) An analysis of supervision skills in youth probation. *Australian and New Zealand Journal of Criminology*, 45(2), 255–73.

Walker, S., Annison, J. and Beckett, S. (2019) Transforming rehabilitation: The impact of austerity and privatisation on day-to-day cultures and working practices in 'probation'. *Probation Journal*, 66(1), 113–130.

Westaby, C., Fowler, A. and Phillips, J. (2019) Managing emotion in probation practice: Display rules, values and the performance of emotional labour. *International Journal of Law, Crime and Justice*, 61, 100362.

Worrall, A. and Mawby, R.C. (2014) Probation worker cultures and relationships with offenders. *Probation Journal*, 61(4), 346–57.

9
WORKING WITH PEOPLE IN PRISON

IN THIS CHAPTER, YOU WILL EXPLORE

1. How the aims and ambitions of imprisonment translate into practice at the coal face of service delivery

2. The design and delivery of interventions such as offending behaviour programmes and the Offender Personality Disorder Pathway

3. The extent to which endeavours to work alongside people in prison reduce (re)offending and promote successful (re)integration into wider society post release.

INTRODUCTION

The material presented to you in this textbook has detailed how and in what ways attempts have been made to justify prison and probation services (see Chapters 3 and 4), organise systems of punishment in custodial and community settings (see Chapters 5 and 6) and legitimise the personal and professional pains of punishment (see Chapters 7 and 8). This has not only helped you to critically engage with long-standing attempts to make sense of these services but question who arrives at their door. To build upon this commentary, the third and final section, *implementation and impact*, will explore how the prison and probation service work alongside individuals who have broken the law. The authors have purposively chosen the phrase *working with* to begin this chapter and the next to illustrate how endeavours to protect the public and reduce reoffending, whether in community or custodial settings, should focus on working alongside people rather than on people – getting to know them as individuals, their risk factors and unmet needs. In addition, the authors contend that the phrase working with goes some way to illustrate how rehabilitative efforts require help, support and guidance from an array of professionals, services and institutions to avoid further lawbreaking.

In contemporary times, attempts to work with people serving a custodial sentence have been driven by a stated ambition to rehabilitate individuals during their time in custody and prepare them for release into the wider community (see Chapters 3 and 4 for a more detailed discussion). In the past, such endeavours were influenced by the concept of reformation but in more recent times, rehabilitative opportunities have typically been driven by an attempt to reduce risk and prevent further lawbreaking (see Chapter 1 for further discussion). According to official discourse, people serving a custodial sentence should be able to access interventions that 'address the risk of harm, reduce the likelihood of reoffending and promote successful reintegration' (HM Inspectorate of Prisons, 2017: 55). As such, prisons throughout England and Wales strive to offer a variety of opportunities for people to address psychological issues and improve well-being, as well as educational programmes, vocational courses and employment opportunities. Whilst rehabilitative opportunities vary between prisons depending on the role and function of the establishment, available resources and staffing levels (see Chapter 5 for further discussion), HM Inspectorate of Prisons expect prisons to provide:

- Appropriate interventions to address the risk of harm, reduce the likelihood of reoffending and promote successful reintegration
- Advice and help to manage financial commitments while in custody
- Advice on managing housing and finding suitable accommodation on release
- Support for people who are particularly vulnerable. (HM Inspectorate of Prisons, 2017a)

Human rights standards require planning for release to begin when an individual arrives at prison. In England and Wales, every person serving a custodial sentence is allocated a case manager who will work alongside them to create a custody plan that is designed to address their specific needs, manage risk of harm and reduce the likelihood of further lawbreaking. Such efforts are undertaken to ensure that prior to release, people serving a custodial sentence 'have an up-to-date plan for addressing outstanding rehabilitation needs' and have been 'given all necessary practical support ready for their day of release' (HM Inspectorate of Prisons, 2017a: para. 1). With a particular focus on offending behaviour programmes and the Offender Personality Disorder Pathway, this chapter will explore how and in what ways this stated ambition translates into practice. In doing so, the chapter will explore some of the challenges which surround the design and delivery of prison-based interventions and encourage you to consider the degree to which these interventions can address the plethora of needs amongst people serving a custodial sentence whilst simultaneously responding to the challenges that surround attempts to (re)settle people into the wider community.

OFFENDING BEHAVIOUR PROGRAMMES

Offending behaviour programmes are interventions that aim to change a person's thinking, attitudes and behaviours that may lead to lawbreaking (HM Government, 2018). They are an important component of prison life as they encourage prosocial attitudes and goals that are designed to help people develop new skills such as problem-solving skills, perspective taking skills and self-management. In England and Wales, there are a range of offending behaviour programmes available in community and custodial settings that are designed to tackle acts such as: sexually motivated crime, domestic violence, general patterns of lawbreaking and drug-related crime (HM Government, 2018). In the main, they are delivered in group settings but in some circumstances one-to-one support is also available. Offending behaviour programmes typically use techniques associated with cognitive behavioural therapy to support individual growth and change. Cognitive behavioural therapy is a form of talking therapy that combines cognitive and behavioural therapy to challenge cognitive distortions and behaviours, improve emotional regulation and develop personal coping strategies. It is based on the idea that a person's thoughts, feelings and behaviours are interconnected. Participants work with a trained facilitator or psychologist to identify, break down and understand their problems. By focusing on the interaction of thoughts, emotions, feelings and actions, personal therapy goals and strategies can be developed, monitored and evaluated over time.

The design and delivery of offending behaviour programmes are also influenced by principles of the Risk, Needs and Responsivity model (see Chapter 2 for a detailed discussion) which helps to target the right programmes for the right people so that the level of support provided by a programme matches a person's risk of reoffending; programme content covers areas that are relevant to a person's needs, and the approach can be adapted to respond to people's circumstances, abilities and strengths (Ministry of Justice, 2018). The insight afforded by such principles provides an important step towards the provision of suitable rehabilitative opportunities as evidence suggests that offending behaviour programmes are more effective when they are properly targeted within a culture that supports rehabilitation (Ibid). Taking into consideration Figure 9.1 below, take a moment to think about the extent to which the prison place provides a culture that supports rehabilitation.

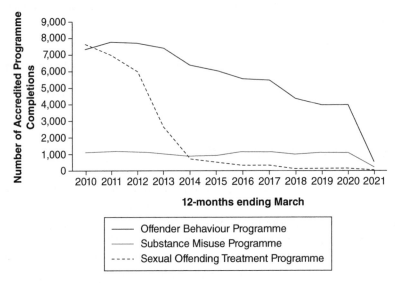

Figure 9.1 'Number of completions for accredited programmes in custody, 12-months ending March 2010 to 12-months ending March 2021'

Table 6.2 in Ministry of Justice (2022) HMPPS Annual Digest 2020/21. Available at: https://assets.publishing.service. gov.uk/government/uploads/system/uploads/attachment_data/file/1047798/HMPPS-annual-digest-2020-21_vFINAL. pdf (last accessed 27 July 2022)

In England and Wales, offending behaviour programmes fall into two broad categories: accredited programmes and non-accredited programmes. The term accreditation, in the criminal justice field, describes the process of reviewing, validating and improving interventions that have been designed to reduce reoffending (Ministry of Justice, 2014). Accreditation gives confidence that a programme is based on the best available evidence, is monitored to make sure it is delivered as intended and is evaluated to ensure specified outcomes are achieved (Ibid). The Correctional Services Advice and Accreditation Panel (CSAAP), originally established in 1999 as the General Accreditation Panel, helps HM Prison and Probation Service to accredit programmes by reviewing programme design, quality assurance procedures, findings and evaluations. To achieve accreditation, programmes must demonstrate sound evidence that techniques help to create individual change, assessment tools will reliably target the right people, and there is a commitment to monitoring the quality of programme delivery as well as ongoing evaluative work. There are three possible outcomes from the accreditation review: full accreditation, accreditation maintained subject to addressing areas of concern, and accreditation lapsed. Programmes are typically accredited for five years after which they are reviewed to ensure that they continue to meet accreditation criteria.

Although accredited programmes are overseen by a central interventions unit, prisons that deliver accredited programmes must have a local management structure. This typically consists of a programmes manager who is responsible for the day-to-day operation of programmes, from ensuring that programme facilitators have access to resources to ensuring that participants are not transferred to another prison whilst involved in a programme. A treatment manager is responsible for overseeing the selection process, (ensuring people are allocated to programmes that can work with their level of risk and need) and is required to ensure that a programme maintains its integrity and quality of delivery. Interventions facilitators are required to prepare and deliver individual and group-based interventions for programme participants. Forensic psychologists play an integral role in the design and delivery of offending behaviour programmes, supporting 'individuals to go on to lead better lives' and helping the prison service to 'strengthen its rehabilitative ethos' (HM Government, 2018a: para. 3).

Offending behaviour programmes are further divided into medium intensity programmes and high intensity programmes. In England and Wales, medium intensity programmes typically cater for people serving a custodial sentence who have been assessed as a medium risk of reoffending. They are managed by an interventions manager or trainee forensic psychologist and typically last between 35 and 60 hours, over a four-to-ten-week period (subject to change depending on the programme and individual need). Medium intensity programmes are delivered in groups of up to ten participants and often have supplementary individual sessions to create more personalised approaches where and when required. Examples of medium intensity programmes include but are not limited to:

- *Alcohol-Related Violence*: a cognitive behavioural programme designed for men who have a history of violence following alcohol consumption

- *Building Better Relationships*: a cognitive behavioural programme for adult men convicted of intimate partner violence

- *Building Skills for Recovery*: a psychosocial programme for adult men and women who are dependent on one or more substances, including alcohol

- *Drink Impaired Driving Programme*: for adult men and women who have more than two but less than five drink driving convictions, or a single conviction that involved a particularly high level of alcohol

- *Horizon*: designed to help men who have been convicted of sexually motivated crimes to address factors that have contributed to their behaviour, such as poor self-regulation and issues with relationships more generally

- *New Me Strengths*: a strengths-based programme for men with learning difficulties who are assessed as having a medium risk of further lawbreaking

- *Resolve*: a cognitive–behavioural group that aims to reduce violence in men who have been assessed as medium risk who have a history of using violence

- *Thinking Skills Programme*: a medium intensity programme for men and women convicted of almost any crime.

High intensity programmes, managed by qualified psychologists, are typically offered to people who are at high or very high risk of reoffending. The duration of high intensity programmes varies between participants given that progression is directed by ability to demonstrate understanding and application of programme content. People who participate in high intensity programmes can expect to complete around 200 hours of group work and individual sessions, spread over nine to 12 months. Examples of high intensity programmes include but are not limited to:

- *Kaizen*: adopts a biopsychosocial approach for males who are considered to be at high risk due to the nature of the crimes they have committed

- *Becoming New Me+*: targets the same criminogenic need as Kaizen but is adapted to meet the needs of adult males who have a learning difficulty

- *Healthy Sex Programme*: a bolt-on course for adult men who have previously completed a programme such as Kaizen, Becoming New Me+ or Horizon but still demonstrate outstanding needs with regard to their sexual interests. Although it is not necessary for Healthy Sex Programme participants to be high risk, they often are due to the nature of their sexual interests

- *Healthy Identity Intervention*: delivered on an individual basis and aims to address the social and psychological factors that underpin acts of terrorism

- *Identity Matters*: also delivered on an individual basis and designed for people who are affiliated to a gang.

Non-accredited programmes do not have recognition from CSAPP as they have not been through the accreditation process. Though they are numerous and varied across the prison estate, they typically work to equip participants with specific knowledge and skill sets over a short period of time. Examples of non-accredited programmes include but are not limited to:

- *A–Z*: a group-based intervention for people serving a custodial sentence who possess little motivation to engage with available opportunities

- *Choices and Changes*: delivered on an individual basis to young adults who have been identified as having low psychosocial maturity

- *Motivation and Engagement*: aims to encourage participants (with a particular focus on those showing signs of personality disorder) to meaningfully engage in interventions and explore how change is possible.

Alongside offending behaviour programmes, people serving a custodial sentence may also be eligible for one-to-one support from a forensic psychologist. This is typically offered to people who have a specific learning need that requires a greater level of support than that offered by standard, group-based interventions, have complex risk-related needs that are better addressed through bespoke, one-to-one support, and/or are unable to engage in group-based work.

Recent developments in the What works literature highlights how multi-modal and integrated interventions (which suggest that behaviour is best explained through interactions between biological, psychological and sociological factors) produce more successful results than those that rely on one perspective and/or single practice (Gannon et al., 2019; Papalia et al., 2019). As such, biopsychosocial approaches are commonly delivered across prisons in England and Wales to better understand and respond to the complex and often multifaceted levels of need amongst people serving a custodial sentence. An example can be found in the Integrated Theory of Sexual Offending, which suggests biological, cultural, social, individual and psychological traits are all involved in the commission of a sexually motivated crime. This is, according to its advocates, because genes, social learning and neuropsychological systems interact to generate specific issues, such as offence-related thoughts and fantasies, negative/positive emotional states and social difficulties that can lead to 'sexually abusive actions' (Ward and Beech, 2006: 46). A further example can be found in the General Aggression Model, which explores how personal and situational factors influence cognitions, feelings and arousal which in turn affect a person's appraisal and decision-making processes that may influence a decision to react aggressively (Allen et al., 2018). Though not an offending behaviour programme, the section below on the Offender Personality Disorder Pathway exemplifies how and in what ways a multi-modal approach attempts to engage some of the people most in need in the custodial estate.

OFFENDER PERSONALITY DISORDER PATHWAY

Personality disorder is a complex biopsychosocial disorder that develops because of interactions between biologically based vulnerabilities, early experiences with significant others and social factors that intensify problematic personality traits. It is suggested that people with a personality disorder may display unusual or extreme behaviour traits, have mild problems or severe difficulties managing themselves and relating to others, and/or pose harm to either themselves or others. Someone who behaves in a way consistent with a personality disorder diagnosis often adopts behaviour that is inflexible and hard to change despite changing contexts and situations. Often these traits are present since adolescence and result in significant distress or impaired functioning in a number of different areas such as interpersonal relationships. What constitutes a personality disorder is, however, not without its critics. As Pilgrim (2001: 255) argues, the concept of personality disorder is fundamentally flawed and acts as a 'dustbin category of problematic behaviour'.

For many years, services failed to respond adequately to personality disorders, believing that it was untreatable. This situation changed following the brutal attacks against the Russell family by Michael Stone who, although a diagnosed psychopath, did not meet the criteria for treatment under the Mental Health Act 1983 and, as such, could not be detained indefinitely despite the obvious risk to the public. This led to the introduction of the Dangerous and Severe Personality Disorder service in prisons and secure hospitals. However, it became increasingly evident that there might be other personality disordered lawbreakers who may benefit from services associated with the Dangerous and Severe Personality Disorder pathway but did not meet the admission criteria. This in turn led to the development of a comprehensive strategy for the treatment and management of personality disordered lawbreakers and resulted in the introduction of the Offender Personality Disorder Pathway in 2011.

The Offender Personality Disorder Pathway, developed to meet the strategic aims of both the Ministry of Justice and Department of Health, provides a variety of psychologically informed services for people serving a custodial sentence who have been identified as having difficulties with their personality that are, in the main, linked to their lawbreaking. Interventions offered on the Offender Personality Disorder Pathway are multidisciplinary in nature, incorporating expertise from a variety of professionals such as consultant psychiatrists, clinical and/or forensic psychologists, occupational therapists, prison officers and social workers across services based within and beyond HM Prison Service. The aim of the Offender Personality Disorder Pathway is to reduce the risk of harm to others, reduce serious lawbreaking and improve prosocial behaviour and psychological health by ensuring people with a personality disorder are a shared responsibility of the criminal justice system and National Health Service, identified as having complex needs early on in their sentence that present as a high risk of serious harm, and are subject to arrangements for lifelong management as a pathway of active intervention (National Offender Management Service, 2008).

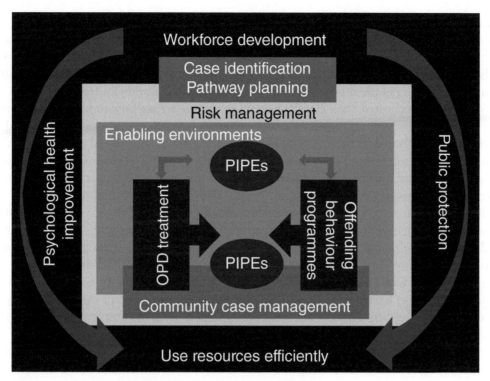

Figure 9.2　Illustration of Offender Personality Disorder Pathway

Source: National Offender Managament Service (2015) The Offender Personality Disorder Pathway Strategy 2015. Available at: www.england.nhs.uk/commissioning/wp-content/uploads/sites/12/2016/02/opd-strategy-nov-15.pdf (last accessed 27 July 2022), p. 7

Figure 9.2 illustrates the key features of the Offender Personality Disorder Pathway, which is indicative of a commitment to: a consistent and coherent process of offenders moving along a range of different criminal justice and health interventions: starting in the community, moving through the sentence, and back to the community at the end of sentence, via custody where applicable (National Offender Management Service, 2015: 6).Though there is more work to do to establish the prevalence of personality disorders amongst those involved in the criminal justice system, it has been estimated that '58% of male remand prisoners, 64% of male sentenced prisoners and 50% of female prisoners (remand and sentenced combined) have a personality disorder' (National Institute for Clinical Excellence, 2014: 3). Whilst there is a well-established association between personality disorders and lawbreaking, the nature of the relationship is less well understood (Davison and Janca, 2012). What we do know is that frameworks which recognise and integrate responses to a wide variety of issues such as personality traits, comorbidity issues, mood disorders, motivation for lawbreaking, maladaptive cognitions, beliefs and attitudes, and situational factors are helpful when considering how to assess, manage and help people during their time in prison and beyond (Ibid).

Whilst it is suggested that 20,000 people in prison across England and Wales meet the Offender Personality Disorder Pathway criteria, current provision is extremely limited. This is attributed to the financial burdens of the services required and long waiting lists. It is, therefore, unsurprising to find vulnerable prisoner units (see Chapter 11 for a more detailed discussion) holding people with serious and complex issues that should be cared for elsewhere more able to respond to their ongoing risk and needs. This is not an ideal situation given that the Offender Personality Disorder Pathway itself recognises how some people require a more holistic approach when it comes to efforts to meet risk and need, led by principles of trauma-informed care that are, where possible, embedded within the environment where they reside (known as integrated interventions). As a result, people who require support from the Offender Personality Disorder Pathway should (in theory) have access to a personality disorder unit, therapeutic community or secure hospital/service. Though not necessarily regarded as an intervention per se, psychologically informed planned environments, commonly referred to as PIPE units, are an integral part of an individual's journey on the Offender Personality Disorder Pathway. The following section will now explore each of these interventions in more detail.

Personality disorder units

People serving a custodial sentence can reside in a personality disorder unit for between two and five years, depending on the severity and/or complexity of their personality disorder as well as bed availability. The design and delivery of treatment in personality disorder units are typically modelled on Livesley's (2009) integrated approach to treatment, which suggests interventions should be based on generic change mechanisms and be divided into general and specific treatment strategies. General strategies should be applied throughout the course of an individual's participation in a personality disorder unit to build a therapeutic alliance, ensure therapeutic consistency, provide validation and build motivation. Specific interventions can be added to this as and when needed to respond to specific problems as they arise. In addition, Livesley suggests that participation should be thought of as a series of phrases (with each addressing different problems and issues related to psychopathy) and change in behaviour should be described using the stages of change model (Prochaska and DiClemente, 1983) to provide an orderly way to combine interventions.

Phases include: *establishing safety, containment of symptoms, regulation and control, exploration and change,* and *integration and synthesis.* Establishing safety is related to the safety of all involved in a personality disorder unit – staff and residents alike. Support and structure can be provided through crisis intervention services as well as in-patient treatment to help individuals achieve stability. Once a person is deemed stable, the focus is to contain unstable emotions and cognition whilst restoring impulse control, through the creation of positive relationships between everyone working and living in the unit. Regulation and control are created through the application of specific interventions that explore links between behaviour, emotional reactions, cognition and external factors. In doing so, it is anticipated that a person will build and develop a skill set that can be applied to achieve positive change. During the phase of exploration and change, people are supported to address maladaptive cognitive processes. This stage requires an individual to have achieved a certain level of stability given that some interventions may specifically focus on a person's experience of trauma. Though Livesley suggested that participants will rarely achieve a new sense of self, they should be able to achieve a more coherent sense of self, which will allow them to self-regulate more effectively and respond to the challenges that their personality disorder can create (integration and synthesis).

The aim of Livesley's (2009) model is to develop a framework for treating personality disorder that is consistent with existing evidence, treatment efficacy and behavioural change. Whilst there is little insight into the optimal way to organise interventions and support for people with personality disorder, the framework is intended to provide a flexible structure for organising support in a variety of settings using individual and group therapy. Whilst available therapies differ between personality disorder units, examples include (but are not limited to):

- *Dialectical behavioural therapy*: a type of talking therapy that is designed to help people learn and manage difficult emotions so that they are more able to change harmful and/or unhealthy behaviour

- *Cognitive analytical therapy*: another form of talking therapy that focuses on relationship patterns based on the belief that early life experiences influence the way we relate to others and treat ourselves

- *Mentalisation behavioural therapy*: a long-term psychotherapy that helps people to improve their capacity to mentalise and focus on what is going on in their mind, other people and how this can be used to understand and alleviate problematic behaviours

- *Schema therapy*: designed to address unmet needs and help people break patterns of thinking, feeling and behaviours which are often tenacious, and to develop healthier options

- *Eye movement desensitisation and reprocessing*: helps the brain to process distressing memories and reducing their influence, which allows individuals to develop ways to move on with their lives more effectively

- *Psychoeducation*: involves learning about and understanding mental health and well-being

- *Art therapy*: a form of psychotherapy that uses the medium of art to address emotional issues which may be confusing and distressing

- *Music therapy*: can be used to help individuals accomplish goals such as reducing stress, improving mood and self-expression..

Personality disorder units also offer numerous opportunities for people to engage in less formal group experiences to build interpersonal skills.

Therapeutic community

The origins and development of the therapeutic community can be traced to two independent traditions: the hierarchical movement and the democratic movement. The hierarchical therapeutic community derives from Synanon, a self-help community for substance users, established by Charles Dederich in San Franscisco in 1958. Contemporary hierarchical therapeutic communities provide a social psychological intervention which uses self-help and behaviour modification techniques to help individuals address underlying issues and difficulties that surround their substance use. The democratic therapeutic community began with the work of Maxwell Jones during the Second World War and was developed at the Henderson Hospital, Surrey (United Kingdom) during the 1960s. The democratic therapeutic community specialises in supporting individuals with moderate to severe personality disorders as well as complex emotional and interpersonal issues. It provides a psychosocial treatment approach that is intended to help troubled individuals understand, and as far as possible, lessen or overcome their psychological, social and/or emotional issues and difficulties (Stevens, 2013).

Roberts (1997: 3) suggests that the therapeutic community movement:

implicitly adopts the view that deviant behaviour, much of which is deemed criminal, represents a breakdown of the relationship between the individual and the structured society of which he or she is, by virtue of time and place of birth, a member.

As a result, it is unsurprising to find that the programme has gone on to form a close relationship with the criminal justice system in England and Wales (as well as further afield). In 1962 the first and only therapeutic community prison opened in England. The inception of HM Prison Grendon is (largely) attributed to a government report from 1932 which concluded that 'a certain amount of persistent crime could be related to abnormal mental factors' alongside a recommendation to implement an "experimental approach" for 'mentally disordered offenders' (Shuker, 2010: 466).

HMP Grendon is a prison with a difference as it incorporates essential components of therapeutic community treatment into its day-to-day organisation and structure. Approximately 200 adult men are housed in HMP Grendon across six separate residential units, or TCs as they are more commonly referred to. People serving a custodial sentence in HMP Grendon are required to take responsibility for the treatment setting to which they belong. This includes the interpersonal, domestic and treatment components which characterise the general institution. Residential structures and group work emphasises open communication, involvement, participation and shared problem solving. This, in theory at least, enables staff and participants (referred to as residents) to make joint decisions, address conflict and be mutually accountable for the prison environment (Shuker, 2010).

Since its inception, HMP Grendon has focused its attention on people convicted of violent and sexually motivated crimes as well as those with a personality disorder. Although concerns have been raised about the feasibility of experimental studies of democratic therapeutic community treatment, a significant number of studies have demonstrated reductions in the utilisation of psychiatric services, especially acute inpatient admissions, following therapeutic community treatment of personality disorder (see Davies and Campling, 2018). In recent years, a ministerial ambition to understand and indeed respond to the links between lawbreaking and personality disorder has stimulated a renewed interest in the treatment of personality disorders. Whilst there is evidence to suggest that democratic therapeutic communities go some way to improve outcomes for people in custody with personality disorders it is important to recognise that more research is required to establish how and in what ways prison-based therapeutic communities improve mental health and reduce lawbreaking amongst those in their care.

Psychologically informed planned environments

Psychologically informed planned environments (PIPEs) were developed in 2010 as part of a government initiative to provide specific services for people in prison with diagnosed personality disorders as well as those with personality difficulties. They are defined as 'specifically designed environments where staff have additional training to develop an increased psychological understanding of their work. This enables them to create a supportive environment which can facilitate the development of those living there' (Turley et al., 2013: 6). The PIPEs approach draws on several theoretical models to focus on the importance of relationships. Through consideration of social environments, PIPEs are supported by the implementation of psychologically informed practice and the inclusion of planned, structured elements. Whilst not an intervention or programme per se, there are three diverse types of PIPEs in prison settings: *Preparation*, *Provision* and *Progression* PIPEs. *Preparation* services aim to increase an individual's level of motivational and relational capital before taking part in programmes and/or interventions. *Provision* services work to increase engagement in programmes and interventions and *Progression* units provide opportunities for consolidation of individual change as well as a gradual step down of support post-participation in treatment.

Whilst PIPEs have evolved because of numerous personality disorder strategies, it is not a requirement for participants to have a diagnosis of personality disorder. In England

and Wales, participants are expected to reside in the unit for a minimum of six months and a maximum of two years, have a suitable security category and/or status and be considered amenable to mainstream prison location. PIPEs units may provide structured sessions for participants as well as creative sessions and key worker sessions, based on principles of the Good Lives Model (see Chapter 2 for further discussion). Harvey and Ramsden (2016: 21) identify a number of principles that should underpin psychologically informed practice such as: the development of a practitioner's understanding of and ability to have psychologically informed conversations with those in their care; the development of a practitioner's reflective capacity to facilitate a thoughtful, self-aware and non-reactive approach to people in their care; and the augmentation of the reflective capacity of systems around justice-involved people who present with challenging personality traits.

PIPEs have also been implemented in probation approved premises for those who have completed a period of treatment in custody to ensure that support and guidance is continued into the community. In England and Wales, the Offender Personality Disorder Pathway target population for probation approved premises are individuals managed by the probation service who are over the age of 18. Men are eligible if they are assessed as presenting a high or very high risk of serious harm to others at any point during their sentence and are considered likely to have a severe personality disorder for which there is a clinically justifiable link with that person's risk. These criteria apply to women too but without the necessity to be high risk (Skett et al., 2017). The aim of the Offender Personality Disorder Pathway is to reduce serious repeat offences, improve psychological well-being of justice-involved people, produce a competent and trained workforce and use resources efficiently (Ibid). Whilst such approaches can, and indeed do, help many people to gain stability during their time in prison, there are some people who require a different level of support and care which cannot be provided in a prison setting.

Secure hospitals and secure services

In the United Kingdom, secure services are divided into three levels of security: high, medium and low. At the time of writing, there are three secure hospitals in England and Wales (Ashworth, Rampton and Broadmoor), with an overall capacity of 750 people, for those who present as a 'grave and immediate' danger to the public and/or themselves (Völlm and Clarke, 2018: 5). Most admissions to secure hospitals are made under Part III of the Mental Health Act 1983, which means they must be classified as having a learning disability, mental illness and/or a psychopathic disorder, and be considered an immediate danger to themselves and/or the public. Secure hospitals also care for people who have not committed a crime but are considered to be a serious danger to the public. Of the three hospitals mentioned above, only Rampton provides services for women, D/deaf male patients and male patients with intellectual disabilities (Ibid). In 2013, the average bed cost per annum at Broadmoor Hospital was £325,000 (Lamb, 2013). This is more than 12 times the cost in a category B male prison (£26,606 per person, per annum) during this time (Ministry of Justice, 2014a).

There are approximately 60 medium secure units in England and Wales, providing a total of 3,500 beds for people who are considered to be a 'serious danger to the public' (Völlm and Clarke, 2018: 5). People sentenced to prison can be transferred to a medium secure unit for psychiatric treatment by warrant of the Secretary of State (see sections 47–49 of the Mental Health Act 1983). This means that their remaining sentence tariff governs whether discharge into the community at the time of treatment completion is an option, unless their sentence lapses during their psychiatric detention, in which case community discharge is at the discretion of the responsible clinician. Low secure services are for those who 'pose a significant danger to themselves and others' (Völlm and Clarke, 2018: 6). Admissions are a mix between those stepping down from higher secure services and those coming from general psychiatric settings. Treatment in secure settings varies from medication and nursing care to psychological therapies. Once a person's mental health has stabilised, offence-related work begins. As both prisons and secure settings now acknowledge (to varying degrees) the role of trauma in lawbreakers' lives, the following section will explore how and in what ways trauma is recognised when working alongside people in prison.

TRAUMA

The links between childhood adversity, trauma and involvement in the criminal justice system are well evidenced. Even before entering prison, those serving a custodial sentence are more likely to have experienced abuse and trauma than the rest of the general population. Such experiences often put people at a higher risk of substance use, post-traumatic stress disorder, poor mental health and coping skills that are exacerbated by the prison place, recognised as 'inherently traumatic places that dehumanise people in the name of security and control' (Langness et al., 2020: para. 1). But what do we mean by the term trauma and how does it influence how we work alongside people in prison?

'In general, trauma can be defined as a psychological, emotional response to an event or an experience that is deeply distressing or disturbing. When loosely applied, this trauma definition can refer to something upsetting, such as being involved in an accident, having an illness or injury, losing a loved one, or going through a divorce. However, it can also encompass the far extreme and include experiences that are severely damaging' (The Centre for Treatment of Anxiety and Mood Disorders, 2021: para 1). Albeit with a focus on females, Messina et al. (2020: 638) differentiate between three levels of work required to create services that are *trauma informed*, *trauma responsive* and *trauma specific* for justice-involved people. Being trauma informed means having universal knowledge about trauma and adversity. This requires staff in penal settings to understand the concept of trauma and its link to poor mental health, substance use, behavioural challenges and physical health problems. Staff also need to understand how trauma can relate to childhood experiences and brain development as well as how individuals may be affected by and cope with trauma and victimisation. McCartan (2020: 8) eloquently summarises how to work in a trauma informed fashion, advocating 'a change in perspective from "what's wrong with you?" to "what happened to you?" After becoming trauma informed, a service then needs to become trauma responsive by reviewing policies and practices and incorporating available information into all operational practices. To become trauma specific, services must provide therapeutic approaches that are specifically designed to focus on trauma.

Whilst the design and delivery of imprisonment makes trauma informed, trauma responsive and trauma specific care a difficult task, efforts have been made (albeit in recent times) to understand trauma and its varying forms amongst people serving a custodial sentence. Research conducted by Durr (2020) found that prisons who implement trauma-informed services experience substantial decreases in institutional violence as well as reductions in self-harm, assaults, and suicide attempts. Alongside this, a recent evaluation of the Healing Trauma Intervention found trauma-informed care to have a positive impact on the well-being of women who completed the programme (Petrillo et al., 2019). Such occurrences are not exclusive to England, with the research in keeping with findings from the United States of America (Durr, 2020).

Increasingly, developments in understanding trauma have come to inform the provision of resources in the criminal justice system. With greater emphasis placed on supporting women, for example, to deal with psychological distress through the provision of gender-responsive approaches. Such endeavours are important developments in contemporary penology as scholars such as Malloch et al. (2014) note how gender-responsive approaches not only require an awareness of the differences between men and women but a need to respond to women in ways that focus on safety and reconnection. Utilising trauma as a lens to understand and work alongside people in prison also provides an opportunity to revitalise and reorientate conversations about what works – with indicators of 'successful' treatment outcomes extending beyond traditional desires to achieve a reduction in deficits and skill acquisition (the focus of most offending behaviour programmes), towards interpersonal healing, as well as an understanding of one's perception of themselves, the world around them and others.

CONTEMPORARY CHALLENGES

Whilst prison-based interventions, such as offending behaviour programmes, are recognised as a key component of an individual's personal progression, which may, for some people, include a decision to desist from lawbreaking, we must remember that such endeavours are not without their challenges. Literature in and around the notion of what works suggests that the effectiveness of a given intervention is reliant on the extent to which an individual is ready, motivated and able to engage with the challenges associated with undertaking a programme and/or intervention in prison. Olvr et al. (2011) suggest that individuals who need interventions the most (for example, those who are considered high risk with many criminogenic needs) are the ones who are least likely to complete it. This raises significant questions about how we work alongside people who are considered most in need of help and support but most likely to disengage with services during their custodial sentence.

Attrition is a key concern amongst professionals involved in the design and delivery of rehabilitative opportunities as non-completion of an intervention and/or programme has been shown to increase an individual's risk of future lawbreaking (Lockwood and Harris, 2015). Though it could be argued that the mediating factor in the non-completion of programmes and future lawbreaking is motivation (an internal factor) we must also recognise the role and responsibility of extenuating factors. When considering the effectiveness of prison-based interventions it is important to consider the environment within which the programme is delivered and how characteristics of the environment can impede participation and engagement. Prisons are places where people are held against their will. They are hostile environments with a strong and present anti-social (sub)culture. As a result, people in prison often feel that they must act in a manner that is consistent with anti-social norms to survive and achieve self-preservation (see Chapter 7 for a more detailed discussion). Consequently, they are not the most therapeutic environments or, in the main, able to ignite and support personal growth and change. This is unsurprising when you consider the justifications of imprisonment (see Chapter 3 for further discussion), culture within prisons, and failings of the penal system more broadly to meet basic human needs (see Chapter 11 for further discussion).

Specialist interventions such as therapeutic communities, personality disorder units and PIPEs have been created in prisons across the globe (to a greater or lesser degree) to provide a counterculture to the prison culture that aims to break down custodial norms, values and attitudes by creating a sense of community that is more supportive of change and personal growth. Though a step in the right direction, access to these environments is limited and, perhaps more importantly, we cannot forget that these interventions are still based within a highly politicised institution, populated by a wide variety of people with different life experiences and sentences that ultimately have an impact on how and to what extent they can be worked with. For example, the length of a person's custodial sentence has a significant impact on the scope, nature and depth of work that can be undertaken with them to reduce reoffending in the community. The effectiveness of short-term prison sentences (under 12 months) has been debated for decades given that people do not spend long enough in prison to work with practitioners and services in a genuinely meaningful way that affords lifelong change and reduces further offending. The evidence base highlights this failure too, noting how 63 per cent of people sentenced to less than 12 months in prison reoffend in the 12 months following their release (Prison Reform Trust, 2022). Rather than limiting the use of short-term prison sentences, the opposite is true, with 44 per cent of people in prison in 2020 were serving a sentence of less than six months (Ibid).

Whilst prison-based interventions are a vital component of an individual's journey, it is important to acknowledge the role and responsibility of society in a person's journey back into the community post imprisonment. People can engage in every offending behaviour programme on offer whilst in prison and make a genuine commitment to change, but if they are not given support in the wider community to apply their learning and create a lifestyle that most people take for granted, such endeavours may be short lived (see Chapters 3 and 5 for further discussion). This is a particularly important consideration for people serving a custodial sentence as prison-based initiatives are delivered to people from (predominately) socially excluded sections of society, characterised by a lack of economic opportunity, disproportionate levels of poor mental and physical health, substance use and barriers to educational achievement, employment and housing in an environment that compounds and exacerbates unmet needs. Upon release from prison, people are expected to apply the skills and resources that they have learnt during their custodial sentence so that they can reintegrate into the same wider community that failed them in the first place, which is now additionally reluctant to help and support them due to their criminal record.

Establishing a true version of what works in both theory and practice is a challenging task as it raises questions about what is important when delivering interventions in prison. Is it important to provide opportunities for people serving a custodial sentence to break away from the prison culture? Is it important to provide opportunities to address unmet needs? If so, how can this be done? Should efforts focus on improving well-being during a custodial sentence? Or providing opportunities for people to consider the challenges which will face them upon release into the wider community? Whatever the answer, the discussion throughout this section highlights how prison-based interventions such as offending behaviour programmes are just one part of a person's journey from custody to the community. For the journey to be sustained beyond the prison gates, support and help from society is also required.

WORKING WITH PEOPLE THROUGH THE PRISON GATE

Resettlement work in the community has been shown to be important in reducing further lawbreaking and possibly more important than interventions delivered in custodial settings (HM Inspectorate of Prisons, 2021). This is largely because the transition from prison to the community can be extremely challenging, with newly released people facing numerous obstacles such as a lack of access to suitable housing and employment, financial insecurity and debt, stigma, history of drug use, poor mental health, and pressure to rebuild familial and personal relationships. It is, therefore, unsurprising to find a 34 per cent reoffending rate amongst people serving determinate sentences of 12 months or more within a one-year follow-up period, alongside a higher reconviction rate of 60 per cent for those serving sentences of less than 12 months (Ministry of Justice, 2016).

To address this issue, the Offender Rehabilitation Act 2014 extended statutory post-release supervision to all those given a custodial sentence. As part of the Transforming Rehabilitation (TR) reforms, Through-the-Gate resettlement services were introduced in 2015 with the aim of providing a seamless transition between prison and the community. Following their return to the community, individuals subject to a short prison sentence now serve a period on licence and then receive a top-up period of post-sentence supervision (Cracknell, 2020: 341). Though no additional funds were made available, an extra 45,000 people required supervision because of this change. Raynor (2020: 327) has commented that, 'Superficially this looked like an improvement in services for a neglected group in undeniable need, who were serving prison sentences usually too short to offer any rehabilitative content but long enough to lose accommodation or jobs.' But the lack of additional funding 'not only placed extra pressure on an already overwrought system but was only ever likely to enhance feelings of resentment and disconnection among those delivering services and those requiring them' (Millings et al., 2019: 92).

In July 2018, the Ministry of Justice announced £22 million a year additional funding to improve resettlement for the remaining period of the community rehabilitation company contracts (House of Commons Justice Committee, 2021). An enhanced version of Through-the-Gate was introduced in 2019 to offer tiered support focused on meeting accommodation, employment, training and education, finance, benefit, debt and relational needs. The new approach to resettlement, outlined in the probation reform programme is being developed alongside Offender Management in Custody. This means that every person serving a custodial sentence will have a prison-based offender manager and community-based offender manager. The community-based offender manager is responsible for all pre-release activities from the point of handover from the prison offender manager, (or from the start of sentence for those with less than ten months to serve at the point of sentence). To build relationships, community-based offender managers are required to have at least three contacts with the person serving a custodial sentence pre-release. This includes the Offender Management in Custody handover meeting alongside at least two additional meetings (HM Prison and Probation, 2021: 73). The Target Operating Model specifies that community-based offender managers should offer two weeks of enhanced post-release support with two additional contacts to ensure barriers into interventions or contingences that may need enacting are speedily recognised and acted on (HM Prison and Probation Service, 2021: 73). Though promising, the degree to which such endeavours successfully work with people through the gate is questionable.

A joint inspection report by HM Inspectorate of Probation and HM Inspectorate of Prisons (2016), *An Inspection of Through the Gate Resettlement Services for Short-Term Prisoners*, illustrates a sizeable disparity between the needs of people serving a custodial sentence (of less than 12 months) and ability of the prison place to conduct sufficient work to meet those needs prior to release (Figures 9.3 and 9.4).

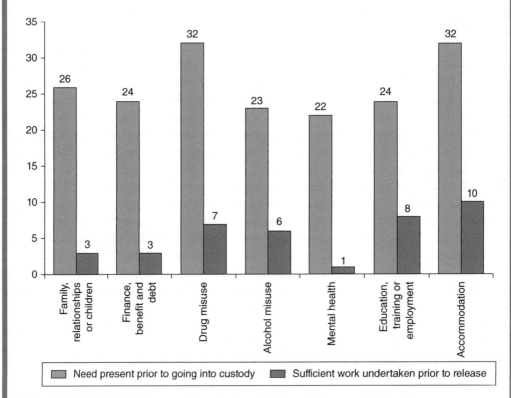

Figure 9.3 Work to address needs amongst males serving a custodial sentence

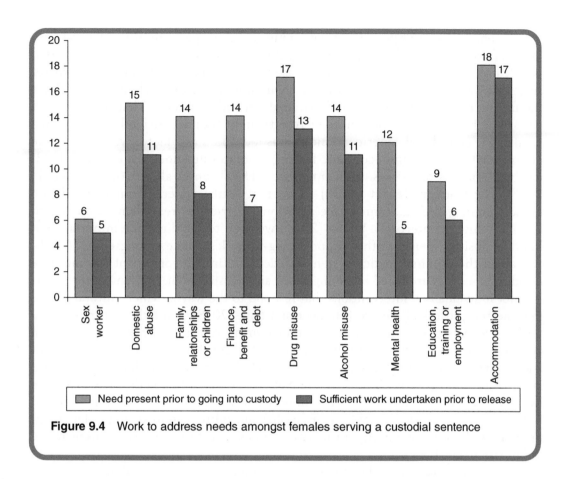

Figure 9.4 Work to address needs amongst females serving a custodial sentence

BAME groups are greatly overrepresented in the prison population. As of March 2020, 27 per cent of people in prison were from a BAME background, compared with only 13 per cent of the general population (HM Inspectorate of Prisons, 2020). People who identify as Black are imprisoned at an even more disproportionate rate – making up

13 per cent of the adult prison population but just three per cent of the general population (Ibid)). Whilst HM Inspectorate of Prisons inspections consistently show that people from BAME groups experience worse outcomes than their white counterparts, across a wide range of measures during their time in prison, little is known about the impact of such failures in the short, medium and long term. That said, research on BAME individuals' experiences of resettlement found that while participants' needs were considered generic, ethnicity was identified as a factor which alongside other social, political and economic factors, mediates but does not define individuals' experiences of the resettlement process (Jacobson et al., 2010; Sharp et al., 2006). The Corston Report (2007) noted that whilst general primary needs are broadly similar, BAME women face additional barriers in resettlement compared to their white counterparts. Young (2014) went on to highlight the importance of building positive identities that support long-term desistance amongst BAME individuals in the criminal justice system, particularly in the context of the multiple disadvantages that are faced by young Black and Muslim men. In doing so the report calls for individualised interventions that respond to the way in which cultural factors mediate the process of change (Shingler and Pope, 2018) Similarly, research by the Griffin Society suggests that racial discrimination, as well as family stigma, have been cited as barriers to resettlement (Owens, 2010) alongside isolation, cultural differences and language barriers for some people from BAME communities (Shingler and Pope, 2018). A recent report by HM Inspectorate of Probation reinforced the view that there 'was scope to engage more with ethnic minority service users before they are released from prison, to work more within their familial and cultural context, and to link them up more with local community organisations and support services' (HM Inspectorate of Probation, 2021: 10).

Taking into consideration the discussion presented to you in this section, is it surprising to find that the total number of recalls to prison have been increasing since October 2016 (HM Government, 2020)?

RECALL TO PRISON

People released from prison are subject to terms and conditions. Standard licence conditions require that individuals refrain from criminal activity, maintain good behaviour, attend regular appoints with their community offender manager and notify them of any changes to accommodation arrangements or employment, for example. If a community offender manager does not think that standard conditions are sufficient then they can recommend additional conditions which can include (but are not limited to) prohibited activity requirements, prohibited contact requirements, programme attendance requirements and/or exclusion requirements. Failure to comply with these terms and conditions can result in a recall to prison.

There are three distinct types of recall: *fixed term* recall, *standard* recall and *emergency* recall. Of those recalled between April 2019 and March 2020, 38 per cent were standard recalls, 37 per cent were fixed term recalls, 8 per cent were breach of home detention curfews and 17 per cent were emergency recalls (HM Inspectorate of Prisons, 2020a). The most common reasons for recall include poor behaviour/non-compliance (43 per cent), further charges (23 per cent), failure to reside at an agreed address (12 per cent) and being out of touch with probation services (9 per cent) (Ibid). People who have been recalled now make up approximately 9 per cent of the prison population.

In 2018, HM Prison and Probation Service produced an analytical summary indicating that recalled people had higher levels of assessed risk of serious harm and more complex needs than the general prison population (Fitzalan et al., 2018). In parallel, Dominey and Gelsthorpe (2020: 395) note how women, but by no means exclusively, are often 'trapped in a cycle of imprisonment, release from prison and then imprisonment again' because of their complex needs resulting from poor physical and mental health, drug and alcohol addiction, homelessness and victimisation. This raises questions about the legitimacy of imprisonment as well as the prison's ability to meet the needs of those serving a custodial sentence (see Chapter 11 for further discussion). Particularly during a global health pandemic when the ability to work with people in prison was significantly affected by unfolding COVID-19 restrictions that meant access to basic services was jeopardised.

recommended reading

If you would like to engage in further reading, you may find the following resources particularly useful:

Hjørnevik, K. and Waage, L. (2019) The prison as a therapeutic music scene: Exploring musical identities in music therapy and everyday life in a prison setting. *Punishment and Society*, 21(4), 454–72.

As part of a wider study into prison-based music therapy, this paper explores the role of music in music therapy and everyday life within a low security prison in Norway. In doing so, the paper explores how the prison as a music scene can form an important part of a prison's emotional geography, supporting the performance of caring and autonomous identities amongst people serving a custodial sentence.

Muirhead, J., and Fortune, C. (2016) Yoga in prison: A review of the literature. *Aggression and Violent Behaviour*, 28, 57–63.

Through a concise review of the evidence base, this paper highlights how yoga may be of use in rehabilitative efforts given its ability to improve factors related to reoffending such as impulsivity and aggression, as well as variables that can increase a person's ability to participate in interventions that are able to reduce their risk of future lawbreaking.

Woods, D., Breslin, G. and Hassan, D. (2017) A systematic review of the impact of sport-based interventions on the psychological well-being of people in prison. *Mental Health and Physical Activity*, 12, 50–61.

This study reviews the impact of sport-based interventions on the psychological well-being of people in prison. Findings suggest that although it can be suggested that sport-based interventions have a positive impact on psychological well-being within prisons, future studies should aim to enhance research designs and include psychological change theory into their design.

references

Allen, J., Anderson, C. and Bushman, B. (2018) The General Aggression Model. *Current Opinions in Psychology*, 19, 75–80.

Corston, J. (2007) *The Corston Report: A Report of a Review of Women with Particular Vulnerabilities in the Criminal Justice System*. London: Home Office. Available at: https://webarchive.nationalarchives.gov.uk/ukgwa/20130128112038/http://www.justice.gov.uk/publications/docs/corston-report-march-2007.pdf (last accessed 30 June 2022).

Cracknell, M. (2020) Post-sentence supervision: A case study of the extension of community resettlement support for short sentence prisoners. *Probation Journal*, 67(4): 340–57.

Davies, S. and Campling, P. (2018) Therapeutic community treatment of personality disorder: Service use and mortality over 3 years' follow up. *The British Journal of Psychiatry*, 182(S44), s24–7. Available at: www.cambridge.org/core/journals/the-british-journal-of-psychiatry/article/therapeutic-community-treatment-of-personality-disorder-service-use-and-mortality-over-3-years-followup/B2C09BED69F397E1790A46FFD3A0E8D1 (last accessed 30 June 2022).

Davison, S. and Janca, A. (2012) Personality disorder and criminal behaviour. *Current Opinions in Psychiatry*, 25(1), 39-45.

Dominey, J and Gelsthorpe, L. (2020) Resettlement and the case for women. *Probation Journal*, 67(4), 393–409.

Durr, P. (2020) *Trauma-Informed Work with People in Contact with the Criminal Justice System*. Clinks. Available at: www.clinks.org/sites/default/files/2020-09/Clinks%20Evidence%20Library%20Trauma-informed%20work%20with%20people%20in%20contact%20with%20the%20criminal%20justice%20system%202020.pdf (last accessed 30 June 2022).

Fitzalan H., Howard, F., Travers, R., Wakeling, H., Webster, C. and Mann, R. (2018) *Understanding the Process and Experience of Recall to Prison*. London: HM Prison and Probation Service.

Gannon, T.A., Olver, M.E., Mallion, J.S. and James. M. (2019) Does specialized psychological treatment for offending reduce recidivism? A meta-analysis examining staff and program variables as predictors of treatment effectiveness. *Clinical Psychology Review*, 73, 1–18.

Harvey, D. and Ramsden, J. (2016) Contracting between professionals who work with personality disorder. *Probation Journal*, 64(1) 20–32.

HM Government (2018) Offender behaviour programmes and interventions. Available at: www.gov.uk/guidance/offending-behaviour-programmes-and-interventions (last accessed 30 June 2022)

HM Government (2018a) Working in the prison and probation service. Blog post. Available at: https://prisonjobs.blog.gov.uk/2018/05/04/psychologists-in-the-prison-service-finding-the-real-story-inside (last accessed 30 June 2022).

HM Inspectorate of Prisons (2017) *Criteria for Assessing the Treatment of and Conditions for Men in Prisons*. Available at: www.justiceinspectorates.gov.uk/hmiprisons/wp-content/uploads/sites/4/2018/02/Expectations-for-publication-FINAL.pdf (last accessed 30 June 2022).

HM Inspectorate of Prisons (2017a) Interventions. Available at: www.justiceinspectorates.gov.uk/hmiprisons/our-expectations/prison-expectations/rehabilitation-and-release-planning/interventions/?highlight=interventions (last accessed 30 June 2022).

HM Inspectorate of Prisons (2020) *Minority Ethnic Prisoners' Experiences of Rehabilitation and Release Planning: A Thematic Review*. Available at: www.justiceinspectorates.gov.uk/hmiprisons/wp-content/uploads/sites/4/2020/10/Minority-ethnic-prisoners-and-rehabilitation-2020-web.pdf (last accessed 30 June 2022).

HM Inspectorate of Prisons (2020a) *A Thematic Review of Probation Recall Culture and Practice. A Review by HMIP*. Available at: www.justiceinspectorates.gov.uk/hmiprobation/wp-content/uploads/sites/5/2020/11/Recall-thematic.pdf (last accessed 30 June 2022).

HM Inspectorate of Prisons (2021) *Effective Practice Guide – Custody and Resettlement*. Available at: www.justiceinspectorates.gov.uk/hmiprobation/research/the-evidence-base-probation/specific-types-of-delivery/custody-and-resettlement/?highlight=resettlement (last accessed 30 June 2022).

I IM Inspectorate of Probation (2021) *Race Equality in Probation: The Experiences of Black, Asian and Minority Ethnic Probation Service Users and Staff*. Available at: www.justiceinspectorates.gov.uk/hmiprobation/wp-content/uploads/sites/5/2021/03/Race-Equality-in-Probation-thematic-inspection-report-v1.0.pdf (last accessed 30 June 2022).

HM Inspectorate of Probation and HM Inspectorate of Prisons (2016) *An Inspection of Through the Gate Resettlement Services for Short-Term Prisoners*. Available at: www.justiceinspectorates.gov.uk/cjji/wp-content/uploads/sites/2/2016/09/Through-the-Gate.pdf (last accessed 30 June 2022).

HM Prison and Probation Service (2021) *The Target Operating Model for Probation Services in England and Wales. Probation Reform Programme*. Available at: https://assets.publishing.service.gov.uk/government/uploads/system/uploads/attachment_data/file/959745/

HMPPS_-_The_Target_Operating_Model_for_the_Future_of_Probation_Services_in_England___Wales_-__English__-_09-02-2021.pdf (last accessed 30 June 2022).

House of Commons Justice Committee (2021) *The Future of the Probation Service: Eighteenth Report of Session 2019–21*. HC 285. (House of Commons Justice Committee 2021).

Jacobson, J., Phillips, C. and Edgar, K. (2010) *'Double Trouble?' Black, Asian and Minority Ethnic Offenders' Experiences of Resettlement*. Prison Reform Trust. Available at: https://prisonreformtrust.org.uk/wp-content/uploads/2010/12/Double-Trouble.pdf (last accessed 30 June 2022.

Lamb, N. (2013) Broadmoor Hospital. *Health written questions answered on 25th April 2013*. Available at: www.theyworkforyou.com/wrans/?id=2013-04-25d.153318.h (last accessed 30 June 2022).

Langness, M., Jagannath, J. and McCoy, E. (2020) Prisons are traumatizing but it is possible to reduce some of their harm. Urban Wire blog. Available at: www.urban.org/urban-wire/prisons-are-traumatizing-it-possible-reduce-some-their-harm (last accessed 30 June 2022).

Livesley, W. (2009) An integrated approach to the treatment of personality disorder. *Journal of Mental Health*, 16(1), 131–48.

Lockwood, B. and Harris, P.W. (2015) Kicked out or dropped out? Disaggregating the effects of community-based treatment attrition on juvenile recidivism. *Justice Quarterly*, 32, 705–28.

Malloch, M., McIvor, G. and Burgess, C. (2014) 'Holistic' community punishment and criminal justice interventions for women. *Howard Journal of Criminal Justice*, 53(4), 395–410.

McCartan, K.F. (2020) *Trauma-Informed Practice*. HM Inspectorate of Probation Academic Insights. 2020/05. Available at: www.justiceinspectorates.gov.uk/hmiprobation/wp-content/uploads/sites/5/2020/07/Academic-Insights-McCartan.pdf (last accessed 21 August 2021).

Messina, N., Zwart, E. and Calhoun, S. (2020) Efficacy of a trauma intervention for women in a security housing unit. *Archives of Women Health and Care*, 3(3). Available at: www.antoniocasella.eu/archipsy/Messina_2020.pdf (last accessed 30 June 2022).

Millings, M., Taylor, S., Burke, L. and Ragonese, E. (2019) Through the Gate: The implementation, management and delivery of resettlement service provision for short-term prisoners. *Probation Journal*, 66(1), 77–95.

Ministry of Justice (2014) Freedom of Information Request. Available at: https://webcache.googleusercontent.com/search?q=cache:yA7YIdUdTncJ:https://assets.publishing.service.gov.uk/government/uploads/system/uploads/attachment_data/file/326267/meaning-accreditation-body.doc+&cd=1&hl=en&ct=clnk&gl=uk (last accessed 30 June 2022).

Ministry of Justice (2014a) *Costs per Place and Costs per Prisoner*. National Offender Management Service Annual Report and Accounts 2013–14. Management Information Addendum. Available at: https://assets.publishing.service.gov.uk/government/uploads/system/uploads/attachment_data/file/367551/cost-per-place-and-prisoner-2013-14-summary.pdf (last accessed 30 June 2022).

Ministry of Justice (2016) Offender Management Statistics Quarterly Bulletin, England and Wales: July to September 2015. Available at: www.gov.uk (last accessed 6 July 2021).

Ministry of Justice (2018) Offending behaviour programmes and interventions. Available at: www.gov.uk/government/statistics/offender-management-statistics-quarterly-july-to-september-2015 (last accessed 27 July 2022).

National Institute of Clinical Excellence (2014) Mental health of people in prison. Available at: www.nice.org.uk/guidance/ng66/documents/mental-health-of-people-in-prison-draft-scope2#:~:text=Among%20people%20serving%20community%20sentences%2C%20an%20estimated%2047%25%20are%20likely,combined)%20have%20a%20personality%20disorder (last accessed 30 June 2022).

National Offender Management Service (2008) Risk of harm guidance and training resources. http://nomsintranet.org.uk/roh/index.htm

National Offender Management Service (2015) *The Offender Personality Disorder Pathway Strategy 2015*. Available at: www.england.nhs.uk/commissioning/wp-content/uploads/sites/12/2016/02/opd-strategy-nov-15.pdf (last accesed 30 June 2022).

Olvr, M.E., Stockdale, K.C. and Wormith, J.S. (2011) A meta-analysis of predictors of offender treatment attrition and its relationship to recidivism. *Journal of Criminology and Clinical Psychology*, 79(1), 6–21.

Owens, E. (2010) *Exploring the Experiences of Minority Ethnic Women in Resettlement: What Role, If Any, Does Ethnic Culture Play in the Resettlement of Black (African-Caribbean) Women Offenders in the UK?* The Griffins Society, Research Paper, 2010/01. Available at: www.thegriffinssociety.org/system/files/papers/fullreport/research_paper_2010_01_e.owens_.pdf (last accessed 30 June 2022).

Papalia, N., Spivak, B.S., Daffer. M., and Ogloff, J.R.P. (2019) A meta-analytic review of the efficacy of psychological treatments for violent offenders in correctional and forensic mental health settings. *Clinical Psychology, Science and Practice*, 26(2), e12282.

Petrillo, M., Tomas, M. and Hanspal, S. (2019) *Healing Trauma: Evaluation Report*. Portsmouth: Institute of Criminal Justice Studies. Available at: https://researchportal.port.ac.uk/portal/en/publications/healingtrauma-evaluation-report(e5bcaab5-a4df-48c9-ba99-a3f8cec6223c).html (last accessed 1 July 2022).

Pilgrim, D. (2001) Disordered personalities and disordered concepts. *Journal of Mental Health*, 10(3), 253–65.

Prison Reform Trust (2022) *Prison: The Facts*. Bromley Briefings Winter 2022. Available at: https://prisonreformtrust.org.uk/wp-content/uploads/2022/02/Winter-2022-Factfile.pdf (last accessed 27 July 2022).

Prochaska, J. and DiClemente, C. (1983) Stages and processes of self-change of smoking: Towards an integrative model of change. *Journal of Consulting and Clinical Psychology*, 51(3), 390–5.

Raynor, P. (2020) Resettlement after short prison sentences: What might work in England and Wales? *Probation Journal*, 67(4): 326–39.

Roberts, J. (1997) History of the therapeutic community. In E. Cullen, L. Jones and R. Woodward (eds) *Therapeutic Communities for Offenders*. New York: John Wiley and Sons, 3–22.

Sharp, D., Atherton, S. and Williams, K. (2006) *Everyone's Business: Investigating the Resettlement Needs of Black and Minority Ethnic Groups in the West Midlands.* Birmingham: Government Office West Midlands.

Shingler, J. and Pope, L. (2018) *The Effectiveness of Rehabilitative Services for Black, Asian and Minority Ethnic People: A Rapid Evidence Assessment.* Available at: https://assets.publishing. service.gov.uk/government/uploads/system/uploads/attachment_data/file/721977/_the-effectiveness-of-rehabilitative-services-for-BAME.pdf (last accessed 9 October 2022).

Shuker, R. (2010) Forensic therapeutic communities: A critique of treatment model and evidence base. *The Howard Journal of Crime and Justice,* 49(5), 463–77.

Skett, S., Goode, I. and Barton, S. (2017) A joint NHS and NOMS offender personality disorder pathway strategy: A perspective from 5 years of operation. *Criminal Behaviour and Mental Health,* 27, 214–21.

Stevens, A. (2013) *Offender Rehabilitation and Therapeutic Communities: Enabling Change the TC Way.* Abingdon: Routledge.

The Centre for Treatment of Anxiety and Mood Disorders (2021) What is trauma? Available at: https://centerforanxietydisorders.com/what-is-trauma/ (last accessed 28 July 2022).

Turley, C., Payne, C. and Webster, S. (2013) *Enabling Features of Psychologically Informed Planned Environments.* Ministry of Justice Analytical Series. Available at: https://assets. publishing.service.gov.uk/government/uploads/system/uploads/attachment_data/ file/211730/enabling-pipe-research-report.pdf (last accessed 1 July 2022).

Völlm, B. and Clarke, M. (2018) *Secure Hospital Care for Carers.* Available at: https://institutemh.org.uk/images/research/7778_Secure_Hospital_Care_Brochure_A5_V5_Online. pdf (last accessed 1 July 2022).

Ward, T. and Beech, A. (2006) An integrated theory of sexual offending. *Aggression and Violent Behavior,* 11(1), 44–63.

Young, L. (2014) *The Young Review: Improving Outcomes for Young Black and/or Muslim Men in the Criminal Justice System.* London: BTEG, Clinks, The Barrow Cadbury Trust.

10

WORKING WITH PEOPLE IN THE COMMUNITY

```
IN THIS CHAPTER, YOU WILL EXPLORE

1.  The range of interventions delivered in the community and the settings in which this work
    is undertaken

2.  The evidence on the contribution interventions make to reducing reoffending, and to pub-
    lic protection and supporting rehabilitation

3.  How newer forms of monitoring and surveillance based on technologies are reformulating
    our understandings of control in the community.
```

INTRODUCTION

In the previous chapter we considered work undertaken by prison staff to protect the public and reduce reoffending. In this chapter we turn our attention to the Probation Service. There are of course strong synergies between both organisations, particularly around resettlement, as we saw in the previous chapter. However, it is perhaps fair to say that most people have a better understanding of what goes on within the prison setting than what happens in probation, largely as a result of its heightened representation in popular media and other sources. Probation work, with the exception of unpaid work, tends to be hidden from public view. Most people's idea of probation work is an individual reporting to a probation officer as part of their supervision. However, in practice, probation work encompasses a range of interventions that are delivered in a number of settings. In this chapter, we explore these various aspects of probation work, which despite the organisational changes we outlined in previous chapters, have largely been a consistent feature of probation work. Whilst probation work is predominantly community facing there are by definition areas of overlap with prison work, particularly around resettlement and recall which we discussed in Chapter 9 and we will consider probation's role in resettlement further in this chapter. Despite there being obvious points during the sentence where the work of the prison and probation services converge (for example, sentence planning, risk management, parole and release on licence) there have also been criticisms that they operate too much in their own individual silos (Carter, 2003). Contemporary policy developments have therefore attempted to bring these two institutions closer together. This was the rationale behind the creation of the National Offender Management Service (NOMS) in 2003. This has been far from straightforward (Worrall and Mawby, 2011), which is perhaps unsurprising given their distinctive cultures and working practices which have developed over many years. The fact that senior management positions within NOMS were dominated by Prison Service staff has led to concerns that probation has been taken over by its larger criminal justice partner and its voice weakened in subsequent policy developments. However, we would agree with Canton and Dominey (2018: 228) that 'joint work does not depend on merger; the best inter-agency work draws on the complementary skills, resources and authority of partner agencies'. Ultimately, our contention is that regardless of whether probation work is undertaken in custodial or community settings it requires skilled and motivated workers.

KEY QUESTIONS TO CONSIDER WHEN READING THIS CHAPTER

1. To what extent are community-based interventions able to meet the needs of all people sentenced to a community order?

2. How do prison and probation work overlap during the sentence?

3. How do community-based sanctions enhance integration with the wider community?

COURT WORK

The courtroom has been described as a 'shop window' for probation (Robinson et al, 2022); it is the place where supervision begins. Within the court setting, one of probation's most important roles is to help sentencers decide the suitability of a community sentence and if imposed, what requirements or combinations of requirements are suitable. The four main areas of advice provided to court by the NPS are: 1) bail services, 2) a bail accommodation and support service (BASS), 3) court work other than assessments and reports, and 4) assessments and reports, pre-sentence. The probation instruction Determining pre-sentence reports: PI04/2016 (Ministry of Justice and HM Prison and Probation Service, 2021) indicates that a pre-sentence report (PSR) should contain as a minimum but not be limited to:

- Offence analysis and the pattern of offending, beyond a restating of the facts of the case

- Relevant offender circumstances, with links to offending behaviour highlighted, as either a contributing factor or a protective factor

- Risk of harm and likelihood of reoffending analysis, based on static predictors and clinical judgement

- The outcome of pre-sentence checks with other agencies or providers of probation services, including if any checks are still outstanding

- The addressing of any indications provided by the court

- Sentence proposals that are commensurate with the seriousness of the offence and will address the offender's assessed risk and needs. (HM Inspectorate of Probation, 2017: 20).

There are three types of reports prepared for the courts by the Probation Service:

1. *Standard delivery (adjourned) reports.* Based on a full Offender Assessment System (OASys) assessment (an electronic risk assessment system used by both the Prison and Probation Services) and suitable for *medium* and *high* seriousness cases when the court has indicated a possible community sentence or where a custodial sentence is being considered

2. *Fast delivery written pre-sentence reports.* Can be completed on the day of sentence by probation court officers. This type of report will only be suitable where a case is of *low* or *medium seriousness* and where the court indicates that a community sentence is being considered. This report may also be suitable where the court is considering custody. These reports are prepared by a probation officer and may include a full assessment of the offender using OASys

3. *Fast delivery oral pre-sentence reports.* An oral report is usually completed within 24 hours of conviction due to a limited amount of information required by the sentencing court. Reports are completed by probation practitioners to help the sentencing court determine the person's suitability for the sentence envisaged by the court, helping to avoid delays.

Driven by the government's agenda to provide *speedy justice*, the Criminal Justice Act 2003, implemented in 2005, paved the way for more reports to be delivered quickly. Importantly, the Act removed the requirement for PSRs to be written, and official guidance capitalised on this opportunity to save resources by encouraging the use of oral reports delivered on the day and introducing a new fast delivery report (a shorter format written report to be completed on the day or in up to five days) to be used 'wherever possible and appropriate' (National Probation Service, 2005: para. 2.5). This focus on speed and timeliness has led to a shift from standard to oral reports. In 2006, these *standard delivery* reports made up 77 per cent of all pre-sentence reports prepared by the Probation Service in England and Wales, but by 2016 the proportion of such reports had declined to just 7 per cent. Furthermore, 2016 saw the number of *stand-down* PSRs – those delivered orally in court on the day of request – exceed the number delivered in writing (that is, standard and fast-delivery written reports) for the first time (Ministry of Justice, 2017). In 2019/20, 98,154 PSRs were produced, of which 3 per cent were standard delivery reports, 45 per cent were fast delivery (short format) written reports and 52 per cent were oral reports. The COVID-19 pandemic and the resultant shutdowns of courts led to a 76 per cent fall in PSRs. Numbers have been returning to pre-pandemic levels since the courts reopened. The current service-level targets for the production of reports are that 60 per cent should be in the form of oral reports, 30 per cent in the form of fast delivery reports and only 10 per cent should be standard delivery reports (HM Inspectorate of Probation, 2017: 21).

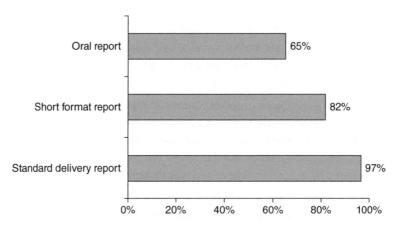

Figure 10.1 The quality of pre-sentence information and advice by type of court report

(*Source*: HM Inspectorate of Probation 2020: 10, Available at: www.justiceinspectorates.gov.uk/hmiprobation/wp-content/uploads/sites/5/2020/08/2020.04-The-quality-of-pre-sentence-information-and-advice-provided-to-courts.pdf)

Focusing on speed has reduced the quality of reports (see Figure 10.1). An analysis of the quality of pre-sentence information and advice provided to courts by HM Inspectorate of Probation (2020) found that the quality of pre-sentence information and advice varied by type of report; nearly all of the standard delivery reports were judged to be sufficiently analytical and personalised to the service user, but this dropped to about two in three of the oral reports. The quality of pre-sentence information and advice not only impacts upon the court's decision making but also has an impact post-sentence, with high-quality PSRs assisting responsible officers in timely and sufficient assessment and sentence planning following allocation of the case. As Robinson

(2017: 350) observes 'the obvious trade-off is one between speed at court and the need for more work post-sentence to acquire a comprehensive understanding of the service user's risks, needs, skills and strengths, enabling service delivery to be sufficiently focused and personalised'.

Concordance between the sentence proposed and the sentence imposed helps to demonstrate the influence of probation officers and sentencer confidence in probation advice. Data for January to December 2020 indicates that community sentences were proposed in 91 per cent of cases and were imposed in 53 per cent of cases. Suspended sentence orders, which are technically custodial sentences, were imposed in 32 per cent of cases where a community sentence had been recommended. Research by Gelsthorpe and Raynor (1995) found that better-quality PSRs were more likely to influence sentencers to use community sentences rather than imprisonment. Good reports were those which identified their information sources, were concise, showed a clear timeline and were logical, consistent and well written.

A study of Transforming Rehabilitation (du Mont and Redgrave, 2017) found that the relationship between frontline delivery and the courts had been fractured; National Probation Service (NPS) court teams were increasingly unaware of the services provided by community rehabilitation companies (CRCs). Other research reported probation court staff feeling that they had lost sources of information and quality control that they had benefited from in earlier years. A survey of 582 magistrates found that confidence in probation services was generally low. For example, over a third of magistrates (37 per cent) were not confident that community sentences were an effective alternative to custody. Around half reported they did not have sufficient information about the services and interventions on offer from probation (HM Inspectorate of Probation, 2016). As Maguire (2020: 265) points out, we still do not know enough about why reports, and the type of report, are requested in some cases and not in others or how courtroom dynamics influence these decisions.

Concerns have also been raised regarding the role that pre-sentence reports play in reproducing discrimination and bias (Maguire, 2020: 264). Gelsthorpe's (1992) study of social enquiry reports (the forerunner of pre-sentence reports) found that women were much more likely to be portrayed in reports as suffering from stress and psychological difficulties than men, and their offending explained by accounts of depression and emotional distress. Hudson and Bramhall's (2005) study suggested that a conflation of race with risk contained within pre-sentence reports contributed to the construction of Muslims of Pakistani heritage as criminal *others*. As Maguire (2020: 265) notes:

Reliance on actuarial risk assessment tools that cannot contextualise the social, cultural, and historical factors underpinning the over-representation of certain marginalized ethnic groups in the criminal justice system means that the character, family, and community background of the ethnic minorities are more likely to be interpreted as risky leading to more punitive treatment.

Court work can be challenging because as Robinson et al. (forthcoming) contend, 'it takes the worker out of their own practice setting and into one with its own rules, rhythms and culture'. The preparation of good quality reports can provide an opportunity for probation practitioners to influence sentences and encourage them to avoid the harmful consequences of imprisonment. However, under the guise of *speedy justice*, PSRs have been downgraded somewhat and this has had a negative impact on sentencing outcomes (HM Inspectorate of Probation, 2020). One of the major challenges facing the reunified Probation Service will be to secure the confidence of sentencers, not only to increase *market share* but more importantly to reduce the potential for disproportionate sentencing outcomes.

UNPAID WORK

The Council of Europe Probation Rules defines unpaid work as 'a community sanction or measure which involves organising and supervising by the probation agencies, of unpaid labour for the benefit of the community as real or symbolic reparation for the harm caused by an offender' (Geiran and Durnescu, 2019: 53). Unpaid work was introduced in England and Wales as part of the Criminal Justice Act 1972. Originally known as community service, it was delivered as a standalone sentence as a direct alternative to imprisonment. Following a successful pilot (see Harding, 2013) it was rolled out nationally in 1975 and has since evolved through various changes which altered the focus and name of the order, reflecting broader policy intentions. Although unpaid work is the favoured term used in England and Wales in relation to this sanction, internationally community service is still the more recognised term. The requirement to undertake unpaid work accounted for 33 per cent of community orders and 29 per cent of suspended sentence orders. Under current legislation, an unpaid work requirement can be imposed for between 40 and 300 hours, depending on the seriousness of the offence, and should be completed within 12 months. Unpaid work is overseen by a dedicated unpaid work team in each probation area although throughout delivery of the sentence, all risk and enforcement decisions and appropriate action will remain with the probation practitioner. Unpaid work projects vary from maintaining the grounds of parks, churches, cemeteries, local football, cricket and sports clubs and schools through to helping to run clubs for elderly and vulnerable adults with learning difficulties. Following a rigorous risk assessment, individuals can also be placed directly with charities and community groups, for example to help run charity shops. Members of the public can nominate projects for unpaid work teams to complete.

Unpaid work is now an important sentencing option in most jurisdictions. Part of its appeal lies in its flexibility as it can be used as a means of reparation, a rehabilitative measure, a punishment or an alternative to imprisonment. Unpaid work is reparative in the symbolic sense that the individual who has offended makes amends to the community rather than to the victims of their crime (McIvor et al., 2010). It has been argued that unpaid work can have an important *communicative* function (Duff, 2001) as a type of public reparation in which the censuring of the offender is accompanied by opportunities for them to express their understanding of what they have done and their commitment to the community. It also provides opportunities for the community to accept that in completing community service the offender has sufficiently apologised for the crime. However, as Carr and Neimantas (forthcoming) point out that 'the symbolism of high visibility jackets and signage spelling out "Offenders working your community" convey a particular message that is more stigmatising than inclusive'.

Unpaid work is seen as rehabilitative in the sense that it can provide an opportunity to enhance life and vocational skills, which are supportive of desistance. However, as Carr and Neimantas (forthcoming) note, despite its potential for developing 'employment and wider social capital, as well as to communicate positive messages about reparation, there has been insufficient attention paid to these possibilities to date'. The Target Operating Model for the latest probation reforms places a new emphasis on utilising 20 per cent of hours for employment, training and education (where relevant) so as to provide individuals with inbuilt learning and rehabilitative opportunities (HM Prison and Probation Service, 2021: 99). However, unpaid work is also closely associated with punishment involving a restriction in liberty in the sense that the individual must give up part of their free time to complete the requirements of the order with the threat of further sanctions if they do not. In 2014, the Ministry of Justice published research on community orders with punitive requirements, including results from a survey of service users. Key findings related to unpaid work were as follows (HM Inspectorate of Probation, 2021b):

- Nearly two-thirds of service users thought that unpaid work made them less likely to commit crime, but around one in five disagreed
- Compliance with unpaid work was higher in relation to:
  - service users who thought their probation practitioner listened to them 'a lot' compared with 'a little' in deciding the type of unpaid work
  - service users who felt the unpaid work was 'not demanding at all' compared with those who said it was 'very' demanding
  - older service users, those without an accommodation need, and those with children
- Service users were more likely to report that they had breached their order when they had an unpaid work requirement in the sentence (controlling for factors including the likelihood of reoffending).

On the face of it, unpaid work is a straightforward concept and therefore easier to *sell* to the public than probation supervision, which generally occurs behind closed doors and the methods utilised perhaps opaquer. Unpaid work is measurable in the sense that work carried out by offenders on community service can be quantified both financially and in terms of hours completed (McIvor, 2016). However, as McIvor et al. (2010) state, it shares a common characteristic of all penal sanctions in that its aims are in practice 'unclear and conflicting' and this is reflected in the way that it has been implemented over time. In most jurisdictions, community service is available as a sanction of the court, as a sentence in its own right or as a legislated alternative to a prison sentence at first sentence or following the imposition of a sentence of imprisonment. It may be imposed as a *stand-alone* option without additional support, as a condition of a supervisory penalty or alongside another order. In some jurisdictions community service operates as an alternative to imprisonment for fine default, as an alternative to prosecution, as a condition of pre-trial release or as a condition of parole. As McIvor (2016) notes, this also has a bearing on the types of offenders or offences for which it is considered suitable, as well as the nature and range of activities that it may involve—and the relative emphasis placed on punishment, reparation and rehabilitation can be seen to vary across jurisdictions and over time within jurisdictions. Moreover, there has been little research into the views, perceptions and experiences of those subject to unpaid work.

Doubts have also been raised that despite its increased usage, there is little evidence of its effectiveness. There have been no systematic reviews on the impact of unpaid work on reoffending rates. However, the following factors have been highlighted for improving the rehabilitative effect of unpaid work (HM Inspectorate of Probation, 2021b):

- Work that is experienced as useful and rewarding
- Opportunities to develop employment-related skills
- Staff following the principles of prosocial modelling, demonstrating good behaviours
- Providing clear information and consistent application of the rules
- Commencing the work promptly and being able to work regularly.

Although it was originally intended to be an alternative to imprisonment, the unprecedented growth of the prison population suggests that unpaid work is instead replacing other non-custodial options such as fines and is therefore having a net-widening effect (McIvor et al., 2010). This is particularly concerning in the event of a community order being breached since at this point it is possible that a more intrusive penalty (such as imprisonment) will be imposed than would have been warranted by the original offence (McIvor et al., 2010). As with all community-based sanctions, appropriate assessment in terms of the individual's suitability for unpaid work as well as ensuring the range of placements available meet the needs of the individual's circumstances is the key here.

A challenge for the reunified Probation Service will therefore be to ensure that quality placements are made available, overseen by skilled workers and perceived as legitimate by those subject to such sanctions.

ACCREDITED PROGRAMMES

As we discussed in Chapter 4, since the mid-1990s there has been substantial interest in the development and delivery of programmes as part of the evidence-based approach that was advocated as a means of improving the standing and impact of probation work. The first wave of accredited programmes was rolled out in England and Wales in 2000 (Robinson and Crow, 2009: 111). There are both accredited and non-accredited programmes delivered by the Probation Service. Courts may order that an individual undertakes an accredited programme as part of a community order or suspended supervision order but they cannot specify that non-accredited behavioural programmes are undertaken. In recent years, the use of accredited programmes has been replaced to a large extent by non-accredited interventions. The number of individuals starting accredited programmes in general fell by 44 per cent in the five-year period to 2015. Numbers seem to have steadied since then, but HM Inspectorate of Probation found variations between programmes (HM Inspectorate of Probation, 2019: 51). Statistics suggest that Black, Asian and minority ethnic individuals are under-represented on accredited programmes even though they are more likely to complete the intervention than white offenders if they are referred to one (HM Inspectorate of Probation, 2020a: 36).

There are a range of programmes currently accredited for delivery in the community by the Correctional Services Accreditation and Advice Panel (Ministry of Justice, 2021). They are cognitive–behavioural programmes in the main, and cover general offending, violence, domestic violence, sexual offending, substance misuse and extremism (some of which we discussed in Chapter 9). Not all accredited programmes will be available in each probation area, and it is for the regional directors to commission those they think are most needed according to local needs and offending profiles. However, the Thinking Skills programme and Building Better Relationships programmes will be delivered in each region by the interventions teams. It is also planned to bring delivery of accredited programmes into a single team so sexual offending teams delivering the accredited Sexual Offending Programme will sit in the interventions team. Interventions Teams will also deliver structured interventions targeted at lower-risk individuals who are not suitable for an accredited programme. Structured interventions are designed to fit with the broader sentence plan. The three areas of need identified for structured intervention are attitudes, thinking and behaviour, domestic abuse and emotional management (HM Prison and Probation Service, 2021: 113).

Individuals eligible and suitable to undertake an accredited programme are identified at the pre-sentence or pre-release stage. When an individual is sentenced to an accredited programme requirement the interventions teams will be informed on the day of sentence. Where a probation practitioner identifies a need for an accredited programme as part of a licence condition or post-sentence supervision, they will be referred to the interventions team to enable them to plan programme delivery. A formal referral is made when the probation practitioner judges that the individual is *programme-ready* (HM Prison and Probation Service, 2021: 111). The assessment of programme-ready made by the probation practitioner ensures motivational work has been completed and that there are no practical reasons such as ability to attend, substance misuse or other commitments (work, family, etc.) that will prevent an individual from completing the programme.

THE EFFECTIVENESS OF COMMUNITY-BASED PROGRAMMES

Research into the effectiveness of offending behaviour programmes in England and Wales has shown only modest positive results, which have mainly been found in some (but not all) prison-based studies where compliance is perhaps understandably higher (Raynor, 2007: 2). Evidence suggests that programmes are most effective when they are properly targeted and provided within a probation culture that supports rehabilitation and staff development and are delivered by staff who are properly trained. Programmes are also more likely to work if they are offered as part of a package of rehabilitative activity and support, which includes supervision by a skilled practitioner and help with practical issues such as finding a job or accommodation. As McNeill and Weaver, (2010): 16) point out:

> there is more to effective programmes than designing them well; they need to be run well; that requires the right organisational arrangements, the right staff skills and the right qualities of relationships between those on supervision and probation staff – both within programmes and beyond them.

Attention also needs to be paid to the offender's motivation and to the impact of their social context on the outcomes of the intervention (Farrall, 2002).

HM Prison and Probation Service (2021: 179) has identified common features of effective programmes that align with the evidence base of what works to reduce reoffending. These principles will be used by effective interventions panels in the future probation model:

- There is a credible rationale for how, why, and for whom, the activity will work.

- The activity should have a structure that allows it to be replicated.

- There is a selection process so that the activity is targeted at appropriate individuals.

- The activity should be designed to equip individuals with useful skills while aiming to ensure that no one will be disadvantaged or harmed.

- The activity is quality assured to ensure it is delivered as designed.

- The activity design shows a commitment to research and evaluation as demonstrated by having a clear, systematic and manageable process for the monitoring of outcomes. This should include evidence of whether intended benefits occur, and harm and disadvantages are avoided.

Most of the group interventions currently available are located within the RNR model we discussed in Chapter 2 and are based on cognitive behavioural therapies (CBT). However, newer programmes developed by HMPPS have adopted a biopsychosocial model that seeks to integrate the three core principles of the RNR model (risk-needs-responsivity) with desistance and strengths-based approaches such as the Good Lives Model (also discussed in Chapter 2). In a recent critique of group interventions, Renehan and Henry (forthcoming) have argued that an over-emphasis on individual deficits and cognitive skills can undermine the potential for group interventions to support people facing social and structural disadvantage. Instead, the authors argue that group interventions should be seen as part of a wider system of criminal, social and community justice that is trauma informed (see Chapter 7 for further discussion) and be sensitive to the person's individual vulnerabilities and circumstances (including adverse childhood experiences). Such an approach would move beyond the mechanics of programme delivery requiring emotionally literate and skilled facilitators attuned to both the emotional and practical challenges that individuals face in desisting from crime.

RESETTLEMENT WORK

The origins of post-custodial supervision in England and Wales can be traced back to the 19th century, when people leaving prison were offered help on a voluntary basis from a small number of discharged prisoners' aid societies (Maguire et al., 2000). It was not until the 1990s that post-custodial supervision became mandatory for large numbers of released prisoners under the provisions of the Criminal Justice Act 1991. As Maruna and LeBel (2002) note, most resettlement reforms focus on either risk- or needs-based strategies. Risk-based resettlement strategies focus on increasing surveillance backed up with new technologies such as electronic tagging and urine testing. Needs-based strategies focus on providing assistance to former offenders in overcoming addiction or learning basic skills, with an emphasis on those needs associated with the risk of reoffending.

Between January 2020 and December 2020, 53,253 people were released from custody. Of those released, 47 per cent were serving determinate sentences of less than 12 months whilst 8 per cent were female (HM Inspectorate of Probation, 2021). Resettlement has been shown to be important in reducing reoffending, possibly more important than interventions carried out in custody (HM Inspectorate of Probation, 2021a). Basic resettlement needs on leaving prison, or moving on from approved premises, include somewhere to live, a means to support oneself via paid employment, and access to benefits. As we discussed in Chapter 9, the transition from prison to the community can be extremely challenging. Individuals released from prison face numerous obstacles to successful reintegration, including a lack of access to suitable housing and employment, financial insecurity and debts, stigma, rebuilding familial and personal relationships, a problematic history of drug and alcohol dependency, and high incidence of mental disorder. For many individuals, their life-course experience has been an extension and confirmation of long-experienced marginalised status (Social Exclusion Unit, 2002). These problems are not unique to England and Wales as 'many countries struggle to manage any continuity of services "through the gate" or to overcome the structural disadvantages of the social environments from which many prisoners come' (Raynor, 2020: 328). As Moore (2011: 133) notes, 'Resettlement is not a uniform process or a universally agreed end-state but encompasses complex individuated transitions within social structures of differentiated, and unequal, life opportunity.'

Perhaps unsurprisingly, reoffending rates among those released from prison are high. The Offender Rehabilitation Act 2014 extended statutory post-release supervision to all those given a custodial sentence. Failing to comply with the requirements of Post Sentence Supervision (PSS) would be dealt with through breach proceedings at the magistrates' court. In the event of the breach being proven, sanctions would be considered, including a return to prison for up to 14 days, a fine, hours of unpaid work or a period of curfew (Dominey and Gelsthorpe, 2020: 393). Findings from an empirical study of practitioner and service users' perspectives in a CRC case study area (Cracknell, 2020) suggested a number of issues with Through the Gate arrangements. These included ambiguities regarding the correct use of enforcement procedures; the antagonistic relationship between third sector and CRC staff, primarily centred around transferring cases and concerns over the use of *light touch* supervision and uncertainties over what the rehabilitative aims of this sentence meant in practice. Service users experienced PSS as a frustrating 'pass-the-parcel' experience, where resettlement support was constantly stalled and restarted at each juncture of the sentence (Cracknell, 2020: 340). In 2017, HM Inspectorate of Probation concluded that 'CRCs are making little difference to their prospects on release … If Through the Gate services were removed tomorrow, in our view the impact on the resettlement of prisoners would be negligible' (House of Commons Justice Committee, 2021: 130).

Within the Offender Management in Custody (OMiC) framework that we discussed in Chapter 9, each person will have a prison offender manager in prison, and then a probation offender manager (community offender manager) who will come into the prison to support the person before release. Further to this, there are also plans to introduce teams based in the prison that specialise in short sentences, which aim to reduce the number of workers a person needs to liaise with (House of Commons Justice Committee, 2021). All individuals serving shorter prison sentences (fewer than ten months left to serve at the point of sentence) will have a community-based probation practitioner (COM), focusing on resettlement from the day of sentence as well as after release. Sentence plans for those with ten months or more of their sentence left to serve will be completed by prison offender managers until the handover to the community when the COM will complete a pre-release risk and needs assessment (HM Prison and Probation, 2021: 73). The COM is responsible for all pre-release activities from the point of handover from the prison offender manager (or from the start of sentence for those with fewer than ten months to serve at the point of sentence). The handover meeting provides the opportunity for the COM to be informed of engagement with any prison-based services. The handover from the prison offender manager to the COM provides enhanced information exchange including ensuring awareness of the experience and assessments of those with protected characteristics (HM Prison and Probation, 2021: 70). It will be a requirement for the probation practitioner (COM) to have at least three contacts with the person in prison prior to their release to help build a good relationship with them. This includes the current OMiC handover meeting, with at least two additional meetings (HM Prison and Probation, 2021: 73). The Target Operating Model specifies that COMs should offer two weeks of enhanced post-release support with two additional contacts to ensure barriers into interventions or contingencies that may need enacting are speedily recognised and acted on (HM Prison and Probation 2021: 73).

A key component of the new resettlement model is the Dynamic Framework. The Dynamic Framework is a commissioning mechanism to enable regional probation directors to procure rehabilitation and resettlement interventions across England and Wales (see Figure 10.2). It is 'dynamic' in the sense that organisations will be able to qualify at any point in time during the term of the Dynamic Framework, which it is anticipated will be in place for a period of seven to ten years, with the opportunity to extend this upon appropriate notification to the market (HM Prison and Probation, 2021: 85). The Framework will primarily be used to award contracts. However, there is flexibility built into the Framework agreement to extend this to grants if required (HM Prison and Probation, 2021: 85). Services from the Framework will be used for individuals on community orders and those supervised on licence in the community. It is hoped that it will encourage the participation of a range of suppliers including smaller suppliers and is responsive to

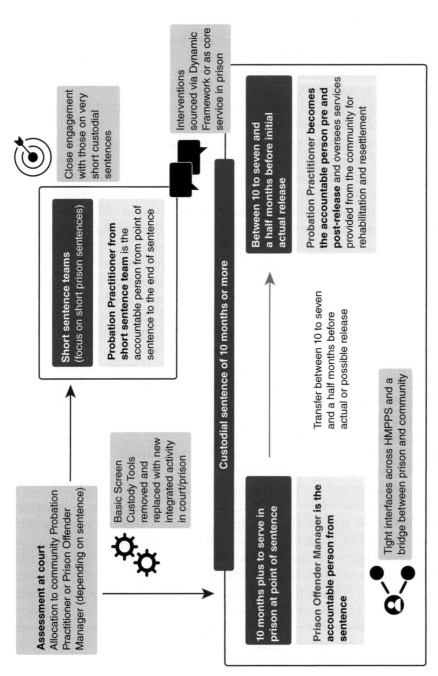

Figure 10.2 Outcome of the approach to resettlement under the unified probation service

(*Source*: HM Prison and Probation Service 2021: 71, Available at: https://assets.publishing.service.gov.uk/government/uploads/system/uploads/attachment_data/file/1061047/MOJ7350_HMPPS_Probation_Reform_Programme_TOM_Accessible_English_LR.pdf) (last accessed 10 October)

the needs of local areas (House of Commons Justice Committee, 2021). This is important because interventions which build social capital are likely to be better delivered by specialist local providers. The total value of contracts to be commissioned through the Probation Service Dynamic Framework will exceed £100 million per year once the system has reached a steady state (House of Commons Justice Committee, 2021). There will be a women's services category in the Dynamic Framework to provide services specifically designed for women, recognising the often-important protective factor for women of maintaining relationships and contact with children. These will be designed to take into account of the geographically dispersed nature of the women's estate.

ELECTRONIC MONITORING

As Hucklesby and Holdsworth (2020: 6) note, electronic monitoring (EM) 'is not in and of itself a criminal justice sanction or measure. It is a tool which is used to monitor conditions which are imposed by courts or prisons'. EM is a blanket term used to describe a range of surveillance and monitoring technologies deployed with a number of uses. It is provided via a worn device referred to as a personal identification device (PID) or more commonly a 'tag' which is fitted to the ankle or wrist. At any one time around 8,000 people in England and Wales are monitored electronically as part of a community sentence or following release from prison (HM Inspectorate of Probation, 2022). England

38,960	Number of prisoners eligible for release on home detention curfew in 2020/2021[2]
26%	Percentage of eligible prisoners released on home detention curfew – January to March 2021[2]
10%	Percentage of home detention curfews that are recalled to custody, October 2019 to September 2020[2]
87,894	Number of community orders started (including suspended sentence orders), April 2020 to March 2021[2]
3,924	Number of people on community orders (including suspended sentence orders) monitored by electronic monitoring on 31 March 2020[3]
2,968	Number of people post-release from custody monitored by electronic monitoring on 31 March 2020[3]
19, 265	Number of community curfew requirements issued[4]
473	Number of community GPS-enforced requirements issued[4]
1,565	Number of community alcohol abstinence monitoring requirements (AAMR) issued (live in Wales from November 2020 and England from 31 March 2021)[5]

Figure 10.3   Electronic monitoring in context

(*Source*: HM Inspectorate of Probation 2022: 5, www.justiceinspectorates.gov.uk/hmiprobation/wp-content/uploads/sites/5/2022/01/Electronic-monitoring-thematic-inspection.pdf)

and Wales have more people on EM than anywhere in Europe and as a proportion of sentences has even outstripped the United States where it was first introduced (see Figure 10.3).

The tag is linked to a transceiver installed in the individual's place of residence (using radio-frequency technology). Some prisoners are released early subject to a curfew which requires them to be at home for between nine and 12 hours a day, allowing them to live at home and to work during the final weeks of their sentence. This is known as a home detention curfew and lasts a minimum of 14 days and a maximum of three months for those serving less than 12 months, and a maximum of four and a half months for those serving between 12 months and four years. The tagging device sends a regular signal to a monitoring centre which confirms the presence of the person in their place of curfew.

If the individual is absent or tries to tamper with the equipment, the monitoring centre is alerted and the breach investigated. If the curfew is breached, either by the person leaving the property during the curfew hours or because of the person tampering with the device, the contractors will act immediately. This will usually result in the person being returned to custody where they will stay until their automatic release date. Studies have reported varying breach rates with EM, often around 30 per cent, with breaches tending to happen earlier on. Many of those who breach EM subsequently complete their orders and access to support is critical, providing information and reassurance to enable those tagged to complete their orders (HM Inspectorate of Probation, 2021c). Hucklesby et al. (2016) make an important distinction between supervision and support. Supervision relates to the supervisory oversight that can be imposed in addition to the technical controls of EM and is provided by a probation practitioner. Support, on the other hand, is normally provided by monitoring staff and generally involves the provision of information and practical assistance.

EM was introduced in England and Wales in the 1990s as a cost-effective means of reducing the prison population. It was first used as a as an alternative to pre-trial detention but nowadays it can be found at any stage of the criminal justice process, from pre-trial to execution of sentence and as part of the post-release supervision of released prisoners (Geiran and Durnescu, 2019). Like unpaid work, EM has been popular with policy makers and politicians worldwide because of its versatility and its potential to fulfil many different sentencing purposes and objectives including compliance, punishment and rehabilitation. It plays an important role in risk management as a means of locating individuals for whom it has concerns and restricting their movements in time and place. It can be a means of reassuring the public with the promise that individuals can be supervised more closely and more intensively in the community than traditional forms of supervision. As we have noted, the nature of community supervision is not fully understood by the general public who are also not always readily persuaded of the punitive and controlling functions of community sanctions. Imprisonment appears to be able to offer greater reliability in the sense that it is more difficult, for example, to break into someone's house if you are imprisoned! EM is currently used in the following ways in England and Wales:

- *Curfew*. A requirement added to a community sentence or as a licence condition at the point of release from custody. It specifies a time range during which the individual must remain within their home – often a 12-hour period (typically 7pm until 7am) but can be for as long as 16 hours a day. Curfew requirements can be up to 12 months long. It is monitored with a radio frequency (RF) tag, linked to a base station within the home.

- *Home detention curfew* (HDC). A form of curfew used with those in the last months of a prison sentence. Suitable candidates are released early and must live at a designated address (typically their home) with a curfew, monitored with an RF tag. HDC numbers increased after changes in the eligibility rules in 2017.

- *Exclusion zone monitoring*. A newer form of EM, rolled out in 2019. It uses global positioning system (GPS) enabled tags to monitor an individual's location and can raise an alert if the individual crosses into an excluded zone. The individual's location is recorded at all times and can be made available to police to confirm locations at the time of an offence.

- *Sobriety tagging*. A new form of tagging, initially piloted in Wales in 2020. It uses a specialised tag that can detect alcohol in small quantities in perspiration from the skin of an individual and provides a way to detect whether the person tagged has been drinking alcohol. Its intended use is to monitor compliance with alcohol abstinence monitoring requirements (AAMR), typically used with those where alcohol consumption is a contributing factor in their offending behaviour, but who are not alcohol dependent.

- *Special uses*. EM also has a variety of other more limited uses, such as with the small number of TACT (Terrorism Act) offenders who are often subject to GPS tagging within intensive offender management (IOM) schemes.

The sentencing White Paper *A Smarter Approach to Sentencing* (Ministry of Justice, 2020) sets out proposals to expand the use of EM and make it more flexible. This includes a proposal to give probation services powers within a prescribed range of circumstances to vary EM requirements to support individuals' living and working patterns and encourage increased compliance. The government's proposals include extending the length of time that individuals can be subject to EM from 12 months to two years and introducing a home detention order which provides a 'lengthy and restrictive curfew' monitored by GPS.

EM potentially fulfils the traditional role of surveillance in terms of bringing about behavioural change on the grounds the people tend to behave differently if they think that the monitor will catch them out and that there will be consequences for their behaviour. However, there has been much debate about the extent to which EM can positively contribute to the processes of rehabilitation and desistance. Nellis (2015) argues that EM is not rehabilitative in itself but is able to facilitate other rehabilitative measures. It has been argued that in the best case scenario EM imposes an external control that offers some respite from behaviour that might be associated with offending and that this might lead to changes of habit and lifestyle that might be conducive to supporting desistance. The structure provided by curfews can also assist with employment. It could also support compliance with rehabilitative interventions and programmes. As Hucklesby and Holdsworth (2020: 7) note, EM 'does not and cannot stop wearers from doing what they want to do'. That EM depends to this extent on the active compliance of the individual could be viewed 'as a limitation (because violation is possible) or as a strength (because it implies trust and affords offenders the opportunity to demonstrate that they can act reliably)' (Canton and Dominey, 2018: 82). On the other hand, some of these controls can disrupt employment and family relationships, thus obstructing processes of desistance. A study by Fitzalan Howard (2018) found that the experiences of people tagged varied, but most regarded EM favourably compared to a term in custody. Those tagged mainly complied with the curfew due to fear of punishment and were less confident that their long-term outcomes or criminal behaviour had really changed.

Unlike arrangements in other European countries, EM in England and Wales is delivered by private companies rather than the Probation Service, although enforcement decisions are taken and acted upon by the Probation Service. Debates continue about the use of EM and its relationship with other forms of supervision. Should the surveillance of EM be accompanied by the support of personal intervention or might it stand alone, especially where there seems to be no particular need for rehabilitative measures? The Council of Europe Recommendation (2014) states that while EM may be used as a stand-alone measure, 'In order to seek longer term desistance from crime it should be combined with other professional interventions and supportive measures aimed at the social reintegration of offenders' (Rule 8). Many countries in Europe have combined EM with rehabilitative interventions to much better effect than England and Wales, where communication between probation and EM providers has usually been poor (Hucklesby and Holdsworth, 2020). A recent inspection (HM Inspectorate of Probation, 2022) found that electronic monitoring could provide people on probation monitoring with a period of stability and a reason to break contact with criminal associates. However, electronic monitoring is often treated as an 'extra', rather than an integral part of an individual's supervision. Inspectors found that practitioners did not always discuss electronic monitoring with individuals on probation and that there were missed opportunities to acknowledge positive progress or to signpost people who had completed alcohol monitoring to further sources of support.

The fact that most EM is unregulated (although there a requirement to comply with human rights conventions) has raised concerns about how this sanction is governed. Concerns have been raised because the equipment, software and sometimes support structures are provided by the private sector, which holds vast amounts of personal data that can be exploited and used for purposes for which it was not intended. Moreover, the costs of developing bespoke tracking systems and the commercial conditions under which they are produced creates financial pressure to find new groups to track in order to recover development costs and generate economies of scale. The Council of Europe Probation Rules on the regulation and practice of EM state that 'the level of technological surveillance shall not be greater than is required in an individual case, taking into consideration the seriousness of the offence committed and the risks posed to community safety' (Geiran and Durnescu, 2019: 63). There is also the issue of consent. As we have noted, EM intrudes into the lives not only of those under supervision but also their families – because it is a sentence of the court it does not require consent from either. Tags are bulky and many people (particularly women) feel stigmatised by having to wear one. There is a danger that we put too much faith in the technology both in terms of its accuracy – there have been cases where the equipment has been faulty and given wrong information – and is worrying when we are talking about people's liberty. Claims for its usefulness have perhaps been somewhat overstated.

EM was originally seen as a means for potentially reducing the prison population. There is little evidence that it has achieved this. England and Wales have high levels of imprisonment but also have high levels of EM whereas Germany has low levels of imprisonments and low levels of EM. Whilst it is hard to demonstrate that the use of EM has done much in any country to arrest an increase in the prison population, some might argue that increases would have been steeper but for EM. Some positive effects have been found in the use of EM with sexual offenders and when it is used as an alternative to custody and combined with other interventions that target offending-related needs (HM Inspectorate of Probation, 2021c). Like other 'alternatives to custody' EM's influence on the size of the prison population is complex and uncertain. There is also little evidence that EM reduces reoffending. Studies into the efficacy of home detention curfews have showed varying results – from improvements in reoffending of 10 per cent in the most favourable studies to no improvement in the least favourable. A systematic review of 17 relevant studies (Belur et al., 2017) found that EM had no statistically significant effect on reducing reoffending, except for sexual offenders and when EM was compared to a short prison sentence as an alternative to custody.

APPROVED PREMISES

Approved premises (APs) refers to accommodation approved under section 13 of the Offender Management Act 2007. As Carr (2018) observes, they are a relatively invisible part of the criminal justice system, even though they play a key role in the transition from prison to community, providing accommodation for the purposes of assessment, supervision and management. They provide key workers and a programme of purposeful activity that is intended to help with reducing reoffending and reintegration into society. The regime within APs varies depending on the locational context and resident composition (Reeves, 2016). AP residents are:

> **subject to random drug tests and room searches and may be required to engage in various chores around the hostel, for example, cleaning and gardening. Residents may be required to attend a range of offence-based or life skills programmes, such as anger management or one-to-one work with their probation supervisor or hostel key worker. (Irwin-Rogers and Reeves, 2020: 547)**

APs act as a halfway house between prison and home and in some jurisdictions are known as *halfway houses*. Originally called probation hostels, they acted as places of residence for people on bail or subject to community sanctions (Irwin-Rogers and Reeves, 2020). Nowadays they provide intensive supervision and monitoring for those who present a high or very high risk of serious harm and are mostly used for people on licence, but they also accommodate small numbers of people on bail or community sentences. There are a hundred APs across the country with over 2,250 bed spaces and a normal length of stay of three months, but this can be longer depending on the availability of safe move-on arrangements (HM Prison and Probation Service, 2021: 20). Residents are subject to a curfew during which they must reside within the AP. Minimum curfews are from 11pm to 6am or 7am, depending on the AP. Extra curfew conditions can be set by the court as part of the licence conditions. Because APs cater mainly for individuals presenting higher risks of serious harm, staff work closely with Multi-Agency Public Protection Arrangements (MAPPA) and a range of organisations including local authorities and housing providers.

APs are staffed 24 hours a day and impose various constraints on residents' freedoms that are determined locally by their supervising officer and staff from the APs. During their stay, residents are required to engage in a minimum number of hours per week of purposeful activity, work on their offending-based behaviours and attitudes and attend relevant treatment or intervention programmes (HM Inspectorate of Probation, 2021d). An inspection report by HM Inspectorate of Probation (2017a) found that APs were exceptional at protecting the public but that the quality of resettlement and rehabilitation services was mixed. There are too few hostels and provision is geographically patchy. Inspectors found that provision was routinely oversubscribed and estimated a 25 per cent shortfall in demand for beds in APs (HM Inspectorate of Probation, 2017a: 64). As we discussed regarding the Joseph McCann case, the lack of available accommodation in APs was highlighted as a factor in the failure to ensure that he was suitably monitored in the community. In terms of overall capacity, women are particularly poorly served – there are just six hostels for women in England and Wales (HM Inspectorate of Probation, 2017b).

As Irwin-Rogers (2017: 389) notes, 'with no bars on the doors and no guards to physically coerce residents into compliance, the effective functioning of APs depends primarily on the voluntary cooperation of residents'. Positive relationships between staff and residents are therefore important in ensuring that the objectives of the APs are achieved. As Irwin-Rogers and Reeves (2020: 548) point out, this can be either assisted or hindered by seemingly innocuous practices such as the use of an open office door policy which can remove 'the boundary between staff and residents' areas, can allow for informal interactions and may enhance trust'. However, care needs to be taken that staff do not become overly involved with residents and respond unhelpfully to crises (HM Inspectorate of Probation, 2021d). In addition, due to the risk of burnout from staff, it is important that they receive necessary support from their line managers and have some time and space away from residents. All APs are expected to be *enabling environments.* Enabling environments are places where there is a focus on creating a positive and effective social environment and where healthy relationships are seen as key. Some APs are designated psychologically informed planned environments (PIPEs) which have been developed as part of the Offender Personality Disorder Strategy (Department of Health and National Offender Management Service, 2011). PIPEs APs offer placements to men who are deemed at high risk of reoffending because of their complex personality traits and attachment histories (Chapman-Gibbs et al., 2019). This means that additional expert psychological input from NHS clinicians is provided to help APs manage individuals with personality disorders (see Chapter 9 for a more in-depth discussion of PIPEs).

Many residents in APs will have committed sexual offences and this can pose particular challenges for APs as they are often stigmatised and encounter hostility and moral condemnation from the community (see Chapter 12). There is also the issue that because of the stigma attached to their offences those convicted of sexual offences tend to form groups within shared accommodation. These social groups have been found to be highly significant to how individuals conceptualise themselves and their social identities (Reeves, 2016). As Reeves (2013) notes, group membership conveys more than simply a network of social contacts, it also serves to practically and emotionally support members and help them cope with the challenges of life in the APs. On the other hand, it can also reinforce negative, criminal identities (HM Inspectorate of Probation, 2021d). As Marston and Reeves (forthcoming) contend, 'although the approved premises offers many benefits and holds much potential, its capacity for transformative change is considerably hampered by the churn of demand and by a risk management culture that understandably tends to dominate the field'.

VICTIM WORK

Over the past 30 years there has been an increasing emphasis on victim-focused work driven by a complex range of social, political and ideological forces (Green, 2020). Victim contact work became a responsibility of the Probation Service through the first

Victims' Charter in 1990. At that time the service was limited to contact with the families of homicide victims when the individual was approaching release from custody. Victim contact was extended further in 1996 as part of the revised to include contact at the beginning of the sentence and to cover a wider range of victims, those where the individual was sentenced to at least 12 months in custody for sexual and/or violent offences. Probation practitioners have specific obligations to keep the victim informed of developments and any application to the Parole Board for release. They provide advice to the Parole Board as it considers applications for release, much as they provide advice to courts on sentencing.

The Criminal Justice and Court Services Act 2000 placed victim contact work on a legislative footing for probation services. The government's *Victim Strategy* (2018) included commitments for increased funding for services, easier opting-in to the Victim Contact Scheme and improved training for victim liaison officers. Other key elements of probation victim work include restorative justice, facilitating mediation and victim awareness programmes. Burrows (2013: 386) observes that victim awareness work 'targets knowledge (for example, the consequences of offending for both specific and potential victims), attitudes/cognitions (including denial and minimisation), and emotions (for example, encouraging offenders to care and develop empathy)'.

The Victim Contact Scheme is an information-sharing service, with victim liaison officers based in each probation area. Just over 40,000 victims of violent and sexual offences are actively managed under the NPS Victim Contact Scheme. Victim liaison officers hold on average 215 cases each, due to staff shortages (HM Inspectorate of Probation, 2020a: 38). Victim liaison officers provide victims with information about the offender's journey through custody and prepare and support victims in the run-up to a person's release. The HMPPS Victims team, which is part of the Public Protection Group, is responsible for policy and strategy regarding work with the victims of violent and sexual offences. A senior manager in each of the Probation Service regions is responsible for operational management of the statutory Victim Contact Scheme. It also liaises with other agencies and acts in an advisory capacity on complex or high-profile cases. Accurate and timely information, providing a professional and fair service, and involving all key agencies have been found to be important for building victim confidence (HM Inspectorate of Probation, 2021e). Victims often do not access services which may help them. Reasons include lack of knowledge about available services; not wanting victim services or believing they do not need them; lack of access to services; fear of re-victimisation, re-traumatisation or blame by service providers; and lack of eligibility for services (HM Inspectorate of Probation, 2021e).

The Target Operating Model for the latest probation reforms (HM Prison and Probation Service, 2021) focuses on the following to improve services provided to victims of crime:

- **Expanding the Victim Contact Scheme to support victims of offences characterised by stalking and harassment where individuals are sentenced to a custodial sentence of under 12 months**

- **Establishing a revised and enhanced 'opt in' process to enable victim contact for cases approaching a review by the Parole Board that provides an additional opportunity for contact including where victims have previously opted out of the scheme**

- **Expanding the Victim Contact Scheme to recognise changes in the Victims' Code for Victim Liaison Officers to be responsible for contact with victims of unrestricted patients**

- **Enhancing the type of information provided to victims to include the prison security category via the annual contact letter**

- **Enhancing the capability of the Victim Contact Scheme to support complex and Terrorism Act cases.**

(HM Prison and Probation Service, 2021: 121)

CONCLUSION

We began this chapter by considering the role of the probation worker in the court setting. We then discussed the different types of court reports produced and changes in their usage driven by the need to provide *speedy justice*. We then considered probation's role and responsibilities in respect of those released from prison on licence and post-sentence supervision. We discussed the challenges facing released prisoners in reintegrating into the community following a custodial sentence and attempts to address this including those in the most recent probation reform programme. We also looked at issues of recall. We then looked at the development of unpaid work which in England in Wales has also been called community service and community payback in England and Wales. We explored terminology that has been used to promote the different intentions of this sanction which also highlights the contested nature of its purpose. We then outlined the range of accredited programmes that are delivered by the Probation Service in the community and the available evidence regarding their efficacy. Our attention then turned to the development of electronic monitoring, its various usages and the available evidence for its efficacy in reducing the prison population. We then looked at approved premises and how they operate within the criminal justice field before finally discussing probation's role in providing a service to victims of crime.

recommended reading

Robinson, A. (2011) *Foundations for Offender Management*. Bristol: Policy Press.

This book provides a comprehensive introduction to criminal justice work, focusing on key areas of practice and law.

McNeill, F., Durnescu, I. and Butter, R. (2016) *Probation: 12 Essential Questions*. London: Palgrave Macmillan.

This volume poses a series of key questions about the practice of probation as an integral part of the European criminal justice system. The contributors' questions address the legitimacy, and perhaps continued existence, of probation.

Canton, R. and Dominey, J. (2017) *Probation*. Abingdon: Routledge.

Setting probation in the context of the criminal justice system, this text explores its history, purposes and contemporary significance. It explains what probation is, and the practical realities of working with offenders in the community.

references

Belur, J., Thornton, A., Tompson, L., Manning, M., Sidebottom, A. and Bowers, K. (2017) *What Works Crime Reduction Systematic Review Series: No. 13: A Systematic Review of the Effectiveness of the Electronic Monitoring of Offenders*. London: University College London.

Burrows, J. (2013) Victim awareness: Re-examining a probation fundamental. *Probation Journal*, 60(4), 383–99.

Canton, R. and Dominey, J. (2018) *Probation*. Abingdon: Routledge.

Carr, N. (2018) Space, place and supervision. *Probation Journal*, 65(2), 131–4.

Carr, N. and Neimantas, L. (forthcoming) Community service and rehabilitation: Untapped potential. In L. Burke, N. Carr, E. Cluley, S. Collett and F. McNeill, F. (eds) *Reimagining Probation Practice: Re-forming Rehabilitation in an Age of Penal Excess*. Abingdon: Routledge.

Carter, P. (2003) *Managing Offenders, Reducing Crime: A New Approach*. London: Home Office.

Chapman-Gibbs., Mannix, K. and Harvey, D. (2019) Relational risk management in a Psychologically Informed Planned Environment (PIPE) approved premises. *Probation Journal*, 66(3), 356–69.

Council of Europe. (2014). *Recommendation CM/ Rec 2014 (4) of the Committee of Ministers to Member States on Electronic Monitoring. Adopted 19th February 2014*. Strasbourg: Council of Europe.

Cracknell, M. (2020) Post-sentence supervision: A case study of the extension of community resettlement support for short sentence prisoners. *Probation Journal*, 67(4), 340–57.

Department of Health and National Offender Management Service (2011) *Response to the Offender Personality Disorder Consultation*. London: Department of Health and National Offender Management Service.

Dominey, J and Gelsthorpe, L. (2020) Resettlement and the case for women. *Probation Journal*, 67(4), 393–409.

Duff, R.A. (2001) *Punishment, Communication and Community*. Oxford: Oxford University Press.

du Mont, S. and Redgrave, H. (2017) *Where Did It All Go Wrong? A Study into the Use of Community Sentences in England and Wales*. London: Crest Advisory.

Farrall, S. (2002) *Rethinking What Works with Offenders: Probation, Social Context and Desistance from Crime*. Cullompton: Willan.

Fitzalan Howard, F. (2018) *The Experience of Electronic Monitoring and Implications for Practice: A Qualitative Research Synthesis*. HM Prison and Probation Service Analytical Summary. London: HM Prison and Probation Service.

Geiran, V. and Durnescu, I. (2019) *Implementing Community Sanctions and Measures*. Council of Europe Guidelines. Available at: https://rm.coe.int/implementing-community-sanctions-and-measures/1680995098 (last accessed 2 July 2021).

Gelsthorpe, L. (1992) *Social Inquiry Reports: Race and Gender Considerations*. Home Office Research and Statistics Department. Research Bulletin 21. London: Home Office.

Gelsthorpe, L. and Raynor, P. (1995) Quality and effectiveness in probation officers' reports to sentencers. *British Journal of Criminology*, 35(2), 188–200.

Green, S. (2020) Victim-focussed work with offenders. In P. Ugwudike, H. Graham, F. McNeill, P. Raynor, F.S. Taxman and C. Trotter (eds) *The Routledge Companion to Rehabilitative Work in Criminal Justice*. Abingdon, Oxon: Routledge, pp. 502–15.

Harding, J. (2013) Forty years on: A celebration of community service by offenders. *Probation Journal*, 60(3), 325–31.

HM Inspectorate of Probation (2016) *A Thematic Inspection of the Provision and Quality of Services in the Community for Women Who Offend*. Available at www.justiceinspectorates. gov.uk/hmiprobation/wp-content/uploads/sites/5/2016/09/A-thematic-inspection-of-the-provision-and-quality-of-services-in-the-community-for-women-who-offend.pdf (last accessed 19 February 2022).

HM Inspectorate of Probation (2016) *Tansforming Rehabilitation: Early Implementation 5*. Manchester: Her Majesty's Inspectorate of Probation. Available at: www.justiceinspectorates.gov.uk/hmiprobation/wp-content/uploads/sites/5/2016/05/Transforming-Rehabilitation-5.pdf (last accessed 1 July 2022).

HM Inspectorate of Probation (2017) *The Work of Probation Services in Courts*. Manchester: HM Inspectorate of Probation. Available at: www.justiceinspectorates.gov.uk/hmiprobation/inspections/courtwork (last accessed 1 July 2022).

HM Inspectorate of Probation (2017a) *Probation Hostels' (Approved Premises) Contribution to Public Protection, Rehabilitation and Resettlement*. Manchester: HM Inspectorate of Probation. Available at: www.justiceinspectorates.gov.uk/hmiprobation/inspections/ap (last accessed 1 July 2022).

HM Inspectorate of probation (2017b) Probation Hostels (Approved Premises) contribution to public protection, rehabilitation and resettlement. Available at: www.justiceinspector-ates.gov.uk/hmiprobation/wp-content/uploads/sites/5/2017/07/Probation-Hostels-2017-report.pdf (last accessed 1 August 2022).

HM Inspectorate of Probation (2019) *Report of the Chief Inspector of Probation*. Manchester: HM Inspectorate of Probation. Available at: www.justiceinspectorates.gov.uk/hmiproba-tion/inspections/report-of-the-chief-inspector-of-probation (last accessed 1 July 2022).

HM Inspectorate of Probation (2020) *The Quality of Pre-sentence Information and Advice Provided to Courts*. Research and Analysis Bulletin 2020/4. Manchester: HM Inspectorate of Probation. Available at: www.justiceinspectorates.gov.uk/hmiprobation/wp-content/uploads/sites/5/2020/08/2020.04-The-quality-of-pre-sentence-information-and-advice-provided-to-courts.pdf (last accessed 1 July 2022).

HM Inspectorate of Probation (2020a) *An Inspection of Central Functions Supporting the National Probation Service*. Manchester: HM Inspectorate of Probation. Available at: www.justicein spectorates.gov.uk/hmiprobation/inspections/nationalnps (last accessed 1 July 2022).

HM Inspectorate of Probation (2021) *Custody and Resettlement*. Available at: www.justicein-spectorates.gov.uk/hmiprobation/research/the-evidence-base-probation/specific-types-of-delivery/custody-and-resettlement/ (last accessed 1 August 2022).

HM Inspectorate of Probation (2021a) *Effective Practice Guide – Custody and Resettlement*. Manchester: HM Inspectorate of Probation. Available at: www.justiceinspectorates.gov.uk/hmiprobation/research/the-evidence-base-probation/specific-types-of-delivery/cus tody-and-resettlement/?highlight=resettlement (last accessed 6 July 2021).

HM Inspectorate of Probation (2021b) *Effective Practice Guide – Unpaid Work*. Manchester: HM Inspectorate of Probation. Available at: www.justiceinspectorates.gov.uk/hmiproba tion/research/the-evidence-base-probation/specific-types-of-delivery/unpaid-work/?highlight=community%20service (last accessed 1 July 2022).

HM Inspectorate of Probation (2021c) *Effective Practice Guide – Electronic Monitoring*. Manchester: HM Inspectorate of Probation. Available at: www.justiceinspectorates.gov.uk/hmiprobation/research/the-evidence-base-probation/specific-types-of-delivery/elec tronic-monitoring/?highlight=Electronic%20monitoring (last accessed 11 July 2021).

HM Inspectorate of Probation (2021d) *Effective Practice Guide – Approved Premises*. Manchester: HM Inspectorate of Probation. Available at: www.justiceinspectorates.gov.uk/hmiprobation/research/the-evidence-base-probation/specific-types-of-delivery/approved-premises/?highlight=approved%20premises (last accessed 13 July 2021).

HM Inspectorate of Probation (2021e) *Effective Practice Guide – Victim Work*. Manchester: HM Inspectorate of Probation. Available at: www.justiceinspectorates.gov.uk/hmiproba

tion/research/the-evidence-base-probation/specific-types-of-delivery/victim-work/?highlight=Victims (last accessed 13 July 2021).

HM Inspectorate of Probation (2022) *The Use of Electronic Monitoring as a Tool for the Probation Service in Reducing Reoffending and Managing Risk.* Available at: www.justicein spectorates.gov.uk/hmiprobation/wp-content/uploads/sites/5/2022/01/Electronic-monitoring-thematic-inspection.pdf (last accessed 1 July 2022).

HM Prison and Probation Service (2021) *The Target Operating Model for Probation Services in England and Wales: Probation Reform Programme.* London: HM Prison and Probation Service. Available at: https://assets.publishing.service.gov.uk/government/uploads/system/uploads/attachment_data/file/1061047/MOJ7350_HMPPS_Probation_Reform_Programme_TOM_Accessible_English_LR.pdf (last accessed 1 July 2022).

House of Commons Justice Committee (2021) *The Future of the Probation Service: Eighteenth Report of Session 2019–21.* HC 285.

Hucklesby, A. and Holdsworth, E. (2020) *Electronic Monitoring in Probation Practice.* HM Inspectorate of Probation Academic Insights 2020/08. Manchester: HM Inspectorate of Probation. Available at: www.justiceinspectorates.gov.uk/hmiprobation/wp-content/uploads/sites/5/2020/12/Academic-Insights-Hucklesby-and-Holdsworth-FINAL.pdf (last accessed 1 July 2022).

Hucklesby, A., Beyens, K., Boone, M., Dunkel, F. McIvor, G. and H., Graham (2016) Creativity and effectiveness in the use of lecetronic monitoring: A case study of five jurisdictions. *Journal of Offender Monitoring*, 27(2), 31–47.

Hudson, B. and Bramhall, G. (2005) Assessing the 'other' – Constructions of 'Asianness' in risk assessments by probation officers. *British Journal of Criminology*, 45(5), 721–40.

Irwin-Rogers, K. (2017) Staff–resident relationships in approved premises. *Probation Journal*, 64(4), 388–404.

Irwin-Rogers, K., and Reeves, C. (2020) Post-release residential supervision. In P. Ugwudike, H. Graham, F. McNeill, P. Raynor, F.S. Taxman and C. Trotter (eds) *The Routledge Companion to Rehabilitative Work in Criminal Justice.* Abingdon, Oxon: Routledge, pp. 545–57.

Maguire, M., Raynor, P., Vanstone, M. and Kynch, J. (2000) Voluntary after care and the probation service: A case of diminishing responsibility. *Howard Journal*, 39, 234–48.

Maguire, N. (2020) Pre-sentence reports: Constructing the subject of punishment and rehabilitation. In P. Ugwudike, H. Graham, F. McNeill, P. Raynor, F.S. Taxman and C. Trotter (eds) *The Routledge Companion to Rehabilitative Work in Criminal Justice.* Abingdon, Oxon: Routledge, pp. 256–67.

Marston, P. and Reeves, C. (forthcoming) Approved premises: Futures of control in the community. In L. Burke, N. Carr, E. Cluley, S. Collett and F. McNeill (eds) *Reimagining Probation Practice: Re-forming Rehabilitation in an Age of Penal Excess.* Abingdon: Routledge.

Maruna, S. and LeBel, T.P. (2002) Revisiting ex-prisoner re-entry: A buzzword in search of a narrative. In S. Rex and M. Tonry (eds) *Reform and Punishment.* Cullompton: Willan, pp. 158–80.

Mawby, R.C. and Worrall, A. (2011) 'They were very threatening about do-gooding bastards: Probation's changing relationships with the police and prison services. *European Journal of Probation*, 3(3): 78-94.

McIvor, G. (2016) What is the impact of community service? In F. McNeill, I. Durnescu and R. Butter (eds) *Probation: 12 Essential Questions*. London: Palgrave Macmillan.

McIvor, G., Beyens, K., Blay, E. and M. Boone (2010) Community service in Belgium, the Netherlands, Scotland and Spain: A comparative analysis. *European Journal of Probation*, 2(1), 82–98.

McNeill, F. and Weaver, B. (2010) Changing lives? Desistance research and offender management. *Glasgow University School of Social Work/ The Scottish Centre for Crime and Justice Studies*. Available at: https://www2.uwe.ac.uk/faculties/HLS/research/Documents/Changing-lives.pdf. (last accessed 2 August 2022).

Ministry of Justice (2017) *Offender Management Statistics Quarterly: July–September 2016*. London: Ministry of Justice.

Ministry of Justice (2020) *A Smarter Approach to Sentencing*. CP 292. London: Ministry of Justice.

Ministry of Justice (2021) *Correctional Services Accreditation and Advice Panel (CSAAP): Currently Accredited Programmes*. London: Ministry of Justice. Available at: https://assets.publishing.service.gov.uk/government/uploads/system/uploads/attachment_data/file/960097/Descriptions_of_Accredited_Programmes_-_Final_-_210209.pdf (last accessed 9 July 2021).

Ministry of Justice and HM Prison and Probation Service (2021) Determining pre-sentence reports: P104/2016. Available at: www.gov.uk/government/publications/determining-pre-sentence-reports-pi-042016 (last accessed 13 July 2022).

Moore, R. (2011) Beyond the prison walls: Some thoughts on prisoner 'resettlement' in England and Wales. *Criminology and Criminal Justice*, 12(2): 129–47.

National Probation Service (2005) Criminal Justice Act 2003 – New sentences and the new report framework. Probation Circular 18/2005.

Nellis, M. (2015) *Standards and Ethics in Electronic Monitoring. Handbook for Professionals Responsible for the Establishment and Use of Electronic Monitoring*. Strasbourg: Council of Europe.

Raynor, P. (2007) Accredited programmes. In R. Canton and D. Hancock. (eds) *Dictionary of Probation and Offender Management*. Cullompton: Willan.

Raynor, P. (2020) Resettlement after short prison sentences: What might work in England and Wales? *Probation Journal*, 67(4), 326–39.

Reeves, C. (2013) 'The others': sex offenders' social identities in probation approved premises. *The Howard Journal of Crime and Justice*, 52(4), 383–98.

Reeves, C. (2016) The meaning of place and space in a probation approved premises. *The Howard Journal of Crime and Justice*, 55(1), 151–67.

Renehan, N. and Henry, O. (forthcoming) Groupwork Interventions: Reimagining groupwork by embedding personal, judicial, moral, and social rehabilitation into practice. In L.

Burke, N. Carr, E. Cluley, S. Collett and F. McNeill (eds) *Reimagining Probation Practice: Re-forming Rehabilitation in an Age of Penal Excess*. Abingdon: Routledge.

Robinson, G. (2017) Stand-down and deliver: Pre-sentence reports, quality and the new culture of speed. *Probation Journal*, 64(4), 337–53.

Robinson, G. and Crow, I. (2009) *Offender Rehabilitation: Theory, Research and Practice*. London: SAGE.

Robinson, G., Halsall, P. and Nixon, M. (2022) Court work and assessment: Laying the foundations for effective probation practice. In L. Burke, N. Carr, E. Cluley, S. Collett and F. McNeill (eds) *Reimagining Probation Practice: Re-forming Rehabilitation in an Age of Penal Excess*. Abingdon: Routledge.

Social Exclusion Unit (2002) *Reducing Re-Offending by Ex-Prisoners: Report by the Social Exclusion Unit*. London: Office of the Deputy Prime Minister.

11

UNDERSTANDING VULNERABILITY IN PRISON SETTINGS

IN THIS CHAPTER, YOU WILL EXPLORE

1. The concept of vulnerability
2. Existing attempts to define vulnerability in prison contexts
3. The extent to which imprisonment exacerbates rather than alleviates vulnerability.

INTRODUCTION

Her Majesty's Prison and Probation Service claim to be 'committed to treating all people fairly' during their time in prison (HM Government, 2021: para. 1). Though positive, the extent to which this can be realised at the coal face of service delivery is questionable, particularly as this stated ambition requires prisons to treat people in their care with 'consistency, impartiality and respect' (Howard League for Penal Reform, 2022: para. 2). Under section 149 of the Equality Act 2010, the Ministry of Justice has an ongoing legal duty to pay *due regard* to the need to eliminate unlawful discrimination, harassment, victimisation and other prohibited conducted under the Equality Act; advance equality of opportunity between people who share a protected characteristic and those who do not; and foster good relations between different groups of people who share a relevant protected characteristic and those who do not. This is an important piece of legislation for the prison service given the significant and varying levels of risk: need; susceptibility to harm and neglect; inability to cope with the prison environment; vulnerability to self-harm and suicide; as well as poor health amongst people serving a custodial sentence (to name just a few examples).

With a particular focus on health and healthcare, this chapter will explore the Equality Act 2010 and the concept of vulnerability, with a specific focus on what it means to be vulnerable in a prison context. Whilst it is recognised that there are different strands of vulnerability (for example, physical vulnerability, social vulnerability and emotional vulnerability) and some people are more vulnerable than others, this chapter explores the extent to which all people serving a custodial sentence are inherently vulnerable given the constraints of imprisonment, the abrasive properties of the prison place, and the prevalence of troubled (and indeed troublesome) lived experience(s). As such, you will be encouraged to consider how imprisonment not only fails to meet the needs of those serving a custodial sentence but exacerbates social inequality amongst those living in penal environments. In doing so, the chapter will make a case for all people serving a custodial sentence to be considered inherently vulnerable given that the prison place acts as both a repository for and site of vulnerability.

KEY QUESTIONS TO CONSIDER WHEN READING THIS CHAPTER

1. To what extent can a prison meet the needs of all people serving a custodial sentence?

2. Does imprisonment exacerbate social inequality amongst citizens?

3. Should all people serving a custodial sentence be considered inherently vulnerable?

THE EQUALITY ACT 2010

To ensure principles of the public sector equality duty are embedded in every aspect of its work, the Ministry of Justice publish equality objectives which detail three overarching ambitions: to ensure that the benefits of the justice system are felt by both business and citizens across the whole of the United Kingdom; to promote equality in core operational and policy work; and to embed quality and inclusion into policies, services and occupational cultures (HM Prison and Probation Service, 2021). To achieve this, HM Prison and Probation Service (2021: 4) note how it is 'vital that custodial institutions are decent and safe, offering a positive rehabilitative environment respectful of human rights' to enable people to 'do their best'. To promote an ethos of fairness and decency, the prison service is required to incorporate principles of equality and inclusion into policy and practice to 'help change the lives of a diverse cohort of offenders' (HM Prison and Probation Service, 2021: 4).

The implementation of such principles is, however, questionable, especially when considered alongside the evidence. Edgar and Tsintsadze (2017) note how Black people are over-represented in prison segregation units, are more likely to have force used against them, and are more likely to be on a basic regime (see Chapter 5 for a more detailed discussion of the incentives and earned privileges scheme). Older people serving a custodial sentence are not being provided with accessible accommodation, appropriate support or age-specific programmes (Age UK, 2019) and people with learning disabilities find it 'disproportionately difficult to navigate' imprisonment 'due to the inherent structural, procedural, and communicative barriers that exclude, disadvantage, and oppress this group' (Gormley, 2022: 257). These occurrences become even more alarming when considered alongside the principles and prescriptions of the Equality Act 2010 which makes it illegal to discriminate against or harass an individual because of a protected characteristic:

- *Age.* You must not be treated less favourably for being a particular age or within a range of ages unless the treatment can be justified.

- *Disability.* A person has a disability if they have a physical and/or mental impairment which has a substantial and long-term effect on their ability to carry out day-to-day activities. If you are disabled, the Equality Act 2010 protects you from discrimination as it requires employers and service providers to make reasonable adjustments to address any disadvantage that you may face.

- *Gender reassignment.* You must not be discriminated against because you are transitioning or intend to transition from your sex assigned at birth. To be protected from gender reassignment discrimination, you do not need to have undergone any specific treatment or surgery.

- *Marriage and civil partnership.* You must not be discriminated against at work because you are married or in a civil partnership, whether your partner is of the same or the opposite sex.

- *Pregnancy and maternity.* The Equality Act protects women from being discriminated against because they are pregnant, suffering from pregnancy-related illness or a new mother. Protection from discrimination at work also extends to maternity leave.

- *Race.* The Equality Act protects people from discrimination because of race, colour, nationality, ethnicity or national origins.

- *Religion and belief.* You must not be discriminated against because of religion or belief, or because of a lack of religion or belief. A belief should affect your life choices and/or the way you live for it to be included in the definition.

- *Sex.* You must not be discriminated against because of your sex.

- *Sexual orientation.* You must not be treated less favourably because of your sexual orientation, whether you are attracted to your own sex, the opposite or both. (Equality and Human Rights Commission, 2021)

To illustrate the prevalence of protected characteristics amongst people serving a custodial sentence in England and Wales, we will now explore data from a recently published report by HM Prison and Probation Service (2021).

- *Age.* As of 30 September 2021, 32.5 per cent of people serving a custodial sentence were aged between 30 and 39. People under the age of 30 constituted 31.8 per cent of people serving a custodial sentence, with 35.6 per cent falling into the over-40 categories.

- *Disability.* Of the 2012 Surveying Prisoner Crime Reduction sample, 36 per cent identified as having a disability – 18 per cent had anxiety and depression, 11 per cent had some form of physical disability and 8 per cent had both. (The figures do not add up to 36 per cent because of rounding.)

- *Gender reassignment.* In 2019, there were 163 people in prison identifying with a gender different to the sex assigned to them at birth. One hundred and twenty-nine people reported their legal gender as male, 32 as female and two did not state their legal gender. Although the numbers indicate approximately 0.2 per cent of the prison population identify as transgender, as people in prison may choose not to disclose their gender identity, the figure is likely to underestimate the total number of transgender people across the custodial estate.

- *Marriage and civil partnership.* No data is cited in HM Prison and Probation Service (2021) report for this characteristic.

- *Pregnancy and maternity.* On 28 October 2019, there were just under 4,000 women in prison. Of these, 47 were pregnant, accounting for approximately 1 per cent of the female prison population.

- *Race.* As of the 30 September 2021, people who identified as white made up 72 per cent of the prison population in England and Wales, with those belonging to BAME groups making up 27 per cent.

- *Religion or belief.* Approximately 35,200 people in prisons across England and Wales identified as Christian in 2021. A further 24,500 identified as having no religion, while 13,700 identified as Muslim.

- *Sex.* Males represent 96 per cent of the prison population in comparison to females who make up just 4 per cent.

- *Sexual orientation.* In 2019/2020, 97.2 per cent of people serving a custodial sentence identified as heterosexual with 2.8 per cent identifying as lesbian, gay or bisexual. (HM Prison and Probation Service, 2021)

Although this provides a valuable insight into the characteristics of people in prison in England and Wales (with a specific focus on legally protected attributes) it must be treated with caution given that the report does not provide comparisons with the population as a whole and/or changes over time. That said, as this is an annual report, valuable insights can be drawn from the data that help us to further engage with the nature and extent of vulnerability amongst people serving a custodial sentence.

DEFINING VULNERABILITY

The term vulnerability is used to denote a condition or situation whereby people or communities, their assets and/or livelihoods are susceptible to injury, loss, or disruption (Wisner, 2009). This may be due to a lack of access to resources (material/economic vulnerability); the breakdown of social support, ties, and patterns (social vulnerability); a lack of strong national and local institutions (organisational vulnerability); limited access to political power and representation (political vulnerability); and/or adoption of certain beliefs and customs (cultural vulnerability). Prior to the introduction of the Care Act 2014, a vulnerable adult was defined as a person 'who is or may be in need of community care services by reason of mental or other disability, age or illness; and who is or may be unable to take care of him or herself, or unable to protect him or herself against significant harm or exploitation' (cited in Department of Health, 2000: 8–9). Since its introduction, 'any person who is aged 18 years or over and at risk of abuse or neglect because of their needs for care and or support' (National Health Service, 2017: 2) may be defined as 'at risk'. Taking into consideration your learning from previous chapters, as well as the above definitions, let us now further examine the characteristics of people serving a prison sentence that may render them vulnerable and/or at risk during their time in prison.

- It is estimated that 7 per cent of the prison population in the United Kingdom have a learning disability, compared to 2 per cent of the general population. Though informative, this is a conservative estimate given that there are currently no national systems in place in prisons throughout England and Wales to screen, identify and record whether a person has a learning disability (Warner, 2018).

- Research suggests that people serving a custodial sentence disproportionality experience problems with substances before, during and after imprisonment. Dolan et al. (2008) note how the percentage of people serving a custodial sentence who have been identified as having an issue with substance use ranges from 40 per cent to 80 per cent.

- Long-term illnesses disproportionately affect people in prison. Compared to equivalent community-based populations, people in prison consult primary care doctors three times more frequently, other primary healthcare workers 80 times more frequently, receive inpatient care at least ten times more frequently and have a higher mortality and morbidity rate from chronic disease (Wright et al., 2020).

- Estimates regarding the number of people in prison who have a physical disability vary. A survey conducted by the Ministry of Justice in 2012 found 18 per cent of people serving a custodial sentence had a physical disability of some kind (Cunniffe et al., 2012). The Institute of Psychiatry estimates that over 50 per cent of people serving a custodial sentence have poor mental health, including depression, post-traumatic stress disorder and anxiety. Around 15 per cent have specialist mental health needs, and around 2 per cent have acute and/or serious mental health problems (Mental Health Foundation, 2019).

- Although there are no universally accepted definitions of old age in prisons, with thresholds varying from 45 to 70, HM Prison and Probation Service consider people who are 50 and above to be elderly (HM Government, 2020). 'As of March 2020, there were 5,176 people aged over 60 in prison in England and Wales. A further 8,588 people were aged 50–59. These represent 6% and 10% of the prison population, respectively, which was 82,990 as of the same period. 1,790 prisoners were aged 70 or over. As of December 2016, 234 prisoners were aged 80 or over, with 14 in their 90s' (HM Government, 2020: para 16).

Prison practitioners have a common law duty of care to people in prison. Safeguarding in a prison context is about keeping people safe; protecting them from abuse and neglect; and ensuring those who are unable to protect themselves are provided with a level of protection that is equivalent to that provided in the community (National Offender Management Service, 2019). Such endeavours, according to official discourse, are underpinned by six key principles: *empowerment, prevention, proportionality, protection, partnership* and *accountability*. As discussed in Chapter 3, HM Inspectorate of Prisons regularly inspect prisons to ensure that they are upholding their legal and moral duties with regard to keeping people safe during their time in custody. The following expectations, according to HM Inspectorate of Prisons, are particularly relevant to this discussion:

- The prison provides a safe and secure environment which actively reduces the risk of self-harm and suicide.

- Prisoners at risk of self-harm or suicide receive individualised care from a multidisciplinary team, and have unhindered access to help, including from their families.

- Prisoners, particularly vulnerable adults at risk – as defined in the Care Act 2014 – are provided with a safe and secure environment which protects them from harm and neglect.

- Adults at risk are appropriately located and supported by trained staff who are resourced to meet their needs. (HM Inspectorate of Prisons, 2021)

Before moving on, take a moment to reflect on your learning so far and consider the extent to which adults in prison are not only inherently vulnerable but at risk, as per the definitions provided to you in this chapter. In doing so you may find it useful to think about the characteristics of the prison population (see Figure 11.1 below) alongside the *pains of imprisonment* outlined in Chapter 5.

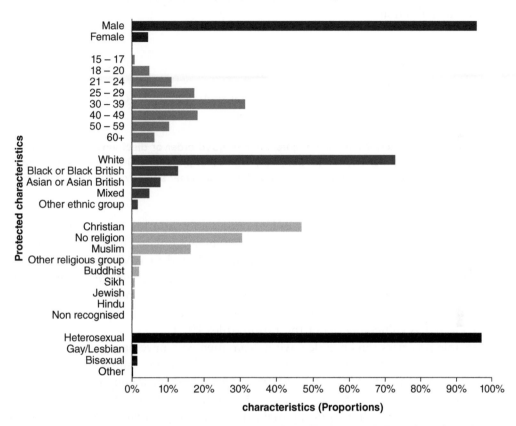

Figure 11.1   Prison population by protected characteristic, England and Wales (2019/2020)

Source: See Figure 1.1. on page 6 of Ministry of Justice (2020) Her Majesty's Prison and Probation Service Offender Equalities Annual Report 2019/20. Available at: https://assets.publishing.service.gov.uk/government/uploads/system/uploads/attachment_data/file/938316/hmppo offender cqualitics 2019-2020.pdf (last accessed 29 July 2022)

To further illustrate how, and in what ways, people in prison are inherently vulnerable, the next section will explore vulnerable prisoners, age, sex, sexual orientation, gender reassignment and disability. In doing so, the discussion will require you to draw on your learning from Chapter 3 (with a particular focus on the work of Mathiesen, 1974) so that you can critically engage, once again, with the purpose of imprisonment, what it achieves and who it benefits in a contemporary society. Alongside this, you may also wish to consider the extent to which the prison place alleviates or compounds vulnerability amongst those serving a custodial sentence and what this tells you about our priorities as a modern civilisation.

Vulnerable prisoners

In England and Wales, people serving a custodial sentence can be offered different protections under the Prison Rules 1999 which state:

> **where it appears desirable, for the maintenance of good order or discipline or in his own interests, that a prisoner should not associate with other prisoners, either generally or for particular purposes, the governor may arrange for the prisoner's removal from association. (Rule 45, Prison Rules 1999)**

According to this rule, governors can isolate people in prison for their own protection and/or to ensure stability within a prison. People who are isolated for their own protection are known as *vulnerable prisoners*, colloquially referred to as VPs, and are typically housed in vulnerable prisoner units that are removed from the general prison population. According to HM Prison and Probation Service, all prisons, regardless of function, whether male or female, open or closed, should have the ability to accommodate people who are classed as vulnerable as per the Prison Rules 1999.

Vulnerable prisoners can 'include anyone from men who have been convicted of rape or murdering children to those who have been accused of being informers, or who have simply run up prison debts' (Maguire, 2019: para 4). Whilst most people who have committed sexually motivated offences are housed in vulnerable prisoner units for their own safety, some remain (by choice) in the mainstream prison population (Howard League for Penal Reform, 2016). As the number of people serving a custodial sentence for sexually motivated crimes has increased in recent times, several prisons have diversified to meet the changing demographics of the prison population.

HMP Whatton is an example of such diversification, claiming to offer a forward-thinking therapeutic focus that is designed to prepare men for life after release. To be eligible for HMP Whatton, men should not be in denial or maintain innocence about their crimes and be able to engage in a range of accredited offending behaviour programmes such as the Sex Offender Treatment Programme (see Chapter 9 for further discussion). Alongside this, HMP Whatton offers several adapted programmes for people with learning difficulties and disabilities, such as Becoming New Me and New Me Coping alongside a programme for D/deaf prisoners that uses British Sign Language. All admissions are screened for signs of autism upon entry to the prison which means that courses can be adapted to those with additional needs or requiring alternative approaches. The prison has a range of services for older prisoners in conjunction with Age UK as well as palliative care and dementia care facilities. Whilst it has been suggested that holding people convicted of sexually motivated crimes together increases programme engagement, little is known about the experience of imprisonment amongst those held in these institutions.

Although we know that many people serving a custodial sentence possess characteristics that, by definition, render them vulnerable and at risk, there is more work to do before we can claim to understand the nature and prevalence of vulnerability in prisons across the globe. Recent discussions about neurodiversity amongst justice-involved people illustrate how the notion of vulnerability, particularly within a prison context, does not neatly fit into legislation and/or official frameworks as it is a complex, evolving, multifaceted concept that requires organisations to ensure individuals are held responsible for their crimes whilst simultaneously acknowledging that they also have unmet and/or differential needs that render them vulnerable and (potentially) at risk.

Neurodiversity is an umbrella term used to refer to a group of conditions that are typically categorised as neurodevelopmental disorders. This may, for example, incorporate learning difficulties and disabilities such as dyslexia, dyscalculia and dyspraxia; attention deficit hyperactivity disorder; autism spectrum disorders, developmental language disorders, tic disorders (including Tourette's syndrome and chronic tic disorder); and cognitive impairments due to acquired brain injury. A joint report by three criminal justice inspectorates in 2021 found neurodiversity to be more prevalent in the criminal justice system than the wider community, with as many as one in three people in the criminal justice system affected by neurodiversity in comparison to 15 per cent of the general population (UserVoice, 2021). Although the report highlighted some of the difficulties that neurodiverse people experience that further disadvantage them both during and after their experience of the criminal justice system, current provisions were, at best, 'patchy, inconsistent and uncoordinated' (Criminal Justice Joint Inspection 2021: 13–14).

Age

The shift towards longer custodial sentences alongside an increase in the use of imprisonment for sexually motivated crimes, including historic sex offences, has created an ageing prison population. People aged 50 and over now comprise 16 per cent of the prison population and over the last decade, the percentage of people over 50 has risen faster than any other age group (House of Commons Health and Social Care Committee, 2018), even though only 0.2 per cent of indictable offences are committed by people over 60 (Tarbuck, 2001). This shifting demographic requires further attention as older people in prison have greater healthcare needs in comparison to their younger counterparts (Fazel et al., 2001), 85 per cent of older people in prison having more than one major illness including a diagnosed psychiatric illness. Older people in prison are more likely to suffer from social isolation through fear of victimisation from younger counterparts and be held in prisons which are unfit for their needs and lacking in reasonable adjustments (House of Commons

Health and Social Care Committee, 2018). They are provided with limited opportunities to remain active and productive if they cannot participate in the usual prison regime and are often released homeless, without social care support or being registered with a general practitioner (Ibid). For those serving longer sentences, 'relationships with people outside prison may suffer due to deaths, divorce and difficulties families face in travelling long distances to visit' (Pocock and Sutton, 2014: 26). With an increasing number of older people in prison, it stands to reason that there will be rising numbers of natural deaths in prison and although some prisons are now establishing evidence-based approaches to palliative care there is still considerable variation in standards of end-of-life care (Ibid).

In 2014, Toby Harris (a Labour Party politician in the House of Lords) led a review of the 83 self-inflicted deaths of young people in custody aged between 18 and 24 from April 2007 to the end of 2013. The *Harris Review: Changing Prisons, Saving Lives* was subsequently published in 2015 with more than a hundred recommendations. Harris (2015) highlights how each of the deaths represents a failure by the state to protect the young people concerned and suggests that this failure is all the greater as lessons have not been learnt and not enough has been done to bring about substantive change in custodial environments for young people. Harris reiterates how all young adults in custody are vulnerable and suggests that there needs to be a shift in the philosophy of imprisonment which would require a new statement of purpose for prisons that focuses on rehabilitation and respect for human rights.

Ethnicity

Despite making up just 14 per cent of the general population, people from BAME backgrounds make up 25 per cent of the adult prison population across England and Wales, with over 40 per cent of young people in custody coming from BAME backgrounds (Lammy, 2017). The over-representation of BAME people within prisons reflects wider societal issues including poverty and discrimination (to name just two examples) and is an issue that extends beyond England and Wales. Statistics from America also indicate an over-representation of marginalised communities, with more African American people in prison than college (Handa, 2020). To date, there have been numerous studies into race relations in prison, as well as several reports conducted by official bodies such as the Prisons and Probation Ombudsman which demonstrate how BAME groups are more likely to endure negative experiences whilst in prison as a result of racism (Chistyakove et al., 2018).

The racist murder of Zahid Mubarek in HM Young Offender Institute Feltham in March 2000 highlights how a catalogue of failures by the prison service contributed to the preventable death of a young person in their care. In more recent times, Mohamed Sharif, a Muslim man serving a custodial sentence at HMP Bristol in 2014, was left severely brain damaged following an attack by a fellow resident who had previously told staff he would 'only share a cell with a white person' shares striking similarities with the murder of Zahid Mubarek (Prison Reform Trust, 2021: 9). Despite efforts to embark upon progressive programmes of activity, the over-representation of people from BAME backgrounds in prison and under-representation of prison staff from BAME groups, particularly at senior levels, reiterates how more needs to be done within and beyond the prison place to tackle racism (see Chapter 5 for a more detailed discussion). The recent publication of the *Prison Strategy White Paper* reflects such concerns as it fails to consider how the stark levels of disproportionality for BAME groups in prison will be addressed (Ministry of Justice, 2021). This, according to Clinks (2020: para. 1) is 'extremely concerning' as 'any future prison strategy should have equality and fairness at its core.'

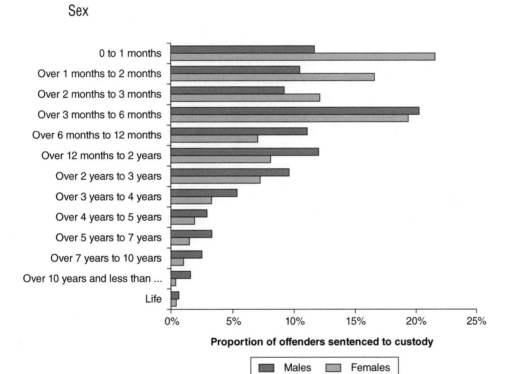

Figure 11.2 Proportion of people sentenced to immediate custody by custodial sentence, length and sex in 2019

See Figure 5.12 in Ministry of Justice (2020) National statistics. Women and the Criminal Justice System, 2019. Available at: www.gov.uk/government/statistics/women-and-the-criminal-justice-system-2019/women-and-the-criminal-justice-system-2019 (last accessed 29 July 2022)

The pattern of women's lawbreaking is quite different from that of men and, because their actions usually involve less violent crimes, they are often given shorter sentences (see Figure 11.2). In 2017, 73 per cent of women were sentenced to less than 12 months in prison (Prison Reform Trust, 2019). The tendency to send non-violent women to prison for short periods of time is myopic as short-term prison sentences do not allow for prolonged assessment and treatment plans which further serves to exacerbate the difficulties in addressing health and social care needs amongst already vulnerable people (Pocock and Sutton, 2014). In addition, there has been a significant increase in the number of women imprisoned in England and Wales – with more than 2,200 women in prison now than 25 years ago (Prison Reform Trust, 2019). Although women constitute a small percentage (approximately 5 per cent) of the overall prison population, they present a significant challenge to prison healthcare.

This is largely because women in prison have high rates of trauma and multiple layers of disadvantage that predispose them to poor mental health and self-harm tendencies. Borrill et al. (2003) examined drug and alcohol use amongst white and Black British women in prison to explore possible associations between self-harm, suicide attempts and family violence. In doing so, they found drug dependence and reported violence from family or friends were more common amongst white women. Self-harm and attempted suicide were generally more common amongst white women, but BAME women (dependent on substances) had the highest proportion of women reporting self-harm.

Women often require specific health and social care interventions that take account of their gender as well as their circumstances and needs, not only while in prison but also on return to the community. For example, maternity care in prisons is sparse due to the limited number of women's prisons providing a dedicated mother and baby unit. This shortcoming in prison-based healthcare is further compounded by the fact that pregnant women may move several times during their sentence and consequently may end up being released before they can attend vital antenatal services (Pocock and Sutton, 2014). The *United Nations Bangkok Rules* emphasise that 'when sentencing or deciding on pre-trial measures for a pregnant woman or a child's sole or primary caretaker, non-custodial measures should be preferred where possible and appropriate, with custodial sentences being considered when the offence is serious or violent' (United Nations Office on Drugs and Crime, 2011: 4) but according to Minson (2014) the law and sentencing guidance are inconsistently applied.

Research on the impact of long-term imprisonment found that long prison sentences (defined as sentences during which 10 years or more will be served in custody) 'uniquely affect women' (Vince and Evison, 2021: 5). This is largely due to separation from their children and family, the loss of relationships, experiences of abuse and trauma in pre-prison life, the strain on their mental health, and the lack of control, privacy and trust inside prison. These findings are reflected in the statistics, which consistently highlight how 'women in prison are often even more affected and have disproportionately higher level of mental health, suicide, self-harm, drug dependence and other health needs compared to men in prison' (Public Health England, 2018: 5). Although gender-specific approaches are a crucial step in the right direction, more understanding, commitment and change are required to ensure that the issues and needs of women serving a custodial sentence are recognised and addressed. In her seminal report, Baroness Corston suggests that 'prisons cannot be the right place for managing these types of behaviours, which stem from deep-rooted long-term complex life experiences such as violent and/or sexual abuse, lack of care and/or post-traumatic stress disorder, in addition to a personality disorder' (Corston, 2007: 15). Rather than expecting the prison service to respond to and resolve such vulnerabilities, Corston suggests that women who engage in low-level lawbreaking and self-harm should be diverted from prison into appropriate care and support in the community.

Sexual orientation and gender reassignment

Though there are many people serving a custodial sentence who have characteristics that are protected under the Equality Act 2010, evidence suggests that prisons are still failing to meet their public sector equality duties. For example, although research notes how homosexual men in prison have a higher risk of self-harm and attempted suicide compared to their heterosexual peers (Read and McCrae, 2016), processes such as Assessment, Care in Custody and Teamwork continue to overlook the reality of people's needs First developed in 2005, Assessment, Care in Custody and Teamwork is the care planning process for people in prison across England and Wales who are identified as being at risk of suicide or self-harm. The process requires certain actions to be taken, at certain points in time, to ensure that a person's risk of suicide and self-harm is reduced. Any member of staff who receives information or observes behaviour which may indicate a risk of suicide or self-harm must consider opening an Assessment, Care in Custody and Teamwork plan by completing a concern and keep safe form.

Within an hour of a plan being opened, staff must complete an immediate action plan with the person of concern to ensure they are safe from harm. A trained assessor must interview the person of concern within 24 hours of the concern and keep safe form being submitted. A multidisciplinary case review meeting must take place within 24 hours of the document being opened. Frequency of conversations with the person of concern, observations and support must be agreed and recorded in the Assessment, Care in Custody and Teamwork plan. Staff must complete a CAREMAP giving detailed information about the actions that have been taken to support the person of concern and reduce the risk of suicide or injury. Frequency of action must reflect the level of risk being managed. An Assessment, Care in Custody and Teamwork plan will be closed when a person of concern is no longer considered to be a risk but will be held for seven days and re-opened if additional concerns arise.

Despite such efforts only around one quarter of those who take their own lives have been identified as at risk of suicide or self-inflicted death (Liebling, 2007). Though able to portray an illusion that something is being done about suicide and self-inflicted death in prison, policies and processes such as Assessment, Care in Custody and Teamwork fail to acknowledge the potential vulnerability of every person serving a custodial sentence, merely reinforcing the idea that some people are 'vulnerable' which implies that everyone else is 'invulnerable' (Medlicott, 2001: 58). In more recent times Assessment, Care in Custody and Teamwork has suffered criticism for overlooking the reality of the needs of people serving custodial sentences, making no reference to the needs of lesbian, gay, bisexual and transgender people in prison or considering how some individuals are exposed to 'the double jeopardy of sexual assault and related suicidal tendencies' (Read and McCrae, 2016: 13). Such shortcomings are of particular concern for transgender people in prison given that they are 7.5 times more likely to attempt suicide in the community than someone who is cisgender (Apter, 2018). Whilst the number of transgender people in prisons across England and Wales is unknown, what is clear is their risk of suicide when they are denied a place in a prison that corresponds to their gender identity.

Disability

According to the Equality Act 2010, a person has a disability if they have a physical or mental impairment which has a substantial and long-term adverse effect on their ability to carry out normal day-to-day activities. Research by Reed and Lynn (2000) found that none of the prison doctors and only a quarter of nurses interviewed in their study had specialist mental health training. In 2006 the National Health Service took over responsibility for administering healthcare provision in prisons in England and Wales. Formerly, this was the responsibility of the Prison Healthcare Service which employed its own clinical staff. The rationale for this change was to improve the quality of care provided to people in prison (Pocock and Sutton, 2014). Underpinning this move was the *principle of equivalence*, which suggests that people serving a custodial sentence should have access and quality of service that is equivalent to that of the general public (the principle of equivalence will be discussed in further detail in the next section).

Although the delivery of effective of healthcare in prison is dependent on the strength of the partnership between health and prison services (Watson et al., 2004), the continuity of care between these two organisations is fractured. Information sharing between healthcare services in the prison and community organisations is hindered by the fact that many people in prison are moved around the prison estate during their sentence (Pocock and Sutton, 2014). As a result, people are often released from prison without a proper assessment of their social care needs and/or prescribed medication, with the wrong medication and/or not registered with a general practitioner (House of Commons Health and Social Care Committee, 2018). Moreover, as Macdonald et al. (2012) note, the lack of standardised procedures to identify if a person serving a custodial sentence has significant health problems means that help and support are often only acquired by personal choice and/or if a member of staff raises concerns about an individual's well-being.

A report by HM Inspectorate of Prisons recommended that improvements were required in over half of prisons inspected in terms of the provision of mental healthcare

(House of Commons Health and Social Care Committee, 2018). Guidelines introduced in England and Wales following the Bradley Report stipulate that people in prison with severe mental health problems should be transferred to a mental health unit within 14 days of the first medical recommendation for transfer. A second medical opinion and all administrative tasks, including finding a bed, should also be completed within this time frame. However, this is rarely the case and the House of Commons Health and Social Care Committee (2018) found that only a third of the transfers from prison to hospital were completed within 14 days and two-thirds took longer, with around 7 per cent of people in prison waiting more than 140 days. The independent review of the Mental Health Act 1983, published in 2018, considered the context of transfers from prison to hospital (HM Government, 2018). It concluded that resolving delays in transfers was not simply a matter of increasing the number of beds available but instead was more about ensuring that the pathway between institutions operated effectively. It has subsequently introduced a range of measures designed to hold prisons to account if they fail to provide the complete paperwork necessary for such transfers. But the degree to which such measures have an impact at the coal face of service delivery are questionable.

There is limited data available on the prevalence of protected characteristics across the prison population even though HM Prison and Probation Service note that 'in order to prevent abuse and neglect, prisons are required to ensure that a prisoner's needs are comprehensively assessed and that those needs are met' (National Offender Management Service, 2016: 6). Identifying and responding to the needs of those serving a custodial sentence is important given that many are from marginalised and disadvantaged communities with a variety of attributes that render them vulnerable. When we consider the gravity of such obligations, alongside ongoing cuts to public expenditure which disproportionality affect those who live and work in penal settings, it is unsurprising to find an abundance of evidence which documents how prisons are failing to meet their statutory duties. Taking this into consideration, the next section will discuss how and in what ways the prison place acts as a *site of vulnerability*, exacerbating rather than alleviating vulnerability and risk amongst those serving a custodial sentence.

THE PRISON PLACE AS A SITE OF VULNERABILITY

According to the World Health Organization (WHO, 2014: 18), governments have a 'a special duty of care for those in places of detention which should cover safety, basic needs and recognition of human rights, including the right to health.' Despite this, a recent report by the House of Commons Health and Social Care Committee (2018) highlighted how the government is failing in its duty of care towards those serving a custodial sentence: 'a prison sentence is a deprivation of someone's liberty, not a sentence to poorer health or healthcare' (House of Commons Health and Social Care Committee, 2018: 11). This is a powerful statement because it demonstrates how the prison place, as a social institution, holds the potential to exacerbate rather than alleviate vulnerability amongst those sentenced to custody. To further illustrate this point, the following section will explore (through a lens of health and healthcare) a series of controversial issues, such as funding cuts and staff shortages, self-harm and violence, substance use and adverse childhood experiences to illustrate how the prison place acts as a site of vulnerability.

Funding cuts and staff shortages

The United Kingdom spent approximately £5.63 billion on its prison system in 2020/21, one of the highest amounts in the last ten years. However, when compared with 2010/11, the United Kingdom is spending around £60 million less than it did, mainly due to the austerity policies pursued by the coalition government of the time (HM Treasury, 2021). The subsequent shortage of prison officers (see Chapter 5 for a more detailed discussion) had a direct impact on the health of people in prison, with many individuals unable to attend healthcare appointments due to a lack of available escorts or not able to access prescribed medication due to staff shortages (MacDonald, 2018). Successive reports by HM Inspectorate of Prisons (2016: 8) have routinely criticised the conditions in English prisons, describing them as 'unacceptably violent and dangerous places'. Much of this has been attributed to funding cutbacks and staff shortages, so much so that the Ministry of Justice has conceded that staff shortages, in an increasingly volatile environment, have been detrimental to ensuring 'security, stability and good order in prisons' (House of Commons Committee of Public Accounts, 2017: 12).

Self-harm and violence

Deteriorating standards within prisons have seen rates of deaths, incidents of self-harm and violence increase to record highs in past years. Though the terms suicide and self-inflicted death are often used interchangeably, they are, in fact, referring to different things. A self-inflicted death is a socially negotiated process where the final decision to end life is influenced by the interpretations and expectations of significant others (Scott and Codd, 2010). It is a social problem whereby those who take their own lives are responding to given situation (for example, imprisonment) or context (for example, the prison place). It occurs when somebody takes their own life but only becomes a suicide if the person intended to die. The Safety in Custody statistics demonstrate how in the 12 months to March 2020, there were 286 deaths in prison. Of these, 80 were defined as self-inflicted (Ministry of Justice, 2020).

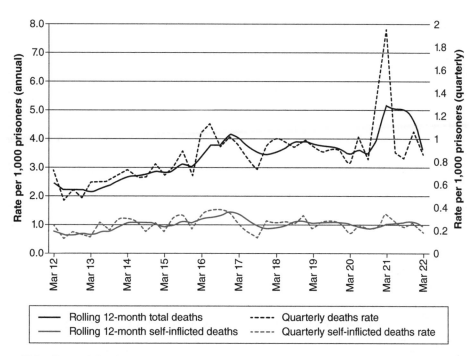

Figure 11.3 Rate of deaths per 1,000 people in prison between March 2012 and March 2022

Incidents of self-harm reached a record high of 63, 328 in the 12 months to December 2019, up 14 per cent from the previous 12 months (Ministry of Justice, 2020). The number of individuals self-harming increased by 3 per cent in the 12 months to December 2019 to 12, 977 and the number of self-harm incidents per individual increased by 11 per cent from 4.4 to 4.9 (Ibid). Although it has been suggested that prisons in Britain have evolved into 'death traps' because of budgetary cuts, staff shortages and acute overcrowding (Wright, 2014) such issues are not exclusive to the United Kingdom. The World Health Organization estimates as many as 40 per cent of people in prison across Europe suffer from some form of mental illness and as a result are up to seven times more likely to take their own lives than people in the wider community (Penal Reform International, 2007: 4).

Adverse childhood experiences

Whilst we have discussed trauma elsewhere (see Chapter 9 for further discussion), it is important to revisit it in this chapter given that poor health, particularly amongst those serving a custodial sentence, can be attributed in a large majority of cases to adverse

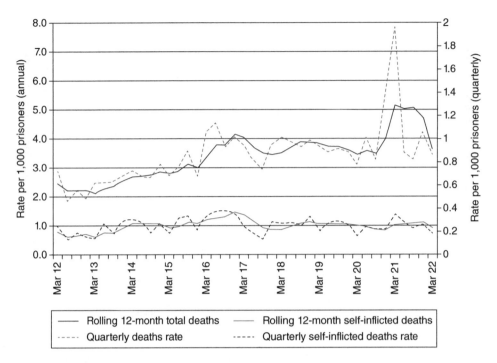

Figure 11.4 Quarterly 12-month rolling rate of deaths per 1,000 prisoners, 12 months ending March 2012 to 12 months ending March 2022, with quarterly rates

citied in HMPPS (2022) www.gov.uk/government/statistics/safety-in-custody-quarterly-update-to-december-2021/safety-in-custody-statistics-england-and-wales-deaths-in-prison-custody-to-march-2022-assaults-and-self-harm-to-december-2021

childhood experiences (ACEs). ACEs are traumatic and/or stressful experiences such as physical, emotional and/or sexual abuse, living in a household affected by domestic violence and/or substance use, that take place before the age of 18 (Ford et al., 2019). Individuals who have such experiences are at an increased risk of poor health across their life course, including poor mental health, the early development of chronic health conditions, such as asthma, diabetes and premature mortality (Ibid). They are also more at risk of a range of health-harming behaviours such as, but not limited to, substance use, poor educational attainment and violence, most of which can be found amongst people serving a custodial sentence.

In 2018, the Public Health Collaborating Unit at Bangor University and Public Health Wales undertook the first adverse childhood experiences prevalence study in a Welsh prison setting. The aim of the ACEs prisoner survey was to measure the prevalence of ACEs amongst people in prison and examine associations between ACEs and lawbreaking. Adults (468) between the ages of 18 and 69 years serving a custodial sentence between

February and June in 2018 participated in the survey. Findings note how 31 per cent of the sample reported that they had no educational qualifications, with just over 32 per cent attaining a college degree or university level qualification (Ford et al., 2019). Findings also show how less than half of the sample had been in employment prior to imprisonment, with just over one in ten not in employment due to long-term sickness or disability (Ibid).

The survey measured exposure to 11 types of adverse childhood experiences before the age of 18 amongst the sample group. The study found that eight in ten people had experienced at least one ACE, with just over 45 per cent reporting exposure to four or more (Ford et al., 2019). An adverse childhood experiences and resilience study in 2017, which asked Welsh citizens in the general population if they had experience of the same ACEs found that just under 12 per cent of males had similar experiences.

Substance use

Between a third and a half of new receptions into prisons in England and Wales have a problematic relationship with substances, with more than 75 per cent of adult males and 69 per cent of adult females injecting drugs whilst in prison (Weild et al., 2000). This is a serious issue for the prison service given that people who engage in such behaviour are at an increased risk of exposure to communicable diseases, which further increases when drug paraphilia, such as needles and syringes, are shared between multiple people (Public Health England, 2018: 19) and the ability to diagnose and treat diseases such as hepatitis C is limited in comparison to the wider community. Pressure to move people around the prison system, largely because of overcrowding, has a further impact on the availability and sustainability of help and support – especially for long courses of continuous treatment which may be contingent on the individual remaining in a certain prison establishment (Pocock and Sutton, 2014: 27).

The prison service also has to contend with a widespread increase in the use of new psychoactive substances in recent years. Manufacturers of these drugs develop new chemicals to replace those that are banned which means that the chemical structures of new psychoactive substances are constantly changing to stay ahead of the law. As such, they can have unpredictable and severe physical and psychological effects on people who use them, with the psychological effects sometimes so severe or enduring that intervention under the Mental Health Act is required (House of Commons Health and Social Care Committee, 2018: 27). A report by User Voice (2016) for the National Health Service confirms that the use of new psychoactive substances, namely Spice, causes serious health and security problems in prison. This is largely because people with mental health needs and problems associated with substance use have little to no choice other than to take huge risks with their physical and psychological health due to limited-service provision (Webster, 2016). But how is this the case when prison-based services are required to mirror their community-based counterparts?

Establishing principles of equivalence within sites of vulnerability

The right to the highest attainable standard of healthcare is enshrined in internal law through the Universal Declaration of Human Rights 1948 and obligations outlined in the 1966 International Covenant on Economic, Social and Cultural Rights. The latter established the principle of equivalence with regard to healthcare (regardless of status), which includes the right to freedom from discrimination, non-consensual medical treatment and experimentation. Both are relevant to the prison place, which has traditionally been a site of such practices. The notion of equivalence was intended to cover the policy, standards and delivery of primary healthcare, as well as some specialist outpatient services, in custodial establishments. Although the principle of equivalence has guided healthcare improvements across English prisons, it has been criticised for failing to acknowledge how people in prison are disadvantaged across a wide and often complex range of health measures, even before they begin their custodial sentence, which are often neglected and compounded during their time in prison. As such, critics have argued that the level of health-related needs of people in prison means that the scope and accessibility of healthcare is, in fact, greater than that required in the community (Lines, 2006).

In 2000, the United Nations developed the *Availability, Accessibility, Acceptability and Quality* framework, colloquially referred to as the AAAQ framework, to create more appropriate standards of prison healthcare. Although the four components are pertinent to the provision of prison healthcare today, the extent to which such ambitions can be realised in custodial environments is tentative. For instance, the AAAQ framework reasserts the state's duty to promote the highest attainable healthcare for its citizens through the principles of availability, but for people serving a custodial sentence their imprisonment, by definition, means that community-based facilities are restricted. Although the state has a responsibility to ensure that certain services are available to people in prison, the degree to which this is possible is highly contested. On average people in prison missed 15 per cent of all medical appointments. This is largely because of a lack of prison staff to move them from residential wings to healthcare appointments (House of Commons Public Accounts Committee, 2017). As such, the degree to which the prison service can uphold principles of accessibility requires further consideration. The third principle – of acceptability – establishes the need for services to be appropriate for all citizens. However, given the heterogeneous nature of the prison population, the degree to which these principles can be met in practice is debatable. Finally, the provision of good quality healthcare requires investment in, as well as the provision of, a skilled workforce, which, as noted previously, has often been absent in prisons in the United Kingdom.

Whilst the AAAQ framework provides a more sophisticated measure for highlighting shortfalls in service provision beyond the principle of equivalence, its impact to date has been limited. According to Exworthy et al. (2012: 273) the 'limits of the AAAQ framework perhaps lie in the potential difficulty in translating its idealism, conceptual complexity, and legal language into practice'. It has subsequently been suggested that for the AAAQ principles to be effectively implemented at the front line of service delivery, appropriate healthcare should be independent of the delivery of punishment to ensure prisons do not 'become places of double punishment' that 'imperil prisoners' health' (Ismail, 2019: 3). That said, it is important to recognise that for some people, imprisonment provides an opportunity to access healthcare that they are unable to source in the wider community (MacDonald et al., 2012). This in itself is, however, testimony to the authors' contention that prisons act as both a repository for and site of vulnerability, with access to equitable healthcare an issue for people entwined in the criminal justice system before, during and after a prison sentence.

Considering the extent to which the prison place acts as both a repository for and site of vulnerability is an important component of your studies as it contributes towards a bigger conversation about why we send people to prison (see Chapter 3), how prison cultures evolve (see Chapter 7) and why the prison place struggles to demonstrate its worth in a contemporary justice system (see Chapter 2). This is in no way an attempt to negate the risk and criminogenic need of people serving a custodial sentence; rather, it is a purposeful effort to demonstrate how people can simultaneously be both a risk and at risk during their time in prison and beyond.

recommended reading

If you would like to engage in further reading, you may find the following resources particularly useful:

Christyakova, Y., Cole, B. and Johnstone, Y. (2018) Diversity and vulnerability in prisons in the context of the Equality Act 2010: The experiences of Black, Asian, minority ethnic (BAME), and foreign national prisoners (FNPs) in a northern jail. *Prison Service Journal*, 235, 10–16.

This article explores the experiences of BAME and foreign national prisoners in a Category B adult male prison and details how the prison is responding to and managing vulnerability with regard to race, post the 2010 Equality Act.

Maguire, D. (2019) Vulnerable prisoner masculinities in an English prison. *Men and Masculinities*, 24(3), 501–18.

Drawing on the experiences of people in a vulnerable prisoner unit (VPU) in an English prison, this article highlights how people defined as 'vulnerable prisoners' adopt strategies to cope with the realities of prison life.

Wainwright, V., McDonnell, S., Lennox, C., Shaw, J. and Senior, J. (2016) Treatment barriers and support for male ex-armed forces personnel in prison: Professional and service user perspectives. *Qualitative Health Research*, 27(5) 759–69.

This article highlights how ex-armed forces personnel consider prison an opportunity to access help and support but find it difficult to ask for help and access consistent resettlement opportunities.

references

Age UK (2019) Older prisoners (England and Wales). Available at: www.ageuk.org.uk/globalassets/age-uk/documents/policy-positions/care-and-support/ppp_older_prisoners_en_wa.pdf (last accessed 1 July 2022).

Apter, C. (2018) When will the prison service act upon the vulnerability of transgender people? *Mental Health Today*. Available at: www.mentalhealthtoday.co.uk/innovations/when-will-the-prison-service-act-upon-the-vulnerability-of-transgender-people (last accessed 1 July 2022).

Borrill, J., Burnett, R., Atkins, R., Miller, S., Briggs, D., Weaver, T. and Maden, M. (2003) Patterns of self-harm and attempted suicide among white and black/mixed race female prisoners. *Criminal Behaviour and Mental Health*, 13(4), 229–40.

Chistyakova, Y., Cole, B., and Johnstone, J. (2018) Diversity and vulnerability in prisons in the context of the Equality Act 2010. *Prison Service Journal*, 235, 10–17.

Clinks (2020) The Prison Strategy White Paper – A lost opportunity to address racial disparity. Available at: www.clinks.org/publication/prison-strategy-white-paper-lost-opportunity-address-racial-disparity (last accessed 1 July 2022).

Corston, J. (2007) *The Corston Report: A Report of a Review of Women with Particular Vulnerabilities in the Criminal Justice System*. London: Home Office. Available at: https://webarchive.nationalarchives.gov.uk/ukgwa/20130128112038/http://www.justice.gov.uk/publications/docs/corston-report-march-2007.pdf (last accessed 30 June 2022).

Criminal Justice Joint Inspection (2021) *Neurodiversity in the Criminal Justice System: A Review of Evidence*. Available at: www.justiceinspectorates.gov.uk/cjji/wp-content/uploads/sites/2/2021/07/Neurodiversity-evidence-review-web-2021.pdf (last accessed 1 July 2022)

Cunniffe, C., Van de Kerckhove, R., Williams, K. and Hopkins, K. (2012) Estimating the prevalence of disability amongst prisoners: Results from the Surveying Prisoner Crime Reduction (SPCR) survey. Research Summary 4/12. Ministry of Justice. Available at: https://assets.publishing.service.gov.uk/government/uploads/system/uploads/attachment_data/file/162358/estimating-prevalence-disability-amongst-prisoners.pdf.pdf (last accessed 1 July 2022).

Department of Health (2020) No secrets: Guidance on developing and implementing multi-agency policies and procedures to protect vulnerable adults from abuse. Available at: https://assets.publishing.service.gov.uk/government/uploads/system/uploads/attachment_data/file/194272/No_secrets__guidance_on_developing_and_implementing_ multi-agency_policies_and_procedures_to_protect_vulnerable_adults_from_abuse.pdf (last accessed 29 July 2022)

Dolan, K., Khoei, E., Brentari, C. and Stevens, A. (2008) *Prisons and Drugs: A Global Review of Incarceration, Drug Use and Drug Treatment*. Beckley Foundation Drug Policy Programme. Available at: www.beckleyfoundation.org/wp-content/uploads/2016/04/BF_Report_12.pdf (last accessed 1 July 2022).

Edgar, K. and Tsintsadze, K. (2017) *Tackling Discrimination in Prison: Still Not a Fair Response*. Prison Reform Trust. Available at: www.prisonreformtrust.org.uk/wp-content/themes/chd/old_files/Documents/Tackling%20discrimination.pdf (last accessed 1 July 2022).

Equality and Human Rights Commission (2021) Protected characteristics. Available at: www.equalityhumanrights.com/en/equality-act/protected-characteristics (last accessed 1 July 2022).

Exworthy, T., Samele, C., Urqia, N. and Forrester, A. (2012) Asserting prisoners' rights to health: Progressing beyond equivalence. *Psychiatric Services*, 63(3), 270–5.

Fazel, S., Hope, T., O'Donnell, I., Piper, M. and Jacoby, R. (2001) Health of elderly male prisoners: Worse than the general population, worse than younger prisoners. *Age and Ageing*, 30: 403-7.

Ford, K., Barton, E., Newbury, A., Hughes, K., Bezeczky, Z., Roderick, J., and Bellis, M. (2019) *Understanding the Prevalence of Adverse Childhood Experiences (ACEs) in a Male Offender Population in Wales: The Prisoner ACE Survey*. Available at: https://research.bangor.ac.uk/portal/files/23356885/PHW_Prisoner_ACE_Survey_Report_E.pdf (last accessed 1 July 2022).

Gormley, C. (2022) The hidden harms of prison life for people with learning disabilites. *The British Journal of Criminology*, 62, 261–278.

Handa, L. (2020) Racism, police violence and mass incarceration: The legacies of slavery and segregation in the United States. *Blog post*. Available at: https://blogs.lse.ac.uk/human-rights/2020/08/12/racism-police-violence-and-mass-incarceration-the-legacies-of-slavery-and-segregation-in-the-united-states (last accessed 1 July 2022).

Harris, T. (2015) *The Harris Review: Changing Prisons, Saving Lives*. Available at: https://assets.publishing.service.gov.uk/government/uploads/system/uploads/attachment_data/file/439859/moj-harris-review-web-accessible.pdf (last accessed 1 July 2022).

HM Government (2018) Modernisng the Mental Health Act. Increasing choice, reducing compulson. Final report of the Independent Review of the Mental Health Act 1983. Accessed at: https://assets.publishing.service.gov.uk/government/uploads/system/uploads/attachment_data/file/778897/Modernising_the_Mental_Health_Act_-_increasing_choice__reducing_compulsion.pdf (last accessed 28 July 2022)

HM Government (2020) The older prisoner cohort. Parliamentary Business. Available at: https://publications.parliament.uk/pa/cm5801/cmselect/cmjust/304/30405.htm (last accessed 1 July 2022).

HM Government (2021) Equality and diversity. Available at: www.gov.uk/government/organisations/her-majestys-prison-and-probation-service/about/equality-and-diversity (last accessed 1 July 2022).

HM Inspectorate of Prisons (2016) HM Inspectorate of Prisons Annual Report 2015–16: Prisons unacceptably violent and dangerous, warns Chief Inspector. News release.

Available at: www.justiceinspectorates.gov.uk/hmiprisons/media/press-releases/2016/07/hm-inspectorate-of-prisons-annual-report-201516-prisons-unacceptably-violent-and-dangerous-warns-chief-inspector (last accessed 1 July 2022).

HM Inspectorate of Prisons (2021) Safeguarding. Available at: www.justiceinspectorates.gov.uk/hmiprisons/our-expectations/prison-expectations/safety/safeguarding/#:~:text=The%20prison%20provides%20a%20safe,receive%20effective%20care%20and%20support (last accessed 1 July 2022).

HM Prison and Probation Service (2021) Prisons Strategy White Paper: overarching equalities statement. Available at: https://assets.publishing.service.gov.uk/government/uploads/system/uploads/attachment_data/file/1038766/pswp-equalities-statement.pdf (last accessed 1 July 2022).

HM Treasury (2021) *Public Expenditure: Statistical Analyses 2021*. Available at: https://assets.publishing.service.gov.uk/government/uploads/system/uploads/attachment_data/file/1003755/CCS207_CCS0621818186-001_PESA_ARA_2021_Web_Accessible.pdf (last accessed 1 July 2022).

House of Commons Committee of Public Accounts (2017) *Mental Health in Prisons*. Available at: https://publications.parliament.uk/pa/cm201719/cmselect/cmpubacc/400/400.pdf (last accessed 1 July 2022).

House of Commons Health and Social Care Committee (2018) *Prison Health*. Available at: https://publications.parliament.uk/pa/cm201719/cmselect/cmhealth/963/963.pdf (last accessed 4 July 2022).

Howard League for Penal Reform (2016) *Living among Sex Offenders: Identity, Safety and Relationships at Whatton Prison*. Available at: https://howardleague.org/wp-content/uploads/2016/03/Living-among-sex-offenders.pdf (last accessed 4 July 2022).

Howard League for Penal Reform (2022) *Justice and Fairness in Prisons*. Available at: https://howardleague.org/our-work/transform-prisons/justice-and-fairness-in-prisons/#:~:text=A%20just%20and%20fair%20prison,and%20not%20by%20the%20prison (last accessed 9 October 2022).

Ismail, N. (2019) Contextualising the pervasive impact of macroeconomic austerity on prison health in England: A qualitative study among international policymakers. *Biomedical Central Public Health*, 19(1), 1043–7.

Lammy, D. (2017) *The Lammy Review: An Independent Review into the Treatment of, and Outcomes for, Black, Asian and Minority Ethnic Individuals in the Criminal Justice System*. Available at: www.gov.uk/government/organisations/lammy-review (last accessed 4 July 2022).

Liebling, A. (2007) Prison suicide and its prevention. In Y. Jewkes (ed.) *Handbook on Prisons*. Cullompton: Willan, pp. 423–46.

Lines, R. (2006) From equivalence of standards to equivalence of objectives: The entitlement of prisoners to health care standards higher than those outside prisons. *International Journal of Prisoner Health*, 2(4): 269–80.

MacDonald, M. (2018) Overcrowding and its impact on prison conditions and health. *International Journal of Prisoner Health*, 14(2), 65–8.

MacDonald, M., Williams, J. and Kane, D. (2012) Inequalities in healthcare for prisoners in Europe: A review. *Diversity and Equality in Health Care*, 2(9): 243–51.

Maguire, D. (2019) Vulnerable Prisoner Masculinities. *Blog Post.* Available at: www.russell-webster.com/magmasc/ (last accessed on 29 July 2022)

Mathiesen, T. (1974) *The Politics of Abolitionism.* London: Martin Robertson.

Medlicott, D. (2001) *Surviving the Prison Place: Narratives of Suicidal Prisoners.* Aldershot: Ashgate.

Mental Health Foundation (2019) 'Jail can be scary' … mental health in prison. Blog post.

Ministry of Justice (2020) Safety in custody statistics, England, and Wales: Deaths in prison custody to March 2020; assaults and self-harm to December 2019. Available at: https://assets.publishing.service.gov.uk/government/uploads/system/uploads/attachment_data/file/893374/safety-in-custody-q4-2019.pdf (last accessed 4 July 2022).

Ministry of Justice (2021) *Prisons Strategy White Paper.* Available at: www.gov.uk/government/publications/prisons-strategy-white-paper (last accessed 4 July 2022).

Minson, S. (2014) *Mitigating Motherhood: A Study of the Impact of Motherhood on Sentencing Decisions in England and Wales.* The Howard League for Penal Reform.

National Offender Management Service (2016) Adult Safeguarding in Prison (PSI 16/2015) Available at: https://assets.publishing.service.gov.uk/government/uploads/system/uploads/attachment_data/file/905158/psi-16-2015-adult-safeguarding-in-prisons.pdf (last accessed 28 July 2022).

National Offender Management Service (2019) Adult safeguarding in prison. PSI 16/2015. Available at: www.gov.uk/government/publications/keeping-adult-prisoners-safe-psi-162015 (last accessed 4 July 2022).

Penal Reform International (2007) Health in prison: Realising the right to health. Available at: https://cdn.penalreform.org/wp-content/uploads/2013/06/brf-02-2007-health-in-prisons-en_01.pdf (last accessed 4 July 2022).

Pocock, L. and Sutton, J. (2014) Health needs of prisoners. *InnovAiT: Education and inspiration for general practice,* 8(1): 24–7.

Prison Reform Trust (2021) *Bromley Briefings Prison Factfile.* Winter 2021. Available at: https://prisonreformtrust.org.uk/wp-content/uploads/2022/01/Bromley_Briefings_winter_2021.pdf (last accessed 4 July 2022).

Public Health England (2018) Health and Justice Annual Review 2017/18. Public Health England/World Health Organization. Available at: https://assets.publishing.service.gov.uk/government/uploads/system/uploads/attachment_data/file/725776/Health_and_Justice_Annual_Review_2017-2018.pdf (last accessed 4 July 2022).

Public Health England (2018) *Gender Specific Standards to Improve Health and Wellbeing for Women in Prison in England.* Available at: https://assets.publishing.service.gov.uk/government/uploads/system/uploads/attachment_data/file/687146/Gender_specific_standards_for_women_in_prison_to_improve_health_and_wellbeing.pdf (last accessed 29 July 2022)

Read, M. and McCrae, N. (2016) Preventing suicide in lesbian, gay, bisexual, and transgender prisoners: A critique of UK policy. *Journal of Forensic Nursing,* 12(1), 13–18.

Reed, J.L. and Lynn, M. (2000) Inpatient care of mentally ill people in prison: Results of a year's programme of semi-structured inspections. *British Medical Journal*, 320(7241), 1031–4.

Scott, D. and Codd, H. (2010) *Controversial Issues in Prisons*. Maidenhead: Open University Press.

Tarbuck, A. (2001) Health of elderly prisoners. *Age and Ageing*, 30(5): 369–70.

United Nations Office on Drugs and Crime (2011) The Bangkok Rules. Available at: www.unodc.org/documents/justice-and-prison-reform/Bangkok_Rules_ENG_22032015.pdf (last accessed 28 July 2022)

User Voice (2016) *Spice: The Bird Killer. What Prisoners Think about the Use of Spice and Other Legal Highs in Prison*. Available at: (last accessed 4 July 2022).

User Voice (2021) *'Neuro … What?' Neurodiversity in the Criminal Justice System*. Available at: www.uservoice.org/wp-content/uploads/2021/07/Neurodiversity-in-the-Criminal-Justice-System.pdf (last accessed 4 July 2022).

Vince, C. and Evison, E. (2021) Invisible women: Understanding women's experiences of long-term imprisonment. Prison Reform Trust. Available at: www.prisonreformtrust.org.uk/wp-content/uploads/2022/02/invisible_women.pdf (last accessed 29 July 2022).

Warner, M. (2018) Out of the shadows: The untold story of people with learning disabilities in prison. 1854 blog post. Available at: www.1854.photography/2018/11/out-of-the-shadows-prison (last accessed 4 July 2022).

Watson, R., Stimpson, A. and Hostick, T. (2004) Prison health care: A review of the literature. *International Journal of Nursing Studies*, 41(2), 119–28.

Webster, R. (2016) The true horrors of using NPS in prison. Blog post. Available at: www.russellwebster.com/the-true-horrors-of-using-nps-in-prison (last accessed 4 July 2022).

Weild, A.R., Gill, O., Bennett, D., Livingstone, S., Parry, J. and Curran, L. (2000) Prevalence of HIV, hepatitis B, and hepatitis C antibodies in prisoners in England and Wales: A national survey. *Communicable Disease and Public Health*, 3(2), 121–6.

Wisner, B. (2009) Vulnerability. In R. Kitchin and N. Thrift (eds) *International Encyclopaedia of Human Geography*. Oxford: Elsevier, pp. 176–82.

World Health Organization (2014) *Prisons and Health*. Available at: www.euro.who.int/__data/assets/pdf_file/0005/249188/Prisons-and-Health.pdf (last accessed 4 July 2022).

Wright, N., Hankins, F., Hearty, P., Allott, D. and Allgar, V. (2020) Long-term condition management for prisoners: Exploring prevalence and compliance with QOF monitoring. *Research Square*. Available at: www.researchsquare.com/article/rs-45365/v1 (last accessed 4 July 2022).

Wright, O. (2014) Rise in prison suicides being fuelled by staff shortages, warns watchdog. *Independent*. Available at: www.independent.co.uk/news/uk/politics/rise-in-prison-suicides-being-fuelled-by-staff-shortages-warns-watchdog-9662758.html (last accessed 4 July 2022).

12

UNDERSTANDING VULNERABILITY IN COMMUNITY SETTINGS

IN THIS CHAPTER, YOU WILL EXPLORE

1. How the concept of vulnerability, introduced in the previous chapter, applies to those on probation.

2. The specific needs of some groups on probation and the evidence for the best way of working with them

3. The challenges for practitioners in working with specific types of criminal behaviour such as domestic abuse and sex offending.

INTRODUCTION

In the previous chapter you were introduced to the notion of vulnerability as it manifests itself among different groups within the custodial setting. Many of those in prison will have pre-existing vulnerabilities that are often compounded by imprisonment or re-emerge following their release. In this respect we argued that prison is both a *repository for* and *site of* vulnerability. It is perhaps unsurprising then that those who come into contact with prison and probation services will often have experienced both sanctions during their criminal careers. As is the case with those in prison, people under probation supervision tend not to be representative of society as a whole. They have in many cases experienced a range of vulnerabilities because of their marginalisation (see Figure 12.1).

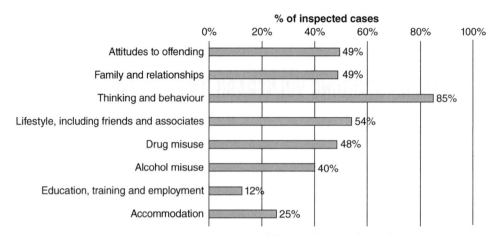

Figure 12.1 Factors linked to offending identified by inspectors. Probation inspections 2018/2019 and 2019/2020

(*Source*: HM Inspectorate of Probation 2020: 33, Available at: www.justiceinspectorates.gov.uk/hmiprobation/wp-content/uploads/sites/5/2020/12/2019-2020-Annual-Report-Inspection-of-probation-services-1.pdf (last accessed 10 October 2022))

Many people under probation supervision have no qualifications and some have special educational needs. A disproportionate number have been excluded from school, have been unemployed or never had a job. A significant number of those on probation will have become serious drug users or dependent on alcohol, or both, and many suffer with anxiety, depression other mental health conditions (such as psychosis) or personality disorders (HM Inspectorate of Probation, 2019). Probation practitioners work with some of the most challenged and challenging individuals in society, to reduce their reoffending and at the same time protect us from the harm they might cause us. In this chapter we initially focus on how the needs of Black and minority ethnic (BAME) individuals and women service users are being met (or not as the case may be) in the community before moving on to aspects of probation work that brings it into contact with individuals the nature of whose offending raises specific challenges for practitioners.

KEY QUESTIONS TO CONSIDER WHEN READING THIS CHAPTER

1. Does contemporary probation practice adhere to principles of equality and diversity?

2. Is it more appropriate to treat those convicted of domestic abuse and sexual offences in the community?

3. Is enough being done to meet the needs of those on probation experiencing mental health problems?

The proportion of ethnic minority individuals subject to court-ordered supervision in 2019, 16.1 per cent, is closer to their representation in the community as a whole (14 per cent, in the 2011 census) than for the prison population (HM Inspectorate of Probation, 2021: 9). Figures for the proportion on prison licence are not published but are likely to be higher because of the higher proportion of ethnic minority prisoners, 27 per cent (HM Prisons and Probation Service, 2020: 7). There is no published data on outcomes for probation service users by ethnicity, nor for key aspects of probation practice like breach or recall rates. The proportion of ethnic minority staff in the NPS is 13.7 per cent (HM Prisons and Probation Service, 2020), which is close to HMPPS's target of 14 per cent, and slightly below the ethnic minority working age population of the UK in the 2011 census. There is no aggregate published information for CRCs. The overall proportion of BAME staff in the NPS 'does not necessarily reflect the diversity in communities at a local level and there is a particular shortage of ethnic minority men' (HM Inspectorate of Probation, 2021: 9).

Calverley et al. (2004) in their study of Black and Asian individuals on probation found that there was no evidence that minority ethnic groups had distinctively

241,350	Number of people under probation supervision[1]
14%	Proportion of the population of England and Wales that is non-white[2]
27%	Proportion of the prison population in England and Wales that is non-white (31 March 2020)[3]
16%	Proportion of those on court-ordered probation supervision[4] that is non-white[5]
13.7%	Proportion of NPS staff who are non-white (31 March 2020)[6]
13.8%	Proportion of NPS staff in senior management grades who are non-white (31 March 2020)[7]
9%	Proportion of the national court-ordered probation caseload where data on ethnicity is missing[8]
25%	Proportion of mixed-heritage service users in employment at the start of a community sentence compared with 31% on average for white service users in 2019/2020[9]
62%	Proportion of mixed-heritage service users in settled accommodation at the start of a communiy sentence compared with 65% on average for white service users in 2019/2020
38	The number of stop and searches per 1,000 black people conducted by the police compared with four per 1,000 white people[10] (April 2018 to March 2019)
X 3	The likelihood of a black person being arrested by the police, compared with a white person[11] (April 2015 to March 2019)

Figure 12.2 Race equality in probation

(*Source*: HM Inspectorate of Probation 2021: 6. Available at: www.justiceinspectorates.gov.uk/hmiprobation/wp-content/uploads/sites/5/2021/03/Race-Equality-in-Probation-thematic-inspection-report-v1.0.pdf (last accessed 11 October 2022))

different or greater criminogenic needs than white people on probation. Overall, though, they were more likely to experience the kinds of disadvantage (poverty, low-educational achievement, school exclusion and unemployment) that are known to be risk factors for involvement in crime. The Young Review (Barrow Cadbury Trust, 2014) also found that Black young men felt stereotyped as involved in gangs and Muslim youth felt labelled as involved in terrorism and extremism; both groups felt that their treatment within the criminal justice system reflected this. The risk agenda (see Chapter 2) which dominates criminal justice operations also impacts disproportionately on Black, Asian and minority ethnic (BAME) young men, who are more likely to be perceived stereotypically. The Lammy Review into the treatment of, and outcomes for, BAME individuals in the criminal justice system identified a number of key areas requiring explanation or reform, including addressing issues that contribute to entry into the system as well as broader questions of staff diversity, legitimacy and trust (Carr, 2017). In response, HM Inspectorate of Probation (2021a: 4) has subsequently raised the lack of published data across probation providers as requiring 'urgent attention'.

A recent inspection of the quality of pre-sentence reports produced on Black, Asian and minority ethnic individuals uncovered considerable variation between probation areas in the proportion of ethnic minority service users appearing before the courts who receive a PSR, and in the number of instances where custody is proposed (HM Inspectorate of Probation, 2021a: 9). In 21 of the 51 reports inspected, the quality of PSRs on BAME individuals was insufficient, with not enough analysis of the service user's diversity (HM Inspectorate of Probation, 2021a: 9). In many cases there was insufficient analysis of factors relating to the service user's maturity or their experience of racism or trauma. Some people had experienced trauma in their upbringing, for example violence in the childhood home, parental mental illness or witnessing people dying because of crime. Some had been exposed to trauma by living in, and then escaping, countries where there was conflict and war, and witnessing violence and killings that contributed to poor mental health and desensitised them to violence (HM Inspectorate of Probation, 2021a: 45). The standard report framework now includes a heading about trauma, but this was not always explored properly and on occasions traumatic experiences were discounted (HM Inspectorate of Probation, 2021a: 30).

There is a commitment in the Target Operating Model (TOM) for probation services in England and Wales that 'a higher proportion of more detailed reports will be completed for these groups' (HM Prisons and Probation Service, 2021: 48). The TOM acknowledges that this will require more time to complete. Improvements in quality control of reports and training on how to work best with interpreters are also required (HM Inspectorate of Probation, 2021a: 10). The Ministry of Justice is currently working on strategies to 'de-bias' the courts and pre-sentence reports are the first trial. Staff will be receiving training resources on:

- The use of language and terminology

- Improving confidence in talking about difference

- Improving cultural competence

- Stereotyping and de-biasing decision making

- Quality assurance. (HM Inspectorate of Probation, 2021: 15)

According to HM Inspectorate of Probation (2021a) since Transforming Rehabilitation (TR), the number of services for Black, Asian and minority ethnic service users has decreased, and there are fewer resources devoted to work on equality and diversity. Probation staff had fewer links with organisations in the community that can support BAME individuals, and services that provide culturally appropriate services were rarely commissioned. Only around a quarter of those interviewed had received referrals or assistance in an area known to affect reoffending (such as accommodation, drugs and alcohol, and mental health), leaving a substantial three-quarters without this sort of support (HM Inspectorate of Probation, 2021a: 47). There were few programmes to address racially motivated offending, and ethnic minority staff were frequently expected to take on these cases without support or consultation.

EXPLORING VULNERABILITIES AMONG FEMALE SERVICE USERS

Many women who end up in the criminal justice system do so after experiencing a number of vulnerabilities beforehand. For example, experience of both sexual and violent victimisation in childhood and adulthood is high among criminalised women. Whilst males may experience similar circumstances, females are 'differentially affected by exposure to the same criminogenic conditions' (Mears et al., 1998). Annison and Brayford (2015: 3) identify three broad categories of vulnerabilities experienced by women caught up in the criminal justice system.

- Domestic circumstances and problems such as domestic violence, childcare issues, being a single parent

- Personal circumstances such as mental illness, low self-esteem, eating disorders, substance misuse

- Socio-economic factors such as poverty, isolation and employment.

Women in conflict with the law have frequent experiences of victimisation and gendered violence as children, adults or both (Sheehan et al., 2011). Examples include a history of care and general exploitation alongside violence in intimate relationships (Corston, 2007). The number of childhood traumatic events experienced by criminalised women has been 'positively correlated with lifetime number of arrests' (Messina and Grella, 2006: 1842). Domestic abuse can play a major part in crimes committed by females. Sixty per cent of females supervised in the community or in custody, who have an assessment, have experienced domestic abuse.

As Sharpe (2020: 611) notes, 'women's involvement in crime is closely bound up with the gendered experiences of social life' in two distinct ways: 'First, patriarchal cultures and structures facilitate gender violence and limit justice and therapeutic support to those who endure it, second, women's caring responsibilities over-determine female poverty and low-paid or precarious employment'. Studies of criminalised women have consistently shown that they are highly likely to experience poverty and economic marginalisation. A large proportion experience homelessness or insecure housing, unemployment and left school early with few formal qualifications or none at all (Sheehan et al., 2011). Many live with the painful emotional legacy of the history of state care and welfare neglect. Physical ill-health and substance misuse problems are common. A study by Annison et al. (2019: 387) found that poor health was likely to have a detrimental impact on attempts they were trying to make to stabilise their lives, and that they were struggling (and often failing) to engage in a meaningful way, mainly because of the lack of flexibility within services to work around their range of needs. The difficulties that many women who come into contact with the criminal justice system experience in their lives often make it difficult for them to comply with community penalties or indeed to engage with statutory services (Malloch and McIvor, 2011: 327). Provision is often inconsistent, and the range of accredited programmes provided for women is limited. The Thinking Skills Programme is the main offer, but take-up is low, which makes it difficult to evaluate results (HM Inspectorate of Probation, 2020: 37).

Cuts to public services, the introduction of Universal Credit, reduced disability benefits, increased demands on single parents to re-enter employment while cutting the benefits those in work can receive have all impacted disproportionately on women (Barr and Christian, 2019). Many criminalised women are therefore disadvantaged not only in terms of material resources but also socially and as a result of government policy. In addition to its material and potentially criminogenic impact on already marginalised groups, austerity has damaging emotional effects, producing humiliation, anxiety, shame, harassment, stigma and depression. As Sharpe (2020: 618) contends, 'structural barriers to (re)gaining a home, an income, and one's own children for a woman with a criminal past and little social or state support may be nearly impossible'.

Women's Centres, which were actively promoted by Baroness Corston in her report (see Chapter 10) became the prototype for how to provide women-only resources effectively. Crucially, the centres were seen as community resources for *all* women, rather than just catering for those who had been convicted of a crime. Those at risk of offending, because of their high level of need, were also welcomed. The centres do not, in themselves, provide an alternative to custody unless part of a specified activity requirement (a formal requirement of a court order) but are a conducive environment where women are actively encouraged to engage with their workers to address their offending (Criminal Justice Joint Inspection, 2011: 27). A report by HM Inspectorate of Probation (2016) found strengths and examples of good practice in the women's centres visited. Women had either direct access to specialist services, or an opportunity for referral to them, including mental health services, support for drug and alcohol misuse, debt counselling, benefits and other financial advice, family support including parenting, domestic abuse services, and education, training and employment. The one-stop-shop approach to accessing services for women was a key strength. The use of holistic interventions, where the work undertaken with women was tailored and personalised to their needs, and the availability of wraparound services in support of women attending the centres were also key strengths. Interventions to help with confidence and self-esteem, relationships, emotional well-being and substance misuse supported women and built good foundations for offending behaviour work (HM Inspectorate of Probation, 2016: 43). However, the inspectors also raised a number of concerns in relation to the existing and future provision of women's centres. They found inconsistencies in the way women who had offended could access support from a women's centre. The proximity of the centre and access to public transport were important factors in women being able to access services. The inspectors also found strategic differences between areas in the way women's services were thought about or prioritised, and this also had an impact on the availability of women's centres. They identified good examples of focus on services for women in areas which had senior managers with specific responsibilities for women's offending, action plans for women, and dedicated single points of contact within teams, giving specialist advice and support to other staff in relation to women who had offended. Provision for women was less evident in areas where there was an absence of dedicated leadership for women's offending (HM Inspectorate of Probation, 2016: 44).

In 2018, the Ministry of Justice published a female offender strategy which launched a new programme of work to improve outcomes for women convicted of crime and build on the identified needs outlined above (see Chapter 11 for further discussion). The strategy contained over 50 commitments which ranged from publishing guidance for police working with vulnerable women, to creating residential women's centres (RWCs) as an alternative to prison. The strategy has three main priorities: earlier interventions, an emphasis on community-based solutions and, where custody is used as a last resort for the most serious offences, delivering better custody (HM Prisons and Probation Service, 2021: 187). The strategy revisits the need for a distinct approach to working with females, specifically one which is gender responsive, trauma informed and partnership led. Aimed at reducing the number of women serving short-term custodial sentences, the strategy recognises the complex link between women's victimhood and their own offending behaviour and the differing operational challenges that this presents. However, Booth et al. (2018) contend that the strategy fails to clearly outline the specific pathways, resources and changes to bring about improvements in the current system. This view appears to be borne out by a recent report from the National Audit Office (NAO, 2022) that found that the Ministry of Justice had made only limited progress on its female offender strategy because it had not prioritised investment in this work and had allocated only limited funding and resources to the programme because it had prioritised other strategic aims, including dealing with the COVID-19 pandemic.

There are also wider issues at play here that are detrimentally affecting women subject to probation supervision. Firstly, there has been a fall in the use of community orders for women (as there has been for men). As we noted in Chapter 6, this has corresponded with an increase in the use of suspended sentence orders, which put women at risk if they reoffend (Ministry of Justice, 2018). The number of women under supervision recalled to prison has more than doubled post TR, with 1.458 women recalled in the year leading up to June 2017 (Prison Reform Trust, 2017). In order to address these trends, the Target Operating Model (TOM) for the current probation reform programme outlines several components to enhance sentencers' confidence and improve compliance. These include:

- The introduction of a tiering framework that recognises the specific complexity factors present amongst women and will be the main vehicle for directing organisational resource to working with women.

- All probation practitioners will be appropriately trained to work with women. A modular training package called 'Power' has been developed to improve consistency. It is accessible to all staff who work with female offenders. Although the full roll-out of this training is not yet complete, feedback from staff has been positive.

- Women who are subject to probation services will be given the option to have a female probation practitioner.

- Probation regions may choose to enhance provision through the use of semi-specialist 'women concentrators' (probation practitioners who champion specific considerations in dealing with women).

- Individuals will be allocated to their probation practitioner within five working days of sentence. Where possible, the supervised individual will remain with the same probation practitioner throughout their supervision. In line with research on effective supervision, this will allow for continuity of contact and support the building of a constructive relationship with service users.

The evidence for working with criminalised women in the community is now well established. Many women could be more successfully supported in the community where reoffending rates are better. Some factors (such as childcare provision or domestic abuse) make participation in probation work more difficult for women than for men, and it is broadly recognised that approaches to tackling women's offending need to be gender-specific and acknowledge the following factors:

- Women who offend are more likely to have been victims of physical, emotional or sexual abuse, or exploitation. They are more likely to have mental health problems and are more likely to self-harm than men.

- Women are a distinct group of offenders within the criminal justice system with specific needs that cannot be met through general systems designed with men in mind.

- Women tend to be lower risk – they are less likely to be serious or violent offenders, are more likely to be acquisitive, committing offences such as shop theft or less serious fraud crimes.

- Interventions that work are less confrontational than some interventions effective for men. They focus upon the future – are optimistic, look to build positive relationships, are mindful of trauma, abuse and victimisation, and are based within the desistance paradigm, stressing strengths, maturation and self-worth.

- Interventions that work with women who offend are based around confidence and self-esteem building – increasing skills in relationships and parenting, improving physical and mental well-being, and tackling substance misuse. (HM Inspectorate of Probation, 2016: 18)

Research suggests that gender-responsive interventions (particularly cognitive–behavioural programmes) show more promise than gender-neutral approaches. A gender-responsive approach may include creating programme content and material that reflects the realities of women's lives and addresses the issues of the participants (HM Prisons and Probation Service, 2021: 187). Such approaches should be supportive not punitive and should be delivered outside of custodial settings. Transforming the criminal justice system to make it more 'women-friendly' (Malloch et al., 2014: 396) not only requires the resources to support women in and out of the criminal justice system but also to engage with the structural and cultural oppression that women face and the economic marginalisation and poverty that underpin the processes of criminalisation for many women. Ultimately, as Malloch and McIvor (2011: 340) note, 'the efficacy of community disposals and how they are experienced by women and workers is always, to some extent, determined by other circumstances which impact on both offending behaviour and routes out of offending'. Women also tend to be disproportionately victims of domestic abuse.

WORKING WITH PERPETRATORS OF DOMESTIC VIOLENCE

Over 1.2 million women and 750,000 men in England and Wales experience some form of domestic violence (World Health Organization, 2013). This amounts to around 40 per cent of all criminal cases. This corresponds to approximately 7 per cent of women reporting having been victims of domestic violence each year. On average two women a week are killed by a male partner or former partner (that is, around 33 per cent of all female homicide victims). Statistics tell us that one in four women (28 per cent) and one in six men have experienced some form of domestic abuse since the age of 16 (British Crime Survey, 2009). Women are at greater risk of repeat victimisation and serious injury, with 89 per cent of those suffering four or more incidents being women. Added to this is the fact that children are not included in the definition of domestic violence and are often the most hidden and marginalised victims (Devaney and Lazenbatt, 2016). Research indicates that children were present in over half of cases (55 per cent) when domestic violence took place. One in seven (14 per cent) of children and young people under the age of 18 will have lived with domestic violence at some point in their childhood. Victims of domestic abuse may experience a range of abusive behaviours from their partners, with psychological abuse being characterised by hostility, deprecation, indifference and lack of attention towards the victim's opinions and emotional needs. In recent years attention has been drawn to the notion of *coercive control* in domestic abuse. This involves a range of acts designed to make a person subordinate and/or dependent by isolating them from sources of support, such as family and friends, exploiting their resources and capacities for personal gain, depriving them of the means needed for independence by controlling their money or bank accounts. Section 76 of the Serious Crime Act 2015 created a new offence of controlling or coercive behaviour in an intimate or family relationship. For the purposes of the Act, the behaviour must be engaged in *repeatedly* or *continuously*. Another, separate, element of the offence is that it must have a *serious effect* on someone and one way of proving this is that it causes someone to fear, on at least two occasions, that violence will be used against them.

In some countries – such as the United States of America – coercive control is not illegal unless it escalates to physical violence. Some academics argue that criminalising coercive behaviour is not a complete solution to domestic abuse because most criminal justice systems rely on physical evidence to charge people with specific acts such as assault or rape. However, coercive control is not a specific act. It is a pattern of behaviours and it tends to leave less physical evidence than violence. Nevertheless, coercive control is still abuse and it can cause long-lasting psychological trauma for those who experience it. While the case of Sally Challen has drawn media attention to the operation of coercive control in murder conviction cases, such cases only show the sharp end of coercive control, women's criminalisation in less extreme circumstances of coercive control has been less publicised (Barr and Christian, 2019: 417). For example, Light et al. (2013) highlight that almost half of women in prison have carried out their offence to support someone else's drug use. Women's Aid (2019) have found that two-thirds of domestic violence survivors' partners held money from them as a form of control.

It is important to remember that abusive behaviours can be many and varied. The stereotypical view has been that domestic abuse describes male violence towards women in intimate relationships. This is understandable given that the majority of domestic abuse (more than 77 per cent) is committed by men against women (Home Office, 2013) but it is not always the case. Women can abuse men, there can be abuse in same sex relationships and trans-generational abuse. Numerous studies have found that victims believe that the psychological abuse they experienced was as bad as or much worse than the physical violence and had a longer-term adverse effect on them. It is now recognised that experiencing domestic violence can typically provoke feelings such as shame, low self-esteem, fear, self-blame and guilt. This can in turn creating unique patterns of psychological and emotional responses within victims, which often manifest in severe psychological illnesses. These can include post-traumatic stress disorder, depression and anxiety disorders, sexual problems, substance abuse and suicidal tendencies. Psychological and emotional manipulation, which are common mechanisms of domestic violence, incrementally erode the victim's sense of self and perceived ability to function independently, serving to bind a victim into a psychologically dependent and socially isolated relationship.

The TOM for the current probation reforms (HM Prison and Probation Service, 2021: 193) suggests that the following could improve outcomes for women under probation supervision who are affected by domestic abuse:

- Provide the opportunity to disclose abuse
- Provide the opportunity to ask for and receive help and support
- Ensure they receive a sensitive and safe response
- Recognise and meet the safeguarding needs of children affected by domestic abuse
- Enable referral and support to access appropriate services to meet needs.

It also identifies the role of advocacy services in helping to explore and access services in the community and identify and achieve personal goals as well as short-term trauma-focused counselling or cognitive–behavioural approaches to treating trauma, which can improve the health of survivors of domestic abuse

It is estimated that approximately 20 to 50 per cent of women suffer physical, emotional or sexual abuse at some point during their lifetimes, but in reality this may only be the tip of the iceberg (Devaney and Lazenbatt, 2016: 20). Domestic abuse can be a very private form of behaviour and we know that victims of domestic abuse are less likely than victims of other forms of violence to report their experiences to the authorities. Most domestic abuse is never reported to the police (four in five victims of partner abuse did not report the abuse to the police in 2015), though it may be known to social services, housing and health professionals. Victims may be reluctant to report cases and the abuse remains hidden; individuals may not see the violence as criminal behaviour, or may not wish their abuser to be criminalised, or indeed known. Additionally, taboos, fears and feelings of guilt and shame also account for a high rate of non-responsiveness particularly for male victims. Domestic abuse is clearly then a key concern for the probation service.

A study by Ellis Devitt et al. (2021) drawing on first-hand accounts of those convicted of domestic abuse offences sought to identify who the perpetrators of domestic abuse are, and how they came to be in order to better understand how current interventions could be enhanced by this information. The authors identified four key points for practice and practitioners:

1. Do not let concerns that perpetrators may be justifying or excusing their DA detract from the importance of such accounts being given at all. Stories themselves can be an important part of sense-making and reflexivity.

2. Male to female domestic violence can threaten masculinity, and therefore may see additional levels of defence as individuals seek to preserve it.

3. Older perpetrators may struggle more than younger perpetrators when it comes to problematic beliefs about gender roles, in part reflecting the generation they were born into, and their confusion about what value they have in the family dynamic.

4. Finally, perpetrators may withhold information, or be more inclined to tell 'success' stories which position themselves as reformed, changed and compliant, due to perceived risks about what might happen if they don't. It is crucial that practitioners working directly with DA perpetrators understand this and encourage perpetrators to talk about these issues without fear of repercussions.

Several risk factors relating to domestic abuse have been identified (Ministry of Justice, 2010). These include a history of violent behaviour, anti-social behaviours and attitudes, relationship instability, employment instability, mental health problems and personality disorder, an abusive childhood, low self-esteem, and hostile attitudes towards women. Therefore, understanding why and how perpetrators of domestic violence change their behaviour is an important goal for the development of policy and in improving practice. However, as Renehan (2020: 384) observes, 'despite almost four decades of domestic abuse perpetrator rehabilitation, there is little consensus on what causes men to be violent towards their partners let alone what interventions should look like'. Given that the perpetration of domestic violence is heterogeneous, it is very likely that interventions will be differentially effective for various individuals. The fundamental bedrock for work with perpetrators is a comprehensive and holistic assessment of the individual within the context of their relationship and family, alongside the influence of community and social values and processes, that seeks to address, as a minimum, a number of key issues (Devaney and Lazenbatt, 2016: 115):

- The nature, quality and dynamics of the relationships between the perpetrator and their current or previous partner from the perspective of both parties
- An assessment of the nature of the risks posed, based on a full consideration of both static and dynamic risk factors
- A full social history of the individual and their family, and prior life experiences
- A professional assessment of any learning difficulty, substance use or mental health difficulties that may complicate the assessment or intervention
- Openness on the part of the perpetrator to acknowledge the need for change in the desired direction and to take responsibility for making and sustaining that change.

PROGRAMMES FOR WORKING WITH PERPETRATORS OF DOMESTIC ABUSE

Gondolf (2002) conceptualises the three prevailing approaches to domestic violence perpetrator programmes as cognitive–behavioural, psychodynamic and pro-feminist treatment. Although these treatment modalities have a limited research base and mixed support, they appear to be the most commonly used approaches to domestic violence perpetrator interventions (Dixon et al., 2012).

- *Cognitive–behavioural programmes* attribute violence to learned behaviours that perform an expressive, instrumental function. Consequently, they emphasise that desistance must be learned through a process of cognitive restructuring.
- *Psychodynamic approaches* emphasise the personality and emotional disposition of the perpetrator as being central to desistance, by facilitating the recognition and reconciliation of latent feelings of emasculation that precipitate abusive impulses.
- *Pro-feminist approaches* view violence as originating from patriarchal values about women's roles, and typically aim to reorient the way men exert power and control over their partner by focusing on attitudinal as well as behavioural change.

Domestic abuse programmes vary considerably, not just in philosophical orientation but also in format, duration, approach and who is involved. There is a tension between whether programmes should be more orientated towards rehabilitation efforts or, alternatively, hold the perpetrator to account for their behaviour, drawing some programmes more in one direction than the other. However, there does appear to be a consensus around some core objectives of perpetrator programmes (Devaney and Lazenbatt, 2016: 99), which are to help individuals stop being violent and abusive, help them learn how to relate to their partners in a respectful and equal way, show individuals non-abusive ways of dealing with difficulties in their relationships and cope with their anger, and keep their current, past or future partner safer from further violent and abusive behaviour.

Three accredited programmes have been used by probation and prison staff to address domestic abuse – Building Better Relationships, Healthy Relationships, and Kaizen. These programmes are accredited by a government-appointed panel on the basis that they are grounded in sound behaviour change theory, and that there are plans for them to be evaluated. The last HMPPS domestic abuse programme to be evaluated – the Integrated Domestic Abuse Programme or IDAP – was discontinued five years ago (Gibbs, 2018). The authors reported that for the majority of participants (both men and their female partners) participation in the programme and the accompanying support for partners resulted in positive benefits and improvements in abusive behaviour. The Building Better relationships programme retains elements of the power and control model on which the Integrated Domestic Abuse Programme was based and recognises the influence of a patriarchal culture. However, it takes a more holistic approach, locating aggression in the context of environmental, social and stress factors in a person's lifetime. Facilitators undergo five days training on the Building Better Relationships programme, which is based on a 400-page manual (Renehan, 2021). Facilitators are expected to adopt a therapeutic strengths-based, solutions-focused approach. Facilitators are also encouraged to engage men in discussions about their 'thoughts, emotions and relationships and how these connect to perceptions and anger arousal' (Renehan, 2020: 389). Rather than solely viewing domestic violence as primarily being caused by either individual failings or societal power structures, the programme explores the nature of domestic abuse from an ecological perspective. This

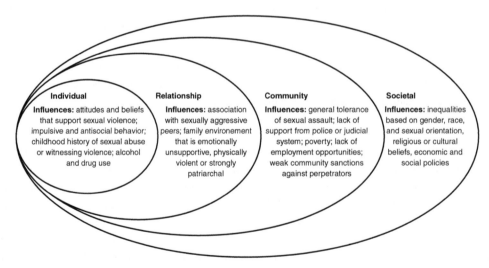

Figure 12.3 The Ecological Model

(*Source*: Centers for Disease Control and Prevention (2004) *Sexual Violence Prevention: Beginning the Dialogue*. Available at: www.cdc.gov/violenceprevention/pdf/svprevention-a.pdf (last accessed 11 October))

acknowledges that the way society is structured is an influence upon, and also influenced by, how people think and how this relates to how they act (see Figure 12.3).

Multi-agency risk assessment conferences (MARAC) are another key policy mechanism aimed at addressing domestic abuse. They operate along similar lines to the MAPPA arrangements (see Chapter 1). There are around 290 MARACs operating in England and Wales. The aims of MARAC are: to share information to increase the safety, health and well-being of victims – adults and their children; to determine whether the perpetrator poses a significant risk to any particular individual or to the general community; to construct jointly and implement a risk management plan that provides professional support to all those at risk and reduces the risk of harm; to reduce repeat victimisation; to improve agency accountability; and to improve support for staff involved in high-risk domestic violence cases. All local agencies can refer cases. This is then referred to an independent domestic violence advisor (IDVA) who meets the victim and undertakes a risk assessment of the risk posed. A screening checklist guides the process. Cases assessed as high risk will be referred to MARAC. The MARAC meeting draws up a plan designed to offer protection to the victim from repeat victimisation which is then overseen and co-ordinated by an IDVA. You may be wondering what the difference is between MARAC and the MAPPA system. In general terms, MARACs concentrate on managing the risks to the victim, whereas MAPPA concentrates on managing the risks posed by the perpetrator. MARAC cases are not inevitably eligible to be MAPPA cases. Some MARAC cases do not result in a conviction. However, where the case is being actively managed at MAPPA level 2 or 3, the MAPPA meeting takes the lead over the MARAC meeting.

EXPLORING VULNERABILITIES AMONG PEOPLE WITH MENTAL HEALTH ISSUES

As with those convicted of sexual offences – which we consider later in this chapter – this work is full of dilemmas for practitioners around personal values, individual freedoms and proportionate responses to risk. Individuals in the criminal justice system with mental health problems present a real dilemma for society, falling as they do so awkwardly between the control mechanisms of the criminal justice and health systems. Skeem and Louden (2006) note that these individuals are often failed by services that are not geared towards the needs of this population. This is because many mainstream community health services sometimes deem their needs too complex and struggle to meet their clinical needs (Vaughan and Stevenson, 2002) whilst criminal justice organisations such as the Probation Service are not always designed to meet the unique challenges that individuals with mental illness can at times pose. As a result, society's response is often deeply conflicted and ambivalent.

Research suggests that on the whole mentally disordered individuals reoffend at lower rates than those without a mental disorder (Robinson, 2011) yet at the same time there has been a ratcheting up of concerns about dangerousness following a small number of high-profile killings by former psychiatric patients. Clearly some mentally disordered individuals are very dangerous but exactly who – or in what circumstances – is difficult to determine. It could be argued that if anything, mentally disordered individuals pose more danger to themselves than to others. Brooker et al's. (2012) study into the prevalence of mental health disorders among a cohort of those under supervision in one probation trust in England and Wales found that around 39 per cent of supervised individuals experienced a mental illness whilst on probation with half of that population having a past or lifetime disorder. In common with previous studies of prison populations, the researchers also found a strong correlation evident in terms of the co-occurrence of comorbidity (the presence of a mental illness and a personality disorder) and of dual diagnosis, (a mental illness and substance use). Such findings appear to replicate and reinforce those found in studies undertaken in other jurisdictions. Worryingly, Brooker et al. (2012) also found that the prevalence of psychosis was ten times higher than in the general population and suicide levels were rising among those being supervised in the community (accounting for one in eight deaths amongst individuals on probation) at the same time as they were declining among those in prison, where traditionally rates of suicide have been high.

Probation practitioners therefore have a significant role in the supervision of individuals with mental health problems in terms of helping them access services and alleviate personal and practical difficulties that might increase their vulnerability. Moreover, exposure to the criminal justice system in itself can induce feelings of social isolation and stigma that might lead to a deterioration in an individual's mental state. In the absence of mental health professionals, it often falls on probation staff to recognise mental health issues and to make appropriate recommendations to the court. For this reason, the Bradley Report (2009) recommended that all probation staff should receive mental health awareness training, having found that existing provision was often non-existent or wholly inappropriate. A study by Brooker et al. (2011) found that only a third of psychotic disorder cases were recorded in probation case files. Brooker et al. (2011) also found that a large proportion of those with a current mental illness were not receiving treatment: for example, 60 per cent of those with a mood or anxiety disorder were not receiving any treatment, and only half of those with a current psychosis were receiving any support from mental health services. Moreover, the research suggests that mental health problems are under-identified by probation staff with only 33 per cent of individuals identified as having a psychotic disorder subsequently recorded in probation files as having such a disorder. This under-identification could be partly explained by the limited opportunities available to probation staff to receive any form of mental health awareness training, with many grades of probation staff receiving no formal training in this area.

Criminality often involves significant levels of stress and anxiety that can exacerbate mental health problems. A combination of mental health problems and/or personality disorder and substance use can have a detrimental impact on treatment outcomes (DiClemente et al., 2008). This is often compounded by a lack of engagement with therapeutic services, poor motivation and relapse (Long et al., 2018). Many of these individuals are likely to have low levels of *health literacy* and do not access mental health services until they are at crisis point (Sirdfield and Brooker, 2020: 6). McArt (2013) warns that there is a danger that an increasing focus on the punitive aspect of community sentences could limit sentencers' options by making the punitive aspects mandatory in many cases. For those with a range of needs related to mental health, making sentences more onerous could create demands that they cannot meet in the community, thus resulting in a further period of imprisonment, thereby continuing the cycle of a lack of treatment in a place of punishment. However, recently a more nuanced understanding of offending among people with mental illness has emerged (Eno Louden et al., 2018) based on strong evidence suggesting that serious mental illness is not a strong predictor of reoffending symptoms and their symptoms are not directly related to the offences they commit. Instead, those with a mental illness tend to display more general risk factors for offending (such as criminogenic personality patterns) compared with non-disordered individuals. In this respect, 'mental illness appears to be an indicator of risk – because it is correlated with factors related to offending – rather than a causal mechanism itself' (Eno Louden et al., 2018: 573).

The past two decades have brought about a substantial amount of attention to individuals with mental illness and has resulted in a number of initiatives reflecting a noticeable shift in perceptions of best practice in managing this group in the criminal justice system. We considered one of them, the Offender Personality Disorder Pathway in chapter 9. Here we turn our attention to another, the Mental Health Treatment Requirement (MHTR). The main purpose of the MHTR is to ensure that individuals appearing before the courts with mental health issues are able to access appropriate treatment in the community (Scott and Moffatt, 2012). It is intended to target individuals committing middle-range offences rather than the least severe end of the continuum where fines or conditional discharges might be more appropriate or those whose levels of seriousness mean that imprisonment or detainment under the Mental Health Act is inevitable. The MHTR is a *bespoke* sentence and as such the nature of the treatment is not specified but in order to include an MHTR in a community order the sentencer must be satisfied that three criteria have been met, notably: they require treatment for mental-health-related needs; there are concerns regarding future engagement; and the court considers that it is not appropriate to divert them from the criminal justice system altogether (Scott and Moffatt, 2012).

An MHTR requires individuals to engage in specific treatment for a specified period of time, the nature of which depends on the condition. As such, it provides sentencers with the option to impose a criminal justice sanction on individuals with mental health problems who have committed relatively minor offences. The MHTR can be used in relation to any mental health issue including personality disorders and any mental health condition susceptible to treatment, such as low-level depression or anxiety. The type of treatment is not defined and can cover a wide range of interventions. Treatment should be based on the individual being assessed as able to be treated for their mental health problem either in a community setting or as an outpatient in a non-secure setting (National Offender Management Service (NOMS, 2014). MHTRs are rarely made as stand-alone sanctions and are usually combined with a supervision requirement to support the rehabilitative endeavour and provide additional assistance. There must be a named registered medical practitioner or registered psychologist overseeing the treatment who will work collaboratively with probation staff, whose focus will be on addressing other matters in relation to offending and monitoring compliance with the order. In imposing an MHTR the recipient's consent is required, reflecting 'the treatment ethos of voluntary and motivated participation' (Pakes and Winstone, 2013).

Implementation of the requirement has not been without problems. Perhaps the most telling has been the low take-up rate – as of March 2020, less than 1 per cent of all court orders (HM Inspectorate of Probation, 2021). The following challenges in delivery have been identified:

- Lack of access to appropriate mental health services
- Some mental health workers being reluctant to treat someone when this is attached to a court order
- The need for greater understanding of issues of service user consent and stigma attached to mental health treatment – some may be unwilling to acknowledge that they have mental health problems
- The need for continuous engagement between criminal justice agencies, health commissioners and treatment providers on all issues of service user health in the community. (HM Inspectorate of Probation, 2021)

In 2018 new pilots were announced to help people with mental health, alcohol and substance abuse issues to address the underlying causes of their offending. The Community Sentence Treatment Requirements (CSTR) established in five areas of England bring together health and justice services to assess, and where appropriate divert, people from short custodial sentences and improve access to treatment. They provide individualised treatment packages coordinated by the probation practitioner in partnership with liaison and diversion schemes and health providers. An assistant psychologist is allocated to the service user to help them improve engagement and coping skills through psychologically informed interventions. Early evidence has shown increased confidence among sentencers, resulting in more CSTRs being issued in those areas.

Working with high-risk individuals with personality disorders presents a range of complex challenges for probation practitioners and can induce feelings of being 'helpless and de-skilled, confused and hopeless' (Murphy and McVey, 2010). The lives of many of those who are in contact with the criminal justice system is often a result of unresolved past trauma and so the work can involve 'bearing witness to someone's distress and trauma by working with them to try and work out how to build a safe relationship, distinct from those in the past that may have been traumatizing' (Cluley and Marston, 2018: 90). Probation staff are therefore faced with a range of contradictions that involve 'being caring whilst detaining; knowing about early life trauma whilst managing a "perpetrator"; meeting high levels of need and deprivation whilst managing high levels of risk' (Fellowes, 2018: 154). Caught between the non-compliance of service users and the system's reliance on custodial sanctions, practitioners and the influence of adverse familial and statutory relationships, practitioners need to persevere in the face of chronic mistrust and paranoia, sometimes for years (Fellowes, 2018: 159). Therefore, as valuable as psychologically informed practice is, it is also a challenging relational and emotional endeavour. If staff are to offer supervision attuned to service users' particular needs, then the wider system needs to afford opportunities for this work to be both safe and sustainable (Fellowes, 2014).

Research suggests that for workers in this field emotional resilience, more effective outcomes and improved service delivery are all more likely within a structured and supportive organisational climate where staff possess high levels of professional competency (Shaw et al., 2011: 42). However, in her study of probation officers who worked as personality disorder leads on the Offender Personality Disorder Pathway, Fellowes (2018) found that the complexity of the work was not always acknowledged in the policies and procedures that govern the organisation of probation. Similarly, with regard to the PIPEs (see Chapter 9) early evidence suggests that this is an effective model for achieving a high-quality relational environment where residents feel better equipped to deal with impulsive behaviours and challenging interactions. Whilst these findings are encouraging and appear to support the aims of the pathway there is still work to be undertaken to ensure that the psychologically informed theory and principles that underpin this approach are meaningfully applied to traditional probation procedures.

Developments such as the MHTR, the Offender Personality Disorder Pathway and the recent interest in neurodiversity (see Chapter 13) can be viewed as positive developments in terms of addressing the needs of offenders under the supervision of the Probation Service in the community even if the potential of these initiatives has not yet been fully realised. They are grounded in notions of effective multi-agency collaboration, which is essential to successful rehabilitation given the complex nature of the psychological, social and forensic problems presented by individuals subject to community supervision. However, at a more fundamental level, there is, and there has been for some time, a strong argument for diversion – that is, to take individuals with mental health issues out of criminal justice contexts, where appropriate, and link them up with other community facilities. One of the Bradley Report's recommendations was for all police custody suites and criminal courts to have access to liaison and diversion services. These services identify and, where appropriate, divert people with mental health problems, learning disabilities and other support needs away from the criminal justice system and into treatment and care. Operating at the interface between criminal justice and mental health services, liaison and diversion services could play an important part in ensuring that the mental health needs of those in contact with, or at risk of entering, the criminal justice system are identified and addressed. It is of course equally imperative that local commissioning bodies and authorities ensure that there are adequate and appropriate services available in local areas that offenders can be diverted to (Scott and Moffatt, 2012: 8). It has been estimated that diverting individuals away from short prison sentences towards effective treatment in the community could lead to savings of over £20,000 per case (Sainsbury Centre for Mental Health, 2009: 5). The roll-out of liaison and diversion services achieved 100 per cent coverage across England in March 2020. An evaluation of the trial scheme (Disley et al., 2016) reported that service users viewed the liaison and diversion services positively and found them helpful at a challenging time.

EXPLORING VULNERABILITIES AMONG PEOPLE CONVICTED OF SEXUAL OFFENCES

The estimated number of sexual assaults in England and Wales each year exceeds 600,000. Prior to the reunification of probation, the National Probation Service was responsible for the supervision of all registered sexual offenders convicted of a sexual offence and serving a current sentence – one in five of all individuals supervised (see Figure 12.4).

Sexual offending by its nature is an emotive and complex subject, and the impact of such offending on victims can be profound. The level of media and public interest in how such cases are managed has increased in recent years, partly because of the number of high-profile cases reported. This can be an extremely difficult area of practice and can challenge practitioners' values and beliefs and be exceptionally emotionally demanding. Dealing with denial, minimisation or justification are inevitable for practitioners given the nature of these offences and society's attitudes towards those who commit them. Research suggests that reoffending rates for those convicted of sexual offences are relatively low, certainly in relation to other offences (Harris and Hanson, 2004). However, the nature of the offences – and the undoubted harm they can cause – makes it sometimes difficult to view them in a rational and unemotional way. Those convicted of sexual offences are perhaps the most vilified of all offenders. The social construction of sex offenders as highly

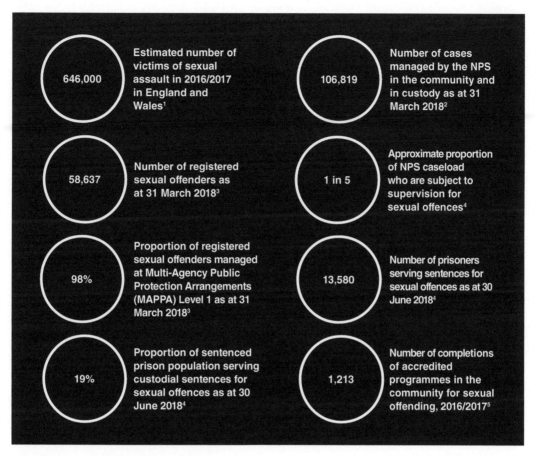

Figure 12.4 Sexual offences in context

(*Source*: HM Inspectorate of Probation 2019: 6, Available at: www.justiceinspectorates.gov.uk/hmiprobation/
wp-content/uploads/sites/5/2019/01/Management-and-Supervision-of-men-convicted-of-sexual-offences-2.pdf
(last accessed 11 October 2022))

dangerous, mentally abnormal and morally contaminated' (Boone and van de Bunt, 2016) and community intolerance and vilification can make their integration extremely difficult. Their needs and rights to fair treatment and privacy have to be balanced by the need to protect both specific victims and in some cases the community at large. There can therefore be complex decisions and judgements about what degrees of intrusiveness or restriction would be both appropriate and effective in individual cases. This is one of the areas where the dilemmas about rights and responsibilities towards public protection are uppermost for practitioners because being too risk averse may ironically increase stigma and social isolation, which in turn can increase the risks posed by individuals.

An inspection of the management and supervision of men convicted of sexual offences (HM Inspectorate of Probation, 2019) found that the theories underpinning effective practice with this group were not understood by probation practitioners sufficiently well, and the methods and tools are not embedded into practice. Consequently, many staff committed to doing their best when working with these individuals struggle to balance a positive, forward-looking approach with one focused on public protection. This is an enduring requirement throughout probation, but it is so often in stark relief when supervising sexual offenders. Yet as McAlinden (2006: 210) observes:

> **sexual abusers are men and women and, in a growing number of cases, adolescents or children; ... there are different levels of risk and ... not all sexual offenders pose the same degree of high risk; and ... in tandem with this, recidivism research has shown that most sexual offenders will not reoffend given appropriate treatment and support.**

The definition of a sexual offence has changed over time, although it can generally be split into four categories:

- Sexual acts with contact
- Non-contact sexual acts
- Abusive images/audio/text of children
- Solicitation and trafficking (HM Inspectorate of Probation, 2019: 7).

The Probation Service uses a number of different tools to inform assessments, assess risk and identify protective factors for people convicted of sexual offending:

- *OASys* is the assessment tool used by the Probation Service for all those under its supervision. It does not focus specifically on sexual offending but provides the opportunity for responsible officers to gather a wide range of information about an individual and their needs and risk factors.

- *The ARMS tool* was introduced in 2015. While it is used as a risk assessment tool by police, it is used by the Probation Service to aid the understanding of dynamic risk and protective factors for men who have committed sexual offences. Probation is responsible for completing ARMS assessments for registered sexual offenders (RSOs) subject to probation supervision, where the NPS is the lead agency. It is only suitable for use with men who have committed sexual offences.

- *Risk Matrix 2000 (RM2000)* is a tool used to predict the risk of reconviction for adult men convicted of sexual offences. It uses static information about an individual and their offending to provide an actuarial assessment of their risk of reoffending. Actuarial risk assessment is the most prominent and common approach to the assessment of sexual offenders in both research and practice; however, without a clinical input, such assessment can become mechanical. However, Grove et al. (2000) found from a meta-analysis of 136 studies that actuarial risk assessment greatly outperforms sole clinical judgement in predictive terms. (HM Inspectorate of Probation, 2019: 15)

Current approaches to people convicted of sexual offences therefore contain both constructive measures (such as attending accredited programmes, psychological or psychiatric input, Circles of Support and Accountability) and restrictive measures (such as residing at approved premises, and restrictions on associations, movements or activities). We will consider these later on in this section. There is growing evidence that our current community risk management approaches are managing risk effectively and sexual recidivism rates are falling (Thornton and d'Orazio, 2016). Hanson and Morton-Bourgon (2005) found that the strongest predictors of sexual reoffending were sexual deviancy, anti-social orientation, criminogenic attitudes and intimacy deficits. Adverse childhood experiences, general psychological problems and clinical presentation had no predictive value. The strongest predictor of non-sexual reoffending was an anti-social orientation.

There were approximately 646,000 victims of sexual assault in 2016/17 in England and Wales and around one in five of those on NPS caseloads were subject to supervision for sexual offences (HM Inspectorate of probation 2019: 6). Although crime surveys strongly suggest that the rates of sexual crime have remained steady, in recent years there has been an increasing number of these types of offences reported. This does not necessarily mean that more crimes have been committed. It could be that people are increasingly willing to come forward to report sexual crimes, and that this may well be linked to publicity surrounding Operation Yewtree in 2012, the police investigation into sexual abuse allegations surrounding Jimmy Savile and other media personalities. It may also reflect the improved approach by the police to recording crime following on from an inspection showing that an estimated one in four sexual offences that should have been recorded as crimes were not (HM Inspectorate of Constabulary, 2014). However, it is still the case that many instances of abuse go unreported or are not taken seriously enough particularly where children and young children are concerned, as highlighted in the independent inquiry into child sexual exploitation in the Telford area (Murray 2022).

However, it still appears to be difficult to convert recorded sexual offences into convictions. Official statistics for 2017 indicate that only 8 per cent of recorded sexual crime leads to charges. Unfortunately, although people are coming forward, more than 50 per cent of the recorded crime suffers from evidential problems – including the victim not wishing to take matters forward – and this tendency is increasing in line with the rise in recorded sexual crime. More encouraging, once a sexual allegation is proceeded with, there is around a 55 per cent conviction rate (7,000 convictions in 2016/17), 60 per cent of which lead to a custodial sentence averaging 60 months duration. Those convicted of sexual offences are clearly receiving increasingly long sentences and, although the figures fluctuate over time, they now comprise around 16 per cent of the England and Wales prison population, at around 14,000 individuals in prison. Despite the punitive response of the criminal justice system, it still remains the case that the majority of those convicted of sexual offences are managed in the community, either because they received a community sentence, or because they have been released following a long custodial sentence.

A meta-analytic review of sexual offending based on 17 samples from 12 countries (Cortoni et al., 2017) found that around 2 per cent of all recorded sexual crimes are committed by females. The most common group of female perpetrators were adolescents (twice as many as adults). Around one third of female perpetrators are coerced or co-offend (with a male or female), and their offending often takes place within the context of broader child maltreatment. A significant number of these individuals have previously sexually offended alone, or subsequently do so.

IS TREATMENT FOR SEXUAL OFFENDING EFFECTIVE?

The history of sex offender treatment has three identifiable phases in which the following approaches have been dominant (Robinson, 2011). Psychoanalytical therapy was mostly developed in the USA but largely fell out of favour during the 1970s when it was believed that *nothing works*. At the same time behavioural approaches were receiving attention and initially focused on desensitisation and reducing deviant patterns of arousal. In a separate development – during the late 1980s and early 1990s – academics began to explore patterns emerging from large numbers of evaluations of interventions with general offender populations which suggested that cognitive behavioural work produced the most promising treatment results. Cognitive behavioural work is premised on the belief 'that schemas – or core beliefs – are stable cognitive patterns which develop in early life as part of normal cognitive development and are shaped by events and relationships; schemas result in underlying assumptions which are conditional beliefs, and which trigger automatic thoughts – cognitions that automatically and temporarily flow through one's mind and will often reflect persistent cognitive distortions' (Craissati, 2005). Recidivist sexual offenders would be expected to hold deviant schema, or habitual patterns of thought and action, that facilitate their offences (Hanson and Harris, 2000).

As we saw in Chapter 11, there are a number of accredited programmes offered by HM Prison and Probation Service to those convicted of sexual offences. They are designed to address the level of actual and potential risk. There is an accredited programme ('Horizon') designed for adult men who have been convicted of a sexual offence and are judged to be at medium or higher risk of reoffending. It supports participants to develop optimism and skills to strengthen their prosocial identity and plan for a life free of offending. Unlike earlier programmes, it is available to those who deny their offences. i-Horizon has recently been introduced in the community for those who have committed internet offences but is not available in custody. Horizon includes the 'New Me MOT' as part of their accreditation. This is a toolkit that can be used by probation officers to provide ongoing support to programme completers (HM Inspectorate of Probation, 2019). Offender behaviour programmes for those convicted of sexual offences utilise a range of techniques such as group discussions, individual and group exercises, role-play, personal reflection and goal setting.

Some recent meta-analytic reviews have concluded with some cautious optimism. Loesel and Schmuker (2005) examined 69 studies comprising more than 20,000 sexual offenders and found that those receiving treatment sexually reoffended 6 per cent less than the untreated controls – that is, 11 per cent versus 17 per cent sexual recidivism, equating to a reduction of over a third in the rate of reoffending. A meta-analysis by Hanson et al. (2002) comprising 43 studies reporting on prison-based, community-based treatments, and treatment in both settings, found a lower recidivism rate among those who undertook randomised offending behaviour programmes although the results were modest. People who dropped out of treatment reoffended more than those who completed, regardless of the treatment. Later studies suggest that cognitive–behavioural programmes are more effective than earlier treatment programmes. Hanson et al. (2009) reviewed 22 studies and found an 8 per cent difference between the sexual recidivism rate of treated versus untreated sexual offenders (11 per cent and 19 per cent respectively); this equated to a reduction of over 40 per cent in the rate of reoffending. These meta-analyses, as well as a wider body of evaluations of criminal justice interventions, found that well-articulated cognitive-behavioural therapy (CBT) models demonstrated the best results. Most importantly, the analyses reliably show that the treatment effect is greatest in those who pose a higher risk; indeed, those who are deemed to be low risk on assessment tools are repeatedly shown to reoffend at slightly higher levels following treatment than those low-risk offenders who do not receive treatment (Hanson et al. 2009). Olver (2016: 1315) provides some further examples of the iatrogenic effect of programmes essentially *over-treating* low-risk sexual individuals and generating very poor outcomes in terms of sexual recidivism.

Other evaluations have produced less encouraging results. Marques et al. (2005) applied the relapse prevention model (based on ideas of addiction) to those convicted of sexual offences imprisoned in California, USA. They deployed a robust methodology including the use of random allocation of volunteers to treatment and control groups, as well as comparison with those who met the criteria but did not want treatment. There was a follow-up period of five years at risk in the community. The results indicated that there was no treatment effect in terms of significant differences in sexual or violent offending. This was true for the type of offence/victim, the risk level and the length of time before reoffending. Furthermore, although scores on a number of pre–post treatment psychometric measures improved as a result of treatment, none of these changes were significantly associated with subsequent sexual recidivism. The most recent evaluation of note is Mews et al.'s (2017) analysis of the England and Wales prison-based Sex Offender Treatment Programme (SOTP). In essence, it was found that 10 per cent of individuals in treatment sexually reoffended compared to 8 per cent of the matched comparison; furthermore, 4.4 per cent of treated individuals committed at least one child abuse image reoffence compared to 2.9 per cent of the matched comparison group. Of those who were categorised as high or very high risk on the Risk Matrix 2000 (comprising around 25 per cent of the treated sample) 16.9 per cent sexually reoffended as compared to 13.7 per cent of the matched comparison group. Following the evaluation, HMPPS withdrew this programme, and subsequently implemented Horizon and Kaizen – programmes that were already being developed. This moved the focus of interventions for people who commit sexual offences to a strengths-based approach. This approach is supported by existing research that programmes alone will not enable significant change in those convicted of sexual offences who require ongoing practical help and support, tailored to their individual needs (Wakeling and Saloo, 2018).

McCartan (2022) has recently called for the adoption of a more evidence-informed and structured approach to managing those convicted of sexual offences. He highlights the potential of epidemiological criminology (EpiCrim), which is an approach that suggests that crime, including sexual offending, can be prevented and that there are four stages of prevention that relate to different stages of the offending cycle (pre, early stages and post). These stages are:

1. *Primary*: broad-based interventions to prevent sexual abuse and/or victimisation taking place

2. *Secondary*: early detection of sexually abusive behaviour or potential for sexually abusive behaviour

3. *Tertiary*: responding to perpetration and victimisation

4. *Quaternary*: ongoing, supportive interventions that streamline criminal justice responses to reduce risk of sexual offending. (McCartan and Kemshall, 2021)

The strength of this approach is that it acknowledges the importance of a holistic, person-centred and multi-agency approach that looks beyond the offence. Rather than seeing those convicted of sexual offences as a homogenous group, it recognises that different levels of risk require different responses and procedures.

CONCLUSION

In this chapter we have looked at how structural issues such as poverty, gender and race impact disproportionally on some groups. The intersectionality of these issues requires us to consider how various societal structures privilege some groups in society while also discriminating against others. There is a growing body of research that is starting to explore and unpack how various issues interact in ways that both reinforce the oppression felt by these groups and, in some instances, restrict the efforts of support services to support in ways that are experienced as helpful. We considered the potential of culturally sensitive and trauma-informed practices to improve service delivery to these groups. We explored the nature of domestic abuse and the wide-ranging and lasting impact of such behaviours and programmes developed to combat them. We also discussed provision for those on probation experiencing mental illness and disorders and looked at initiatives such as the Mental Health Treatment Requirement and Personality Disordered Offender Pathway. Finally, we considered the vulnerabilities of sexual offenders and the effectiveness of treatment.

recommended reading

If you would like to engage in further reading, you may find the following resource particularly useful:

Ugwudike, P., Graham, H., McNeill, F., Raynor, P., Taxman, F.S. and Trotter, C. (2020) *The Routledge Companion to Rehabilitative Work in Criminal Justice*. Abingdon, Oxon, Routledge.

Covering a variety of contexts, settings, needs and approaches, and drawing on theory and practice, this companion provides definitive overviews of a range of key contemporary theories and models for working with those who commit crimes.

references

Annison, J. and Brayford, J. (2015) (eds) *Women and Criminal Justice: From the Corston Report to Transforming Rehabilitation*. Bristol: Policy Press.
Annison, J., Byng, R. and Quinn, C. (2019) Women offenders: Promoting a holistic approach and continuity of care across criminal justice and health interventions. *Criminology and Criminal Justice*, 19(4), 385–403.

Barr, U. and Christian, N. (2019) A qualitative investigation into the impact of domestic abuse on women's desistance. *Probation Journal*, 66(4), 416–33.

Barrow Cadbury Trust (2014) *The Young Review: Improving Outcomes for Young Black and/or Muslim Men in the Criminal Justice System*. Available at: www.equalcjs.org.uk/sites/default/files/articles/clinks_young-review_report_dec2014.pdf (last accessed 24 August 2021).

Boone, M. and van de Bunt, H. (2016) Dynamics between denial and moral panic: The identification of convicted sex offenders in the community. *Probation Journal*, 63(1): 23-40.

Booth, N., Masson, I. and Baldwin, L. (2018) Promises, promises: Can the Female Offender Strategy deliver? *Probation Journal*, 65(4), 429–38.

Bradley, K.J.C. (2009) *The Bradley Report: Lord Bradley's Review of People with Mental Health Problems or Learning Disabilities in the Criminal Justice System*. London: Department of Health.

British Crime Survey (2009) *Crime in England and Wales 2008/2009*. London: Home Office.

Brooker, C., Sirdifield, C., Blizard, R., Denney, D. and Pluck, G. (2012) Probation and mental illness. *Journal of Forensic Psychiatry & Psychology*, 23(4), 522–37.

Brooker, C., Sirdifield, C., Blizard, R., Maxwell-Harrison, D., Tetley, D., Moran, P., Pluck, G., Chafer, A., Denney, D. and Turner, M. (2011) *An Investigation into the Prevalence of Mental Health Disorder and Patterns of Health Service Access in a Probation Population*. Lincoln: University of Lincoln.

Calverley, A., Cole, B., Kaur, G., Lewis, S., Raynor, P., Sadeghi, S., Smith, D., Vanstone, M. and Wardak, A. (2004) *Black and Asian Offenders on Probation*. Research Study 277. London: Home Office.

Carr, N. (2017) The Lammy Review and race and bias in the criminal justice system. *Probation Journal*, 64(4): 333–6.

Centers for Disease Control and Prevention (2004) *Sexual Violence Prevention: Beginning the Dialogue*. Available at: www.cdc.gov/violenceprevention/pdf/svprevention-a.pdf (last accessed 16 May 2022).

Cluley, E. and Marston, P. (2018) The value of 'bearing witness' to desistance: Two practitioners' responses. *Probation Journal*, 65(1), 89–96.

Corston, J. (2007) *The Corston Report: A Report of a Review of Women with Particular Vulnerabilities in the Criminal Justice System*. London: Home Office. Available at: https://webarchive.nationalarchives.gov.uk/ukgwa/20130128112038/http://www.justice.gov.uk/publications/docs/corston-report-march-2007.pdf (last accessed 30 June 2022).

Cortoni, F., Babchishin, K. and Rat, C. (2017) The proportion of sexual offenders who are female is higher than thought: a meta-analysis. *Criminal Justice and Behaviour*, 44, 145–62.

Craissati, J. (2005) Sexual violence against women: A psychological approach to the assessment and management of rapists in the community. *Probation Journal*, 52(4): 401–22.

Criminal Justice Joint Inspection (2011) *Thematic Inspection Report: Equal but Different? An Inspection of the Use of Alternatives to Custody for Women Offenders. A Joint Inspection by HMI Probation, HMCPSI and HMI Prisons*.

Devaney, J. and Lazenbatt, A. (2016) *Domestic Violence Perpetrators: Evidence-Informed Practice.* London: Routledge.

DiClemente, C.C., Nidecker, M. and Ballack, A.S. (2008) Motivation and the stages of change among individuals with severe mental illness and substance abuse disorders. *Journal of Substance Abuse Treatment,* 34, 25–35.

Disley, E., Taylor, C., Kruithof, K., Winpenny, E., Liddle, M., Sutherland, A., Lilford, R., Wright, S., McAteer, L. and Francis, V. (2016). *Evaluation of the Offender Liaison and Diversion Trial Schemes.* Cambridge: RAND Corporation.

Dixon, L., Archer, J. and Graham-Kevan, N. (2012) Perpetrator programmes for partner violence: Are they based on ideology or evidence? L

egal and Criminological Psychology, 17: 196-215.

Ellis Devitt, K., Coley, D., Hockley, M. and Lawrence, J. (2022) *The Complex Pathways to Violence in the Home: Better Understanding Male Domestic Abuse Perpetration.* Interventions Alliance. Available at: https://interventionsalliance.com/wp-content/uploads/sites/4/2022/01/The-Complex-Pathways-to-Violence-in-the-Home.pdf (last accessed 22 February 2022).

Eno Louden, J., Manchak, S.M., Ricks, E.P. and Kennealy, P.J. (2018) The role of stigma towards mental illness in probation officers' perceptions of risk and case management decisions. *Criminal Justice and Behaviour,* 45(5), 573–88.

Fellowes, E. (2014) 'What's needed as part of probation practice when working with personality disordered offenders? The importance of avoiding errors of logic' – A practitioner response. *Probation Journal,* 61(2), 192–99.

Fellowes, E. (2018) The ultimate shock absorber: Probation officers' experience of working with male service users on the Offender Personality Disorder Pathway. *Probation Journal,* 65(2), 152–69.

Gibbs, P. (2018) *Love, Fear and Control – Does the Criminal Justice System Reduce Domestic Abuse?* London: Transform Justice.

Gondolf, E.W. (2002) *Batterer Interventions Systems: Issues, Outcomes and Recommendations.* Thousand Oaks, CA: Sage.

Hanson, R. and Harris, A. (2000) *The Sex Offender Need Assessment Rating (SONAR): A Method for Measuring Change in Risk Levels.* User Report 1998-01. Ontario: Department of the Solicitor General.

Hanson, R.K. and Morton-Bourgon, K.E. (2005) *The Characteristics of Persistent Sexual Offenders: A Meta-Analysis of Recidivism Studies.* Ottawa: Public Safety Canada.

Hanson, R.K., Bourgon, G., Helmus, L. and Hodgson, S. (2009) The principles of effective correctional treatment also apply to sexual offenders. *Criminal Justice and Behavior,* 36, 865–91.

Hanson, R.K., Gordon, A., Harris, A.J.R., Marques, J.K., Murphy, W., Quinsey, V.L. and Seto, M.C. (2002) First report of the Collaborative Outcome Data Project on the effectiveness of psychological treatment of sex offenders. *Sexual Abuse: A Journal of Research and Treatment,* 14, 169–94.

Harris, A.J.R. and Hanson R.K. (2004) *Sex Offender Recidivism: A Simple Question*. Ottawa, ON: Public Safety and Emergency Preparedness.

HM Inspectorate of Constabulary (2014) *Crime-Recording: Making the Victim Count*. Available at: www.justiceinspectorates.gov.uk/hmicfrs/wp-content/uploads/crime-recording-making-the-victim-count.pdf (last accessed 28 July 2021).

HM Inspectorate of Probation (2016) *A Thematic Inspection of the Provision and Quality of Services in the Community for Women Who Offend*. Manchester: HM Inspectorate of Probation.

HM Inspectorate of Probation (2019) *Management and Supervision of Men Convicted of Sexual Offences: A Thematic Inspection by HM Inspectorate of Probation and HM Inspectorate of Prisons*. Available at: www.justiceinspectorates.gov.uk/hmiprobation/wp-content/uploads/sites/5/2019/01/Management-and-Supervision-of-men-convicted-of-sexual-offences-2.pdf (last accessed 28 July 2021).

HM Inspectorate of Probation (2021) *Mental Health*. Available at: www.justiceinspectorates.gov.uk/hmiprobation/research/the-evidence-base-probation/specific-areas-of-delivery/mental-health/?highlight=Mental%20health (last accessed 21 July 2021).

HM Inspectorate of Probation (2021a) *Race Equality in Probation: The Experience of Black, Asian and Minority Probation Service Users and Staff: A Thematic Inspection by HM Inspectorate of Probation March 2021*. Manchester: HM Inspectorate of Probation. Available at: www.justiceinspectorates.gov.uk/hmiprobation/inspections/race-equality-in-probation (last accessed 4 July 2022).

HM Prisons and Probation Service (2020) *Her Majesty's Prison and Probation Service Offender Equalities Annual Report 2019–2020*. Available at: www.gov.uk/government/statistics/hm-prison-and-probation-serviceoffender-equalities-annual-report-2019-to-2020 (last accessed 7 August 2021).

HM Prison and Probation Service (2021) *The Target Operating Model for Probation Services in England and Wales: Probation Reform Programme*. London: HM Prison and Probation Service.

Home Office (2013) *Information for Local Areas on the Change to the Definition of Domestic Violence and Abuse*. London: Home Office.

Light, M., Grant, E. and Hopkins, K. (2013) *Gender Differences in Substance Misuse and Mental Health among Prisoners*. London: Ministry of Justice.

Loesel, F. and Schmuker, M. (2005). The effectiveness of treatment for sexual offenders: A comprehensive meta-analysis. *Journal of Experimental Criminology*, 1, 117-146.

Long, C.G., Dolley, O. and Hollin, C. (2018) The use of the mental health treatment requirement (MHTR): clinical outcomes at one year of collaboration, *Journal of Criminal Psychology*, 8(3), 215–233.

Malloch, M. and McIvor, G. (2011) Women and community sentences. *Criminology and Criminal Justice*, 11(4): 325–44.

Malloch, M., McIvor, G., & Burgess, C. (2014). 'Holistic' community punishment and criminal justice interventions for women. *The Howard Journal of Criminal Justice*, 53(4), 395–410.

Marques, J., Weideranders, M., Day, D., Nelson, C. and van Ommeren, A. (2005) Effects of a relapse prevention program on sexual recidivism: Final results from California's Sex Offender Treatment and Evaluation Project (SOTEP). *Sexual Abuse: A Journal of Research and Treatment*, 17, 79–107.

McAlinden, A-M. (2006) Managing risk: from regulation to the reintegration of sexual offenders. *Criminology and Criminal Justice*, 6(2): 197–218.

McArt, D. (2013) Mental health conditions of offenders supervised by probation services. *Probation Journal*, 60(2), 190–1.

McCartan, K.F. (2022) *Refining Processes in Policy and Practice in Working with Policy and Practice in Working with People Accused or Convicted of a Sexual Offence.* Available at: www.justiceinspectorates.gov.uk/hmiprobation/wp-content/uploads/sites/5/2022/01/Academic-Insights-McCartan-v1.1.pdf (last accessed 24 February 2022).

McCartan, K. and Kemshall, H. (2020) The potential role of recovery capital in stopping sexual offending: Lessons from circles of support and accountability to enrich practice. *Irish Probation Journal*, 17, 87–106.

McCarten, K. and Kemshall, H. (2021) Incorporating quaternary prevention: Understanding the full scope of public health practices in sexual abuse prevention, *International Journal of Offender Therapy and Comparative Criminology*, 1-23.

Mears, D.P., Ploeger, M. and Warr, M. (1998) Explaining the gender gap in delinquency: Peer influence and moral evaluations of behavior. *Journal of Research in Crime and Delinquency*, 35(3), 251–66.

Mews, A., di Bella, L. and Purver, M. (2017) *Impact Evaluation of the Prison-Based Core Sex Offender Treatment Programme.* Ministry o:f Justice Analytical Series. London: Ministry of Justice.

Messina, N. and Grella, C. (2006) Childhood trauma and women's health outcomes: A California prison population. *The American Journal of Public Health*, 96(10), 1842–88.

Ministry of Justice (2010) *What Works with Domestic Violence Offenders?* London: Ministry of Justice.

Ministry of Justice (2018) *Female Offender Strategy.* Cm 9642. London: Ministry of Justice.

Ministry of Justice (2022) *Improving Outcomes for Women in the Criminal Justice System.* Available at: www.nao.org.uk/wp-content/uploads/2022/01/Improving-outcomes-for-women-in-the-criminal-justice-system.pdf (last accessed 22 February 2022).

Murphy, N. and McVey, D. (2010) Fundamental treatment strategies for optimising interventions with people with personality disorder. In N. Murphy and D. McVey (eds) *Treating Personality Disorder: Creating Robust Services for People with Complex Mental Health Problems.* Abingdon: Routledge.

Murray, J. (2022) Over 1,000 children in Telford were sexually exploited inquiry finds. *The Guardian.* Available at: www.theguardian.com/society/2022/jul/12/over-1000-children-telford-sexually-exploited-inquiry-finds. (last accessed 1 August 2022).

NAO (2022) *Improving Outcomes for Women in the Criminal Justice System.* Report by the Comptroller and Auditor General. Session 2021-22 19 January 2022, HC 1012. London: Ministry of Justice.

NOMS (2014) *Mental Health Treatment Requirements Guidance on Supporting Integrated Delivery*. London: NOMS.

Olver, M. (2016) The risk–need–responsivity model: Applications to sex offender treatment. In D. Boer (ed.) *The Wiley Handbook on the Theories, Assessment and Treatment of Sexual Offending Vol. 1*. Chichester: John Wiley & Sons, pp. 1227–43.

Pakes, F. and Winstone, J. (2013) The mental health treatment requirement: The promise and the practice. In A. Pycroft and S. Clift (eds) *Risk and Rehabilitation: Management and Treatment of Substance Misuse and Mental Health Problems in the Criminal Justice System*. Bristol: Policy Press.

Prison Reform Trust (2017) *'There's A Reason We're in Trouble': Domestic Abuse as a Driver to Women's Offending*. Available at: www.prisonreformtrust.org.uk/Portals/0/Documents/Domestic_abuse_report_final_lo.pdf (last accessed 3 August 2021).

Renehan, N. (2020) Applications of psychotherapy in statutory domestic violence perpetrators programmes: Challenging the dominance of cognitive behavioural models. In P. Ugwudike, H. Graham, F. McNeill, P. Raynor, F.S. Taxman and C. Trotter (eds) *The Routledge Companion to Rehabilitative Work in Criminal Justice*. Abingdon, Oxon: Routledge, pp. 383–96.

Renehan, N. (2021) Building better relationships: Interrogating the black box of a statutory domestic violence perpetrators programme summary and findings. *University of Manchester*. Available at: www.research.manchester.ac.uk/portal/files/195990742/Building_Better_Relationships_Programme_Report_final.pdf (last accessed 1 August 2022).

Robinson, A. (2011) *Foundations for Offender Management: Theory, Law and Policy for Contemporary Practice*. Bristol: The Policy Press.

Sainsbury Centre for Mental Health (2009) *Diversion: A Better Way for Criminal Justice and Mental Health*. London: Sainsbury Centre for Mental Health.

Scott, G. and Moffatt, S. (2012) *The Mental Health Treatment Requirement: Realising a Better Future*. London: Centre for Mental Health.

Sharpe, G. (2020) More sinned against than sinning: Women's pathways into crime and criminalization. In P. Ugwudike, H. Graham, F. McNeill, P. Raynor, F.S. Taxman and C. Trotter (eds) *The Routledge Companion to Rehabilitative Work in Criminal Justice*. Abingdon, Oxon: Routledge, pp. 611–22.

Shaw, J., Minoudis, P., Hamilton, V. and Craissati, J. (2011) An investigation into competency for working with personality disorder and team climate in the probation service. *Probation Journal*, 59(1), 39–48.

Sheehan, R., McIvor, G. and Trotter, C. (2011) (eds) *Working with Women Offenders in the Community*. Cullompton: Willan.

Sirdfield, C. and Brooker, C. (2020) *Maximising Positive Mental Health Outcomes for People under Probation Supervision*. HM Inspectorate of Probation Academic Insights 2020/06. Manchester: HM Inspectorate of Probation.

Skeem, J. and Louden, J.E. (2006) Towards evidence-based practice for probationers and parolees mandated to mental health treatment. *Psychiatric Services*, 57(3), 333–42.

Thornton, D. and d'Orazio, D. (2016) Advancing the evolution of sex offender risk assessment. In D. Boer (ed.) *The Wiley Handbook on the Theories, Assessment and Treatment of Sexual Offending*, Volume II. Chichester: John Wiley & Sons, pp. 667–93.

Vaughan, P. and Stevenson, S. (2002) An opinion survey of mentally disordered offender service users. *The British Journal of Forensic Practice*, 4(3), 11–20.

Wakeling, H. and Saloo, F. (2018) *HMPPS Analytical Summary: An Exploratory Study of the Experiences of a Small Sample of Men Convicted of Sexual Offences Who Have Reoffended after Participating in Prison-Based Treatment*. London: Ministry of Justice.

Women's Aid (2019) Women's Aid responds to government's draft domestic abuse bill. Available at: www.womensaid.org.uk/womens-aid-responds-to-governments-draft-domestic-abuse-bill (last accessed 26 July 2021).

World Health Organization (2013) *Global and Regional Estimates of Violence Against Women: Prevalence and the Health Effects of Intimate Partner Violence and Non-partner Sexual Violence*. Geneva: WHO.

13

BEYOND PUNISHMENT, PRISONS AND PROBATION

INTRODUCTION

Throughout this textbook we have critically engaged with long-standing penological debates that take into consideration the theory, policy and practice of punishment, within and across community and custodial settings that are required to work alongside people who break the law. In doing so, we have explored a wide variety of issues that raise fundamental questions about the design and delivery of punishment, as well questions about who we punish and for what reason(s). In doing so we contend that both prisons and probation have become highly politicised institutions that have been subject to contradictory and, at times, unhelpful political pressures which have obscured their purpose whilst simultaneously undermining their ability to help and support people entangled in the criminal justice system. Although the duty of politicians is to promote the interests of the public, 'it is not always easy for them to separate the public interest from their own priorities and ambitions' (Canton, 2017: 207). Such sentiments become particularly pertinent when we consider the role and function of the contemporary prison and probation service, required to represent a society's attitude towards troubled and indeed troublesome individuals and, perhaps more importantly, what should happen to them if they break the law.

As a society, our reliance on imprisonment appears entrenched despite its dubious record to either deter or rehabilitate people. So perhaps we should heed the quote (widely misattributed to Albert Einstein) that 'the definition of insanity is doing the same thing over and over and expecting different results'. Whilst the human costs and collateral consequences of probation supervision might seem less evident than those of imprisonment, we argue that less imprisonment should not necessarily mean more community sanctions because as we have discussed elsewhere, community sanctions also involve intrusions that are widening the reach and scope of state control (see Chapter 2 for further discussion).

TOWARDS PEACEMAKING CRIMINOLOGY

For decades we have witnessed governments from around the world wage war on those who break the law with little to no avail. There are more than 11.7 million people imprisoned globally (United Nations Office on Drugs and Crime, 2021) and conservative estimates suggest that there are at least three to four times as many people under the supervision of probation services worldwide, even though there are other, more peaceful, ways to work alongside people who have broken the law. Drawing on a variety of ancient teachings and religious perspectives, peacemaking criminology offers a progression of ideas about how to respond to lawbreaking and those who break the law. Although typically overlooked, it is an important offering as it provides an alternative vision of how individuals and communities can work together to create social arrangements that meet the needs of all members of society.

Although a relatively new branch of critical criminology, becoming popular in the early 1990s through the work of Harold Pepinsky and Richard Quinney, peacemaking criminology provides a theoretical blueprint for how principles and values of peace can be applied as a foundation for justice in any given society. Wozniak (2000) suggests that the core themes and characteristics of peacemaking criminology include, but are not limited to: challenging the status quo and confronting inequality in society; highlighting structurally based injustices; examining long-standing definitions associated with endeavours to identify who commits crime; conceptualising social change through liberation; emphasising non-violence instead of punitive attempts to ensure law and order; recognising the needs of all involved in harmful situations; and prioritising social justice rather than criminal justice.

Rather than declaring war on those who break the law, peacemaking criminology calls for society to look at the suffering which takes place amongst and between those involved in such activity. In doing so, peacemaking criminology bears numerous similarities to the concept of social justice, a framework which suggests that everyone deserves equal economic, political and social rights and opportunities. To facilitate this, we propose that the prison and probation service should strive to embody organisations rich in institutional justice capital that are 'sustained by the norms, rules and practices present in the justice institution[s] and creates the conditions and context for growth and for building personal and social capital' (Best et al., 2021: 211). By placing social justice at the heart of its endeavours, peacemaking criminology offers an opportunity for society to consider problems that may have contributed to the harm caused by individuals who break the law. This is because crime has no ontological reality (it is little more than a social construct that can be created by a given society via a series of socio-legal processes) and most events that are defined as a crime can be minor in terms of harm. However, many incidents that do cause harm are not recognised by criminal law and/or processed through agencies of the criminal justice system.

Peacemaking criminologists are not alone in their endeavours to move away from the concept of crime. For many years, critical criminologists have called for a (re)examination of the notion of harm to provide a broader, more inclusive, picture of the harms that individuals and communities may be subject to before, during and after involvement with the criminal justice system. Hillyard and Tombs (2007) suggest that a social harm perspective could provide a more responsive way to consider the multiple and varied causes of human suffering than the notion of crime. This is because it can encompass detrimental activities of local and national states, as well as corporations, on the welfare of individuals and recognise how various forms of harm are not distributed randomly through society. This, in turn, would form the basis of a more accurate picture of the range of harms and causes of human suffering that people endure (many of which fall outside of the parameters of the legal system). It would also allow victims to have greater involvement in the process, able to define the harms that have been created rather than follow ministerial definitions of crime.

Peacemaking criminologists recognise that justice cannot be achieved through efforts to standardise need. Rather, justice can only be achieved when each person's feelings, issues, realities and needs are considered. When we examine the fundamental nature of justice, we see that it is an ongoing process that has something to do with equalising unequal social situations. By examining the conditions that make justice through equalisation possible, it becomes clear that endeavours to do justice must include more than the distribution of something to someone (Sullivan and Tifft, 1998). This is primarily because justice, in effect, is created by people who embark upon a journey to recognise and reconcile difference (Ibid). From a peacemaking perspective, justice requires people to be open and receptive to each other's concerns, needs, feelings, pain and suffering so that they can genuinely see each other, as individual human beings rather than sources of actual and/or perceived conflict.

A social harm approach provides a way in which society can create a more accurate picture of the variants of harm that have an impact on people during their lifetime. For peacemaking criminologists, poverty is defined as a major form of suffering. This is echoed by advocates of social harm perspectives who define poverty as a social harm. Rather than seeking to study poverty as a variable in relation to crime, peacemaking criminologists seek to shed light on how poverty and crime are forms of suffering that need eradication if we are ever to reduce lawbreaking. Although the social harm perspective is still evolving, it goes some way to provide a more valid way of developing a better insight into the harms that affect people over their lifetime. As Canton (2017: 1750) notes, 'they challenge criminal justice to develop practices that go more with the grain of the ways in which conflicts are managed and wrongs are righted in other (than criminal) procedures and in societies that make less use of formal professionalised processes'.

Peacemaking criminology in action

The broad, encompassing nature of peacemaking criminology allows its principles and prescriptions to be expressed in many ways. To illustrate this point, the next section will explore the concept of restorative justice given its ability to recognise the role of pain, hurt and suffering in events and activities that are defined as crime. Restorative justice requires people to take accountability for their actions whilst seeking to develop community-based solutions and support for all people involved in conflict. It is a perspective and practice that views crime as a violation of people and relationships which creates a series of unmet needs. From a restorative justice perspective, justice constitutes attempts to meet the needs created by crime for all involved (Ame and Alidu, 2010). Thus, justice can only be done when the needs created by crime are met. Restorative justice is an umbrella term for a group of approaches which seeks to resolve conflicts by bringing together those with a stake in resolving that conflict and deciding how to move on from it.

As a response to offending, restorative justice differs from most other approaches in that it is not solely focused on what is done to or with the individual who has committed a crime. Indeed, the current appeal of restorative justice has been fuelled by the growing influence of the victim's movement in criminal justice. Nonetheless, the objectives of restorative justice do include offending-focused ones such as encouraging people to assume responsibility for their actions, seeking to reintegrate individuals into their communities and reducing the likelihood of reoffending. As an approach to securing such positive outcomes its novelty lies in the value and importance it places on the involvement of other stakeholders, specifically non-professionals, including but not limited to victims and sometimes members of the wider community in which perpetrators and victims reside. Although there is no one model of restorative justice practice, the most common operational examples of restorative justice are victim–offender mediation and restorative conferencing.

In 2001 the Ministry of Justice funded a seven-year research programme, worth £7 million, into restorative justice. The independent evaluation, led by Professor Joanna Shapland at the University of Sheffield, found no evidence that any types of offences or groups of lawbreakers are more or less suitable for restorative justice processes (Shapland et al., 2008). People who participated in the restorative justice schemes under investigation were found to commit statistically significant fewer offences (in terms of reconvictions) in the subsequent two years than those in the control group. Shapland et al. (2008) also found that individuals in restorative justice programmes are more likely to complete the programme and are less likely to reoffend, demonstrating how for every £1 spent on restorative justice conferencing, £9 was saved in terms of criminal justice expenditure. Taken together the above-mentioned research appears to support Canton's (2017) contention that restorative approaches provide a catalyst for engaging individuals in rehabilitative opportunities that may be more able to motivate some individuals in a way that a court order or interventions by a prison or probation officer cannot. That said, as current restorative justice approaches tend to provide add-ons to traditional modes of punishment, the challenge is to create opportunities to infuse criminal justice policy and practice with more restorative values.

CONCLUSION

Both peacemaking criminology and restorative justice seek to restore a sense of balance to the wider social landscape. While they seek to achieve the same outcome, they do so from different starting points. Peacemaking criminology has been described as a proactive and preventative theoretical perspective, whereas restorative justice is a practice that takes place as a direct response to crime (Hanser, 2009). Despite divergent starting points both frameworks have human interaction at their epicentre, and it is this unorthodox approach to doing justice (in theory at least for this moment in time) that could, and in some cases is, drawn upon to alleviate the pain and suffering of those involved in criminal justice processes and penal institutions. Whilst we do not present these alternative approaches as an all-encompassing remedy to the long-standing issues which surround the theory and practice of punishment, we hope that such offerings, rooted in principles of peace rather than punishment, go some way to enhance not only your insight into the subject area but your ability to critically engage with its offerings. This is an important endeavour for anyone with an interest in penology as it provides an opportunity for you to think beyond the status quo: challenging how we work alongside people who have broken the law, considering why we continue to engage in such practices and contemplating what the term penology could represent in years to come.

references

Ame, R. and Alidu, S. (2010) Truth and reconciliation commissions, restorative justice, peacemaking criminology, and development. Criminal Justice Studies, 23(3), 253–68.

Best, D., Hamilton, S., Hall, L. and Bartels, L. (2021) Justice capital: A model for reconciling structural and agentic determinants of desistance. *Probation Journal*, 68(2), 206–23.

Canton, R. (2017) *Why Punish? An Introduction to the Philosophy of Punishment*. London: Palgrave Macmillan.

Hanser, R. (2009) Conflicts and geographical flashpoints around the world: the effective application of restorative justice and peacemaking criminological perspectives. Contemporary Justice Review, 12(20), 195–205.

Hillyard, P. and Tombs, S. (2007) From crime to social harm. *Crime, Law and Social Change,* 48(1–2), 9–25.

Shapland, J., Atkinson, A., Atkinson, H., Dignan, J., Edwards, L., Hibbert, J., Howes, M., Johnstone, J., Robinson, G. and Sorsby, A. (2008) *Does Restorative Justice Affect Reconviction? The Fourth Report from the Evaluation of Three Schemes.* London: Ministry of Justice. Available at: https://restorativejustice.org.uk/sites/default/files/resources/files/Does%20restorative%20justice%20affect%20reconviction.pdf (last accessed 4 July 2022).

Sullivan, S. and Tifft, L. (1998) Criminology as peacemaking: A peace-oriented perspective on crime, punishment and justice that takes into account the needs of all. The Justice Professional. 11(1–2), 4–34.

United Nations Office on Drugs and Crime (2021) Data Matters 1. Available at: www.unodc.org/documents/data-and-analysis/statistics/DataMatters1_prison.pdf (last accessed 4 July 2022).

Wozniak, J.F. (2000) The voices of peacemaking criminology: Insights into a perspective with an eye toward teaching. Contemporary Justice Review, 3(3): 267–89.

Index

Page numbers in *italics* refer to figures.

technology *see* electronic monitoring (EM); surveillance, monitoring and control

terrorist offenders 23, 257

Thatcher government 98–9

theoretical perspective
prisons and imprisonment 61–81
probation and rehabilitation 87–105

therapeutic community (TC) 124, 223–4

Thinking Skills programme 217, 249, 302

Thomas, T. 21
Marshall, D. and 26, 27

Through-the-Gate resettlement services 230

Tidmarsh, M. 97, 142, 193

training prisons 122

training/qualifications
prison officers 176–7
probation staff 103, 142, 143, 196–9, 200–2, 312

Transforming Rehabilitation (TR) reforms 25, 101–2, 140–1, 301
effect on probation cultures 191–3
Through-the-Gate resettlement services 230

trauma
BAME individuals 300
and trauma-informed services 226–8

treatment requirements: community order 139, 140

Turing, A. 94

United Nations
AAAQ framework for prison healthcare 290
Bangkok Rules 282
Optional Protocol for the Convention Against Torture 130
Standard Minimum Rules for the Treatment of Prisoners (UNODC) 115, 118, 126
Universal Declaration of Human Rights (1948) 289

unpaid work 246–9
community order 139, 140, 246

utilitarian perspective on rehabilitation 91–2

victim contact work 261–3

violent offenders 23

voluntary sector: probation and rehabilitation 100, 101

vulnerability in community settings 297–8
BAME service users 299–301
female service users 301–4
mental health issues 311–16
see also domestic violence/abuse; sexual offenders

vulnerability in prison settings 271–2
defining 275–85
Equality Act (2010) 271, 272–5
prison as site of vulnerability 285–90

Wakefield prison 119, 123

Ward, T. and Maruna, S. 20, 39–40, 42
Good Lives Model (GLM) 54–6

Whatton prison 278–9

women
girls and young women in custody 114
Newgate prison 66
probation workers 142, 201
recall to prison 233, 304
security categorisation 120
social enquiry reports 245
vulnerability in community settings 301–4
vulnerability in prison 282–3
see also gender/sex; pregnancy and maternity

Women's Centres 302–3

Woodcock Report (1994) 126–7

Woolf report 69–70

World Health Organization (WHO) 285–6, 304

World War II and post-war period 67, 97

young offender institutions 114, 115

young people *see* children and young people

Young Review 300

youth court system 113–14